D1280225

CHILD-REARING
VALUES

CHILD-REARING VALUES

VALUES

A Cross-National Study

Wallace E. Lambert
Josiane F. Hamers
Nancy Frasure-Smith

PRAEGER PUBLISHERS
Praeger Special Studies

New York • London • Sydney • Toronto

Library of Congress Cataloging in Publication Data

Lambert, Wallace E
    Child rearing values.

    Bibliography: p.
    1. Parenting--Case studies. 2. National character-
istics--Case studies. I. Hamers, Josiane F., joint
author. II. Frasure-Smith, Nancy, joint author.
III. Title.
HQ755.83.L35   649'.1'0722   78-19747
ISBN 0-03-049086-3

PRAEGER PUBLISHERS
PRAEGER SPECIAL STUDIES
383 Madison Avenue, New York, N.Y. 10017, U.S.A.

Published in the United States of America in 1979
by Praeger Publishers,
A Division of Holt, Rinehart and Winston, CBS, Inc.

9   038   987654321

© 1979 by Wallace E. Lambert

Printed in the United States of America

ACKNOWLEDGMENTS

We have many people to thank. First, we are very much indebted to the Spencer Foundation for research grants that permitted
us to conduct the extensive study described here. In particular,
H. Thomas James, president of the Spencer Foundation, gave us
encouragement and perspective from the start of the project. Finan-
cial support for the Canadian based research was also received
from The Canada Council (grant number S75-1191-X2 to Wallace E.
Lambert) for which we also are very grateful.

Many colleagues and friends around the world gave us substantive suggestions about our research plans, and/or helped us make
personal contacts with potential research associates in the different
countries included in the overall investigation. Specifically, we
would like to express our gratitude to John Berry of Queen's University, Roger Holmes of London University, Otto Klineberg of the
University of Paris, William W. Lambert and Harry Levin, both of
Cornell University, Walter Lonner of Western Washington State College, Nelly Sidoti of the New York Public School System, and Susan
Thomas of the Educational Development Center in Massachusetts.

We are very much indebted to colleagues at McGill, especially
G. Richard Tucker, Donald Taylor, Alison d'Anglejan, and Andrew
Yackley, whose suggestions and encouragement throughout the study
were of immense help. We also thank Chet Olson, James Ramsey,
and Laurel Ward of McGill for their precious statistical advice.

As the investigation got underway, we necessarily made numerous local contacts in foreign settings which means that many
people contributed by supervising the field work or helping us find
skilled interviewers. These same people helped us understand and
interpret the reactions of local parental groups to our research approach. In this regard, we thank William B. Beeman and Naomi
Baron at Brown University in Providence, Rhode Island, for their
assistance with the American east coast sample; Adele Martinez
and Harold Wingard of the San Diego School System for help with the
American west coast sample; Nelson Viera of Brown University and
Valdo Correia of the Fall River, Massachusetts Public School System for their assistance with the Portuguese immigrant sample;
Sandra Trehub of Erindale College, University of Toronto, Yosh
Taguchi, and Mr. Ono for their help with the Japanese immigrant
sample; Clothilde Ferreira and Bryan Foss, both of London University College, for the British sample; Marisa Zavalloni of the Uni-

versity of Paris, for the French sample; Marc Richelle of the University of Liége and Georgette Hamers of the Governmental Psycho-Medico-Social Center in Oostende for help with the Belgian samples; Gustavo Iacono, Guglielmo Belleli, and Carmencita Serena, all of the University of Naples, and Clotilda Pontecorvo-Piperno of the University of Rome for help with the Italian samples; Vasso and George Vassiliou for help with the Greek sample; Maria-Emilia Ricardo Marquez of the Universidade Nova de Lisboa for help with the Portuguese sample; Giyoo Hatano of the University of Tokyo for the Japanese sample; Ellen Grandsard for gathering data for the mixed-ethnic marriage study in Paris, and Florence Callaghan who helped us collect a sample of American teachers in Plattsburgh, New York.

McGill University provided the office space and ambience for a small team of staff and assistants. In particular, we are grateful to Hélène Grégoire who stayed with us throughout the completion of the field studies and participated in all of the data analysis. Catherine Stratford also has been with us throughout the study, and has been enormously helpful as an assistant and an editor. Our secretary, Norma Caretta, typed many versions of the manuscript and contributed not only her technical skill, but also her precious humor and wisdom. Catherina Papastogianni and Gretchen Martin also worked as secretaries at earlier stages of the study. Then, as the writing up began, Janine Lambert helped us enormously with suggestions for improving and clarifying our modes of expression.

Other assistants worked for shorter periods helping with the local interviews, coding, translating, statistical work, and proofreading. We express our sincere thanks to Claire Aecherli, Ann Argyris, Francoise Bouçher, Rosa Caramanico, Murray Cohen, Anna-Lee Dietsche, Antonio da Sousa, Francine Giguère, Samuel Gutman, Yoriko Inove, Violet Jackson, Adele Kirby, Harvyo Lieteau, Deirdre Meintel Machado, Richard Morin, Nicole Mourelatou, Benoîte Noble, Sally Richens, Vincenza Santini, George Tacik, Catherine Tadgell, Valerie Underwood, and Hiroko Yoshino.

The field workers in the various national settings were critically important to the success of the investigation. In this regard, we thank, in the United States, John Castro, Irene Duran, Joseph Fieschko, James Hull, Jo-Beth Hull, Susan Jenkins, Eva Kleederman, Georgia Nigro, and Aida Ramirez; in Greece, Chrysantia Koutougou, Katerine Ioannides, Tom Tavantzis; in Italy, Anna Maria Ajello, Ester Alvino, Angela Fortini, Luisa Fuse; in Portugal, Manuel Joaquim Lopes Agostinho; in France, Christian Louis-Guérin, Monique Weinberger; in Maine, for the Franco-American sample, Bernadette Mayhew; in Great Britain, Sylvia Younson; in

Japan, Y. Ohura; and in Belgium, Marie-Jeanne Bremer and Marie-Christine Kaquet.

We are also grateful to the school boards, principals, teachers, and community leaders who permitted us to conduct the investigations and who in many cases introduced our interviewers to the parents, thereby facilitating home interviews. Finally, and most important of all, we thank the numerous parents throughout the world who willingly took the time to play the role of parents for us in the interviews. It is to these parents, and to new generations of parents to come, that we dedicate this work.

CONTENTS

LIST OF TABLES

LIST OF FIGURES

CHILD-REARING VALUES

1

INTRODUCTION

This book is about the ways children in various parts of the world are brought up. Our focus is as much on parents—those who supposedly do the bringing up—as on children—those who supposedly are brought up. The reader should be forewarned that this is a rather technical account of child rearing, based on numbers and statistical tables, and this emphasis reflects the fact that, as researchers, we were brought up to have a certain faith in empirical documentation of personal accounts, even in an area as delicate as that of child-rearing values. Many people seriously interested in our topic may be bothered by a statistical treatment of this sort. Others, however, may want all the statistical information available, and more. We have tried to keep both in mind, by writing our account in such a way that those not interested in statistical details can skip over the tables of numbers and read the written descriptions of what we believe to be the potentially significant trends in the results. In reality, we are not as scientific and technical as the tables and graphs might suggest. Rather, we view the statistical procedures employed here as restraining devices that put very important limits on our own enthusiasm and imagination and that could very easily exaggerate or bias our interpretations of the trends and patterns of results that we see emerging in the various parts of our study. Once caught up in the topic of child rearing as we have been, one begins to wonder why it has fascinated people from the beginning of social life and still continues to fascinate so many of us today. We have to wonder, too, why we have given in to its fascination to the extent that we have in this investigation. Part of the charm seems to stem from a widely shared belief that understanding the child-rearing practices of our parents can provide us with an opportunity, through retrospection, to explain our own personal strengths or weaknesses. At the same time, by reflecting on our own childhoods, we as adults are able to abstract guidelines for rearing our own children. This view assumes that child rearing is a simple and straightforward phenomenon, that the way parents treat their children in large part determines the ultimate shape of their personalities. Judging from current research, however, this view may be far too simple, for there is an impressive accumulation of evidence that points the other way, suggesting that the shape of the child's personality may have an important influence on the way parents conduct themselves as mothers or fathers (Bell 1968; Harper 1975). This child-to-parent influence apparently starts early. For instance, it has been documented that a mother's milk may begin to flow at the sound of her baby's cry. And it continues into young adulthood, as in the case where parents who have repeatedly had to change their own plans because a teenager "needs" the family car, end up "needing" a second car. This is not to say that children never have wholesome influences on parents as well. The circle closes somewhat pathetically when parents become old, as Jean Chalon (1976) recently explains. There comes a time when statements like "Don't forget your hat," or "Now what have you done?" are children's ways of talking to old and forgetful parents.

Not only do children influence parents, but it is no longer certain that the socialization influences of parents are any more important than, or even as important as, those of peers. In other words, the basic order of cause and effect in child rearing is no longer all that clear, and even the weights that should be assigned to alternative sources of influence are now uncertain. This complexity seems to increase the charm of the topic, especially for behavioral scientists.

Regardless of who brings up whom, the study of variations in child-rearing practices does provide instructive insight into parents' beliefs and values, and this contributes to the widespread interest in the topic. Still, even on this point, it is not all that easy to explain how parental values and beliefs are related to child-rearing practices. For instance, at the conclusion of their comprehensive cross-national study of child rearing, Leigh Minturn and William W. Lambert (1964) are of the opinion that parental beliefs and values may function more to justify than to influence the child-rearing practices in vogue. For instance, in societies where living space is insufficient and children must be taught orderliness, parents are prone to place great value on orderliness and responsibility in child rearing. So, parents' beliefs about child rearing may not have any simple direct causal relationship to child-rearing practices. Even so, one can still learn a great deal about those belief systems through studies of child-rearing practices.

We can also learn much about the children involved in the rearing; the nature of their social interaction and the restrictions placed on it; the expectations others have of them; and the possible consequences the child-rearing practices may have on personality formation. The investigations of Whiting and Child (1953); W. W. Lambert, Triandis, and Wolf (1959); and Campbell (1961) persuade us that early child-training experiences can affect the structure of personality and leave residues that are seen even at the adult level. The data so far available on the issue, however, vary greatly in reliability and representativeness from one study to the next, so much so that one can be sure that new and better investigations will be generated with new and more reliable probing methods and procedures.

One thing is becoming clear: to be valuable, investigations of child-training practices should be both comparative and observational in nature. Research that is neither comparative, nor based as closely as possible on systematic observation of actual familial interaction, reveals its limitations when cross-national evidence finally becomes available. For example, an interesting interview-type study of child-rearing practices in French Canadian families by Philippe Garigue (1962) is by its nature not comparative, and the findings presented as unique features of the French Canadian family may in reality be as descriptive of all Canadians or all families from rural or semiurban settings as they are of French Canadians. A similar study conducted in the Philippines by Guthrie and Jacobs (1966) presents a profile of child-rearing practices that is in many respects as "French Canadian" as Garigue's study of French Canadians.

The fascination with child rearing is particularly high when investigations become comparative, as in Urie Bronfenbrenner's explorations of changes in child-rearing values through time and space (1958), even though his time span, in this example, was limited to 25 years and his space span limited to various centers in the United States. At the end of his 1958 review, Bronfenbrenner hoped that these time and space limits would be extended so that we could learn more about the ways "humanity brings up its children" (Bronfenbrenner 1958). Bronfenbrenner's own interest in the comparative study of child rearing has been sustained and has become a distinctive feature of his important research (for example, Bronfenbrenner 1970; Devereux, Bronfenbrenner, and Rudgers 1969; Devereux, Bronfenbrenner, and Suci 1962).

Like Bronfenbrenner's work, the present study reveals our own captivation with the comparative aspects of child rearing, and although we judge it to be an important contribution, one not quite like any other, we certainly do not claim to resolve all issues with this study. Even at the end, we won't be sure, for instance, who brings up whom—parents, children or children, parents—nor will we know for sure whether the parents' values we deal with have a direct effect on their modes of child training or whether their values reflect mainly their justifications for the way they happen to rear their children. Even though we break away from the typical two- or three-nation comparison (and at times chew off much more than we can really digest), our own samples of "humanity" end as quite modest ones, limited mainly to North America and Europe, particularly the Mediterranean strip, and Japan.

We view this heavy cross-national feature of our work very much as Roger Holmes (1976) views cross-cultural research in general. According to Holmes, cross-cultural data, when compared to "rigorous" data, are basically "weak," but nonetheless "valuable." In fact, he argues, data of this sort become valuable because they are weak. His reasoning is that cross-cultural studies "present us with problems of inference whose solution has a more general validity than might at first appear plausible" (Holmes 1976, p. 118). It is in confronting these problems of inference that one transforms weak characteristics into valuable ones.

In our case, weak cross-cultural data have prompted us to question the scientific status of various basic concepts that are usually taken for granted or ignored. For example, we began by asking ourselves: Are differences in social class also "cultural" differences? Most people's thinking gets fuzzy on these matters because the stereotypes we hold about culture and class are often taken to be facts. Located as we are in the fascinating province of Quebec, we wondered about the "cultural" differences that are said to separate French and English Canadians (see, for example, Lambert 1970; 1974). Are there two distinct cultures in Quebec, or could it be that all long-term residents in Canada, French-speaking or English-speaking, are basically American, even though they happen to be living north of the U.S. border? If this is so, where then are the limits of the American cultural influence? We hoped that our cross-national data on child-rearing values might provide information relevant to such complicated questions, and as we look back on the overall study, we feel we have made important contributions to this end. The point, however, is that these questions, and many others like them, came to our attention only because we found ourselves knee-deep in cross-national data and problems of inference.

Let us follow two examples of what happened as we got into the investigation. On several occasions, when comparing two national groups of parents, say English Canadians and French Canadians, we would find them to have certain different and distinctive patterns of child-rearing values. Then, when we broadened our base of comparison by including another national group, say Anglo-American parents from the United States, we would find that, on those same value dimensions, the original differences were no longer statistically reliable, and, in fact, none of the differences among the three samples reached significance levels. What could have happened to the "statistically significant" differences that had emerged in the two-group comparison? When differences vanish in this way, one is forced to rethink the whole process of making such comparisons and the statistical procedures involved. After much anguish, we are now of the opinion that the three-nation comparison in the example just given provides evidence for a style of child-rearing values common to all three groups, that is, a general "North American" style. With a narrower perspective, the differences that appeared in the two-nation comparisons could be real enough, and one might well expect them to vanish or change substantively as one's perspective is broadened. Thus, if we were to gradually increase the number of national samples in a comparison, we would get progressively closer to making statements about humanity in general, and any differences between pairs of nations that would otherwise be striking ones might, from a world view, be nothing more than local idiosyncrasies. In the present study, we encountered many cases of this sort, especially when we enlarged our frame of reference from two to three or more national groups. Interestingly, it was not always the case that, by simply increasing the number of national groups, we automatically erased distinctive national group differences; instances of what we will call "real" distinctiveness did sometimes remain in the broader comparisons. However, in the more typical cases where differences based on two-group comparisons vanish in a broader context, we will not assume that some artifact of a statistical sort is at work. Instead, we will argue, in these instances, that the statistical results make good common sense: If the perspective is made broad enough, then degrees of similarity among different modes of behavior overshadow differences, because differences would mean that we have selected disparate cases from a finely graded series. In this way, local contrasts get smoothed out, and only "real" exceptions hold up. It is interesting to us that statistical procedures seem to support this sociopsychological view of the reality of narrow versus broad perspectives. Suppose we were to compare groups A and B and find them in some respect different when tested statistically. Then suppose we select a third group, X, to include in a three-way comparison, with two provisos: that the mean score for group X lies at the mean of scores for groups A and B combined and that the spread of scores for group X is the same as that for groups A and B. In technical terms, the between-group variation (or SS between groups) in

this example has not been increased by the addition of group X.
The point is that in cases of this sort, one often finds no statistically
reliable differences among groups A, X, and B (Olson 1976). In
other words, a solid A-B difference can vanish with the introduction
of a third or fourth group. In our view, that is what happens when
the comparison base is broadened in the real world, and we are delighted that the statistical procedures seem to reflect the real world
so well. Statistics can also help isolate "real" exceptions, for it
could turn out that groups A and B will stay different when X is included in the comparison, just as A and X can end up not statistically
different from one another, although both are different from B.*
The main point of all this is that we would never have begun to think
in these statistical terms if we had not been dealing with "weak"
cross-national data.

The meaning of the term "culture" comes into question from
the moment one tries to obtain a national "sample" of parents. For
example, even though we were as careful as possible to include only
bona fide French people in our national sample of French parents,
we began to wonder what Frenchness really is. Our stereotype led
us to believe that French and English parents might well differ in
their child-rearing values, but we were puzzled by within-nation
social-class differences, because another set of stereotypes suggested to us that working-class people are different in some basic
ways from middle-class people. These stereotypes conflicted, and
we began to wonder if social-class membership might not be as
strong, or stronger, a contributor to parents' values as national or
cultural group membership. Thus, we were prompted throughout
our study to pit the influence of social class against that of national
background, and time after time, the outcomes came as surprises.
For example, we have found many instances where French parents
of a particular social-class background are more like English,
Italian, U.S., or Japanese parents of the same social-class strata
than they are like French parents of a different social-class background. As one might imagine, findings of this sort upset our
stereotypes about "cultural" backgrounds to such an extent that we
have used "cross-national" rather than "cross-cultural" as our descriptive term, even though we realize that "cross-national," used
in the sense of a geographical unit, may mean too little, just as

---

*Of course, to be on solid statistical ground, we would need
to know how similar or different the overall populations of our
A's, B's, and X's are, and usually we have no independent means
of knowing this.

"cross-cultural" may mean too much. Hopefully, by getting as much perspective as possible on "culture," in terms of both national group and social class, we will contribute to a better understanding of the concept.

Our data also prompted us to explore the extensity of "Frenchness," for example, by searching for signs of distinctively French child-rearing values not only in France, but also in Belgium, French Canada, and even in French American communities in northern New England. Then the search for Frenchness in child-rearing values prompted us to find a comparable sort of "Englishness" in the values of English, Anglo-Canadian, and Anglo-American parents. If distinctive patterns of Frenchness and Englishness were traceable, then how durable would "old country" child-rearing values be if Italian, Greek, and Portuguese young adults were to immigrate and start their own families in Canada or the United States? Might we find pervasive and distinctive Greek, Portuguese, and Italian child-rearing patterns as well? Attempts to make sense of our cross-national data forced us to come to grips with questions like these, which in turn made us rethink the whole process of interpreting and making inferences about research findings.

As we have gone along, we have accumulated a large number of filing cards summarizing similar, although usually less extensive, attempts by other researchers to deal with the intricacies of child rearing. Although we will refer to certain of these important studies as we proceed, we have been discouraged from trying to provide a full review of the relevant literature on the topic, because such a review would seem to suggest that our study grew in some sensible way out of previous research, which is not the case. Actually, our study grew from commonsense questions that anyone might ask, and it should be seen in that light. Although larger and more extensive than most investigations dealing with child rearing, our study will find its place along with a host of others in some future, up-to-date review of the literature in this rich, technical area of scholarship.

We have to confess that we did not even attempt to explore and incorporate local research, such as unpublished theses, in the nations included in our study, even though such explorations might have helped us make better sense of many of our findings. Nor have we gone deeply enough into the social history of the nations involved, which would have helped us place our study in proper perspective. We have been impressed and awed by the social perspectives provided by G. M. Trevelyan (1942) and Philippe Ariès (1975) for investigations like this one, but unfortunately we do not have the competence to give a broad historical background to our work, and consequently we are wide open to criticisms from Italian, Greek, Portuguese, Japanese, U.S., Canadian, British, Belgian, and French specialists in child rearing, who are informed about the social histories of the settings we have included in this investigation. Compared with social historians like Trevelyan and Ariès, or with specialists in the field of child training like Bronfenbrenner, Sears, and Maccoby, we see ourselves more as research technicians who have bulled our way into a very exclusive china shop. Nonetheless, some of the personal experiences we have had with preliminary presentations of our study give us a type of consolation. Each of us has been asked to present overviews of our findings before local groups of specialists in one or another of the foreign settings included in the investigation: Frasure-Smith in England, Hamers in Portugal and the Netherlands, and Lambert in Canada, the United States, and Greece.

By way of illustration, in the spring of 1976, a group of 30 specialists in child rearing congregated in Athens to listen to and react to our overall findings, especially to the results of our "Greek study." Once the technical and statistical results were presented along with the cross-national comparisons involving "Greek" styles of child-rearing values, a wonderful three-hour discussion developed, and throughout, our ignorance of the details of Greek family life and Greek society sparkled. However, our findings were stubborn "facts" that had to be dealt with by the specialists, and the diversity and number of individual interpretations that came out of the discussion made it crystal clear that no single interpretation or consensus was likely to emerge. In the end, our findings and the interpretations given them, especially when viewed cross-nationally, began to fit into most of the different theories represented at that meeting. We were most gratified that a number of potentially valuable follow-up studies were suggested during that discussion. Thus, we believe that the results presented in the chapters that follow can be instructive for local specialists in child rearing and can strengthen the theoretical and empirical bases of their own work by suggesting new lines of investigation.

THE RESEARCH PROCEDURE

Over the past 25 years, interviews with parents and questionnaires filled out by parents have been the most popular modes of collecting information about parent-child interactions, and they have proven to be efficient and useful methodological approaches. Parents are typically asked to recall and evaluate how they would react and how they would feel in various parent-child situations. Certain investigations using these methods (for example, Sears, Maccoby, and Levin 1957) have become models for cross-national studies (for example, Guthrie and Jacobs 1966). As might be expected, many questions have been raised about the appropriateness of taking interview responses as reliable or valid reflections of actual parent-child interaction, for when interviewed or questioned, parents may be anxious to present themselves in the best possible light, trying not to stray too far in their replies from what is expected of them (Radke-Yarrow, Campbell, and Burton 1970). Although the usefulness of interview and questionnaire procedures is beyond question (Campbell 1961), it is nonetheless true that researchers are now convinced that progress in the field will only be made as more investigations of actual parent-child interactions in normal settings become available (J. W. M. Whiting et al. 1955; B. Whiting 1963; L. Minturn and W. W. Lambert 1964).

But direct observation in natural settings has its problems, too; it is difficult to arrange, it is often unnatural, it is time-consuming, and it is costly. As a consequence, researchers have tried to develop alternatives. In our view, a very promising alternative is that developed recently by Rothbart and Maccoby (1966), a procedure that we adopt for the purposes of our own investigation. In this approach, parents of young children are asked to react to the taped voice of a child as that child seeks attention, help, or comfort, or becomes angry, insolent, or aggressive either toward a parent, a younger sibling, or a same-aged friend, and so forth. Rothbart and Maccoby argue that this method "closely approaches the behavior of a parent in an actual situation," and their findings with U.S. parents suggest that the procedure may be an extremely sensitive and powerful one. We view these reactions to the taped episodes more as reflections of parents' attitudes toward or values of child rearing than as indexes of child-rearing practices, even though we have seen parents become so involved with the episodes that they talk to the tape recorder and sometimes hit the table hard enough to make the instrument jump.

Our research adapts the Rothbart-Maccoby procedure for cross-national and cross-linguistic use and extends the number of taped incidents. We conducted a pilot study in the early 1970s (Lambert, Yackley, and Hein 1971) to test the applicability of the procedure for the Canadian setting as a preliminary to the series of interrelated comparative studies presented in this volume. A secondary aim of the Canadian study was to increase our own understanding of the value orientations of English and French Canadians and to search for the sources of conflict that arise between these two ethnic groups. In this regard the study was an extension of earlier work on Canadian social matters (for example, Lambert et al. 1960; Lambert, Frankel, and Tucker 1966; Lambert and Moore 1966; Aellen and Lambert 1969; Lambert 1967; Lambert and

Klineberg 1967; Lambert and Tucker 1972; Lambert 1968; Yackley and Lambert 1971).

In preparation for the Canadian pilot study, interviews were conducted with a broad sample of English-speaking and French-speaking mothers of first-grade children. These mothers were asked to recall incidents with their six-year-olds that worried, annoyed, or upset them and to describe their own and their husbands' typical reactions to such incidents. Note that we concentrate more on the annoying aspects of child rearing and less on the positive aspects, where, for example, a child might try to be helpful to a parent, take on responsibilities, or show cooperation and considerateness with siblings or peers. Our study then deals more with the everyday "realities" of child rearing, and less with the "pleasures."

From the preliminary survey of mothers, it became clear that a common set of episodes would be appropriate for both English Canadian and French Canadian parents of different social-class backgrounds, even though quite different meanings might be attached to the child's behavior, depending upon the parents' national, ethnic, or social-class background. The series of incidents worked out by Rothbart and Maccoby covered most of the episodes encountered in our pilot study, although new items, representing other problem areas also mentioned frequently by the parents in the pilot study, were added. Since them, the appropriateness of these incidents has been attested to by informants from various nations around the world. For instance, at an international seminar, a group of educators and psychologists from the Far East, Asia, Europe, and North America were given the taped episodes to evaluate, and, for each region represented, it was felt that, with minor revisions, the episodes captured familiar, everyday parent-child interactions.

The final versions of the episodes, adopted either from the Rothbart and Maccoby version or from the Canadian pilot studies, are listed below. Two separate tapes were made for each national setting, one for mothers, another for fathers, with local language or dialect variations worked into the child's statements. The English version follows. (1) Mummy (Daddy) come look at my puzzle. (2) Mummy (Daddy), help me! (3) Does this piece go here? (4) Baby, you can't play with me, you're too little. (5) He can't play with my puzzle. It's mine! (6) Leave my puzzle alone or I'll hit you on the head! (7) I don't like this game. I'm gonna break it. (8) I don't like this game. It's a stupid game, and you're stupid, Mama (Daddy). (9) Ow-w! Baby stepped on my hand! (10) Mummy (Daddy), it hurts! (11) Mummy (Daddy), get me another puzzle. (12) It's not raining now. Can I go across the street and play? (13) Why can't I? I'm gonna go anyway. (14) Can Chris come in and play?* (15) Chris, lemme put the pieces in myself. You watch me. (16) Don't touch the pieces. You don't know how to do it. (17) If you don't leave 'em alone, I'll beat you up.

For each national study children who were native speakers of the language and dialect in question were selected to play the child's role. All statements were rehearsed until the speaker sounded natural and realistic in his or her renditions. We also determined in advance that all of the child speakers could be easily taken as a boy or a girl, so that parents of a six-year-old boy thought that the child they heard on tape was also a boy; similarly, parents of a six-year-old girl took the speaker to be a girl.

From the pilot studies, we learned that for some parents the procedure was somewhat less embarrassing if they were permitted to write rather than speak aloud their reactions. Others preferred to speak their responses. In the investigation, we have collected parental reactions in both ways, as we explain in later chapters. When writing, parents were, of course, told to ignore spelling and punctuation errors because we wanted only their immediate, spontaneous reactions. They were assured in advance that the responses were coded for meanings and feeling, not for style.

Following preliminary phone or letter contacts, visits were made to the homes of parents. In most cases, families were chosen from lists provided by school principals. Each parent was tested individually and separately in order to keep the responses of mothers and fathers independent. The parent being tested was asked to imagine that he (or she) was at home reading, knitting or sewing, or occupied in the kitchen, while the six-year-old child was, in the early episodes on the tape, playing with a puzzle on the floor within hearing distance. Thus, it was not a free play period where the parent had nothing else to do. A younger sibling was with the child. After each of the child's statements, the tape was stopped, and the parent was encouraged to react to the taped statement as if he or she were listening to his or her own six-year-old.

The parents' responses to each item were coded, and then items were tallied and combined to form one of the ten separate scales. Since higher scores on these scales are generally more punitive or restrictive, the names assigned to the scales refer to

---

*Where possible, a "neutral" name, like Chris in English, was used to suggest that a visitor of the same sex as the child was invited in to play. In cases where the language did not provide neutral names, two separate tapes were made with a boy's name on one and a girl's name on the other.

the restrictive end; thus, it is a "Help Withholding" scale rather than a "Help Giving" scale. The total possible ranges of scores and the "neutral points" of the scales (the points where parental attitudes switch from permissiveness to sanctioning) are provided in each of the main statistical tables. The scales are: Help Withholding (Items 1, 2, 3, and 11); Comfort Withholding (9, 10); Temper Control (7); Social Temper Control (6, 17); Insolence Control (8, 13); Siding with Baby vs. Child (4, 5, 6); Attention Denial (9); Autonomy Control (12); Guest Restrictions (14); and Siding with Guest vs. Child (15, 16, 17). For each scale, scores can range from a permissive reaction (assigned a low score), to a restrictive reaction, a moral reprimand, taking the baby's or the playmate's (rather than the child's) side in a dispute, or withholding assistance. For example, in response to the child's statement "Daddy, help me!" (Item 2), a parent's reaction, "Let's see now, where would that piece go," would be rated high in help giving, while another reaction, in the form, "Try it in different places and see how it works," would be rated more toward the help withholding limit, next to an outright refusal or a complete ignoring of the child's request for help. Again for item 8 ("I don't like this game. It's a stupid game, and you're stupid Mama!"), parental reactions could range from overlooking the insolence and trying to understand the child's frustration, to demanding an apology, to reprimanding the child, to physically punishing the child.

Two judges coded the parental responses independently of each other. The details of the item-by-item coding are presented in Appendix A. In the case of parental reactions given in languages other than English or French, one of the coders worked from the language used by the parents in their replies, while the second coder worked from an English translation of the foreign language responses. The native language coder was always a native speaker of the language being coded. Thus, in Montreal we sought the assistance of native speakers of Greek, Portuguese, Japanese, and so on. A third coder was constant throughout the investigation, coding separately all English language versions of all responses. Disagreements between coders were resolved by discussion. Many revisions of the coding procedures were made over a three-year period until intercoder agreement, before any discussion was permitted, had reached at least 80 percent. The majority of the disagreements were due to translation problems, which were easily resolved through meetings of the three judges.

In addition to responding to the taped episodes, parents were also asked to respond to two questionnaires, half completing them before and half after they had listened to the tape. The first questionnaire, referred to as Perceived Differences in Sex-Roles, consisted of 40 items that probe for parents' perceptions of how similar or different boys and girls are in their typical behaviors or reactions. For example, parents were asked whether, from their experience, boys or girls are more likely to be bold and self-assertive, more persistent at tasks, more apt to defy punishment, more helpful around the house, and so on. A parent could say that, in his or her experience, a description applied more to girls (G), more to boys (B), or equally to both (X). The number of "X" answers, indicating no perceived boy-girl difference, was tallied for each parent. In order to make these scores consonant with the coded scores, the total number of "X" scores was subtracted from 40, making a higher score on this converted scale reflect a greater degree of perception of sex-role differences in behavior.

The second questionnaire, referred to as Expected Differences in Sex-Roles, measured parents' opinions as to whether sex-role differences in behavior should exist. In this case, parents were asked to indicate, for example, whether they felt it is "very important for a boy to be bold and self-assertive" (rated 5 on the 5-point scale) or "very important for a boy not to be bold or assertive" (rated 1 on the 5-point scale). Each question was asked twice, once with a boy and once with a girl as reference points. The absolute differences (D scores) were calculated in such a way that the higher the total D score, the more the parent expected sex-role differences in behavior. The two sex-role questionnaires can be found in Appendix B.

THE SAMPLES OF PARENTS

For each national study, we interviewed 40 mother-father pairs of parents, 20 who were from working-class backgrounds and 20 who were from middle-class backgrounds. Half of the sets of parents had a six-year-old boy, and half had a six-year-old girl, and that child was used as the reference person in the interview. Our measure of social class included three features: paternal education, paternal occupation, and the interviewer's opinion of family life-style. All middle-class fathers had at least some university-level education, while working-class fathers had at most completed high school or its European equivalent. This, we felt, was not a sufficient social-class measure by itself, so in addition, we categorized occupations into five major groupings: blue-collar, unskilled blue-collar, skilled; white-collar; business-managerial; and professional. Blue-collar, unskilled jobs included: truck drivers, janitors, day laborers, and unskilled factory workers. Blue-collar, skilled jobs included: barbers, electricians, plumbers, and skilled machine operators. White-collar jobs included: clerks, typists, and keypunch operators. Business-managerial jobs included: company presidents and vice-presidents, stockbrokers, departmental managers, and administrators. Professional jobs included: doctors, lawyers, architects, and researchers.

For our purposes, blue-collar occupations were considered to be working-class, and business-managerial and professional occupations were considered to be middle-class. We have not included the white-collar groups in our study, except when educational levels, as well as interviewer opinions, indicated that a particular white-collar family was unquestionably middle- or working-class. Tables describing the occupation, education, and family size of each group of parents were compiled.

STATISTICAL ANALYSIS

Our major statistical treatment has been analysis of variance, which allows us to examine independently and in interaction the effects of: ethnic or national group membership, social-class background, sex of child referred to, and sex of parent providing the information. For each pair or set of groups compared, separate tables were compiled of mean scores and analysis of variance results.

RELIABILITY

What about the reliability of our data? Could we expect to be able to replicate our results if we were to conduct the study a second time in any particular national setting? Because of limitations of funds and time, complete testing of replicability could not be carried out, but we, nonetheless, do have some evidence that the methods involved are reliable. For instance, we purposely collected two separate French Canadian middle-class samples of parents, and the responses received from the two groups of parents are essentially identical. In fact, it makes little difference whether we use one sample or the other in our comparisons with other groups, for the French Canadian middle-class pattern is the same. Thus, there is apparently a good deal of within-group homogeneity in the reactions we are measuring, and we feel fairly secure that at least the major trends found in our data are reliable.

THE PLAN OF THE CHAPTERS TO FOLLOW

Simple and straightforward as our methodology may appear, it took on surprising degrees of complexity as we applied it in various foreign settings. There was no master plan worked out in advance as to which nations should be included in the investigation. Instead, we jumped around from one national setting to another, something like a hound dog following a trail. The investigation started in Canada and jumped from there to France, from France to Belgium, and then back to French America, all with the purpose of following the trail of "Frenchness." This led us on a search for "Englishness," taking us from English Canada to the "old stock" United States, and from there to England. The results in Canada and the United States made us think of particular immigrant groups—Italian, Portuguese, Greek, and Japanese—which in turn, brought us back to comparable samples of parents still in the "old countries." Then, in Chapter 13 we stop and try to put it all in perspective by conducting a broad-spectrum analysis of ten national groups by linking distinctive national characteristics of child-rearing values with independent cross-national data on values and attitudes and by applying our findings to the school setting, where we explore degrees of match and mismatch of child-training values held by North American teachers, on the one hand, and immigrant parents, on the other.

Thus, this is an extensive investigation, and even though we find it fascinating and exciting at every point, we wonder if readers will share our enthusiasm, because the book is long and sometimes technical. Perhaps we can engender enthusiasm of a somewhat different sort if we ask potential readers to think about the following news release from the United States. Maybe its message will give parents a good reason to study our book carefully; in fact, it might even entice perceptive children to study the book more carefully still!

Son Sues Parents for Malpractice

(Chicago Tribune, April 29, 1978)

Boulder, Colo. (AP) - A 24-year-old man has filed suit in District Court here seeking $350,000 in damages from his mother and father for what his lawyer described as parental malpractice.

Tom Hansen alleged in the suit that his parents had inflicted emotional distress by willfully and wantonly neglecting his needs for food, clothing, shelter, and psychological support at crucial times of his life.

Hansen's attorney, John Taussig Jr., said the issue in the case was not whether parents make mistakes in raising their children, but whether parents should be held responsible for serious damage to the physical and mental health of their offspring.

Hansen's parents, Shirley Hansen of Boulder and Richard Hansen of Hilo, Hawaii, could not be contacted for comment on the suit filed here Wednesday.

Hansen's suit stated that he would be in need of psychiatric care throughout his life because of the "intentional infliction of emotional distress" by his parents.

Hansen said he suffered from malnutrition in his formative years and needs continuing psychiatric care. His suit seeks $250,000 for medical expenses and $100,000 in punitive damages.

2

ENGLISH CANADIAN AND FRENCH CANADIAN STYLES OF CHILD REARING

Is there anything special about child rearing in Canada? Do Canadian parents have unique approaches to child training? Are there any real differences between English-speaking and French-speaking Canadian parents in their orientations to child training? With questions of this sort in mind, we conducted an extensive investigation of the child-training orientations (or values) of English Canadian (EC) and French Canadian (FC) parents, selecting samples representing working- and middle-social-class positions in Canadian society. It was a complex and difficult study to manage. Fathers and mothers of young children (around six years of age) were interviewed in their homes. The interview procedure was novel in that each parent, one at a time, was asked to listen to and then react spontaneously to tape-recorded episodes of a child, one much like their own, in various types of everyday interactions with a parent, with a younger sibling, or with a playmate invited in to play. What the child said and did in each episode was meant to evoke particular types of reactions from parents, and these could range from acquiescence through "laissez-faire," to outright anger. The parent's task then was to imagine himself or herself as the parental partner in these episodes, either in direct contact with the child or as an observer, and to give his or her first reactions. This procedure, first tried out by Rothbart and Maccoby in California (1966), had been used in a pilot study (Lambert, Yackley, and Hein 1971) where its effectiveness and interest value were tested. From previous research, then, we knew that parents get caught up with the taped episodes as though they were actually in interaction with their own children, only occasionally dropping out of the parental role to say "Oh, no. My child would not go that far with me!" or something similar. In fact, we feel that the procedure may be as evocative and natural or more so than actual observations of family interactions. The pilot study also demonstrated that the results of an investigation of this sort are reliable across subgroups of parents, easily scored and analyzed in the statistical sense, and extremely rich in terms of subgroup differences, many of which have great social significance.

Although the Canadian study can be taken as a separate and independent investigation, it will become evident in later chapters that it is really just the first in a series. But because so many questions of a cross-national nature come to mind as we explored the Canadian scene, this study became the focal or reference work for those to follow.

METHOD AND PROCEDURE

In preparation for this study, interviews were conducted with approximately 20 English-speaking and 20 French-speaking mothers of first-grade children. They were asked to recall incidents with their six-year-olds that worried, annoyed, or upset them, and to describe their own and their husbands' typical reactions to such events. From this preliminary investigation, it became apparent that a common set of incidents would be appropriate for both English and French Canadian parents, although quite different local or national interpretations and reactions might be expected in certain instances. The series of incidents worked out by Rothbart and Maccoby also seemed appropriate, although new items, representing other problem areas mentioned frequently by Canadian parents, were added.

Subjects

The informants for this investigation were 80 sets of parents each having a six-year-old child attending public elementary schools in the greater Montreal area. Forty of these pairs of parents were English-speaking Canadians (ECs), meaning that their home language was English and that both parents had been born in Canada, 20 pairs coming from "working-class" or lower socioeconomic home backgrounds (to be discussed below), and 20 others from middle-class backgrounds. Forty sets of parents were French-speaking Canadians (FCs), whose home language was French and who were born in Canada, 20 pairs coming from working-class backgrounds, and 20 pairs from middle-class backgrounds. In each of the four social class-ethnic subgroups, there were ten mothers of girls, ten fathers of girls, ten mothers of boys, and ten fathers of boys, making a total sample of 160 parents (80 couples).

All English Canadian parents were Protestant, and all French Canadian parents were Catholic. Because we wanted to compare "typical" EC and FC parents as much as possible, we decided on EC Protestant families to compare with FC Catholic ones. A separate study now underway will provide a further comparison of EC Protestant and EC Catholic orientations to child training. Although the difference of religion for the two groups does to some extent involve ethnicity as well as religion, the difference is an accurate reflection of the religious affiliation of most English and French Canadians in Montreal, according to the 1971 census returns for the greater Montreal area.

A good deal of attention was given to the assessment of social-class background, for we wanted to be certain that there would be real differences between those classified as working- and middle-class. In anticipation of the cross-national studies to follow, we needed to establish definite guidelines for the two social-class levels that would hold in North American as well as European and Oriental settings. Our initial demarcations for social class were based on Canadian norms developed by Blishen (1967). The Blishen scale was constructed on the basis of 1960 census information and involves three aspects of social class: education, income, and prestige. By means of a form of regression analysis, Blishen assigned scale values (ranging from 25.36 for trappers and hunters to 76.69 for chemical engineers) to 320 different occupations. Initially for the middle-class group, we planned to include only those occupations in the top two deciles of the Blishen scale, and for the working class to include only those occupations in the bottom two deciles, ignoring the somewhat indistinct area between the two groups. However, because of inadequacies in the Blishen scale (the small number of occupations rated, the lack of differentiation on the basis of size of business, and the relative age of the data on which it is based) and because of our fear that the scale would almost certainly not be cross-nationally valid, we decided to discard the Blishen scale in favor of classifying occupations into one of five broad categories: professional, business-managerial, white-collar, blue-collar-skilled, and blue-collar-unskilled. Professional and business-managerial jobs were counted as middle-class, and white-collar, blue-collar-skilled, and blue-collar-unskilled jobs were counted as working-class. We tried to avoid white-collar workers as much as possible, since to some extent they are middle-class and to some extent they are working-class. Thus, decisions about their social status tend to be rather subjective. In addition to the job requirements for the two social classes we added an educational requirement. All middle-class fathers had to have graduated from high school and had some college experience. To fall in our working-class category, fathers could have at most a high school diploma.

Briefly, then, in order to be included in our Canadian samples, a family had to meet the following requirements:

1. Father's occupation
   - middle class: professional or business-managerial
   - working or lower class: white collar, blue collar-skilled, or blue collar-unskilled
2. Father's education
   - middle class: high school diploma plus some college
   - working class: at most a high school diploma
3. Religion of both parents
   - English Canadian: Protestant
   - French Canadian: Roman Catholic
4. Home language of both parents
   - English Canadian: English
   - French Canadian: French
5. Birthplace of both parents
   - Canada
6. Age of child
   - 5 years 6 months to 6 years 6 months
7. Intactness of family
   - parents not divorced or separated
   - biological parents or adoptive parents of a six-year-old child who was less than two years old at time of adoption.

Finding parents who met all of our requirements and who were also willing to let interviewers come into their homes for an hour-long interview proved to be a long and time-consuming task. The major problem lay not in the number of refusals, but in locating people born in Canada who met our other requirements.

Parents' names for the study were obtained in one of three ways: from lists of names of parents of kindergarten and first-grade children provided by a number of school principals, from names suggested by parents whom we did interview, or by parents who could not be interviewed because they did not meet all of the sample requirements, and from responses to a letter sent home with kindergarten and first-grade children in a number of schools describing the study and asking parents if they would be willing to volunteer. The majority of parents were obtained from telephoning the numbers given on the school lists. However, we were unable to continue this procedure because of an increase in concern among principals that the names might be used for some business venture.

This occurred at about midpoint in our study and was the direct result of a large-scale phone campaign by an insurance company. It was then that we turned to the other alternatives just described.

A summary of the background characteristics of our working- and middle-class samples, both English and French Canadian, is given in Table 2.1. The average number of years of education for both French and English working-class fathers was between eight and nine years and for the middle-class groups about 17 years. Thus, our working-class groups consisted primarily of eighth-grade graduates and our middle-class group was made up largely of college graduates with some postgraduate training. In addition to the marked difference in education between the social-class groups, there was also a large difference in the types of occupations held by family heads from the two classes. The working-class fathers from both language groups were primarily blue-collar workers, and there was essentially no difference between the ethnic groups in the number of skilled and unskilled workers. In contrast, the middle-class fathers were either professionals or held business-managerial type positions. It is noteworthy that although the difference is not significant (chi^2, 1 $\underline{df}$ = 3.61) there were more professionals in the French Canadian middle-class sample than in the English Canadian middle-class. This difference is to a large extent representative of the middle-class components of the two language groups (Guindon 1968; Ossenberg 1971; Woolfson 1973) and, given the equivalence in education of our samples, the difference in occupations should not constitute a real difference in social status. However, there was a significant difference between the English and French Canadian middle-class groups in the number of mothers who held positions themselves or attended classes outside the home. There were only two working mothers in the English Canadian middle class in contrast to 11 working mothers in the French Canadian middle class (chi^2, 1 $\underline{df}$ = 7.29, $\underline{p}$ < .01). We have no way of knowing the extent to which this difference affected the representativeness of the families we interviewed.

Taped Stimulus Material

A number of six-year-old children were considered as candidates for the child's role, and the two finally chosen had voice characteristics that were ambiguous enough to be easily taken as either girls or boys when given appropriate names. One was a native speaker of French Canadian style French, the other of Canadian style English. Each child was given scripts of the episodes taken from Rothbart and Maccoby (1966), with certain small adaptations,

TABLE 2.1

Background Characteristics of English Canadian
and French Canadian Samples

Group		Fathers' Years of Schooling	Mothers' Years of Schooling	Number of Children	Fathers' Occupations
English Canadian	X̄	8.9	9.3	3.3	7 blue-collar, unskilled:
Working-	SD	1.6	1.4	1.8	2 janitors
Class					1 orderly
	Range	7-11	6-11	1-8	1 stevedore
(Protestant)					3 drivers
					10 blue-collar, skilled:
					3 printers
					1 mechanic
					1 telephone technician
					1 painter
					3 industrial
	2 working mothers				foremen
					3 white-collar:
					2 office clerks
					1 insurance underwriter
English Canadian	X̄	17.0	14.6	3.4	6 professional:
					1 college
Middle-	SD	2.1	1.9	1.0	professor
Class					3 lawyers
	Range	13-20	11-17	2-6	2 doctors
(Protestant)					14 business- managerial:
					10 managers or executives
					1 accountant
					1 banker
	2 working mothers				1 personnel consultant
					1 stockbroker

Group		Fathers' Years of Schooling	Mothers' Years of Schooling	Number of Children	Fathers' Occupations
French Canadian	X̄	8.3	8.7	3.2	10 blue-collar, unskilled:
Working-	SD	2.4	2.1	1.5	1 janitor
Class					3 day laborers
	Range	3-12	5-12	2-7	5 drivers
(Catholic)					1 station attendant
					9 blue-collar, skilled:
					1 press operator
					1 miller
					2 firemen
					2 mechanics
					1 mailman
					1 painter
	0 working mothers				1 white-collar:
					1 office clerk
French Canadian	X̄	17.4	14.6	2.7	13 professional:
					2 lawyers
Middle-	SD	1.5	2.4	1.0	2 optometrists
Class					3 college
	Range	15-20	9-18	1-4	professors
(Catholic)					1 head librarian
					3 engineers
					2 high school teachers
					7 business- managerial:
					1 accountant
					2 administrators
					1 stockbroker
	11 working mothers				3 managers or executives

Source: Compiled by the authors.

or from the pilot study mentioned above. Their deliveries were rehearsed until they were natural and realistic. Certain mumblings were retained on the tapes so that parents would have a good reason to follow a typed transcript of the child's productions. The transcriptions assured us that the content was fully understood by the parents before they gave us their immediate reactions.*

Procedure

The parents were interviewed at home by a female interviewer, a native speaker of French in the case of French Canadian parents and a native speaker of English in the case of English Canadian parents. While one parent was occupied with the taped episodes, the other filled out the sex-role questionnaire.[†] Parents were encouraged to give their first reaction to each of the child's statements, while the tape was stopped, by writing what they would say or do in each instance. The statements, in either an English Canadian or French Canadian version, were presented via a tape recorder exactly as described in Chapter 1. The parents' responses were also analyzed and coded as described earlier.

Coding sheets based on those of Rothbart and Maccoby, with adaptations, were developed in advance. A great deal of attention was given to the reworking of the coding categories to improve the interjudge agreement in assigning parental reactions to definite places on each scale. To this end, the codes were revised several times and tested until we were satisfied. The final coding sheets are included in Appendix A.

Because of the large number of recodings necessitated by the changes made in the coding schema during the time that the English and French Canadian data were being analyzed, it is difficult and

---

*This approach differs from that used in our work with immigrant groups, in which case the interviewers transcribed the oral responses of the parents rather than having the parents write their answers. This change was introduced to avoid any embarrassment for those with limited writing and reading experience.

[†]With immigrant groups to be described in later chapters, two interviewers went to each home. One interviewer played the tape and transcribed the responses of one of the parents while the other interviewer read aloud the questionnaire and wrote down the responses of the second parent. For half the interviews mothers heard the tape before the fathers, and for the other half fathers heard the tape first.

perhaps misleading to calculate interrater reliabilities for these samples. However, Table 2.2 includes the interrater correlations and percentages of agreement between the two bilingual coders (one English and the other French) who scored the responses of 20 French Canadian middle-class parents. The average interrater correlation for the 17 items was .84, with .70 being the lowest and .96 the highest.

TABLE 2.2

Interrater Correlations and Percentages of Agreement per Item for the Responses of Forty French Canadian Middle-Class Parents

Item	Correlation	Percent Agreement
1	.92	92.5
2	.96	90.0
3	.93	87.5
4	.83	90.0
5	.79	75.0
6	.91	82.5
7	.70	62.5
8	.80	65.0
9	.85	85.0
10	.85	85.0
11	.91	90.0
12	.73	80.0
13	.76	77.5
14	.86	87.5
15	.74	85.0
16	.83	82.5
17	.86	65.0
Mean	.84	81.3

Source: Compiled by the authors.

Parent Questionnaire

Parents completed a questionnaire providing us with their views of a) the expected sex-role behaviors of boys and girls, and b) an estimate of their own perceptions of differences in the sex-role behavior of boys and girls. This questionnaire has been described in Chapter 1 and is presented in full in Appendix B.

In addition there were a number of background questions concerning each parent's education, occupation, place of birth, and religious affiliation, as well as information concerning the family size and the birth date and birth order of the "six-year-old" child.

RESULTS: THE CANADIAN STUDY

The statistical comparisons of the reactions of English and French Canadian parents are summarized in Table 2.3 and Table 2.4. Table 2.3 presents the "statistically significant" comparisons, that is, those at the .01 and .05 levels of confidence. Blanks in Table 2.3 mean that the particular comparison did not constitute a statistically reliable difference, and these we will consider as being cases of no difference. Table 2.4 presents the mean or average scores for each subcategory of respondent, categorized in various ways. For instance, the most complex finding in the tables is a three-way interaction for temper control. One can locate this in Table 2.3 with the entry 4.51 (significant at the .05 level of confidence) for the interaction between the ethnicity of parents (the G factor), the social-class background of parents (the C factor), and the sex of the children involved (the X factor). This finding means that French and English Canadian parents of different social class backgrounds react differently to temper outbursts of their sons in comparison with those of their daughters. The mean scores for this interaction are on page 30 of Table 2.4. We can visualize this interplay of factors by diagraming the scores. Since we shall be drawing conclusions from such outcomes, it may be informative to follow this complex example through as an illustration. None of the others will be as difficult to grasp. When plotted, the means for the GCX interaction for temper control generate the pattern seen in Figure 2.1.

Note first that in Table 2.3 there is no overall ethnic group difference in how parents treat temper displays, and Figure 2.1 reflects that fact. In other words, if an average were taken of all four EC plots it would fall at about the same score position as an average of the four FC plots, somewhere between 58 and 65 (see page 28 of Table 2.4 for the mean EC and FC scores for the temper control dimension). If we were to take averages of the two lower-class and two middle-class plots for each ethnic group we would find that working-class parents in general are, relative to middle-class parents, harsher with temper displays, and this is reflected in the significant overall social class effect (see Table 2.3 and page 28 of

TABLE 2.3

Significant Effects in the Comparisons of English Canadian and French Canadian Parents

Comparisons	Value Dimensions											
	1) Help Withholding (np = 58.6)	2) Siding with Baby vs. Child (np = 42.7)	3a) Temper Control (np = 30.0)	3b) Social Temper Control (np = 41.6)	4) Insolence Control (np = 25.0)	5) Attention Denial (np = 75.0)	6) Comfort Withholding (np = 41.6)	7) Autonomy Control (np = 58.3)	8) Guest Restriction (np = 62.5)	9) Siding with Guest vs. Child (np = 42.7)	10) Perceived Sex-Role Differences	11) Expected Sex-Role Differences
G	<u>10.70</u>	-	-	-	4.80	-	-	-	-	-	-	-
C	-	<u>33.90</u>	<u>8.07</u>	<u>43.10</u>	<u>58.99</u>	-	-	<u>8.95</u>	<u>21.68</u>	<u>38.70</u>	7.26	<u>19.6</u>
X	-	6.31	-	8.37	-	4.63	-	-	5.19	<u>7.59</u>	-	-
P	-	-	-	-	-	6.69	-	-	-	4.38	-	-
GC	-	-	-	-	-	-	-	-	-	-	-	-
GX	-	-	-	-	-	-	-	-	-	-	5.28	-
CX	-	-	-	-	-	-	-	-	-	-	-	3.9
GP	-	<u>10.47</u>	-	5.50	-	-	4.75	-	-	-	-	4.2
CP	-	-	-	-	-	-	-	-	6.71	-	4.53	-
XP	5.39	-	-	-	-	-	-	-	-	-	-	-
GCX	-	-	4.51	-	-	-	-	-	-	-	-	-
GCP	-	-	-	-	-	-	-	-	-	-	4.87	-
GXP	-	-	-	-	-	-	-	-	-	-	-	-
CXP	-	-	-	-	-	-	-	-	-	-	-	-
GCXP	-	-	-	-	-	-	-	-	-	-	-	-

Notes: In this and all subsequent tables, G = Group; C = Social Class; X = Sex of Child; P = Sex of Parent; GC = Group/Social Class; GX = Group/Sex of Child; CX = Social Class/Sex of Child; GP = Group/Sex of Parent; CP = Social Class/Sex of Parent; XP = Sex of Child/Sex of Parent; GCX = Group/Social Class/Sex of Child; GCP = Group/Social Class/Sex of Parent; GXP = Group/Sex of Child/Sex of Parent; CXP = Social Class/Sex of Child/Sex of Parent; GCXP = Group/Social Class/Sex of Child/Sex of Parent.

Entries are significant F values; those underlined are beyond the .01 level of confidence, the others are beyond the .05 level.

Source: Compiled by the authors.

TABLE 2.4

Subgroup Comparisons: English Canadian versus French Canadian Families

Comparisons		1) Help Withholding (np = 58.6)	2) Siding with Baby vs. Child (np = 42.7)	3a) Temper Control (np = 30.0)	3b) Social Temper Control (np = 41.6)	4) Insolence Control (np = 25.0)	5) Attention Denial (np = 75.0)	6) Comfort Withholding (np = 41.6)	7) Autonomy Control (np = 58.3)	8) Guest Restriction (np = 62.5)	9) Siding with Guest vs. Child (np = 42.7)	10) Perceived Sex-Role Differences	11) Expected Sex-Role Differences
(G)	EC	50.65	51.29	65.25	68.93	68.60	82.07	52.31	44.57	49.69	61.41	18.99	13.89
	FC	43.33	54.96	58.75	68.75	62.16	84.95	50.08	44.99	35.00	62.13	19.14	15.41
(O)	WC	47.97	58.71	67.35	76.95	76.67	84.32	53.35	52.28	45.94	67.67	20.67	18.35
	MC	46.01	47.54	56.65	60.73	54.09	82.71	49.04	37.29	38.75	55.86	17.45	10.95
(X)	B	47.04	52.27	60.10	65.27	66.49	79.39	51.12	45.82	40.00	59.15	18.09	15.25
	G	46.94	53.97	63.90	72.41	64.28	87.64	51.27	43.74	44.69	64.38	20.04	14.05
(P)	F	45.39	55.41	60.60	67.28	66.25	87.87	55.92	46.66	42.50	60.03	19.86	15.33
	M	48.59	50.83	63.40	70.40	64.52	79.16	46.48	42.91	42.19	63.50	18.26	13.97
(GO)	WC <u>EC</u>	52.13	58.57	74.00	77.08	81.67	80.40	54.60	52.91	53.13	67.53	21.97	17.65
	MC	49.17	44.01	56.50	60.77	55.53	83.75	50.02	36.24	46.25	55.29	16.00	10.13
	WC <u>FC</u>	43.81	58.84	60.70	76.81	71.67	88.24	52.10	51.66	38.75	67.82	19.37	19.05
	MC	42.85	51.07	56.80	60.69	52.65	81.67	48.07	38.33	31.25	56.44	18.90	11.77

Value Dimensions

(GX)	EC	B	49.53	49.91	62.50	65.67	69.99	77.49	52.51	45.82	47.50	57.81	18.47	16.15
		G	51.77	52.67	68.00	72.19	67.21	86.65	52.11	43.33	51.87	65.00	19.50	11.63
	FC	B	44.55	54.63	57.70	64.86	62.98	81.29	49.73	45.82	32.50	60.49	17.70	14.35
		G	42.11	55.29	59.80	72.64	61.35	88.62	50.44	44.16	37.50	63.77	20.57	16.47
(CX)	WC	B	47.41	58.69	66.20	73.34	80.63	80.45	51.27	48.74	43.13	63.69	19.80	20.67
		G	48.54	58.72	68.50	80.55	72.72	88.19	55.43	55.82	48.75	71.65	21.55	16.03
	MC	B	46.68	45.85	54.00	57.19	52.35	78.33	50.97	42.91	36.87	54.61	16.37	9.83
		G	45.33	49.23	59.30	64.27	55.84	87.08	47.11	31.67	40.63	57.11	18.53	12.07
(GP)	EC	F	50.43	56.53	64.50	68.37	71.37	87.91	62.52	48.74	50.63	59.14	20.20	15.75
		M	50.87	46.05	66.00	69.48	65.83	76.24	42.10	40.41	48.75	63.68	17.77	12.03
	FC	F	40.35	54.30	56.70	66.19	61.13	87.83	49.31	44.58	34.37	60.93	19.53	14.90
		M	46.31	55.62	60.80	71.31	63.20	82.08	50.85	45.41	35.63	63.32	18.75	15.93
(CP)	WC	F	46.97	60.01	64.70	73.69	75.83	88.24	55.02	52.91	42.50	64.57	22.50	19.30
		M	48.97	57.40	70.00	80.21	77.51	80.40	51.68	51.65	49.37	70.77	18.85	17.40
	MC	F	43.82	50.81	56.50	60.87	56.67	87.50	56.81	40.41	42.50	55.50	17.23	11.35
		M	48.20	44.27	56.80	60.59	51.52	77.91	41.27	34.16	35.00	56.23	17.67	10.55
(XP)	B	F	43.44	54.13	56.70	60.88	65.41	84.62	57.23	48.33	40.00	55.85	18.75	16.87
		M	50.64	50.41	63.50	69.65	67.57	74.16	45.01	43.32	40.00	62.45	17.43	13.63
	G	F	47.35	56.69	64.50	73.68	67.09	91.12	54.61	44.99	45.00	64.22	20.97	13.77
		M	46.53	51.26	63.30	71.14	61.47	84.16	47.94	42.49	44.37	64.55	19.10	14.33

(continued)

29

Table 2.4, continued

			Value Dimensions											
Comparisons			1) Help Withholding (np = 58.6)	2) Siding with Baby vs. Child (np = 42.7)	3a) Temper Control (np = 30.0)	3b) Social Temper Control (np = 41.6)	4) Insolence Control (np = 25.0)	5) Attention Denial (np = 75.0)	6) Comfort Withholding (np = 41.6)	7) Autonomy Control (np = 58.3)	8) Guest Restriction (np = 62.5)	9) Siding with Guest vs. Child (np = 42.7)	10) Perceived Sex-Role Differences	11) Expected Sex-Role Differences
(GCX) EC	WC	B	51.21	56.33	76.00	73.33	86.67	76.65	50.85	49.15	50.00	63.14	22.70	22.75
		G	53.06	60.81	72.00	80.83	76.67	84.15	58.35	56.65	56.25	71.91	21.25	12.55
	MC	B	47.86	43.49	49.00	58.01	53.32	78.33	54.18	42.49	45.00	52.49	14.25	9.55
		G	50.47	44.53	64.00	63.54	57.75	89.16	45.85	29.99	47.50	58.09	17.75	10.70
FC	WC	B	43.61	61.05	56.40	73.34	74.59	84.24	51.69	48.33	36.25	64.24	16.90	18.60
		G	44.01	56.63	65.00	80.28	68.77	92.24	52.51	54.99	41.25	71.39	21.85	19.50
	MC	B	45.50	48.21	59.00	56.37	51.38	78.33	47.77	43.32	28.75	56.74	18.50	10.10
		G	40.19	53.93	54.60	64.99	53.93	85.00	48.36	33.33	33.75	56.13	19.30	13.45
(GCP) EC	WC	F	51.53	63.13	73.00	74.16	84.17	86.65	61.69	55.83	48.75	63.35	23.15	20.45
		M	52.74	54.01	75.00	80.01	79.17	74.15	47.52	49.99	57.50	71.71	20.80	14.85
	MC	F	49.35	49.92	56.00	62.59	58.57	89.17	63.35	41.65	52.50	54.93	17.25	11.05
		M	48.99	38.09	57.00	58.96	52.49	78.33	36.69	30.83	40.00	55.65	14.75	9.20
FC	WC	F	42.41	56.89	56.40	73.21	67.50	89.83	48.35	49.99	36.25	65.79	21.85	18.15
		M	45.21	60.79	65.00	80.41	75.85	86.65	55.85	53.32	41.25	69.84	16.90	19.95
	MC	F	38.29	51.71	57.00	59.16	54.76	85.83	50.27	39.17	32.50	56.07	17.20	11.65
		M	47.41	50.44	56.60	62.21	50.55	77.50	45.85	37.49	30.00	56.81	20.60	11.90

30

Section	Cond	Grp	Sex												
(GXP)	EC	B	F	48.17	55.87	61.00	63.01	71.66	85.83	65.01	53.33	50.00	53.89	19.45	18.90
			M	50.89	43.95	64.00	68.34	68.33	69.15	40.01	38.32	45.00	61.73	17.50	13.40
		G	F	52.70	57.19	68.00	73.75	71.09	89.99	60.02	44.15	51.25	64.38	20.95	12.60
			M	50.83	48.15	68.00	70.63	63.34	83.32	44.19	42.49	52.50	65.62	18.05	10.65
	FC	B	F	38.71	52.39	52.40	58.75	59.17	83.41	49.44	43.33	30.00	57.81	18.05	14.85
			M	50.39	56.87	63.00	70.96	66.80	79.16	50.01	48.32	35.00	63.17	17.35	13.85
		G	F	41.99	56.20	61.00	73.61	63.09	92.25	49.19	45.83	38.75	64.05	21.00	14.95
			M	42.22	54.37	58.60	71.66	59.59	84.99	51.69	42.49	36.25	63.47	20.15	18.00
(CXP)	WC	B	F	43.95	59.77	63.40	67.09	78.75	84.24	50.85	48.33	41.25	58.01	21.30	23.40
			M	50.85	57.61	69.00	79.58	82.51	76.65	51.68	49.15	45.00	69.37	18.30	17.95
		G	F	49.99	60.25	66.00	80.27	72.93	92.23	59.19	57.49	43.75	71.13	23.70	15.20
			M	47.09	57.19	71.00	80.83	72.51	84.15	51.69	54.15	53.75	72.19	19.40	16.85
	MC	B	F	42.93	48.49	50.00	54.67	52.08	85.00	63.60	48.33	38.75	53.69	16.20	10.35
			M	50.43	43.21	58.00	59.72	52.62	71.67	38.35	37.49	35.00	55.54	16.55	9.30
		G	F	44.71	53.14	63.00	67.09	61.25	90.00	50.03	32.49	46.25	57.31	18.25	12.35
			M	45.97	45.32	55.60	61.45	50.42	84.16	44.19	30.83	35.00	56.91	18.80	11.80
(GCXP)	EC	B	F	48.35	63.17	78.00	69.17	88.33	83.32	58.35	54.99	50.00	56.04	23.30	27.70
			M	54.06	49.50	74.00	77.50	85.01	69.98	43.35	43.32	50.00	70.24	22.10	17.80
		G	F	54.70	63.10	68.00	79.15	80.01	89.98	65.02	56.66	47.50	70.65	23.00	13.20
			M	51.42	58.51	76.00	82.51	73.34	78.32	51.69	56.65	65.00	73.18	19.50	11.90
	MC	B	F	47.99	48.57	44.00	56.84	54.99	88.33	71.68	51.66	50.00	51.75	15.60	10.10
			M	47.73	38.40	54.00	59.18	51.65	68.33	36.68	33.32	40.00	53.23	12.90	9.00
		G	F	50.70	51.27	68.00	68.34	62.16	90.00	55.02	31.65	55.00	58.11	18.90	12.00
			M	50.25	37.78	60.00	58.74	53.34	88.32	36.69	28.34	40.00	58.06	16.60	9.40

(continued)

Table 2.4, continued

Value Dimensions

Comparisons			1) Help Withholding (np = 58.6)	2) Siding with Baby vs. Child (np = 42.7)	3a) Temper Control (np = 30.0)	3b) Social Temper Control (np = 41.6)	4) Insolence Control (np = 25.0)	5) Attention Denial (np = 75.0)	6) Comfort Withholding (np = 41.6)	7) Autonomy Control (np = 58.3)	8) Guest Restriction (np = 62.5)	9) Siding with Guest vs. Child (np = 42.7)	10) Perceived Sex-Role Differences	11) Expected Sex-Role Differences
WC	B	F	39.56	56.38	48.80	65.02	69.16	85.16	43.36	41.66	32.50	59.99	19.30	19.10
		M	47.65	65.71	64.00	81.66	80.01	83.32	60.01	54.99	40.00	68.49	14.50	18.10
	G	F	45.27	57.39	64.00	81.40	65.84	94.49	53.35	58.33	40.00	71.60	24.40	17.20
		M	42.76	55.88	66.00	79.16	71.69	89.99	51.68	51.65	42.50	71.19	19.30	21.80
(GCXP) FC	B	F	37.87	48.41	56.00	52.49	49.17	81.67	55.52	44.99	27.50	55.63	16.80	10.60
		M	53.13	48.02	62.00	60.26	53.59	75.00	40.02	41.65	30.00	57.85	20.20	9.60
MC	G	F	38.71	55.01	58.00	65.83	60.35	90.00	45.03	33.34	37.50	56.51	17.60	12.70
		M	41.68	52.86	51.20	64.16	47.50	80.00	51.69	33.33	30.00	55.76	21.00	14.20

Note: In this and all subsequent tables, EC = English Canadian; FC = French Canadian; WC = Working Class; MC = Middle Class; B = Boy; G = Girl; F = Female; M = Male.
Source: Compiled by the authors.

32

FIGURE 2.1

G x C x X Interaction for Temper Control

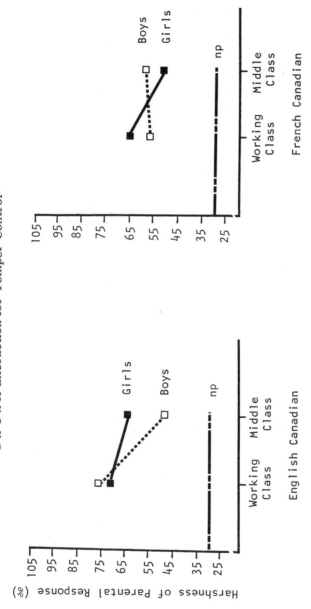

Note: In this and all subsequent figures, G = Significant Ethnic Group; C = Social Class; X = Sex of Child.
Source: Constructed by the authors.

33

Table 2.4). It might seem that the EC parents are the bigger contributors to this social-class effect, but actually the FC-EC difference in this case is not statistically significant since the ethnicity by social-class difference (the GC interaction) was not significant by itself (see Table 2.3 and page 28 of Table 2.4 under temper control).

Our example in Figure 2.1 does however reflect quite different reactions on the part of FC and EC middle- and working-class parents to their sons and daughters. The contrast has at least two components: first, middle-class EC parents compared to middle-class FC parents are relatively lenient with their sons' displays of temper. In fact, we note that it is the middle-class FC parents of boys who go against a rather general middle-class trend of showing more lenience toward temper outbursts. Second, the diagram shows us that working-class EC parents of boys are harsher than working-class EC parents of girls on temper displays, while working-class FC parents of boys are less harsh than working-class FC parents of girls. Questions raised by these outcomes can not all be answered from the data available. Rather the questions that come to mind suggest directions for further research. For example, why should FC working-class parents be particularly harsh on short-tempered girls, while comparable EC parents are particularly severe on short-tempered boys? And why should FC middle-class parents single out boys, while comparable EC parents single out girls? We will try to examine in some detail, questions of this sort as we go along, but in many instances we will not have definitive answers without further research.

Our main purpose here is to assure the reader that there is nothing highly mathematical, forbidding, or mysterious about the numbers presented in these tables. They are simply the numbers assigned by teams of coders who have considered carefully the meaning of each parent's reactions to the episodes provided. These code assignments have been put to a statistical test of reliability or significance, and we are left to construct our interpretations of the ways parents react to their children on the basis of those comparisons that meet acceptable levels of significance. As will be evident, we will give as much attention to cases where the major ethnic or social class groups are similar in their reactions as to cases where they are different.

Parental Reactions to a Child's Requests for Help

The information for this analysis is found in the first columns of Tables 2.3 and 2.4. Note that Canadian parents in general extend assistance or help when it is requested, judging by the mean scores, all of which fall below the neutral or middlemost point on the help withholding dimension. There are, nonetheless, several important subgroup differences among parents in degrees of readiness or eagerness to give help. First, there is a highly significant ethnicity effect (row 1 in Table 2.3 and rows 1 and 2 in Table 2.4, $p < .01$), indicating that EC parents are much less immediate than FC parents in extending help to their children. The strategies employed by the two groups also differ in subtle ways, as is evident in the classification reactions to a child's request for help, depicted in Table 2.5. There is a tendency among FC parents to be more immediate and direct in offering help, whereas EC parents are more prone to delay, to refuse, or ignore the child's requests.

TABLE 2.5

Response Comparisons: English and French Canadian Parents

Reactions to: "Mommy/Daddy, help me."

Reactions	Ethnicity of Parents	
	FC	EC
Direct, immediate, or partial assistance	60	51
Short delay	8	12
Urge child to try alone	8	9
Refuse, ignore, deflect	3	8
Uncodable	1	0
Totals	80	80

Source: Compiled by the authors.

It is of interest that social-class background does not affect parents' tendencies to extend or withhold help. In fact there is only one other source of influence, that of the interaction of sex of parent by sex of child (the XP interaction, row 10 in Table 2.3, and page 29 of Table 2.4, $p < .05$). This interaction is depicted in Figure 2.2 which shows that Canadian fathers of girls are relatively less inclined to give help than are fathers of boys, while Canadian mothers of girls are generally similar to mothers of boys in their readiness to extend help. Although one-sided, there is here a pattern that we will refer to as "same-sex leniency," meaning that a parent favors a same-sex child in his or her reactions to the child's comportment.

A contrast can be made with comparable data from the Rothbart-Maccoby study in the United States (1966), where cross-sex leniency was the general bias evident in most forms of parent-child interactions. Apparently, Canadian parents encourage the child to turn to the same sex parent for help possibly as a means of developing closer ties between mothers and daughters and especially fathers and sons, thereby facilitating identification with the appropriate sexed parent.

FIGURE 2.2

X x P Interaction for Help Withholding

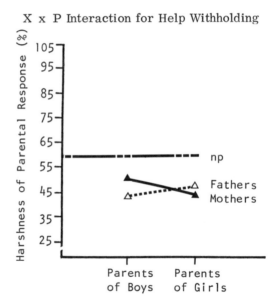

Note: In this and all subsequent figures, P = Sex of Parent.
Source: Constructed by the authors.

Parental Reactions to a Dispute between
a Child and a Younger Sibling

The data for this analysis are to be found in the second columns of Tables 2.3 and 2.4. We find here that Canadian parents in general side against the child and with the baby in such squabbles, that is, all mean scores lie above the neutral point. Next, there is no overall difference between French and English Canadian parents in their reactions, although there is, as we shall see, an important interaction involving ethnicity. However, the major factor determining how parents react in this instance is social class (row 2 in Table 2.3 and rows 3 and 4 in Table 2.4, $p < .01$); it is those from lower social-class backgrounds who demand more of the child (the mean scores are 58.71 for working class and 47.54 for middle class). There is also a difference in the major types of reproval evoked by the incident, as is evident in Table 2.6. We see clearly here the tendency for middle-class Canadian parents to side with the child, seek compromise, or ignore the incident, while the working-class parents more often take sides with the baby against the child.

TABLE 2.6

Response Comparisons: English and French Canadian Parents

Reactions to: "Baby, you can't play with me. You're too little."

Reactions	Parents' Social-Class Background	
	Lower	Middle
Side with child	9	16
Compromise	8	17
Ignore	12	17
Side with baby	46	26
Reprimand child	4	4
Threat of punishment	1	0
Punishment: nonphysical	0	0
Punishment: physical	0	0
Sarcasm	0	0
Uncodable	0	0
Totals	80	80

Source: Compiled by the authors.

In addition to the large social-class differences, there is also a statistically significant mother-father difference (the P effect, row 4 in Table 2.3 and page 28 of Table 2.4, $p < .05$), revealing that Canadian fathers are harsher on the child in the event of a within-family squabble (mean score 55.41) compared to Canadian mothers (mean score 50.83). But the GP interaction (row 7 in Table 2.3, $p < .01$) indicates that there are ethnic differences in how mothers and fathers react. Figure 2.3 reveals that it is the EC mothers (both working- and middle-class) who are the distinctive subgroup, producing the significant P effect. Thus, whereas FC mothers and fathers and EC fathers all have similar reactions to the child-baby squabble (all three subgroups siding against the child), EC mothers are unique in being much less harsh on the child. Note that this is a tendency of both working- and middle-class EC mothers. One wonders why EC mothers in particular should take a softer approach to sanctioning aggression, especially since it puts them, as a subgroup, at odds with the views of their husbands. Could it be that a soft, "psychological" doctrine works its way into various media and is picked up by EC mothers in particular?

FIGURE 2.3

G x P Interaction for Help Withholding

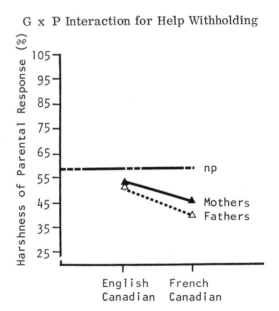

Source: Constructed by the authors.

In summary, how Canadian parents react to a child-baby dispute is determined mainly by social-class background, with the working-class parents being the harsher in admonishing the child for being involved in a dispute with his younger sibling. Ethnicity is a determining factor only to the extent that EC mothers of both social classes tend to be softer and more "understanding" of the dispute than are EC fathers, or FC mothers or fathers.

Parental Reactions to Children's Temper Displays

When a Canadian child shows temper outbursts, he or she can count on stern reactions from parents; the mean scores in this case are well above the neutral point (column 3a in Tables 2.3 and 2.4). Again there is a marked difference in reaction, depending upon the social-class background of the parents, with working-class parents being reliably harsher than middle-class in their reactions (the mean scores are 67.35 versus 56.65, $p < .01$).

The strategies parents use for socializing children who display temper were contrasted and analyzed in detail (see Table A 2.1).* We find that middle-class parents are more likely than working-class parents to divert or ignore the temper display, whereas the working-class parents are more ready to threaten punishment or reprimand the child.

This general social-class effect, however, is tempered by the significant GCX interaction (see Figure 2.1, used earlier as an illustration, $p < .05$). In this case we observe a complex interplay of the social-class background and the ethnicities of parents, coupled with differences in reactions to boys and girls. The pattern suggests that temper outbursts of girls are given relatively harsh treatment by middle-class parents if the girl is EC but also by working-class parents if the girl is FC. Stated otherwise, EC middle-class and FC working-class parents let boys more than girls get away with temper displays. With the data available to us here, we are left completely in the dark as to why these different social-class groups of EC and FC parents should have similar reactions to children's temper displays. There is, for instance, no similar pattern in their expectations of how boys and girls should behave or how they perceive the behavior of boys and girls (columns 10 and 11 in Table 2.3). Could it be that FC girls from working-class backgrounds and EC girls from middle-class backgrounds actually are more prone to use temper and that the respective parental groups are sensitive to this tendency? Could it be that FC working-class girls take EC middle-class girls as models, thereby becoming similar to EC girls in the use of temper in interpersonal relationships? If so, where would the EC middle-class girls get their models? It would be worthwhile

*Tables and figures with the prefix "A" are available in microfiche and photocopy form. These can be ordered from ASIS/NAPS, Microfiche Publications, P.O. Box 3513, Grand Central Station, New York, New York 10017. Remit in advance $3.00 for microfiche copies of each of the sets listed below, or for photocopy, $5.00 up to 20 pages plus 25¢ for each additional page. All orders must be prepaid. Institutions and organizations may order by purchase order; however, there is a billing and handling charge for this service. Foreign orders should add $3.00 for postage and handling.

Set One includes "A" tables and figures from Chapters 2 through 5; NAPS Document #03396 for 95 pages. Set Two covers "A" tables and figures from Chapters 6 through 8; NAPS Document #03397 for 76 pages. Set Three, for supplemental data in Chapters 9 and 10; NAPS Document #03398 for 82 pages. Set Four, for Chapters 11 and 12; NAPS Document #03399 for 37 pages. Set Five, for Chapter 13; NAPS Document #03400 for 83 pages.

to explore this and various other possible explanations for this intriguing finding.

In summary, Canadian parents (both EC and FC) are severe with children who display temper. The degree of severity of socialization is attributable mainly to the social-class background of the families, with working-class parents being decidedly more prone to punish rather than overlook children's temper displays.

Parents' Reactions to a Child's Temper
Outburst Directed to Another Person

The relevant data are to be found in the columns labeled 3b of Tables 2.3 and 2.4. Here again the major tendency of parents is to come down hard on the child who is aggressive toward a sibling or peer; all mean scores are far above the neutral point. The factor determining how harshly parents will react is social-class background ($p < .01$), and again, the working-class parents are much more severe than the middle-class (the means are 76.95 versus 60.73, with a neutral point of 41.6).

An illustration of the differences in strategies used by working- and middle-class parents is given in Table A 2.2 where one episode involving a social display of temper is analyzed. The striking differences represented here are: (a) the tendency for middle-class Canadian parents either to side with the child in the dispute or to overlook the child's threat of aggression, relative to (b) working-class parents who threaten the child with punishment should he/she pursue an aggressive line of conduct.

In this instance, there is no influence of ethnicity. Instead there is an additional difference in parental reactions depending on the sex of the child (the X effect, $p < .01$), and on the interaction of the sex of child and sex of parent (the XP effect, $p < .05$). First, we note that it is the parents of girls in Canada who are particularly severe compared with parents of boys (the respective means are 72.41 versus 65.27) suggesting a sex-linked norm difference in Canada, which makes it especially wrong for girls to direct their temper toward others. By implication this large and statistically significant difference suggests that it is much more permissible for boys to be socially "aggressive," possibly meaning that boys have to learn to "fight for their innings."

The XP interaction throws some light on this antigirl bias, as can be seen in Figure 2.4. The pattern of scores not only reflects the general tendency of both parents to be harsher with girls than with boys, but also that fathers of boys let more instances of social temper pass than do fathers of girls. This illustration of "same-sex leniency" between Canadian fathers and sons appears to reflect some type of mother-father division of socialization responsibilities in the training of boys. Canadian fathers of boys are particularly lenient with social temper outbursts of their sons, while Canadian mothers of boys are more severe. The Canadian mothers are more equitable in their treatment of social temper in boys and girls; it is the Canadian fathers who are distinctive in their lenient treatment of boys who display social temper.

FIGURE 2.4

X x P Interaction for Social Temper Control

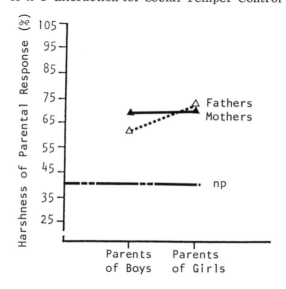

Source: Constructed by the authors.

In summary, the approach Canadian parents use in sanctioning the social temper outbursts of their children is influenced mainly by social-class background. Middle-class parents, both EC and FC, tend to be much less severe, either diverting the child or ignoring the episode, whereas working-class parents come down hard on such actions and reprimand or threaten to punish the child. Girls, in particular, are given harsher treatment for social temper displays than boys. In general it is the opposite-sex parent who leads the attack, fathers being harsher with daughters and mothers being harsher with sons.

Parents' Reactions to Children's Insolence

In Canadian families, children can count on a strong response from parents when they are insolent, at least as insolence is defined through the episodes included in this study (column 4 in Tables 2.3 and 2.4). Note that all mean scores are far above the neutral point. Still there are both ethnic and social-class differences in the ways and the extent to which parents control insolence. With regard to ethnicity, we find that EC parents are reliably more severe than FC parents in the control they apply to displays of insolence, the mean scores being 68.60 and 62.16 ($p < .05$). In addition, there is a huge social-class difference, with working-class parents (both EC and FC) being much more severe than middle-class parents; the means are 76.67 versus 54.09 ($p < .01$). There are then two separate sources of influence on the degree of control exerted on insolence—ethnicity and social class—and there are no interactions in this case. Thus, both EC and FC parents contribute to the social-class differences, even though EC parents in general are harsher than FC parents in their reaction to insolence.

The contrasts in strategies that parents use for controlling insolence are summarized in Table A 2.3 where the ethnic comparisons are listed to the left and the social-class comparisons to the right. As for ethnicity, we find a trend for FC, in contrast to EC parents, to overlook or ignore the child's insolence and to be somewhat less likely to punish the child. The social-class differences are much more pronounced. Middle-class Canadian parents tend to emphasize the delaying or diversion forms of strategies to control the child's insolence, while working-class Canadian parents are more inclined to actually punish him/her in some nonphysical way.

Parents' Reactions to Children's
Demands for Attention

When a Canadian child makes a bid for attention (in the fashion of the episode we included in our study, that is, "Ow, baby stepped on my hand," he is not likely to reach a sympathetic audience, judging from the fact that all means lie above the neutral point on the attention denial scale (column 5 in Tables 2.3 and 2.4). Furthermore, it doesn't matter whether the parent in question is EC or FC, or of working- or middle-class background. In this instance, then, there is a general cross-ethnic and cross-class reaction.

Interestingly, it does matter whether the child involved is a boy or a girl and whether the parent is a mother or father. Note in Table 2.4 that Canadian parents of girls are more likely to deny their daughters' demands for attention than their sons'; the mean scores are 87.64 versus 79.39 for parents of girls versus parents of boys ($p < .05$). In addition, Canadian fathers are more likely than mothers to reject attention demands: the means are 87.87 for fathers and 79.16 for mothers ($p < .05$). The fact that there are no interactions means that both mothers and fathers contribute to the harsher treatment given to girls and that parents of both boys and girls contribute to the mother-father difference in severity. It appears, then, that in Canada girls in particular should not be attention seekers, but when either boys or girls do clamor for attention, it is more the father's than the mother's role to discourage such comportment.

Are there differences in strategies for controlling children's demands for attention? In Table A 2.4 we provide the data for mothers versus fathers, and for parents of boys versus parents of girls. In the first instance, note that Canadian mothers are more ready than fathers to comfort the child and to excuse the baby, whereas fathers clearly side with the baby and ignore the child's attention-getting plea. In the second instance, we find that parents of boys, relative to parents of girls, are more ready to give comfort and less likely to ignore, or side with the baby.

Parents' Reactions to Children's
Requests for Comfort

When the Canadian child asks to be comforted, his parents in general do not comply (column 6 in Tables 2.3 and 2.4). Instead they remain neutral to the request, at least in the episode used for our study (that is, "Mommy/Daddy, it hurts!"). Note that all the means but one in Table 2.4 are slightly above the neutral point (implying a trend toward comfort withholding), the exception being middle-class mothers (see page 29 of Table 2.4) who fall just below the neutral point.

All subgroups of Canadian parents agree on how they should react in this case: there are no ethnic, social-class, sex-of-child, or sex-of-parent main effects. The only statistically significant difference is a GP effect ($p < .05$), indicating that FC and EC mothers and fathers differ in some way in their responses to children's requests for comfort. This pattern is deciphered in Figure 2.5, and here we find a contrast between FC parents who tend to agree on appropriate reactions to comfort requests of children, whereas EC parents have quite different reactions, mothers tending to be much more ready to comfort than fathers. The suggestion here is that in EC, relative to FC families, there may be some division of socialization duties between mothers and fathers, with fathers expected to discourage sissy-like behaviors of children, while mothers play a more tender role. This interpretation is derived from the strategy comparisons of EC and FC parents in Table A 2.5. FC mothers and fathers tend to agree on approaches, either comforting and siding with the child or making interested statements about his or her discomfort. In contrast the EC fathers, relative to mothers, are less prone to nurture the child, restricting their reactions mainly to making interested statements.

FIGURE 2.5

G x P Interaction for Comfort Withholding

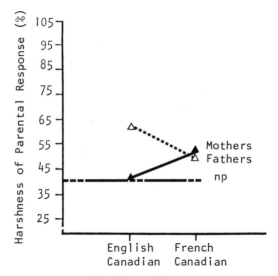

Source: Constructed by the authors.

Parents' Reactions to Children's Bids for Autonomy

When a Canadian child makes a move toward independence, Canadian parents in general grant him permission in the sense that all subgroup means are below the neutral point on the autonomy control scale (column 7 in Tables 2.3 and 2.4). There are no ethnic group differences, meaning that ECs and FCs react in a similar fashion and with the same degree of compliance. There are, in fact, no subgroup differences of any sort except a reliable difference attributable to social-class background ($p < .01$), and, consistent with the trend established so far, it is the middle-, relative to the working-class Canadian parent, who is more willing to encourage the child in his bid for independence (mean scores are 52.28 versus 37.29, $p < .01$). We have to be cautious in interpreting this difference since in the episode used to evoke parental reactions, the child asked if he could go across the street to play. The social-class difference may simply reflect some lesser degree of danger in crossing streets in middle- than in working-class neighborhoods. We feel that the scores reflect something more than this, on the supposition that no streets in a large North American city are safe for six-year-olds to cross on their own. But we will keep this reservation in mind.

What are the strategies used by middle- and working-class parents to cope with their children's autonomy requests? We find that the working-class parents are less ready to permit the child to go on his own, and, correspondingly, more ready to say "no," especially "no" without explanation (available in Table A 2.6).

We went one step further with this analysis. We found that over 30 parents in both working- and middle-class subgroups permitted the child to go but with reservations (Table A 2.6). When these reservations are examined in detail, we get a better idea about the concerns of parents of each social class. Working-, relative to middle-class parents, are more concerned about children dressing appropriately and keeping tidy, while middle-class parents are relatively more concerned about traffic (Table A 2.7). Thus, this evidence suggests that something other than a middle-class/working-class difference in the safety of neighborhoods underlies the social class contrasts we have seen in reactions to children's bids for autonomy.

Parents' Reactions to Children's
Requests for Guest Privileges

Although Canadian parents in all cases permit their children to invite guests in to play (all subgroups are well below the neutral point), there are, nonetheless, important ethnic-group and social-class influences on how willingly parents extend guest privileges to their children (column 8 in Tables 2.3 and 2.4). First, EC parents are clearly less extreme than FC parents in adopting an open-door policy. Although both groups grant permission, there is a systematic difference in degree of willingness, making a highly significant ethnic group contrast ($p < .01$). There is a similar but less pronounced difference for social-class groups in which middle-class parents are systematically more permissive than working-class parents ($p < .05$).

In addition there is a significant CP effect which is depicted in Figure 2.6. Here we find that fathers of both social classes have essentially similar degrees of permissiveness, while middle- and working-class mothers differ in their views, working-class mothers being relatively more neutral compared to middle-class mothers, who are relatively more permissive. This pattern may mean that working-class mothers are perhaps more sensitive about, or more ashamed of, their homes, making them less willing to undergo the inspections of neighbors' children.

FIGURE 2.6

C x P Interaction for Guest Restrictions

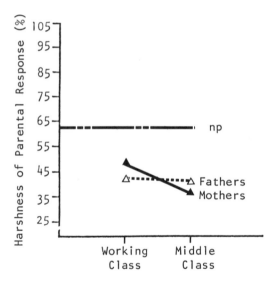

Source: Constructed by the authors.

The ways in which parents react to their children's requests to have a guest over were analyzed (Table A 2.8). These data are fully consistent with the mean score differences just discussed. Thus, FC parents are more inclined to agree with the request, without reservations, whereas EC parents tend to put certain restrictions on their agreement, as though visits by neighbors' children are viewed quite differently by the two groups of parents, perhaps more as invasions of privacy by EC parents and more as visits of extended family members by FC parents.

Working-class parents may also view such visits more as invasions of privacy, whereas middle-class parents may be more anxious to make their children's friends feel at home. Still the data are nonetheless consistent with the notion mentioned above that the working-class parents may be less proud of their dwellings than middle-class parents.

Parents' Reactions to a Dispute
between Child and Guest

In light of the trends presented so far, it is not surprising to find again that Canadian parents have little tolerance when their children get involved in an argument with a guest; mean scores are well above the neutral point (column 9 in Tables 2.3 and 2.4). Although there are no ethnic-group differences in how parents react, there are important social-class contrasts and differences attributable to the sex of the child in question and the sex of the parent. Again, as one might predict at this point, the parents from working social-class backgrounds are much more severe in their reactions to this form of dispute (the mean scores are 67.67 versus 55.86 for working- and middle-class parents, with a neutral point of 42.7, $< .01$).

Canadian parents are harsher on girls than on boys when children become involved in arguments with a guest (the means are 64.38 versus 59.15, $p < .01$). This incidentally is the third instance where girls are treated more harshly than boys, the others being social temper outbursts and attention requests.

Finally, Canadian mothers are harsher than fathers in this case (the means 63.50 versus 60.03, $p < .05$). In fact this is the only episode where Canadian mothers are more demanding of their children than fathers. We have already noted cases of the reverse trend, that is, where Canadian fathers are harsher than mothers, namely for the dispute between child and younger sibling and for the episode where the child demands attention.

We can compare the ways in which parents react to the dispute with a guest (see Table A 2.9). The statement analyzed here is just at the start of a dispute, reflecting a lack of cooperation rather than an argument. Considering first, the social-class comparisons, it is evident that middle-class Canadian parents are more likely than working-class parents to ignore the start of the squabble, and less likely to reprimand the child, threaten him with punishment, or punish him. In other words, the working-class Canadian child who argues with his playmate can expect harsher treatment in the form of reprimands, threats of punishment, or punishment.

Although the differences are small, we note that Canadian parents of boys are somewhat more ready than parents of girls to ignore the child's lack of cooperation and slightly less likely to use threats of punishment. Thus, being antisocial or noncooperative for a Canadian girl means provoking relatively more negative attention from parents, who are less likely than parents of boys to ignore or overlook the beginnings of a dispute. Again, we should keep in mind that precisely the same dialogue is used here for boys and girls, which means that for exactly the same degree of provocation, boys get away with more than girls. The implications of this differential encouragement given to boys rather than to girls are particularly interesting from a social-psychological point of view.

Similarly, we note subtle differences in the ways mothers and fathers react to the noncooperative comportment of their children, and here Canadian fathers, compared to mothers, are slightly more ready to ignore and less likely to side with the guest. Apparently, this form of noncooperation involving someone outside the family becomes a matter more for mothers to attend to than fathers.

Parents' Perceptions of Boy-Girl
Differences in Comportment

As mentioned earlier, this dimension reflects parents' perceptions of the similarities or differences in the ways boys and girls behave; the higher the score, the greater the perceived differences. The scale, we feel, reflects parents' views of how the boys and girls actually conduct themselves. A relatively low score means that in the eyes of the respondent, boys and girls are essentially alike, while a relatively high score means that boys and girls are seen as quite different in their styles of behavior.

Considering the results for this dimension (column 10 in Tables 2.3 and 2.4) note first that there is a significant social class effect ($p < .01$) and several interactions, all at the .05 level of confidence. Although there are no main effects attributable to ethnicity of parents, ethnicity does play its role in interaction with social class and with sex of parent (the GC and GCP interactions). Furthermore, social class and sex of parent interact to influence the final perceptions (the CP interaction).

What then are the perceptions of Canadian parents with regard to the sex-specific behavior of children? First, it is the parents of working social-class background who see significantly more instances of differences in the comportment of boys and girls than do middle-class parents. This finding may mean that working-class parents are more vigilant to sex-role differentiations, that for them being a boy or a girl is no arbitrary matter, but rather one of major importance. It is also possible that if they place importance on such distinctions, their children conform by behaving more in accordance with sex-role prescriptions than is the case for middle-class children, whose parents perceive fewer sex-role distinctions and possibly place less importance on such matters.

With this general social-class difference as background, consider next the three interactions that qualify and modify this trend: a significant GC effect, a significant CP effect, and a significant GCP effect. Since the GCP interaction encompasses the other two we will focus attention directly on it (see column 10, row 12 of Table 2.3 and page 30 of Table 2.4). The pattern is presented in Figure 2.7, and here we can pinpoint the FC middle-class mothers as the single group going against the overall social-class trend. Note that EC mothers, EC fathers, and FC fathers all contribute to the general social-class trend already mentioned. The puzzle, then, is why FC mothers, particularly those of the middle class, have perceptions quite unique and quite different from those of their husbands. Could it be that they are concerned or worried about a drift among children toward unisexism that is less perturbing to FC middle-class fathers? Is it that, in not going along with the middle-class trend on this issue, the FC middle-class mothers are trying to head off a worrisome drift toward unisexism?

Parents' Expectations of Boy-Girl
Differences in Comportment

For Canadian parents, there are no overall ethnic differences in expectations of how boys and girls should behave, although French and English Canadian parents do have distinctive expectations, depending upon the sex of their own child (column 11 in Tables 2.3 and 2.4). This is so because of the significant GX interaction ($p < .05$) which is depicted in Figure 2.8. It is intriguing to find differences in sex-role expectations that apparently stem from the fact that one group of parents has daughters, the other sons. (In the cases where families included both sons and daughters, the parents were asked to direct attention in their reactions to the son or daughter who was six years of age at the time.) On one hand, EC parents of boys, relative to EC parents of girls, appear to expect sharper contrasts in the conduct of boys and girls, as though for them, boys and girls were "made" differently or differed "naturally." On the other hand, it is the FC parents of girls who expect greater boy-girl differences in behavior. One possible interpretation of this fascinating ethnic contrast is that EC parents of

FIGURE 2.7

G x C x P Interaction for Perceived Sex-Role Differences

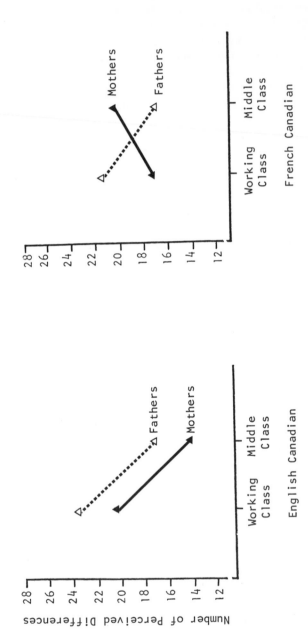

Source: Constructed by the authors.

50

boys for some reason are concerned lest their sons drift away from acceptable standards of masculinity. Perhaps the reason is that manly behavior is defined by the ECs as being aggressive and independent. Boys shouldn't lose such characteristics, and it wouldn't be bad if girls were to adopt them also. For FC parents, the concern takes a different form: daughters should be different from sons, suggesting that FC norms of femininity are valued. Perhaps feminine behavior is defined by FCs as being nonaggressive and dependent. Girls shouldn't lose such characteristics, and boys could adopt them without damaging their identity. But this is only a speculation at this stage. It would now be interesting to explore these EC-FC differences much more carefully.

FIGURE 2.8

G x X Interaction for Expected Sex-Role Differences

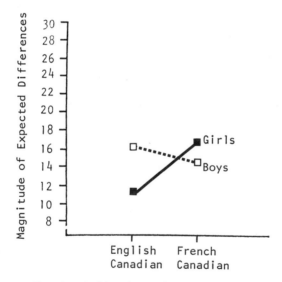

Source: Constructed by the authors.

In addition, there is a major difference in the sex-role expectations of middle- and working-class Canadian parents as reflected in the C effect ($p < .01$), and it is the working-class parents, who, relative to middle-class parents, expect greater sex-role differentiations in behavior. Thus, considering the previous analysis of parents' perceptions, we see now that working-class Canadian parents expect boy-girl differences and perceive greater differences than do middle-class parents. One wonders if, in striving for cognitive consistency, expectations have biased the perceptions of both working- and middle-class parents, that is, that they see what they want to see. And in the working class it may be much more important for men to be men and women to be women; in the eyes of middle-class parents, "masculinity" or toughness is less of a requirement for success.

FIGURE 2.9

C x P Interaction for Expected Sex-Role Differences

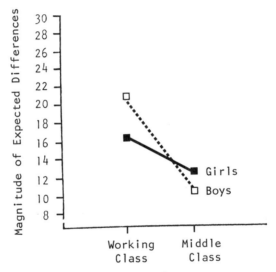

Source: Constructed by the authors.

Finally, there is an interesting CX interaction ($p < .05$) on sex-role expectancies, indicating differences in sex-role expectations of parents from middle and working social-class backgrounds, related to the fact that they have sons or daughters. This interaction is depicted in Figure 2.9. In this diagram we see clearly the general social-class contrast, that is, the two working-class points are well above those of the middle class. But the significant interaction is due to the crossover of lines: whereas working-class parents of boys, relative to working-class parents of girls, have the higher sex-role expectations, it is the middle-class parents of girls who have the higher sex-role expectations. This pattern suggests that working-class parents of boys may be more concerned about their sons maintaining acceptable standards of masculinity, just as middle-class

parents of girls may be more anxious about their daughters maintaining standards of femininity. Note particularly the sharp contrast in the sex-role expectations of working-class compared to
middle-class parents of boys. Thus, in the eyes of working-class
parents, boys apparently have to play a stereotyped masculine role
in order to survive or succeed in the working-class world. If girls
were to be boyish, in this sense, it might be to their advantage as
well. Middle-class parents apparently have a different outlook:
success in the middle-class occupational and social world is not
determined by strictly masculine orientations, and, in fact, a liberal outlook on what is masculine and feminine might be advan-
tageous. At the same time, the middle-class girl had better be
prepared to play a more feminine role.

Fascinating as speculations like these are, we need much
more information on this matter to come to any conclusions about
the differences found here.

SUMMARY AND CONCLUSIONS

The vast array of information just presented can perhaps best
be put in perspective if we first review and highlight the major
trends from each analysis. Then, by looking at the study as a
whole, we can extract those recurring forms of interaction that
characterize Canadian parents' ways of relating to young children.

A Dimension-by-Dimension Review

Requests for Help

Canadian parents in general comply with their children's demands for assistance, but it is the FC, relative to the EC parents,
who are much more inclined to extend immediate and direct help.
There are no social-class differences in reactions. One interaction
involving a one-sided "same-sex leniency" effect suggests that
Canadian boys are encouraged by the differential treatment they get
from mothers and fathers to turn to the same-sexed parent for help,
an interesting and possibly effective means of developing identity
and camaraderie between fathers and sons.

A Dispute with a Younger Sibling

Canadian parents discourage such squabbles by taking the
baby's side rather than the child's in the dispute. There are no
general EC-FC parent differences in response to within-family

disputes, although EC mothers of both social classes are much
easier on the child who becomes involved in the dispute. Thus, EC
mothers as a subgroup are at odds with their husbands and with both
FC mothers and FC fathers in their approach to children's squabbles.
We can only guess as to why this is so. One farfetched idea is that
EC mothers may be in direct line with specialized media (for example, English-language television and daytime radio programs
from the United States) that influence them in the direction of being
more "understanding" or more "psychological" in their approach to
children's disputes. Be that as it may, the major effect in this instance is social class, and it is the parents from working social-
class backgrounds who are decidedly more severe in sanctioning
their children when fighting breaks out.

Temper Outbursts

Both EC and FC parents are harsh in response to their children's displays of temper. Again social class has the major influence on how severely parents react, and it is, again, parents of
working social-class background who are more inclined to punish
temper displays rather than overlook them, which is more a middle-
class means of coping.

Social Temper Displays

When the Canadian child directs his temper to other people,
EC and FC parents alike are severe in their attempts to sanction
him/her. There are differences in severity of treatment, however,
and again it is the working-class parents (both EC and FC) who are
the more demanding. Whereas working-class parents reprimand or
threaten punishment, middle-class parents try more to divert the
child or ignore the episode. Girls, in particular, are given harsher
treatment than boys, and, in general, it is the opposite-sexed parent
who is to be feared, fathers being more severe with daughters,
mothers with sons. This is a second instance of same-sex leniency.

Insolence

Although Canadian parents in general do not tolerate insolence
from their children, there are important differences in degrees of
intolerance because of two separate sources of influence, namely,
ethnicity and social class. EC parents are much harsher than FC
parents, the former tending more to threaten the child with punishment, the latter being more inclined to overlook or ignore examples
of insolence. Working-class parents (both EC and FC) are much
harsher than middle-class, the former threatening or administering
punishment, the latter more prone to divert the child.

Attention Demands

Canadian parents discourage their children from clamoring
for attention, and this is so whether they are FC or EC, middle-
class or working-class. There are differences, nonetheless, in
how mothers, in contrast to fathers, react and differences in how
mothers or fathers react to sons in contrast to daughters. Girls
are treated more severely than boys for attention seeking, and, regardless of the child's sex, fathers are more demanding than mothers.

Comfort Demands

When Canadian children ask for comfort, parents remain more
or less neutral. There are no major ethnic or social-class differences in this general reaction, except to the extent that ethnicity interacts with sex of parent. Thus, FC mothers and fathers have a
common view on how to react to the comfort requests of their children whereas EC fathers are particularly harsh and EC mothers
particularly soft in their reactions. One gets the impression then
that there is more of a division of socialization responsibilities in
the EC family, with EC fathers expected to discourage their children from whining, while EC mothers are expected to play a much
more sympathetic role.

Independence Bids

When the Canadian child makes a move toward autonomy, his
parents generally comply with his request, regardless of their ethnic background. There is, nonetheless, a significant social-class
difference in extent of compliance, and again parents from working
social-class backgrounds are less inclined to encourage the child in
his ventures toward independence.

Having a Guest in to Play

All Canadian parents permit their children to have guests in
to play, but there are marked ethnic differences in degrees of willingness, with the FC parents having a more liberal, open-door attitude on the issue, suggesting that FC parents are more inclined to
see neighbors' children as members of the extended family. Similarly, middle-class parents (EC and FC) are more willing to extend
guest privileges than working-class parents are. It is the working-
class mothers in particular who are reluctant, suggesting that they
as the "homemakers," may be especially sensitive (ashamed?) to
have neighbors' children in their (working-class) homes.

Disputes between Child and Guest

Canadian parents, both EC and FC, have little tolerance for a dispute between their child and a playmate. Consistent with the trend, working-class parents are much more severe with their children in this situation. Also, consistent with another trend, girls in Canadian families, regardless of ethnicity or social class, are treated more harshly than boys for what objectively is the same degree of involvement in the dispute. Finally, mothers are systematically harsher than fathers when their children get in arguments with playmates.

Perceptions of Boy-Girl Differences in Behavior

There is an overall difference in what Canadian parents of different social-class standing consider appropriate behavior for boys in distinction to girls. Working-class parents perceive more contrasts in the ways boys and girls conduct themselves than do middle-class parents. There is, in this case, a complex series of interactions that leads to the conclusion that FC middle-class mothers, the one subgroup that stands out from the others, may have an exaggerated perception of sex-role differentiations. One possible interpretation is that FC middle-class mothers in particular are concerned about a cultural drift toward unisexism.

Expectations of Sex-Role Differences

There is a substantial social-class influence on parents' expectations of how boys and girls should behave, and again it is the working- relative to the middle-class parents, who expect sharper contrasts in the conduct of boys and girls. Thus, working-class Canadian parents, EC and FC, both expect boys and girls to behave differently and perceive essentially what they expect, that is, that boys and girls do have different styles of comportment. In this analysis, there was a complex set of interactions which suggests: (a) that EC parents of boys and FC parents of girls may be concerned about trends toward unisexism, and that (b) working-class EC and FC parents of boys and middle-class EC and FC parents of girls may be worried about their children maintaining standards of masculinity and femininity. Although these possibilities are consistent with the findings of the present study, further research, focused directly on these potential differences in concern about appropriate conduct for boys and girls, would be valuable and instructive.

THE CANADIAN STUDY IN PERSPECTIVE

How then do Canadian parents interact with their children in everyday episodes? Put differently, how does the process of socialization run its course in Canadian families? At best we can only make tentative statements about these important and fascinating matters since our study really only examines aspects of the values and attitudes Canadian parents have toward child training. Also, we have only dealt with small samples of parents from one of Canada's large cities, one where ECs have close contacts with FCs. We cannot generalize about Canada as a whole.

A glance at the entries in Table 2.3 reminds us that there are various types of parental values and attitudes in the Canada we studied. The single most important influence on parental reactions, however, is social-class background. Its effects are seen in all but three of the eleven value dimensions included in the study, and it also plays a role in three interactions. Although these social-class comparisons in general hold as well for English as French Canadian parents, this is not to say that the importance of social class is necessarily a distinctly Canadian phenomenon, for when comparisons are made later with other national settings, it could be that social class plays as important a role in many or all nations. We will see about that in later chapters. What is instructive and interesting, though, is that Canada, one of the New World nations where social-class distinctions are often said to be of little real significance, is characterized by such pervasive and important differences in parent-child interactions that are attributable to social-class background. One begins to wonder whether a powerful myth about a classless society has worked its way into our own belief systems. The fact is that the social-class background of parents makes a good deal of difference in child-training value systems in Canada.

Three other factors play relatively less important roles: the English Canadian-French Canadian ethnicity of parents, the sex of the child, and the sex of the parent. Even so, each has its own distinctive and illuminating influence. We will consider first the role played by ethnicity, since that was the basic question that prompted the research in the first place, and it is the question most parents, educators, and social philosophers might ask first, namely: How different or how similar are English and French Canadian parents in their approaches to child rearing?

Ethnicity

Being French or English Canadian has a direct effect on how parents deal with children's requests for help, children's displays of insolence, and children's requests to have guests in to play. In each instance it is the EC, relative to FC, parents who hold back, in the sense that they are less spontaneous and less immediate in giving help, more controlling and harsh on insolence, and more restrictive in extending guest privileges. These contrasts make good social-psychological sense. For instance, EC parents may be more hesitant to extend help because they are anxious to have their children learn to help themselves, to be independent. Such an interpretation is consonant with the data available on independence training, which, according to McClelland (1961), is emphasized more in the EC than FC communities, and according to Rosen (1959) more in the Anglo-American than the Franco-American communities in the United States.

Similarly, one might develop a convincing argument for the control of insolence which might well be more threatening to EC parents who could feel particularly vulnerable to what seems to be a tendency in the United States for children to break away from adult control and adult direction (see Bronfenbrenner 1970).

That the FC parents have more of an open-door attitude toward guest privileges for playmates is a surprising and interesting outcome. One possible interpretation is that the French-Canadian community, like most ethnic minority communities, may be more inclined to consider other members of the same minority group, including their own children's playmates, as extended family members. To have survived as an ethnic group, they perhaps have had to rely on one another to a great extent and to consider one another as cohabitants of a cultural island. (It is likely, too, that because of their need for strong ingroup ties they may have learned to make sharp distinctions between members of the ingroup and members of the various outgroups that "surround" them.) The EC parents, in contrast, may try to foster self-sufficiency by discouraging a dependence on playmates as agents of entertainment. Regardless of the interpretations, the major outcomes portray EC parents as less supportive and helpful when help is asked for, less permissive of insolence, and less open to guests than FC parents.

There are other more subtle comparisons that emerge through the various interactions. For instance, we found that EC mothers take a distinctively lenient and tolerant stance in two instances—when a squabble breaks out between a child and a younger sibling and when the child asks for comfort. The EC mothers thereby are at odds with their husbands, suggesting that there are more pro-

nounced normative differences between the mother and father roles
in the EC than the FC families. One wonders if there is some more
superficial explanation for this tendency, for example, that EC
mothers may have some special source of influence (such as daytime media inputs in the English language) that contributes to their
distinctive degree of tolerance in these cases, or whether there is
a deeper significance to the ways in which EC mothers fulfill the
maternal role.

The point of special interest is the flexibility and independence
that characterize the mother role in the EC families studied. The
EC mothers are as demanding and harsh as their husbands on matters of help withholding, insolence control, and restrictiveness
with regard to guest privileges. They, nonetheless, are tolerant
and lenient in cases of squabbles between siblings and comfort seeking. In one sense then, it is the EC mother who plays the more
active or flexible role in socializing the child since she, along with
the EC father, plays the role of demanding parent in particular
domains of interaction and, quite independent of the EC father, the
softer more comforting role in other domains.

The ramifications of this pattern could touch the EC child's
interpersonal behavior both within and beyond the family setting.
Consider the effects this attitude of EC mothers could have on the
development of achievement motivation. In his review of a large
number of investigations on achievement strivings, McClelland
(1961) concluded: "In general, the mothers of the 'highs' (in achievement motivation) also show authoritarianism towards their sons,
just as they showed more 'warmth.' They appear to be much more
actively involved than the mothers of the sons with low n achievement.
The fathers of the 'highs,' on the other hand, differ quite markedly
from their wives in that they show less dominating behavior than do
the fathers of the 'lows' " (p. 352). Here McClelland touches on a
set of maternal characteristics that seem to influence favorably the
development of achievement motivation, that is, the maintenance of
both authoritarian and warm tendencies, traits associated with the
EC mothers in our study.

Interestingly, the independent investigations of Rosen (1961)
and D'Andrade (1959) place emphasis on very similar maternal
characteristics. They find that both fathers and mothers contribute
to the development of "achievement training" by the models they
provide and by the goals and expectations they set for the child.
"Independence training" and self-reliance, on the other hand, is apparently developed in contexts where mothers and fathers play quite
different roles in the socialization process. Fathers of high achievement-oriented boys expect their sons to show self-reliance and are
more inclined in general to let the child function on his own. "The

mothers of boys with high achievement motivation, on the other hand, are likely to be more dominant and to expect less self-reliance than the mothers of boys with low motivation" (Rosen 1961, p. 575). This analysis also points to a parental division of socialization responsibilities that parallels in an intriguing manner the EC-FC contrasts emerging from our study.

The parallel, however, is less clear in the case of fathers, since EC fathers are not less dominating than FC fathers, except that they are more prone to withhold help giving. It is interesting though that no comparable mother-father divisions of responsibilities turned up in the FC families studied.

Although the empirical data available are limited, McClelland's cross-national comparisons of achievement motive indexes (derived from a content analysis of children's readers used in various nations) lend some small support to the EC-FC differences we have uncovered. Of the 40 nations included in McClelland's survey, the achievement index for EC Protestants was somewhat higher than that for FC Catholics (the respective standard scores were .39 and .00; see McClelland 1961, p. 461). Interestingly, in our pilot study of EC Catholic parents (Lambert, Yackley, and Hein 1971), there was similar and somewhat stronger evidence for EC mothers to be more active and flexible in socializing their children, relative to FC mothers. The achievement index in McClelland's survey for EC Catholics was the highest of all 40 nations studied (with a standard score of 2.92) compared to an average index (standard score .00) for FC Catholics (McClelland 1961, p. 461).

There are also potentially important ethnic contrasts in how parents think about sex-role differences in the behavior of boys and girls. FC middle-class mothers as a group are particularly perceptive of boy-girl differences in styles of conduct, suggesting to us that these FC mothers may be especially concerned about social movements that would de-emphasize traditional sex-appropriate comportment.

Our findings also indicate that any social erosion of sex-appropriate behavior would also likely be a source of concern to other subgroups of Canadian parents, especially to FC parents of girls and EC parents of boys. What might this intriguing pattern of results mean? Only further research focused on this issue will give us any substantive answers, but one farfetched possibility was suggested. Perhaps in the eyes of EC parents the EC culture is characterized by its economic and social aggressiveness, traditions that may be considered more masculine than feminine. In contrast, the cultural distinctiveness of the FC society may be seen by FCs as being economically and socially nonaggressive, and these values might be more under the control of FC women than FC men. Thus,

FC parents of girls might worry about an erosion of cultural identity that might accompany a shift in their daughters becoming aggressive. By the same token, EC parents of boys might have similar identity concerns should their sons become less aggressive.

There is a parallel comparison at the social-class level: working-class parents of boys have much stronger expectations of sex-role differences than do middle-class parents. This contrast suggests to us that, in the eyes of working-class Canadian parents, boys must be "boys" to succeed in life, whereas middle-class parents are much more liberal on the issue as though for them, the male's success in the middle class calls for something more than "masculine" traits. At the same time we find that parents of girls from working-class backgrounds are relatively less concerned about their daughters being similar to boys, suggesting that from their perspective girls would also find it an advantage to be able to take the harsher side of life. Middle-class parents, in contrast, seem to want their daughters to be different from boys, as though femininity was for them relatively more important and valuable.

Social-Class Background

The influence of social-class background touches parents' relations with children on all the dimensions we examined except help withholding, attention denial, and comfort withholding. On all other dimensions, it is the working-class parents (both FC and EC) who are the harsher or more demanding in the socialization of children. That is, relative to middle-class parents, they are more inclined to side with the baby and against the child when a dispute breaks out; they control displays of temper, social temper, and insolence more severely; they restrict the child more on guest privileges; side more against the child when he argues with a playmate; control more his bids for autonomy; and they both perceive and expect greater degrees of sex-role differentiations in the comportment of boys and girls.

There are only three dimensions that are not affected by social class, one concerned with a child's request for parental aid, another with requests for comfort, and the third with a child's request for the attention or psychological presence of the parent. When a child asks for help, both working- and middle-class parents comply (that is, both means are below the neutral point). However, when a child asks for attention or comfort, both working- and middle-class parents deny the child. Thus, on matters where parents have to cope with requests for help or nurturance, social-class background does not influence parents' reactions. It is instead on matters calling for discipline and on bids for autonomy that working- and middle-class parents differ. The fact is that in these cases they differ to a substantial extent, indicating to us that we are dealing here with major characteristics of Canadian child-rearing values, that is, that the social-class background of parents overrides ethnicity, sex of child, or sex of parent in importance.

The outstanding finding then is that Canadian parents of working social-class backgrounds are decidedly more demanding and more punitive than middle-class parents in their child-training values. Their relative harshness is limited to provocations by the child that call for discipline and to signs of the child's early moves toward independence or autonomy. With the data available here, we can only speculate about the reasons for these parental differences in outlook. It could well be that working-class parents train their children with more severity and exigence as a means of preparing them for the world these parents know well, a world where, because of one's lower status in society, one must be prepared to suffer, to be humiliated, and, especially, to be prepared to do what one is told. It is a world, too, where there is little room for arbitrariness around matters of sex-role comportment. Young boys have to be trained to become men just as young girls must learn to take on the roles of women, although women too can profit from being able to take the bumps of life. Very early or precocious moves toward independence on the part of the child might well worry working-class parents who could lose their child to outside influences before the childhood training has been completed. The training is not all harsh, however, for when aid and nurturence are called for, these discipline-oriented, working-class parents are as ready to help and comfort as anyone else.

The contrasts suggest that middle-class parents use another world of experience as a reference point. They want their children to face experiences and to learn how to think for themselves, to be able to take care of themselves, and to be prepared more to tell others what to do than to follow directives. Early explorations with autonomy would be encouraged, and any standardized views of what constitutes manly and womanly comportment would be questioned. This contrast thus jibes nicely with the developmental stages of achievement motivation (McClelland 1961; Rosen 1961). Strength of achievement motivation, these researchers have found, is clearly associated with social class, and it is the middle-class experience that not only generates relatively more achievement motivation, but it also seems to provide an earlier foundation for autonomy, for flexibility, and for self-reliance.

The middle/working-class contrast also has a quite different significance if one thinks of the effects on personality development of relatively harsh or relatively lenient parental attitudes toward the socialization process. But we must be clear here about what we mean by the terms "harsh," "demanding," "soft," or "psychologi-cal"—terms that we have been using to contrast the approaches of middle- versus working-class Canadian parents. Recently, Stanley Guterman (1970) has seen the need, in his analysis of a wide array of research findings on child training, to differentiate parental "punitiveness" from parental "strictness." Guterman was inter-ested in how conscience or superego is developed in children, and this, of course, led him to Freud. His argument runs as follows:

> The preponderance of the (research) evidence suggests that, if Freud meant by severity of training the degree of punitiveness parents exhibit in disciplining their children, he was mistaken in believing that severity favors greater internalization of ethical standards. The contrary seems to be true: harsh, fear-provoking treatment on the part of parents is associated with a defective development of conscience. The more "psy-chological" or "love-oriented" methods of securing compliance with parent standards and restrictions ap-pear, on the other hand, to encourage a greater devel-opment of internalized controls. (pp. 21-22)

However, if Freud meant something else by severity of training, such as firmness or strictness, the whole picture changes as far as research evidence is concerned. Guterman notes:

> If severity of discipline in the sense of punitiveness favors the development of a weak conscience, sever-ity in the sense of strictness appears to have the op-posite effect. (p. 24)

The evidence Guterman presents looks impressive on this point. Strength of conscience in children is associated with a home life that is "well regulated and orderly" as manifest, for example, by the existence of definite hours for meals, bedtime, and when to be in at night, a home life that, in terms of discipline, is "consis-tent and predictable by the child." Children's strength of conscience is also associated with parents who enforce rules for do's and don't's, who demand "obedience from their children," and who "put pressures on" their children to live up to quite definite parental expectations.

There is a very basic and important distinction being made here, but when we try to apply it to the Canadian social-class dif-ferences, we might at first glance have difficulty deciding which group is which, that is, deciding whether it is the parents of the

middle- or the working-social class in Canada who are the more
punitive or the more strict. As we see it, a strong case can be
made, from the Canadian findings, that it is the working-class
parents who are both the more strict and the more punitive. It is
the working-class Canadian parents who, relative to the middle
class, set more definite limits on what the child can or can't do,
and who put more pressure (albeit of a characteristically more
punitive nature) on obedience to rules and standards. These more
clearly defined limits cover aggression or temper directed toward
siblings, toward peers, and toward parents. It is likely that Canadian working-class children face "disciplinary procedures" that
are "more consistent and predictable" in Guterman's terms. To
this extent the stricter socialization of the working-class Canadian
child may contribute to the development of a relatively strong conscience, in contrast to the development of a relatively weak conscience in the case of middle-class children. If this conclusion
seems odd to those who would be challenged to defend the middle-
class strategies, perhaps they can argue that this potential advantage of lower-class upbringing is offset by the more authoritarian
and demanding models working-class parents provide their children.
Or that the plus of parental firmness and strictness is offset by the
greater degree of working-class parental punitiveness. This last
argument jibes well with what we have seen throughout our study:
Canadian working-class parents are more inclined to use threat-of-
punishment or punishment techniques, while middle-class parents
are more inclined to use "psychological" and "reasoning" approaches
to discipline, making them more lenient and "soft" or, in other
words, less punitive. Of course, this nonpunitive approach could
be easily confused with a "studied neglect" of children, as Bronfenbrenner (1970) might argue.

One wonders what functions are served by this working-class
approach to discipline, characterized by severity in the sense of its
punitiveness and its strictness. If it were dysfunctional, we would
expect it to change. Of course, it may well be that, by the nature
of their social-class status, working-class parents don't have the
time for the slower, more drawn out "psychological" approaches.
Would a change in approach be any more advisable for working-
class parents than the comparable change toward greater strictness
required of middle-class parents to bring them closer to some ideal?
One wonders what an ideal amount of conscience might be. Too
much conscience would likely be debilitating because of the con-
striction and anxiety it entails. The practical question then is:
Which social-class group in Canada has the better mode of developing ethical standards in children, the middle class with its relatively
nonpunitive, nonstrict approach to child training or the working class

with its relatively punitive but strict approach? This question would certainly be worth exploring in future research.

Our findings make contact as well with another extremely rich research domain—that of field independence vs. field dependence—associated first with Herman Witkin (1948; 1969; 1976) and more recently with Witkin and John Berry (1975). Witkin has been interested since the 1940s in the process of psychological "differentiation," that is, in the ways that cognitive subsystems pull apart and become functionally distinctive specializations within the growing personality. For example, with normal development, perception is said to separate itself gradually from thinking and thinking from action or emotion. The interplay of theory and research has been especially interesting in the hands of Witkin and his associates. Empirical methods have been devised (for example, the Rod and Frame procedure and the Embedded Figures test) which reflect different degrees of field dependence-independence and which reveal quite sharp contrasts in perceptual styles. Thus, these empirical tests of a perceptual and cognitive nature very nicely separate subgroups of individuals who, in one case, are field dependent (in the sense that perception is very much controlled by the perceptual field, making any item in the field difficult to "disembed") or field independent (in the sense that the field is less determining and instead the person himself makes use of more internalized frames of reference). Degrees of field independence are taken to be indicators of psychological differentiation. The contrast between subgroups is reflected at perceptual, cognitive, and social-interactional levels. Thus, the field independent person can more easily differentiate parts of a perceptual array, he can also more easily restructure environmental or perceptual inputs to his advantage in various cognitive tasks, and socially he is able to differentiate self from others more readily, making him less easily dependent on others. At the same time as the field independent person proves to be more autonomous, he, nonetheless, has looser ties with social structures and norms and turns out to be less interested in, and sensitive to, others than is the field dependent person.

Although a précis of this work detracts from its real elegance, the major point is that different degrees of field dependence-independence can be traced back very nicely to early child-rearing and socialization experiences, and these links with childhood experiences hold cross-culturally. In essence, child-rearing experiences in which obedience and conformity to parental authority are stressed by "strict and even harsh" child-rearing techniques promote less psychological differentiation (Witkin 1976). Furthermore, less differentiation is found in families in which the mother takes a "dominant and dominating role in the physical and emotional care of the child . . . at the same time as the father is an authority figure who expects obedience and respect from his children" (Witkin and Berry 1975). These characteristics define a "tight" family and provide a contrast with a "loose" family, wherein children are encouraged to be autonomous and where violating parental authority is generally tolerated. Finally, it is of interest to us that girls are typically more field dependent than boys, and this too holds up cross-culturally (Witkin and Berry 1975).

The relevance of Witkin's exciting research program to our own is quite apparent: in our examination of Canadian families it is unmistakably the working-class in contrast to the middle-class parents who promote a "tight" atmosphere in which conformity is demanded, and it is the working-class parents who are more harsh and strict in their demands for conformity. Although Witkin and Berry have not yet focused on social-class differences in field dependence, the coincidence of the present findings with those they have already worked out is promising. The point is that the marked social-class differences in child-rearing values that we have uncovered here in Canadian families may have perceptual, cognitive, and social-interactional consequences on the children involved.

A similar argument could also be made for the ethnic contrasts between EC and FC parents discussed above, for it is the EC parents who are more demanding and harsh in an important subset of episodes (help withholding, insolence control, and guest privileges), suggesting that they may be indirectly promoting more field dependence than is the case for FC parents. But this trend could be offset by the lenience of EC mothers on two other dimensions, the squabble incident and the child's request for comfort. Could it be that EC mothers sense the cognitive consequences of the relatively harsh socialization atmosphere and try to attenuate it with these instances of relative softness?

There is one final point of contact with Witkin on the matter of boy-girl differences in field dependence. Note in the section to follow that we have clear evidence from our Canadian parents of a harsher attitude toward girls than toward boys when social aggression or demands for attention arise. Perhaps this harshness bias that works against girls contributes to the boy-girl differences in field dependence-independence noted by Witkin and Berry.

Parents of Boys versus Parents of Girls

There are three instances in the Canadian study where parents of girls differ in their reactions from parents of boys: in controlling social temper outbursts, denying the child attention, and siding against the child who quarrels with a playmate. In each instance, it is the parents of girls who are the harsher socializers, and there are no counterbalancing instances where parents of boys are the harsher. These three forms of conduct then are particularly annoying to Canadian parents when they originate from girls. When we take into consideration the fact that the taped episodes used in the study were precisely the same in the boy and girl versions, these differences in parental reactions to sons and daughters become doubly interesting. Thus, to the extent that Canadian girls are overdisciplined for social temper displays, for arguing with a playmate, and are more thwarted on requests for attention, one can by the same token argue that Canadian boys are relatively underdisciplined and underthwarted.

When cross-national comparisons are made, we will be able to determine if this discipline bias favoring boys is distinctively Canadian or is instead a more general or even universal phenomenon. Regardless, the bias does characterize the relations between Canadian parents and their children and calls for comment. Apparently we are dealing here with a broadly shared point of view in Canada since no ethnic differences emerged in these cases, nor are they tempered by social class differences. Thus, Canadian parents, in general, appear to bring girls up so that they will not be socially aggressive or attention seekers. To the extent that social aggressivity and attention seeking are negative characteristics for Canadian girls, they are, in comparison, more positive characteristics for Canadian boys. One can look at this boy-girl contrast as the society's way of developing a clear model of the differences expected in adult men and women. The more that adult sex-role models differ, the greater the basis there would be for complementarity in relationships involving men and women and the easier it might be to establish a natural division of socialization responsibilities between mothers and fathers.

There are, however, questions that this contrast brings to mind. Is it valuable or appropriate to differentiate between boys and girls in this fashion from childhood on? If social aggression is a bad trait for girls, how could it be a good trait for boys? It is this matter of training aggression out in one case and in in the other that becomes particularly interesting. If it were a natural proclivity to be socially aggressive, then to discourage it in the case of girls would cause them biological and emotional harm. If it is not a natural tendency and one easy to control, why should boys be encouraged to be aggressive in this already very aggressive world? Apparently Canadian parents feel that to survive in this aggressive world, boys must be given more opportunities than girls to learn to take care of themselves!

Mothers versus Fathers

There are two unambiguous instances in the Canadian study where being a mother rather than a father affects how one reacts to children: one involves attention seeking, the other, disputes between the child and a playmate. In the case of attention seeking, Canadian fathers are harsher in their reactions than mothers, while in the case of siding with the playmate and against the child, Canadian mothers are harsher than fathers. These contrasts suggest that in Canadian families, there is a division of socialization responsibilities, and apparently fathers are expected to take nagging or attention-getting ploys as their speciality, while mothers take on the task of training proper behavior in the child's relations with those outside the family. We have no explanation for why these two particular differences emerge or how the purported division of responsibilities develops. Nonetheless, it would be worthwhile exploring other aspects of socialization in further research to test this general notion—that Canadian fathers are more responsible for keeping peace within the family and Canadian mothers more responsible for smooth relationships with others in the community.

What is noteworthy in the Canadian study is the lack of evidence for "cross-sex permissiveness," that is, we have found no incidents where fathers are differentially harsh with sons and relatively supportive of daughters and where mothers favor sons and show biases against daughters. This is noteworthy because Rothbart and Maccoby (1966) in their study conducted in the United States found a large number of examples of cross-sex permissiveness. In the Canadian study not only have we found no cross-sex permissiveness, we have found examples of same-sex permissiveness.

This U.S.-Canadian contrast is intriguing, and it is on this note of intrigue and at the point where cross-national comparisons begin to interest us that we turn to the next chapter, where we begin the comparison process by moving from Canada to other settings.

3

FRENCH FEATURES OF CHILD REARING:
FRANCE AND FRENCH CANADA

By comparing English Canadian (EC) and French Canadian (FC) approaches to child rearing in the previous chapter, we begin to get a perspective on parent-child interactions in Canada, but these comparisons also start one wondering about other matters: Just how "English" and "French" are English Canadian and French Canadian parents? Thinking along this line led us to enlarge the scope of our investigation in several ways. For one thing it prompted us to follow the tracks of Frenchness from Canada to France, from France to Belgium, and then to the United States, where we found "French Americans," that is, French Canadians or their ancestors, who had brought their families up in the United States and kept their language and possibly other aspects of their Frenchness alive. The parallel question of Englishness also intrigues us and in a later chapter we trace its path from Canada to the United States and back to Great Britain, the main country of origin. For another thing, it prompted us to collect comparable data on various immigrant groups who have been in Canada or the United States long enough to get their own Canadian-based or U.S.-based families started, and the results of this probe are treated in later chapters.

This chapter deals with Frenchness, particularly, the Canada to France comparison. We wondered if there is something distinctively French about child-training values that might emerge when French Canadian and French-French parents are compared. Does some common cultural background permeate child-rearing techniques in these two national settings, or have values evolved in different ways during the two centuries of separate histories of France and French Canada?

Both groups of parents examined here, the French from France (FF) and the French speaking Canadians (FC) may have a common cultural-linguistic heritage, but FF parents are living in a largely unicultural nation where cultural autonomy is never seriously challenged, while FC parents are members of a minority group on a largely English-speaking continent. Although the cultural roots of the FC community go back to France in the sense that most FCs are descendants of French immigrants to Quebec, one wonders, nonetheless, how similar FC and FF families are today, living as they do in separate social environments that have isolated FCs from France and brought them under the largely Anglo-Saxon atmosphere of North America.

The study was conducted in exactly the same fashion in France as in Canada. Principals and teachers of schools in the greater Paris area provided lists of names and addresses of families who were presumed to fit either middle-class (MC) or working-class (WC) criteria. These parents were contacted by phone or mail. Those who could be unambiguously classifiable as being from one social class or the other were then interviewed at home by two research assistants who lived and attended university in Paris. Since no standardized index of socioeconomic standing comparable to the Canadian Blishen scale (1967) is available in France, families were classified as working-class or middle-class according to the occupation and education of the fathers. The French and Canadian samples are compared in Table A 3.1.

The same type of statistical analysis was used for the FC and FF comparison as was used for the EC-FC comparison described in Chapter 2. Furthermore, the FC tape was pretested in Paris, and the child's statements were taken to be those of a typical Parisian by those pretested. As in the Canadian study, FF parents were asked to write their reactions as quickly and spontaneously as possible.

Finally, husbands and wives were tested separately, one filling out the questionnaire while the other reacted to the taped episodes.

RESULTS AND DISCUSSION: THE
FRENCH CANADA-FRANCE STUDY

The reactions of FC and FF parents are compared and summarized in Tables 3.1 and A 3.2. Our standard plan will be to focus first on contrasts that are attributable to national or cultural background, then those traceable to social-class background, then those related to sex of child, and finally those related to sex of parent. The order is arbitrary because in most cases, social-class background is involved in the greatest number of contrasts, more so than national background, sex of child, or sex of parent. The

TABLE 3.1

Significant Effects in the Comparisons of French Canadian and French French Parents

Comparisons	1) Help Withholding (np = 58.6)	2) Siding with Baby vs. Child (np = 42.7)	3a) Temper Control (np = 30.0)	3b) Social Temper Control (np = 41.6)	4) Insolence Control (np = 25.0)	5) Attention Denial (np = 75.0)	6) Comfort Withholding (np = 41.6)	7) Autonomy Control (np = 58.3)	8) Guest Restriction (np = 62.5)	9) Siding with Guest vs. Child (np = 42.7)	10) Perceived Sex-Role Differences	11) Expected Sex-Role Differences
G	12.08	-	-	-	-	-	10.99	26.46	-	4.08	4.22	-
C	-	18.54	4.55	20.87	6.21	7.87	5.43	9.63	-	10.05	-	10.58
X	-	-	-	-	-	-	-	-	-	-	-	-
P	-	-	-	5.63	-	-	-	-	-	5.73	-	-
GC	-	-	-	-	9.39	-	-	-	-	6.27	-	-
GX	-	-	-	-	-	-	-	-	-	-	-	-
CX	5.52	-	-	-	-	-	-	-	-	-	-	-
GP	-	-	-	-	-	-	-	-	-	-	-	-
CP	-	-	-	-	-	-	-	-	-	-	4.59	-
XP	-	-	-	-	-	-	-	-	-	-	-	-
GCX	-	-	-	-	-	-	-	-	-	-	-	-
GCP	6.14	-	-	-	7.31	-	-	-	-	-	-	-
GXP	-	-	-	-	-	-	-	-	-	-	-	-
CXP	-	-	-	-	-	-	-	-	-	-	-	-
GCXP	-	-	-	-	6.54	-	-	-	-	-	-	-

Note: Entries are significant F values; those underlined are beyond the .01 level of confidence, the others are beyond the .05 level.

Source: Compiled by the authors.

pervasiveness of social class is evident in the FC-FF comparisons and is reflected in the large number of entries in Table 3.1.

Differences Attributable to Nationality of Parents

When we compare the group means in Table A 3.2 and relate them to the respective neutral points of each scale, we find first that parents in both countries are inclined to give help when help is requested. Then when a child asks for comfort by complaining that he/she is hurt, we note that he/she will not be fully comforted or receive the complete attention of the parents. When the FC or FF child asks for guest privileges he/she can count on having the request granted. When a quarrel develops between the child and a younger sibling or a friend of the same age, both the FC and FF parents tend to take the side of the baby or the friend, thereby discouraging the child's displays of aggression. Similarly, both FC and FF parents discourage temper outbursts or insolence directed toward the parents.

There are, however, differences in the degrees of severity or permissiveness displayed by FC and FF parents in these everyday situations. The FF parents are generally harsher than the FC parents in situations where their six-year-old requests help, comfort, or makes a move toward autonomy, and each of these main effects is significant at beyond the .01 level of confidence.

Autonomy Control

Perhaps the most striking contrast occurs between FC and FF parents in their different reactions to a child's request to go on his/her own to the other side of the street to play (autonomy control). Here we find that FC parents are much more permissive than FF parents. In fact, the FF parents of both social classes are above the neutral point on the scale, while the FC parents are below the neutral point (Figure 3.1).

The finer details of this sharp contrast are brought out by comparing the types of reactions given by FC and FF parents (see Tables A 3.3 and A 3.4). Here we find that 65 percent (52 out of 80) of the FC parents permit the child, with or without reservations, to leave the house and cross the street. In contrast, 67 percent (54 out of 80) of the FF parents refuse permission, with or without explanations or alternative suggestions. The comparison for permissive reactions on the part of parents then is 65 percent for FC versus only 33 percent for FF parents. It does not seem to us that this difference is due to one setting having greater amounts of traffic to worry about since in both Paris and Montreal, parents have big-

city concerns about automobiles and careless drivers. Traffic concerns turn up in the reservations of both groups of parents, for example, "Yes, but watch out for the cars" or "Yes, but look both
ways before crossing." However, very few FF parents thought it
necessary to give explanations for their refusals; of the 54 parents
who refused permission, 34 gave no explanation or alternative suggestions. When explanations were given for the refusal, many FF
parents urged the child to stay home with such statements as: "You
don't leave the house so late," "You have your little sister to play
with," "We're going to eat soon," and so on.

FIGURE 3.1

Ethnic Group and Social Class Contrasts for Autonomy Control

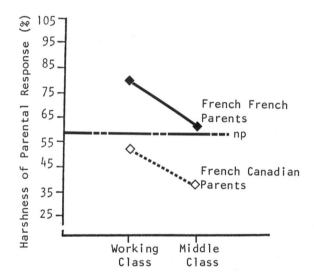

Source: Constructed by the authors.

Incidentally, the FF middle-class parents gave more explanations as to why a child should not leave the house than did working-
class parents. Some 60 percent of the FF middle-class parents ex-
plained their refusals, compared to only 20 percent of the FF
working-class parents.

Help Withholding

Although the child in either the FC or FF family is likely to
be helped when help is requested, the FC child is more likely to

receive help than the FF child ($p < .01$). Moreover, fathers and mothers of different socioeconomic backgrounds from the two national settings do not react to requests for help in the same way, as is evident in the significant GP and GCP interactions for help withholding.

Figure 3.2 presents the GCP interaction which tells us that the FC mother is less inclined than the FC father to extend help. This parental difference is more accentuated in middle-class FC families where the father is even more likely to give help than the working-class FC father, while the middle-class FC mother is less inclined to be helpful than the working-class FC mother.

A completely different picture emerges for the FF family. Except for being generally less willing to extend help than the FC parents, the FF working-class parents show the same pattern of parental differences as did the FC parents, the father being more helpful than the mother. In the FF middle-class family, however, the reverse is true. Here the father's score is surprisingly high, to the point of not offering help at all (the mean score is 56.24 with the np at 58.6). It is the FF middle-class mother who is the more prone to give help. Thus, a child in a working-class family in Quebec can expect more help than a child from the same social-class background in France, and in both cases the father is likely to be more helpful than the mother. In contrast, the six-year-old middle-class child receives as much help from his mother in a FF family as in a FC one, whereas the FC middle-class father is much more helpful than the FC mother, compared to the FF middle-class father who is much less helpful than the FF mother, to the point of offering little help at all.

When the types of reactions of parents are examined in more detail for the three help-withholding episodes, we note that the most pronounced differences occur on the first of the child's three requests (Tables A 3.5 to A 3.7). For example, the child's first request for help evokes quite different reactions from FC and FF parents, the FF being much more likely than the FC to refuse, ignore, or interpolate long delays. With follow-up requests, the FF-FC differences are much less marked.

Comfort Withholding

In this instance, we find the FF parents significantly less inclined to extend comfort than FC parents, and this is a general tendency that is not tempered by any interactions.

Insolence Control

If we think of the help, comfort, and autonomy dimensions as examples of parental willingness to extend or withhold assistance or

FIGURE 3.2

G x C x P Interaction for Help Withholding

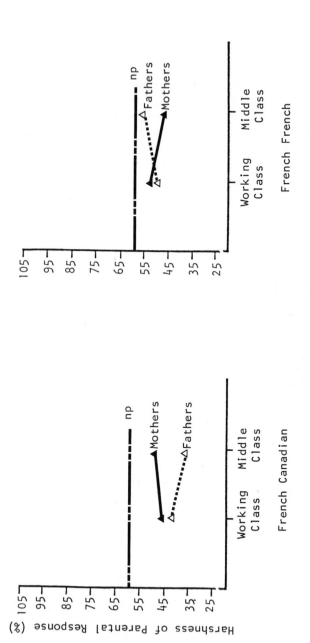

Source: Constructed by the authors.

aid, we can then conclude that FC parents are generally more prone than FF parents to offer aid. There are also differences between FC and FF parents on discipline matters. What is interesting in these cases is the fact that the FF parents no longer stand out as being relatively more severe or harsh.

A complicated pattern of factors determines the approach taken by FF and FC parents in handling episodes of insolence stemming from a six-year-old child. First, whereas social class affects the strategy adopted in French Canada, in the sense that more tolerance toward insolence is displayed by middle- than working-class FC parents, there is essentially no difference between class levels in the FF family (GC interaction, $p < .01$; see also Figure A 3.1). Furthermore, each national group of fathers and mothers reacts differently depending on whether the insolence comes from a son or a daughter (GXP interaction $p < .01$; see also Figure 3.3). This means that in the case of FC parents there is a pattern of same-sex leniency with regard to insolence, whereas FF parents show cross-sex leniency.

But we are forced here to go one step further in the analysis because of a significant 4 factor interaction, GCXP, $p < .01$ (see Figure A 3.2) which indicates that the same-sex versus cross-sex leniency patterns in Canada and France hold only for middle-class families. In working-class families, one parent takes a more dominant disciplinarian role in matters of insolence, although this role is played by the father in the FF working-class family and by the mother in the FC working-class family. Also, in the FC working-class family, both parents (but especially mothers) are harsher on boys than on girls.

This intriguing French Canadian pattern, wherein the mother specializes in the disciplinarian role with regard to insolence at the working-class level while at the middle-class level, the parent of the opposite sex becomes the disciplinarian, has its counterpart in the French-French family, but in France it is a different parent—the father—who assumes the tougher role. Thus, in the FF working-class family, the father will be the disciplinarian for children of both sexes, whereas in French Canada it is the mother. In the FC middle-class family the six-year-old can expect to be treated more severely for being insolent with the opposite-sex parent, while in the FF middle-class family the same-sex parent will likely be the harsher disciplinarian on insolence matters.

The French Canadian middle-class pattern then would encourage sons to aggress toward fathers and daughters toward mothers, a scheme that could lay a groundwork of fear and/or respect for the parent of the opposite sex. In contrast the European French middle-class pattern, with the opposite-sex parent being the easier target

FIGURE 3.3

G x X x P Interaction for Insolence Control Showing Same-Sex and Cross-Sex Leniency Patterns

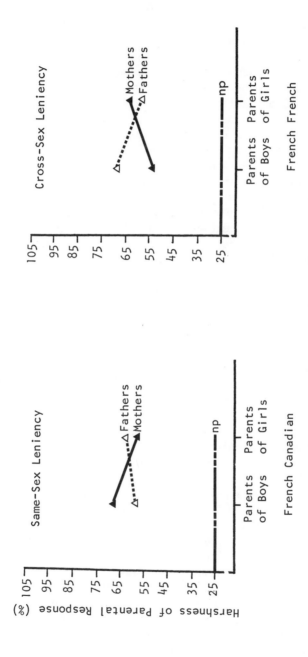

Source: Constructed by the authors.

77

for insolence, would affect the child's development of sex-role
identification in a different way, since the boy would have a fear-
respect orientation toward his father and the girl a similar perspective toward her mother.

Here we make contact with theory derived from Freud.
Mowrer (1950), for example, suggested that children first identify
with the same-sex parent, the intensity of the identification being
determined by the parents' nurturance, affection, competence, and
power. Thus, in the FC middle-class family the same-sex parent
would encourage the child to identify with him or her by playing
down instances of insolence, thereby emphasizing affection as a
mode of developing identification. Just the opposite would take
place in the FF middle-class family: the six-year-old child in
France would apparently expect leniency from the opposite-sex parent although he/she would more likely develop fear and/or respect
for the same-sex parent. Perhaps middle-class parents in France
emphasize a different mode of developing identification than their
counterparts in French Canada, socializing the same-sex child for
what they consider inappropriate behavior through the display of
power rather than affection.

For children in working-class families in France or in Quebec,
the parent to be feared and/or respected is the one who assumes the
dominant role, the mother in the FC family and the father in the FF
family.

There is one final aspect of this France-Quebec contrast needing comment. Although parents in both countries, regardless of
social-class background, tend to be equally harsh on insolence,
they are harsh in quite different ways (data given in Table A 3. 8).
First, the overall harshness of the FC working-class parents is
based on their tendency to use threat of punishment, a reaction that
is virtually absent with the FC middle-class parents or the FF parents of either social class. In contrast the relative leniency of the
FF father toward his daughter is to a large extent due to his ignoring her insolence; six fathers out of ten show this pattern. The
characteristic reaction of the FC middle-class parents is to divert
the insolent child.

Two types of reactions—reprimanding or punishing the insolent
child—were very common both in France and in Quebec. However,
there were important national differences in the use of these tactics
(Tables A 3. 9 and A 3. 10). When we examine the content of the
reprimands, we note, in addition to the fact that reprimanding is
more typical of FF than FC parents, that FF parents favor moral
reprimands, such as "That is no way for a child to speak to his
father," or "That is not a nice way to speak." In contrast, the reprimands of FC parents seem to be more in the form of scolding, for

example, telling the child that his/her statement is wrong, or that, with the attitude displayed, he/she had better change games.

As far as punishing is concerned, there is an even more prominent national contrast. The FF and FC parents favor different types of punishment: FF parents turn more to physical punishment, while FC parents rely more on nonphysical punishment, either restricting the child's freedom by sending the child to bed, putting him in a corner, or taking the game away.

These data make one wonder about physical punishment. Does it provide the child with a model of aggressivity, or does it otherwise influence the development of the child's personality? We are reminded again of Guterman's (1970) review, which indicates that parents' severe and harsh treatment can disturb the development of conscience in the child, and we wonder if the relatively more severe treatment of FF, relative to FC, parents may have negative effects on conscience development. Unfortunately, we have no independent information available in our study to test for effects on conscience or on field independence, although these and other personality characteristics merit cross-national exploration in light of our findings. One also wonders if differences in the aggressivity of the two parents have differential effects on sons and daughters. According to the empirical evidence reviewed by Maccoby (1966) and Sears, Maccoby, and Levin (1957), in most cultures so far studied aggressivity is more accepted from boys than from girls. Interestingly, we have found no significant differences in the ways boys, in contrast to girls, are treated for aggressiveness in FF and FC families, although in the fascinating case of insolence control we did find important national differences in terms of same-sex versus opposite-sex leniency.

Siding with Guest versus Child

There is another significant difference in the reactions of FC and FF parents in their management of a quarrel between child and guest, ($p < .05$). In this case the FC parents are the more severe disciplinarians, relative to the FF parents, even though both parental groups take a strong stand against the aggressive child. There is a qualification, however, indicated by the significant GC interaction (depicted in Figure A 3.3), which tells us that the overall national group difference just mentioned is due mainly to the working-class parents. Thus, we find no social-class differences in reactions to a child-guest dispute in France, whereas in French Canada we find working-class parents bearing down more harshly than middle-class parents on the disputative child. But when we ask why social class differences turn up with our FC sample and not with our FF sample, we have no means, with the data available, to suggest an answer.

Perceived Sex-Role Differences

Finally, FF parents perceive more differences in the comportment of boys and girls than do FC parents ($p < .05$), and interesting as this difference is, here, too, we are left with unanswerable questions: Are there factual grounds for such a Canadian-European difference in perceptions? Could it be that sex-role distinctions are actually better maintained in France (and Europe) than in Canada (and North America)?

Differences Attributable to Social-Class Backgrounds

As mentioned earlier, numerous contrasts attributable to the different socioeconomic backgrounds of the parents were uncovered. In fact, we find the influence of social class showing up on all but three scales, and in two of these instances (help withholding and perceived sex-role differences) social class plays an indirect role in determining how parents react. Actually, the only dimension that is neither directly nor indirectly affected by social class is that dealing with guest restrictions. In this one case we find that FC and FF parents, regardless of social-class background, permit their children to invite guests into the home.

On the many dimensions where social-class differences have their effect it is the middle-class parents, in France and in Quebec, who are the more lenient, that is, the less harsh disciplinarians, and the more inclined to extend comfort, to cater to a child's pleas for attention, or to allow the child autonomy. Middle-class parents also expect fewer sex-role contrasts in the behavior of boys and girls.

Those cases where social-class differences work in conjunction with other factors—for example, through the GCP interaction for help withholding, the GC and GCXP interactions for insolence control, and the FC interaction for siding with guest versus child—have already been mentioned because each involves national group differences as well. However, we want to emphasize that these comparisons are based as much on social class as on national background. First, there are important social-class differences between FF and FC parents with regard to helping. At the working-class level, the FF and FC parents present a similar pattern, with fathers being generally more helpful than mothers. At the middle-class level there are marked national differences: FC middle-class fathers are particularly helpful, whereas FF middle-class fathers are particularly reluctant to help.

In the case of insolence, we find that FC middle-class parents are less punitive than FC working-class parents, whereas in France there is a more complex contrast between social-class levels: in FF working-class families one parent takes charge of disciplining the insolence of both boys and girls, while in FF middle-class families one parent disciplines sons, the other daughters.

Comparable national differences turned up for the case of a child-guest dispute, since in this instance we find no social-class differences in the reactions of FF parents but a prominent difference in FC families, with the working-class being the harsher.

Finally, social class also had an influence on parents' perceptions of sex-role differences as reflected in the CP interaction (depicted in Figure A 3.4). This pattern suggests that in both France and French Canada, working-class fathers perceive more differences in the comportment of boys and girls than do mothers, whereas middle-class mothers see more instances of sex-role differentiation than do fathers. Could this mean that boys and girls actually emphasize sex-role distinctions more in behavior when in the presence of fathers in one case and mothers in the other, or may it mean that, for some unknown reasons, working-class fathers and middle-class mothers have lower thresholds for the perception of differences in the comportment of boys and girls? This matter also merits further follow-up study.

Differences Attributable to the Sex of the Child

There are very few instances where FF or FC parents react differently to sons as compared to daughters. On none of our scales does the sex of the child appear as a main effect, and on only one (namely, insolence control) was the child's sex relevant in an interaction (the GXP and GCXP interactions already discussed). The single case of insolence, however, was extremely interesting and suggested that boys and girls who are insolent toward their parents are treated in quite distinctive ways by a father or a mother depending on (a) the social-class status of the family, and (b) the nationality of the family, French or French Canadian.

Differences Attributable to the Sex of the Parent

As we have already seen, being a father or a mother in France or in French Canada makes a difference in how one responds to a child's request for help, how one reacts to displays of insolence, and how one perceives sex-role differences in behavior. There are two other instances where mothers and fathers, both FF and FC, have different modes of reacting, namely with regard to social temper and a child-guest dispute. It is interesting that both FF and FC mothers are more severe than fathers in their reactions to these two forms of social behavior ($p < .05$ in both cases). This consistent tendency for mothers to take the more dominant role of sanctioning social aggressiveness is worth further study. Why would this task fall to French mothers, whether they are Canadian or European French, more than fathers, and why should parental differences show up on these particular dimensions?

SUMMARY

A coherent set of contrasts and similarities was revealed in this investigation. As we summarize the most prominent of these, it is painfully evident that we are unable to answer fully all questions that come to mind. We have to content ourselves with the thought that the cross-national feature of the investigation has generated a body of factual information, which at least leads us to a set of new questions.

In the first place, there are several rather substantial contrasts between French-French and Canadian French approaches to child rearing, although these are intermeshed with instances of very similar reactions on the part of the two parental groups. We found a completely different attitude in FC, in contrast to FF, families on the issue of a child's request for autonomy. When a child makes a bid for autonomy, as that is indexed in this study, he or she is likely to meet with refusal in the European French setting but with compliance in the French Canadian setting, regardless of the social-class background of the family. In both France and French Canada, parents of middle-class socioeconomic status tend to be more compliant than those from working-class backgrounds, but even so, FF middle-class parents as a group tend to refuse the child's overture for autonomy.

The particular episode used to reflect autonomy was a child's request to cross the street on his/her own to play. It is doubtful that the FF-FC differences we are talking about are simply differences between Montreal and Paris in parental concerns about traffic. Instead, we are of the opinion that the different reactions to the episode reflect differences between FF and FC parents' interpretations of a six-year-old asking to leave parental surveillance and separate himself from the influence of the "foyer," supposedly so important to European French families (Metreaux and Mead 1954). The child's request also reminds one of the social independence that French families purportedly cherish in their associations (or the lack of them) with neighbors and the outside-the-family world in general.

The contrast may also be a reflection of a much broader view that FC parents have of the in-group and of the family-like relations they typically have with other FC neighbors. In other words, it could be that FC parents, as members of a tightly integrated minority group in the North American setting, have developed a relatively broad view of the in-group and their relatively generous reaction to children's requests to visit may stem from their more open perspective. Of course these results could reflect a basic difference between FC and FF parents in the value assigned to independence training, a possibility consistent with McClelland's finding of different levels of achievement motivation in French Canada in contrast to France (McClelland 1961). To decide among these alternative interpretations, we would need a broadly gauged follow-up study.

Other important differences emerged in the ways that FC and FF parents react to a six-year-old in episodes taking place within the home. In three instances—when the child asks for help, for comfort, or starts to quarrel with a same-age friend—he or she is more often ignored in the FF than in the FC family. That is, relative to the FC parents, the FF parents are more likely to withhold both help and comfort and are less likely to intervene when a child-guest quarrel develops. We wonder if this may not reflect the FF parents' way of shaping individuality in their children: by giving them a relatively greater degree of responsibility for their own behavior. By contrast, FC parents seem to be more involved with, and attentive to, the child in these episodes. Furthermore, if the "foyer" is of more importance in the FF than in the FC family, it would follow that the FF child would be discouraged from leaving the family circle for excursions outside at the same time as he or she would be expected to learn to be responsible within the family circle. Independence training then would have a distinctive form for FF parents: they would capitalize on opportunities to teach the child to behave autonomously within the family group but not encourage the child to withdraw from the family group.

Our FC and FF parents also had substantially different modes of dealing with a child's insolence. At one level, we observed a basically similar pattern of reactions in France and French Canada: in both FC and FF working-class families one parent takes on a more punitive role toward insolence, whereas in the middle-class families the parents' reactions are clearly associated with the sex of the child. What is intriguing is that there seems to be a complete reversal of roles played by fathers and mothers in the two settings: mothers are the disciplinarians for insolence in FC working-class families, while fathers take on this role in FF working-class families. At the middle-class level, FC parents show leniency for the same-sex child who becomes insolent, while FF parents show leniency for the opposite-sex child. We have no guesses as to why these fascinating contrasts turned up, but, assuming they are reliable trends, they should be explored in follow-up research.

Finally, there were two other FC-FF contrasts that are noteworthy, and these involved social-class differences. What is interesting is that there are greater social-class differences in parental approaches to discipline in French Canada than in France. In these comparisons the French Canadian working-class parents are relatively prompt and harsh in their reactions to a child's displays of aggressivity directed toward a parent or toward a friend, and these reactions typically involve punishment or the threat of punishment. It is as though the FC working-class parents are particularly concerned about compliance with social norms, that is, concerned that their child behave in a socially acceptable way. Because social aggressiveness is often a very public and visible display, it could be particularly disconcerting. By the same token, FC middle-class parents appear to be less concerned with social norms and conformity, and their reactions to a child's displays of social aggression are much like those of FF parents.

This review of the national contrasts in parental reactions has to be seen in relation to an equally impressive number of similarities in the modes of reaction of these two groups of French-speaking parents. These common perspectives shared by FC and FF parents are most apparent in the large number of cases where the social-class background of the family makes as much difference, or more, as the nationality of the parents. We found, for example, that differences in social-class background had significant effects on nine separate dimensions, and in all nine cases middle-class parents, whether from France or French Canada, were more lenient than working-class parents. This means that FC and FF parents of lower social-class backgrounds are more severe or demanding in child rearing, whether the children are aggressive toward people or things, insolent toward parents, or simply requesting attention, comfort, or autonomy. Working-class parents also expect greater sex-role differentiations. In fact it is only when a child asks for help or for guest privileges that social class does not affect the parents' reactions.

What does this striking social class contrast mean? As we have already argued, it could signify a major divergence in the perspectives of parents. Having experienced one social-class world or the other and assuming one's children will likely have a similar fate, parents in France and French Canada may try to prepare their children for survival and adjustment in the appropriate class structure. The strategy of the working-class parents seems to involve strictness, being negative to requests, and demanding respect and obedience. One wonders whether early rearing differences of this sort would hamper later adjustment for those who might, when adult, want to move out of the social-class positions anticipated for them. It could be that they are being trained to stay within particular social-class boundaries.

Another prominent characteristic of both French and French Canadian parents is their generally consistent tendency to treat boys and girls alike. Only in the case of a display of insolence will a boy and a girl be treated differently. But this one instance is extremely instructive, as we have seen, because of the fascinating sex-linked biases between parents and children in middle-class families—same-sex leniency for FC parents and cross-sex leniency for FF parents. However, the fact that FF parents perceive more sex-role differences than FC parents do does not seem to have influenced differentially their modes of reacting to boys and girls.

Finally, there are few signs of father-mother differences in approach to child rearing for these two samples of French parents. In general mothers and fathers present a common front to their children, leaving little room for the use of divisive tactics. Still, the common front breaks down for middle-class parents when the child is insolent. There is also one other weak spot in the common front: when a child displays aggression in the form of social temper or a quarrel with a peer, the mother (FC or FF) becomes a stricter socializer than the father. There are no counterexamples where fathers are more harsh than mothers. For FC working-class families we also found that the mother is less inclined than the father to extend help and is generally more punitive when the child is insolent. Contrary to a common stereotype, then, and contrary to the descriptions provided by Garigue (1962), in our two examples of French families, the mother emerges as a more active or dominant socializer than the father. Of course, this may be the French male's way of showing his authority, that is, of withdrawing and leaving the details of socialization to the woman. But in any case, the rationale behind the common stereotype of the dominant French father now calls for further investigation.

4

FRENCHNESS IN FRANCE, FRENCH BELGIUM, AND FRENCH CANADA

When, in the preceding chapter, we compared the reactions of French Canadian and French French parents, we found that each group had its own quite distinctive ways of interacting with children, in spite of a common linguistic and "cultural" background. Because these contrasts between French Canadian and French French parents were complex and fascinating ones, we thought it would be worthwhile to go one step further in the analysis by comparing French parents from France and French-speaking, European-based parents from Belgium, and then by bringing all three groups—French French, French Belgian, and French Canadian—into a wider comparison. This we do in this chapter.

Like the French Canadians, the French Belgians or Walloons live in a bicultural nation and they too come into contact continuously with members of a different ethnic subgroup, the Flemish. Unlike the French Canadians, the Walloons live geographically very close to France, and direct contacts between the Walloons and the French from France have always been numerous. In fact, the Walloons have never been isolated from the French for any extended period of time in history.

The Walloons, however, have had many more opportunities than the French to come into close social contact and make political adjustments with people of various national or cultural backgrounds. They live on the northern border of the French-speaking community of Europe and are neighbors to Germanic nations. What is more, their history over the last few centuries has been quite different from that of France, since they have always been linked, politically and socially, with various national/cultural groups. For example, since the Treaty of Verdun in 1814 they have been politically aligned with the Germans, the Austrians, the Spanish, and the Dutch.

In the light of this sociopolitical history, we asked ourselves: Are the value systems of these French-speaking Belgian parents basically similar to those of their French neighbors with whom they share not only the same language but also to a certain degree the same culture, or has the Belgian experience with its broader social contact with different national groups contributed to a substantially different set of values? Although these questions are broad, we will limit our attempts to answer them to parents' child-rearing values, for it is within the home, we believe, that the values and attitudes of nations have their start.

The Walloon study was conducted in exactly the same way as the French and Canadian studies. The interviews were conducted in the metropolitan area of Liége, Belgium's largest all-French city, located near the border separating French-speaking communities from the Flemish and German subgroups. Names of families who fitted our criteria of middle class (MC) or working class (WC) were obtained from school principals and teachers. The parents were contacted by phone or by mail so that appointments could be made to conduct the interviews in homes. Two research assistants who lived in the city and attended universities in Liége conducted the interviews. Classification of the socioeconomic background of the families was based on the occupation and education of the fathers, since no standardized socioeconomic index, comparable to the Blishen index for Canada, has been developed in Belgium. Critical features of the French and Walloon samples are compared in Table A 4.1.

Our standard statistical treatment was applied to the parents' responses. The significant comparisons for each of the 11 scales are presented in Table 4.1 and the mean scores for each subgroup are available in Table A 4.2.

RESULTS: FRENCH BELGIAN AND
FRENCH FRENCH PARENTS

It is evident in Table 4.1 that very few significant differences turn up in the comparison of French Belgian and French French parents. We notice also that there are many more significant contrasts attributable to the parents' socioeconomic backgrounds than to their nationality. The relative importance of social class will again become clear as we discuss in turn each of the possible sources of influence.

TABLE 4.1

Significant Effects in the Comparisons of French French and French Belgian Parents

Comparisons	1) Help Withholding (np = 58.6)	2) Siding with Baby vs. Child (np = 42.7)	3a) Temper Control (np = 30.0)	3b) Social Temper Control (np = 41.6)	4) Insolence Control (np = 25.0)	5) Attention Denial (np = 75.0)	6) Comfort Withholding (np = 41.6)	7) Autonomy Control (np = 58.3)	8) Guest Restriction (np = 62.5)	9) Siding with Guest vs. Child (np = 42.7)	10) Perceived Sex-Role Differences	11) Expected Sex-Role Differences
G	–	–	–	13.19	–	–	–	–	6.43	15.64	–	–
C	–	13.46	10.59	7.16	–	11.36	10.72	6.05	–	–	–	15.05
X	–	–	–	–	–	–	–	–	–	–	–	–
P	–	4.27	–	–	–	–	6.75	–	–	–	–	–
GC	–	–	–	–	–	–	–	–	–	–	–	–
GX	–	–	–	–	–	–	–	–	–	–	–	–
CX	4.17	–	–	–	–	–	–	–	–	–	–	–
GP	–	–	–	–	–	–	–	4.79	–	–	–	–
CP	–	–	–	–	–	–	–	–	–	–	–	–
XP	–	–	–	–	6.09	–	–	–	–	–	–	–
GCX	–	–	–	–	–	–	–	–	–	–	–	–
GCP	7.37	–	–	–	–	–	–	–	–	–	–	–
GXP	–	–	–	–	–	–	–	–	–	–	–	–
CXP	–	–	–	–	–	–	–	–	–	–	–	–
GCXP	–	–	–	–	4.35	–	–	–	–	–	–	–

Note: Entries are significant F values; those underlined are at the .01 level of confidence, the others are at the .05 level.
Source: Compiled by the authors.

Differences Attributable to Nationality of Parents

On three scales the Walloon parents are significantly different from French parents, and all three involve interactions with a same-age friend: the child's request to have a guest over to play and the child's subsequent aggression directed toward his friend. The scales in question are <u>social temper</u>, <u>guest restrictions</u>, and <u>siding with guest versus child</u>, and in all three instances the Belgian parents are harsher or more demanding with their children than are their French counterparts. Not only are they less permissive on guest privileges, but once they do agree, they tend to control the child's social behavior more than the French parents do. This tendency to control is also clear when one compares parental reactions to the socially aggressive child (data available in Tables A 4.3 and A 4.4). The major difference in tactics shows up when the child threatens to strike a friend. Both sets of parents apparently have the same reactions at the beginning of the quarrel, both asking the child to share the toys and cooperate, although even at the start there is a greater tendency for French parents to ignore the quarrel. But as the quarrel progresses to the point of threats of physical aggression, Walloon parents react strongly: the mildest reaction is to reprimand the child, while the majority either punish or threaten to punish the child. There is a large difference in the use of threats of punishment or actual punishment, and the Belgian parents stand out as clearly more severe than French parents ($X^2 = 13.485$, $\underline{p} < .01$). The types of punishment used, however, are similar in both countries, consisting mainly of sending the visitor home, telling the friend that he or she can play with the game alone, or removing the game entirely.

When the child asks to have a friend over to play, there are also distinctive differences in the tactics used by Walloon and French parents. Whereas French parents tend more to agree, without comment, Walloon parents are more inclined either to add some form of stipulation to their acquiescence or to give some type of explanation for their refusal (data in Table A 4.5). Two stipulations frequently given by the Walloon parents are (a) agreement conditional on the friend's parents ("Yes, if his mother agrees."), and (b) an insistence on orderliness ("Yes, if you clean up afterwards.").

Apart from these guest-related episodes that show Walloon parents to be harsher than French parents, certain other group differences turned up in the interactions. A three-way interaction indicates that French and Walloon fathers and mothers of different social-class backgrounds react differently to the child's request for help (Figure 4.1). Social-class differences in readiness to help are more pronounced for our Belgian parents. Furthermore, whereas

FIGURE 4.1

G x C x P Interaction for Help Withholding

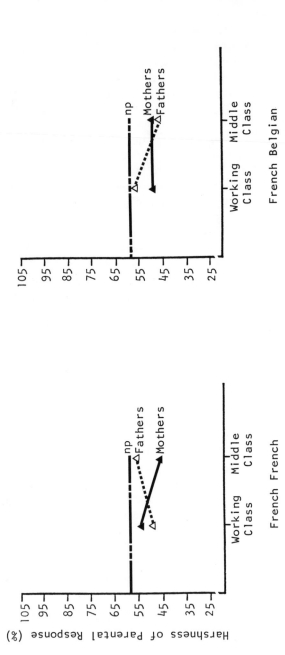

Source: Constructed by the authors.

the French Belgian working-class father is less helpful than the
mother, the opposite is true for our French samples where the
French working-class father is the more helpful parent. However,
the French middle-class father is less inclined to help than the
mother. Thus, at the middle-class level, the French Belgian child
can expect to receive much more help from his or her father than
can his French counterpart, who, in fact, can expect very little help
from the father.

The help-withholding issue has another interesting feature
which cuts across national background (Figure 4.2). Middle-class
boys in both France and French Belgium can expect more parental
help than working-class boys. For girls, the reverse is true, that
is, the middle-class girls are less likely than working-class girls
to receive parental help. Furthermore, the parents' social-class
background has a greater effect on boys than on girls. Thus, when
requesting parental help, the middle-class boy is the most likely to
receive it and the working-class boy, the least.

FIGURE 4.2

C x X Interaction for Help Withholding

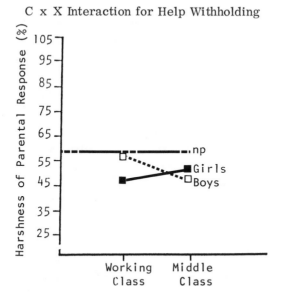

Source: Constructed by the authors.

Although in both countries there are marked social-class differences in parents' reactions to a child-baby dispute, in this instance social-class differences are more pronounced for our French

than for our Walloon parents (Figure A 4.1). French middle-class parents are less inclined than working-class parents to side with the baby in a child-baby dispute. There is no such social-class difference in the French Belgian data, which means that the Walloon child, whether from a working- or a middle-class family, can expect harsh treatment when becoming involved in a quarrel with a younger sibling.

When we examine the actual reactions of parents (data available in Tables A 4.6 to A 4.8), we find that French middle-class parents tend to ignore the dispute or to overlook the child's threat more so than the French working-class parents or the French Belgians of either socioeconomic level. When the child threatens to strike a younger sibling, the Belgian parents, regardless of social class, react with reprimands or threats of punishment, whereas the French middle-class parents are noticeably less severe.

Finally, there are also national-group differences in reactions to insolence, and these appear as part of a complex but interesting interaction, depicted in Figure 4.3, where national background, social class, sex of the parent, and sex of child are all involved. First, working-class families in both France and French Belgium develop a system whereby one parent plays the disciplinarian role toward insolence, while middle-class families in both nations develop a system of cross-sex leniency. The disciplinarian role in the French working-class family is assumed by the father, making the French working-class mother relatively lenient toward displays of insolence. In contrast, in the Walloon working-class family, the mother assumes the disciplinarian role and the father is relatively more permissive. Furthermore, in both the French and the Walloon working-class families, the disciplinarian (that is, the French father and the French Belgian mother) is harsher with an insolent girl than with an insolent boy, making the nondisciplinarian (that is, the French mother and the French Belgian father) more lenient with an insolent girl than with an insolent boy. As a consequence, the father-mother difference in reaction to insolence is greater for girls than for boys.

At the middle-class level, our French families show a pronounced pattern of cross-sex leniency toward insolence, so much so, that the mothers of boys and the fathers of girls come close to allowing their children to be insolent. A similar but less marked pattern of cross-sex leniency emerges for the Walloon middle-class parents, but in their case the pattern is one-sided in the sense that fathers are harsher on insolent boys than on insolent girls, while mothers show no bias one way or the other.

Overall, then, the least complicated difference between French and French Belgian parents is seen in their responses to a child's modes of interacting with a playmate, and in these instances French Belgian parents are more strict and demanding than French parents. The various other differences between the two national groups of parents are based on some combination of national background of the parent, along with social class, sex of the parent, and sex of the child involved.

Differences Attributable to Social-Class Backgrounds

The most striking and pervasive contrasts are again those associated with the socioeconomic background of the parents. We find, for example, that middle-class parents, whether French Belgian or French, show greater leniency toward a six-year-old child than working-class parents on all ten of our scales, and in six cases the differences are large enough to be statistically significant. This means that working-class parents in both France and French Belgium are more demanding or severe on issues calling for discipline (for example, child-baby disputes, temper outbursts, or social temper outbursts), on issues calling for parental aid or attention (for example, requests for attention or comfort), and on bids for independence (for example, autonomy) than are middle-class parents. The working-class parents also have significantly higher expectations that boys and girls will behave differently.

With regard to autonomy control, there are important differences in the reactions of fathers and mothers depending upon their socioeconomic backgrounds (see Figure 4.4). The interplay of factors here means that middle-class parents from both France and French Belgium are less restrictive than the working-class parents in allowing the child to cross the street on his own, and the social-class factor tends to affect fathers in particular. Working-class fathers are very restrictive on the autonomy issue, while middle-class fathers are particularly permissive; they are more ready, in fact, than middle-class mothers to permit their children to try their own wings.

On the help-withholding and insolence-control scales, social-class effects show up in the form of significant interactions, leaving three scales only—guest restrictions, siding with guest versus child, and perceived sex-role differences—where the working-class and middle-class parents in these two settings react in essentially similar ways. Social class, then, has important effects in both the French and French Belgian settings, and these effects tend to take the same form: working-class parents are generally harsher, more restrictive, or more demanding than their middle-class counterparts.

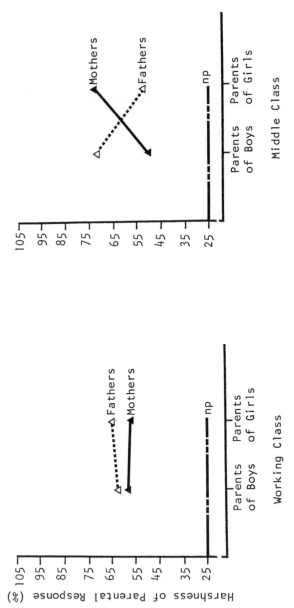

FIGURE 4.3

G x C x X x P Interaction for Insolence Control

French French

94

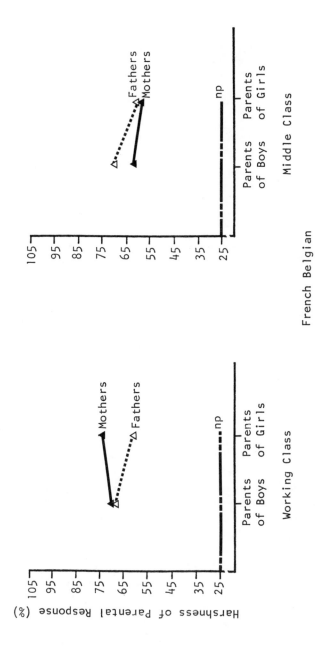

Source: Constructed by the authors.

FIGURE 4.4

C x P Interaction for Autonomy Control

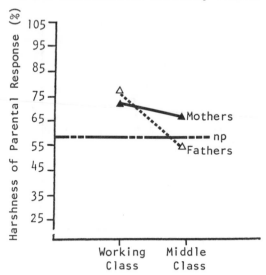

Source: Constructed by the authors.

Differences Attributable to the Sex of
the Child or the Sex of the Parent

As we have already seen, there are important national-group differences in the ways mothers, in contrast to fathers, react to boys in contrast to girls. For example, we have found that the social-class background of the family in both France and French Belgium affects the amount and type of help boys and girls are likely to receive from their fathers; mothers' reactions on the help issue are less affected by social-class status. Then we noted that fathers and mothers in France and French Belgium react in distinctive ways toward an insolent boy and an insolent girl. Finally, we found that middle-class parents in general encourage autonomy more than do working-class parents and that middle-class fathers in the two settings are particularly permissive, while middle-class mothers are particularly restrictive.

SUMMARY: FRENCH VERSUS
FRENCH BELGIAN PARENTS

This comparison of French and French Belgian parents provides us with an interesting array of similarities and contrasts in the ways these parents interact with their children. For instance, French and Walloon parents have similar ways of dealing with a child's temper displays; they both come down hard on such outbursts. Both parental groups discourage a child's bids for attention and comfort, and both groups tend to dampen a child's bids for autonomy. In addition, both groups have similar views on sex-role differentiations. At the same time, Walloon and French parents have quite different approaches to social temper: the Walloon parents are much more severe with aggression directed toward a peer, and they express greater opposition to requests to have a playmate come into the home as a guest, as though they viewed a playmate as some type of intruder within the "foyer." If a guest is permitted in the house, Walloon parents place more restrictions on their children's mode of interaction with the guest, compared to French parents who are more "laissez-aller" even when the child-guest interaction leads to a quarrel.

One wonders if these distinctive concerns of the Walloon parents—a general wariness toward playmates, as though they were intruders, and a relatively greater concern for socially appropriate manners when their children interact with playmates—may not have roots in the history of the nation as a whole. One speculation might run this way: Belgium historically has been a "pawn" in European politics as Toynbee (1947) has argued, and Belgians have earned the reputation of having "hereditary mistrust" of strangers (Thérèse Henriot 1971). Might it be that the Walloon parent considers a child's guest as a threat to the order of the family circle, someone to be dealt with with care and caution? It would be worthwhile to explore this possibility further in future research.

One wonders also whether the relatively strong authoritarian attitude of the Walloon parents—their tendency to lay down the law to their children with no questions permitted, in contrast to the relative permissiveness of the French parents—has a particular impact on, among other things, their children's achievement orientations (McClelland 1966), their development of conscience (Guterman 1970), or their degree of field independence (Witkin and Berry 1975). According to McClelland's research (1966), there is a sizable difference in the achievement scores for the two groups in question, with the French having a much higher "need for achievement" index than the Belgians. Because achievement needs in children are apparently fostered by parents' philosophies about independence training, we may have here an important difference in French and French Belgian approaches to child rearing that could affect their children's motivation.

There were also differences between French and Belgian mothers and fathers in the ways they reacted to requests for help and to displays of insolence, two interesting exceptions to the otherwise general tendency for French and French Belgian mothers and fathers to present a common front to their children. In the case of insolence, there is a clear display of cross-sex leniency in both French and French Belgian middle-class families. For working-class families, however, there is an important national difference in the sense that mothers are the more severe socializers of insolence in our French Belgian families, while fathers are the more severe socializers of insolence in our French samples.

The second exception shows itself on the help-request episodes. In France, working-class fathers are more helpful than working-class mothers, whereas middle-class mothers are more helpful than middle-class fathers. In French Belgium, the pattern is reversed: in working-class families the mother is the more helpful parent, while in middle-class families the father is the more helpful parent.

What is striking in the overall comparison is the fact that social-class background has a greater impact on parents' reactions than does national or cultural background. The social-class differences are not only large and numerous, but they also pattern themselves in similar ways in France and French Belgium. What has been said in the previous chapters about the relative strictness of working-class parents holds for these two European French-speaking groups as well. However, we have found instances here where social-class differences are expressed differently in these two countries. For example, in the case of insolence displays, the working-class family in France and French Belgium is characterized by one parent playing a disciplinarian role, but in France the father is the disciplinarian, for instance, while in French Belgium it is the mother. In middle-class families, on the other hand, the fascinating cross-sex leniency pattern turns up both in France and in French Belgium.

Social-class background also determines how helpful parents are likely to be to boys as compared to girls. Thus, in middle-class French and French Belgian families, boys receive more parental help than girls—a trend that could encourage more independence in girls than in boys—while in working-class families in both settings, girls receive more parental help than boys—a pattern which could foster relatively more independence in boys than in girls. This social-class bias toward boys in middle-class families and toward girls in working-class families is an isolated outcome and does not emerge as a systematic social-class trend. Nevertheless, it would be worthwhile to explore in more detailed follow-up research what these social-class biases in help giving might mean in France and French Belgium.

Finally, social class influences parents' reactions to the autonomy bids of their children, and here middle-class fathers in both France and French Belgium are more inclined than middle-class mothers to encourage the child's request for independence, while in working-class families fathers are more restrictive than mothers on the autonomy issue. Could it be that the father's involvement in the independence training of the child determines whether the child will develop a middle- or a working-class value system? That would be one way in which the social-class standing of the linear family in France and French Belgium could be perpetuated. This possibility, too, deserves further exploration.

A THREE-GROUP COMPARISON: FRENCH CANADIAN, FRENCH FRENCH, AND FRENCH BELGIAN PARENTS

So far we have compared three French-speaking groups of parents two at a time: French Canadian (FC) and French French (FF) parents were compared in Chapter 3, and French Belgian (FB) and French French parents in this chapter. We have seen that FC and FF parents differ on certain aspects of child rearing while FB and FF parents differ on other aspects. We now bring all three groups into one comparison, and, as we do so, it will become very evident that it is the FC parents who are distinctive, differing from both FF and FB groups, the two European-based samples, on a number of issues. As far as Frenchness is concerned, then, the across-the-Atlantic differences end up to be more extensive than the within-Europe differences.

These three-group comparisons are based on the significant contrasts presented in Table 4.2 and the whole set of mean scores available in Table A.28.

National-Group Comparisons

The first major trend is that the FC parents are generally more lenient than either the FF or FB groups on a series of dimensions, and the FB parents are generally the most restrictive and

TABLE 4.2

Significant Effects in the Comparisons of French Canadian, French French, and French Belgian Parents

Value Dimensions

Comparisons	1) Help Withholding (np = 58.6)	2) Siding with Baby vs. Child (np = 42.7)	3a) Temper Control (np = 30.0)	3b) Social Temper Control (np = 41.6)	4) Insolence Control (np = 25.0)	5) Attention Denial (np = 75.0)	6) Comfort Withholding (np = 41.6)	7) Autonomy Control (np = 58.3)	8) Guest Restriction (np = 62.5)	9) Siding with Guest vs. Child (np = 42.7)	10) Perceived Sex-Role Differences	11) Expected Sex-Role Differences
G	6.35	3.71	–	8.24	–	–	5.00	12.91	6.15	7.57	4.61	3.22
C	–	20.92	10.43	24.30	7.75	13.28	9.16	9.90	–	7.12	–	23.42
X	–	–	–	4.13	–	–	–	–	–	–	–	–
P	–	–	–	–	5.00	–	–	–	–	4.15	–	–
GC	–	–	–	–	–	–	–	–	–	5.94	–	–
GX	–	–	–	–	–	–	–	–	–	–	–	–
CX	–	–	–	–	–	–	–	–	–	–	–	–
GP	3.79	–	–	–	–	–	–	–	–	–	–	–
CP	–	–	–	–	–	–	–	–	–	–	–	–
XP	–	–	–	–	–	–	–	–	–	–	–	–
GCX	–	–	–	–	–	–	–	–	–	–	–	–
GCP	5.15	–	–	–	–	–	–	–	–	–	–	–
GXP	–	–	–	–	3.63	–	–	–	–	–	–	–
CXP	–	–	–	–	–	–	–	–	–	–	–	–
GCXP	–	–	–	–	3.57	–	–	–	–	–	–	–

Note: Entries are significant F values; those underlined are at the .01 level of confidence, the others are at the .05 level.

Source: Compiled by the authors.

100

punitive. FB parents also have the highest scores for perceptions and expectations of sex-role differentiations and FC parents the lowest scores, suggesting a possible relationship between severity in child rearing and the degree of attention given to sex-role differences in comportment.

Second, when we rank the three parental groups in terms of degree of restrictiveness, the FB parents are always harsher than FC parents, whereas for the two European groups, the FBs are sometimes more and sometimes less severe socializers than the FF parents (see Table 4.3). The FF parents are the most severe on three issues: help withholding, comfort withholding, and autonomy control, all three dealing with parents' reactions to various requests made by the child, and in these cases FB parents are somewhat (that is, nonsignificantly) more willing than FF parents to give help or comfort and to grant autonomy. On the other hand, FB parents are harsher than FF parents on three issues characterized by a child's comportment with a guest, social temper, guest restriction, and siding with guest versus child. On two of these scales, social temper and guest restriction, the FB parents are also significantly harsher than the FCs. Interestingly, in the case of a child-guest quarrel the FB and FC parents are equally severe, both groups more severe than FF parents.

Both European groups, however, are much less likely than FC parents to comply with requests for help, autonomy, or comfort.

A third trend emerges around the social temper and child-guest dispute episodes, where the FC and FB parents are alike and both different from the FF parents. These two episodes involve a child displaying aggression toward a guest, and we find that our FF parents are more inclined to ignore these forms of social aggression than are FC or FB parents. Perhaps the "laissez-faire" attitude taken by the FF parents in guest-child disputes is uniquely French French, for not only do the FF parents differ from FC and FB parents on this issue, but this is also the only theme that links FC and FB parents, who are both harsher in their reactions than FF parents. We wonder if this common concern with the propriety of children's behavior with visitors to the home stems from the greater experience both FCs and FBs have had in learning to adjust and accommodate to ethnic differences.

Finally, there are differences in the ways our three groups of French-speaking parents extend help to a child and in the ways they control a child's insolence. Not only are FC parents more prone to comply with requests for help than are either of the two European groups, but in both middle- and working-class families, FC fathers tend to be more helpful than FC mothers. The picture is different for the two European groups: French working-class families are

TABLE 4.3

Group Comparisons for Degree of Parental Harshness*

	French Canadians		French French		French Belgians	
	Mean	Rank	Mean	Rank	Mean	Rank
			.01			
Help withholding	43.33	(1)	51.91	(3)	49.68	(2)
			.05			
Siding with baby versus child	54.96	(1)	56.70	(2)	59.96	(3)
			.05		.01	
Social temper	68.75	(2)	67.81	(1)	76.79	(3)
			.01			
			.01			
Comfort withholding	50.08	(1)	65.51	(3)	58.80	(2)
			.01			
Autonomy control	44.99	(1)	71.25	(3)	65.21	(2)
			.01			
					.01	
Guest restriction	35.00	(1)	36.34	(2)	45.66	(3)
			.01			
			.05		.01	
Siding with guest versus child	62.13	(2)	58.07	(1)	65.30	(3)
			.05			
Perceived sex-role differences	19.14	(1)	21.93	(2)	22.79	(3)
			.01			
			.05			
Expected sex-role differences	15.41	(1)	18.00	(2)	19.81	(3)

*Lines connect means that differ at the .05 or .01 level according to the Newman-Keuls test of significance.

Source: Compiled by the authors.

characterized by a more helpful father and French middle-class families by a more helpful mother, whereas the French Belgian working-class mother is the more helpful parent, as is the French Belgian middle-class father.

The different ways in which these three national groups cope with insolence is particularly interesting because we find instances of cross-sex and same-sex leniency, especially at the middle-class social level, and, at the working-class level, distinctive patterns wherein one parent or the other takes the major disciplinarian role. In both French Canada and French Belgium, the disciplinarian role for insolence is taken by the working-class mother, whereas in France, the working-class father is the major disciplinarian. In contrast, at the middle-class level, the two French-speaking European groups show cross-sex leniency on the insolence issue, whereas the French Canadian parents show same-sex leniency.

Social-Class Influences

It is striking that for each of these French-speaking groups middle-class parents emphasize leniency in their relations with children more than working-class parents do. There are only two exceptions to this general contrast between the two social classes. The first involves insolence, and here both the French Canadian and the French Belgian working-class parents are, characteristically, more severe than the middle-class parents, whereas in France the middle-class parents are equally as harsh as their working-class counterparts. The second exception involves the child-guest quarrel, where the French Canadian subgroups show the characteristic social-class difference in degrees of leniency, whereas in France parents from both socioeconomic levels tend to be relatively lenient, and in French Belgium working- and middle-class parents are alike but relatively harsh in reacting to such disputes.

Sex-of-Child Influences

All three French-speaking groups of parents treat boys and girls essentially alike. The only exception to this equal-treatment pattern occurs on the insolence issue where, as already mentioned, there is at the middle-class level cross-sex leniency in our FB and FF families and same-sex leniency in our FC families.

Sex-of-Parent Influences

In all three settings, mothers and fathers are generally similar in their reactions to children. The exceptions to this general
tendency show up on the social temper and child-guest dispute issues
where mothers are the more severe socializers in all three settings.
Apparently, in France, French Belgium, and French Canada, the
mother is expected to be responsible for the child's behaving in a
socially acceptable way with a guest.

OVERALL SUMMARY

What then are the common French value themes that link these
three French-speaking groups of parents? Actually, when FC, FF,
and FB parents are brought into a single comparison, we are struck
more with differences than with common themes. We have found
that the three groups differ markedly in degrees of leniency or
severity in child rearing, with the FC parents being clearly the most
lenient and FB parents the most severe or demanding. Furthermore,
parents' attitudes toward sex roles turned out to be closely related
to their leniency or severity in child rearing: the more severe FB
parents expect and perceive more sex-role differentiations in the
actions of their sons and daughters than do the less severe FC parents.

Although FB parents are, in general, the most demanding of
the three comparison groups, there are two issues—giving help and
permitting autonomy—where the FF parents become number one in
harshness. Apparently FF parents become particularly recalcitrant
when a child asks for help or asks to leave the home, and their relatively noncooperative reaction to such requests may be an expression of their mode of inculcating independence. On the other hand,
the FF parents are particularly lenient on the social temper and
child-guest dispute issues, suggesting that their "laissez-faire"
attitude in such matters may be another way of forcing children to
work things out on their own. FC parents have quite a different perspective on child-guest disputes and social aggression, for it is on
these issues that they are particularly harsh with their children,
as harsh in fact as the FB parents.

Other contrasts emerge. The FC parents, regardless of social
class, are most ready to help, and, in general, FC fathers are more
helpful than FC mothers. This pattern differs from that of the FF
parents, for FF fathers are more helpful than FF mothers at the
working-class level but less helpful than FF mothers at the middle-
class level. The FB pattern is different again: at the working-class

level, FB mothers are more helpful than FB fathers, while at the middle-class level, FB mothers are less helpful than FB fathers.

Similarly, each of our three French-speaking groups has its distinctive mode of coping with insolence. At the working-class level, FC and FB mothers are the harsher socializers of insolence; this is not so in France, where FF fathers are harsher socializers than FF mothers. At the middle-class level, FF and FB parents show cross-sex leniency in their approach to insolence, while FC parents show same-sex leniency.

There are, then, clear national-group differences in child-rearing approaches among our French Canadian, French, and French Belgian parents. At the same time, there are certain common approaches which turn up in unanticipated forms, and these may reflect an underlying theme of Frenchness. For example, all three groups show similar effects of socioeconomic background, for it is the working-class parents in all three settings who are generally demanding more of their children. Likewise, all three groups treat boys and girls with equal severity or leniency, and for all three groups, mothers and fathers generally treat children in the same way, presenting, in other words, a unified front. This equal treatment given boys and girls and the generally similar reactions of mothers and fathers may be real manifestations of Frenchness. The social-class differences, however, may not be features of Frenchness because, as we will see, they turn up in nearly all of our national settings, making them more universal characteristics.

Nonetheless, important French Canadian-European differences were uncovered. Differences of this sort turned up (a) on the amount of aid or assistance parents extend to their children, (b) on parents' reactions to a child's request for autonomy, and (c) on the number of sex-role differentiations that parents see or expect to see in the behavior of boys and girls. In each case, FC parents are more likely than FF or FB parents to be helpful to their children, more willing to permit the child to leave the house alone, and less likely to perceive or expect boy-girl differences in behavior. Perhaps this set of features is due to an American influence on FC parents, a type of "American connection" that modifies Frenchness in the North American context.

What distinguishes the French Belgian from French French parents is essentially the degree of harshness applied to displays of social temper, to requests for guest privileges, and to the child's subsequent behavior with the guest. In these cases, the French Belgian parents are more hard-nosed and demanding than the French French parents, and we wonder if these distinguishing characteristics of the FB parents may be due to a Germanic influence, a type of "German connection" that modifies Frenchness in a quite different direction in French Belgium.

5

FRENCHNESS IN NORTH AMERICA: FRENCH AMERICAN AND FRENCH CANADIAN PARENTS

In this chapter we change our tack in the search for values that link French-speaking people in different sociocultural settings. Here we wonder whether French Canadian styles of child rearing are maintained by French Canadians who have immigrated to the United States—whether, in other words, typical French Canadian child-rearing values still characterize French-speaking Americans who have immigrated or whose parents have immigrated from French Canada to the United States. With this aim in mind, we made contact with colleagues in a French American region in northern New England and through them were introduced to numbers of French American parents living in and around Madawaska, Frenchville, and other small communities in northern Maine.

The whole region is known as the St. Johns Valley, and it is part of the U.S. peninsula that protrudes into the Canadian provinces of Quebec and New Brunswick. The largest village, Madawaska, has a population of about 4,500. Throughout the valley, 70 to 75 percent of the residents have ancestors from Quebec or New Brunswick, and the French language is still a central feature of social life for the majority of residents. The closest "Anglo" community, in fact, is nearly 50 miles to the south of Madawaska, making the valley region in many ways much more French Canadian than American. This is not to say that there is no English or American influence in the area. In fact, until the mid-1960s the vast majority of French American children in the area attended all-English schools. Thus, most French Americans in the valley are bilingual, the one local newspaper is in English, and as would be expected, English-language communication media are evident in all walks of life.

Given the complex misture of cultural influences in the area, we wondered what specific effects these might have on the child-

rearing values of French American parents. Would their orientations to children still reflect their French Canadian heritage, would
they have adopted essentially U.S. norms, or would they have
forged some distinctive amalgamation of child-rearing values?

The sorts of comparisons that these questions entail are not
necessarily simple and unambiguous. The St. Johns Valley area,
the source of our French American (FA) sample, and Montreal, the
source of our French Canadian (FC) sample, are very different
communities in terms of size as well as social structure. Montreal
is a huge metropolitan area with dozens of cultural influences beyond those of the English and French communities, while the valley
region comprises relatively small and isolated villages and towns.
Value differences could exist between the two areas simply because
of differences in degree of urbanization. We might have repeated
our French Canadian study in comparably small communities in
Quebec, but we did not, and the reader should keep the differences
in community size in mind as a reservation.

The only procedural difference between the FC and the FA
studies was a change in the tape recording of the child's voice. Because there are potentially important regional dialect differences
between the French of Montreal and those of the valley, an FA version of our tape was made using the voice of a six-year-old native
of Madawaska. We made sure that the child's tone of voice and
points of emphasis were similar in the Montreal and the Madawaska
versions. All interviews with FA parents were conducted in French
by two native speakers of French, one of whom was a native of
Madawaska.

Because it was difficult to find large numbers of FA families
in the valley who fit our specifications for middle-class standing,
we restricted our study to working-class FA parents only, and,
thus, all comparisons of FA and FC child-rearing practices are
also limited to working-class FC parents.

The background information for our FA and FC samples is
available in Table A 5.1. Most of the fathers in both groups have
"blue-collar" positions. In Madawaska most of the men work in
paper manufacturing, the major industry of the region, while in
Montreal there is more variation in types of employment. Although
the occupational positions of the fathers in the two samples were
fairly equivalent, the educational levels of the groups were a bit different. Few of the fathers had completed high school, and yet the
FA fathers, on the average, had completed some two years more
schooling than their FC counterparts. All of our FC parents had
been born in Canada, whereas the majority of the FA parents had
been born in the United States of FC parents; fewer than half had
immigrated from Canada.

The statistical analyses followed the pattern already described, and the contrasts that turned out to be statistically significant are given in Table 5.1. The mean scores for each subgroup on each scale are available in Table A 5.2.

RESULTS: FRENCH AMERICAN AND FRENCH CANADIAN PARENTS

Is there an FC style of child rearing detectable in the patterns of parent-child interaction in FA families? In spite of the worrisome urbanization differences between Montreal and the valley area, we found a surprisingly large degree of similarity between the reactions of our two samples of parents. In fact, there were only four statistically significant contrasts (see Table 5.1), and only two of these are based on differences between Montreal-based FC and Madawaska-based FA parents. Thus value similarities far outweigh value contrasts in this case.

Group Comparisons

When FC or FA children ask for help, they are likely to receive it. When they get into a dispute with younger siblings or guests, both groups of parents take sides against the child. When they display temper, either toward things or toward people, both groups of parents are severe. Similarly, both groups of parents tend to reject attention-getting ploys, and they hold back and thus discourage children's requests for comforting. On the other hand, both groups of parents tend to give in to children's bids for autonomy or requests for guest privileges. And, finally, the two parental groups have similar sex-role expectation and sex-role perception scores.

Thus, most of our tape-recorded episodes evoke essentially the same responses from the FC and the FA parents. Still, we do find subtle differences in the ways the two groups respond to their children, even in the cases just reviewed where there are no statistically reliable group differences (data available in Tables A 5.3 to A 5.10). For example, when a child asks for help, we note that the FA parents are more inclined to give direct, immediate help, while FC parents are more likely to delay or give only partial assistance. Similarly, when the child makes a gesture for autonomy or requests guest privileges, the FC parents tend to question, qualify, or otherwise temper their agreement while FA parents tend to agree without these reservations.

TABLE 5.1

Significant Effects in the Comparisons of French Canadian Working-Class Parents with French American Working-Class Parents

Comparisons	Value Dimensions										
	1) Help Withholding (np = 58.6)	2) Siding with Baby vs. Child (np = 42.7)	3a) Temper Control (np = 30.0)	3b) Social Temper Control (np = 41.6)	4) Insolence Control (np = 25.0)	5) Attention Denial (np = 75.0)	6) Comfort Withholding (np = 41.6)	7) Autonomy Control (np = 58.3)	8) Guest Restriction (np = 62.5)	9) Siding with Guest vs. Child (np = 42.7)	10) Perceived Sex-Role Differences	11) Expected Sex-Role Differences
G	–	–	–	–	5.46	–	–	–	–	–	–	–
X	–	–	–	6.87	–	–	–	–	–	8.29	–	–
P	–	–	–	–	–	–	–	–	–	–	–	–
GX	–	–	–	–	–	–	–	–	–	–	–	–
GP	–	–	–	11.71	–	–	–	–	–	–	–	–
XP	–	–	–	–	–	–	–	–	–	–	–	–
GXP	–	–	–	–	–	–	–	–	–	–	–	–

Note: Entries are significant F values; those underlined are beyond the .01 level of confidence, the others are beyond the .05 level.
Source: Compiled by the authors.

109

However, when a child threatens to break the game, FA parents threaten punishment, while FC parents tend simply to divert the child. In this one case, then, the FA parents are more severe in their reactions. By way of contrast, when the child's frustrations are directed toward the parents in the form of insolence, the FA parents are relatively less severe in the sense that they are less likely to threaten punishment or to actually punish the child. In fact, this group difference for insolence control, with FC parents showing the harsher reactions, is statistically significant (see Table 5.1). Likewise, when a child-guest dispute shapes up, the FC parents are more inclined to threaten punishment, whereas FA parents rely more on urgings to have the child share.

There is a consistent trend here: FA parents tend to be generally less harsh in situations calling for discipline and more immediate in complying with a child's request for help, for permission to cross the street, or for guest privileges. It is only in the case of temper-directed-toward-things (rather than temper-toward-people) that the FA parents become the more severe socializers. At the other extreme, the sharpest contrast appeared for the episodes involving insolence, and in these cases the FA parents were significantly more lenient in their reactions. Perhaps, then, the U.S. influence on a basic French Canadian child-rearing style takes its start around issues like insolence, where lenience seems to be considered the appropriate parental reaction, and temper-toward-things, where parental harshness seems to be the accepted norm. It would be valuable to test the reliability of these trends in follow-up research.

Differential Reactions to Boys and Girls

There are two instances where parents, whether FC or FA, react differently to boys and girls. One is the social temper issue ($p < .05$) and the other the dispute with guest issue ($p < .01$). It is interesting that in both cases both FC and FA parents are harsher with girls than with boys. Apparently, there is something particular about these two forms of behavior that makes them out of character for FC or FA girls. There is no overall tendency for FC or FA parents to be more severe with girls than boys; instead the bias shows up only on the matters of social temper and child-guest dispute issues.

The intriguing question is why FC and FA parents are especially anxious to curb the socially directed temper and aggressive outbursts of girls. Why girls? Social temper and aggressivity should be just as offensive in boys, unless these parents feel that young men have to learn to take care of themselves, whereas young ladies have to prepare themselves for a more feminine role, keeping peace and being friendly rather than hostile to those inside as well as outside the family. There is some persuasive independent evidence from Parsons and Bales (1955) suggesting that parents in the United States serve as important models for the learning of these types of male and female roles. They argue that the maternal role involves more of the maintenance of warm, integrated interpersonal relationships within the family, while the paternal role involves more of the application of instrumental skills so that the family can cope and adapt to the environment. Perhaps these biases against girls reflect parents' attempts to teach their children appropriate sex roles. But what is perhaps more interesting is that this version of what constitutes acceptable sex roles may be more North American than it is universal. For instance, we find that the tendency for parents to be particularly harsh on girls who display social temper shows up in our EC and FC samples of parents, both working-class and middle-class, and in our sample of FA working-class parents. On the other hand, we find no such pattern in our French French or French Belgian samples.

Mother-Father Differences in Reactions

There is only one instance where mothers and fathers, both FC and FA, have different views of how they should react to the provocations of the child. In other words, there are hardly any signs in these comparisons of parental divergences of opinion, of parental divisions of responsibilities, or of cross-sex or same-sex leniency. This one exception, therefore, becomes all the more informative.

The interaction in question, that for social temper control ($\underline{p} < .01$), is depicted in Figure 5.1. Here we find a sharp contrast between FC and FA parents. FC mothers are more severe than FC fathers in their reactions to social temper displays, whereas FA mothers are less severe than FA fathers. What might this FC-FA difference mean? Note that there is a general trend for FC working-class mothers to be more severe or demanding than FC fathers on most dimensions (data available in rows 5 and 6 of page 1 of Table A 5.2). The pattern for social temper is therefore not uncharacteristic of FC lower-class families. On the other hand, it is apparently uncharacteristic for FA working-class mothers to be softer or easier than their husbands as they are in this case, because, in general, they are at least as demanding and punitive as their husbands. It seems, therefore, that there is something particular about social temper that evokes leniency on the part of FA mothers.

FIGURE 5.1

G x P Interaction for Social Temper Control

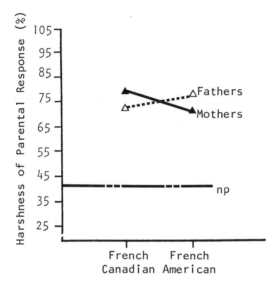

Source: Constructed by the authors.

It is also possible that there could be friction between mothers and fathers on this issue, since the FA fathers seem insistent on curbing their children's social temper while the FA mothers are relatively lenient on the issue, and uncharacteristically so. Perhaps here we see a possible U.S. influence that hits the FA mother, a type of Dr. Spock influence that pushes her toward softer treatment when children have emotional outbursts, including social temper and insolence displays. The FA father, on the other hand, may feel that he, as the "head" of an ethnically distinct group in the United States, may want to be sure that his children learn to curb socially aggressive impulses. It is not that the FA father is generally harsher on discipline matters, for on the insolence issue, he is as lenient as his wife. This suggests that FA fathers tolerate aggression directed to parents but not aggression directed to people outside the family. Whatever the final explanation might be, the main point is that we have isolated two major issues—social temper and insolence—that clearly differentiate the child-training values of FC and FA parents.

SUMMARY: FRENCH AMERICAN VERSUS
FRENCH CANADIAN PARENTS

Our purpose here was to explore the changes that might take place in an ethnic group's values when members of that cultural group immigrate to another national setting. The focus was on French American parents living in northern Maine whose families had emigrated from French-speaking regions of Canada to the United States and whose six-year-old children had been born in the United States. These French American parents were compared with French Canadians, both groups being from lower social-class backgrounds.

The U.S. community in question is situated close to the U.S.-Canadian border, so that many cultural and linguistic props are available to help FA families in the region to maintain their Frenchness. We were certain of the strength of the linguistic prop because all interviews were conducted entirely in French (Canadian style) and with no communication difficulties whatsoever. On the other hand, we had no clear idea about the durability of the French Canadian cultural traditions that had been transplanted in the United States.

What has been a pleasant surprise for us is the apparent depth and strength of FC cultural traditions, in the sense that FA and FC parents have very similar child-training values. We encountered only two instances of statistically significant contrasts between the FC and FA families, one indicating that FC parents are harsher than FA parents in reacting to children's insolence and the other indicating substantive differences between FC and FA parents in coping with children's displays of social temper. FC mothers are relatively harsher than FC fathers in sanctioning social temper, whereas FA mothers are relatively softer than FA fathers on the same issue. We wondered whether this contrast meant that FA mothers had been affected by a general U.S. norm of lenience and softness on the particular matter of social temper, whereas FA fathers, who may feel that they are the main representatives of their ethnically distinct families in the U.S. setting, may be particularly sensitive about their children developing socially aggressive inclinations.

An analysis of the types of reactions made by FC and FA parents to each of the taped episodes revealed several trends that distinguished the groups, apart from those reflected in the main statistical tables. Thus, FA parents were more inclined than FC parents to cater to their children's requests and demands with immediacy and with compliance. FA parents were also clearly less punitive than FCs; rather than punishing or threatening punishment, the FA parents tried more to reason with an insolent child or, if necessary, to reprimand. It was only on the matter of temper directed toward things (for example, breaking a toy) that the FA parents were more punitive than FC parents. We speculated here that the U.S. influence on FC values may get its foothold on two sorts of issues: insolence, where lenience may be the norm for parents in the U.S. setting, and temper-toward-things, which may be upsetting to people in the U.S. setting. These findings at least jibe with stereotypes of the contemporary United States, which has been described as showing "disciplined neglect" of children (Bronfenbrenner 1970) and placing comparatively high value on materialism.

Finally, we found a common FC-FA tendency for parents to be harsher with girls than with boys when displays of social temper or quarrels with a guest surface. This fascinating discouragement of aggressivity in girls (and encouragement of aggressivity in boys) could have important consequences for the French family in North America.

A COMPARISON OF FRENCH AMERICAN,
FRENCH CANADIAN, AND AMERICAN PARENTS

There are other vantage points for exploring the values of French American parents, and in this section we get a broader base of comparison, first by comparing FA parents with American (A) parents of similar (that is, working-class) socioeconomic backgrounds, and then by comparing FA parents with both A and FC parents. The question we have in mind here is: Where do FA values stand relative to those of parents in the host society and relative to parents in French Canada?

The American Working-Class Parents

The U.S. working-class parents we introduce here are part of our "old-stock" sample which will be used as a reference group in several chapters to follow. For a family to be considered "old-stock American," both parents of the six-year-old child and three of the child's four grandparents had to have been born in the United States and to have been native speakers of English. Half of our U.S. sample of families came from the east coast (Providence, Rhode Island) and half from the west coast (San Diego, California). The two halves were combined into a composite sample after statistical analyses showed remarkably little east coast-west coast variation in parental reactions to our taped episodes. We will consider these

as "typical" U.S. parental reactions, just as we consider our FC
data from Montreal as typical of French Canadian parental reactions.*

The background characteristics of the two French-speaking
samples and the working-class U.S. group are available in Tables
A 5.1 and A 5.12. The occupational positions held by all three
groups of working-class fathers are similar, but the U.S. fathers
have on the average about one year more education than the French
Americans, who, in turn, have about two years more education than
the French Canadians. There is also a difference among the samples
in religion. All of the French Canadian and French American parents are Roman Catholic, while about half of the U.S. sample are
Protestant, the other half Catholic, Jewish, or other. Thus, there
are potentially important demographic differences among our
samples of parents, even though they are comparable in terms of
social-class standing.

RESULTS: FRENCH AMERICAN, FRENCH
CANADIAN, AND AMERICAN PARENTS

Tables 5.2 and A 5.13 summarize the statistical findings for
the two-group comparisons: American (A) and French American
(FA) working-class parents, and Tables 5.3 and A 5.14 summarize
the findings for the three-group comparisons: American, French
American, and French Canadian working-class parents. Because
quite different information comes to light depending upon the base of
comparison used, we will shift attention back and forth between the
two-group and three-group comparisons, sometimes focusing mainly on the similarities and contrasts between FA and A parents on a
particular issue, and at other times, on the question of how the FA
parents, with their FC ancestry, have adjusted to the U.S. setting,
a three-group comparison.

Certain trends stand out immediately. For instance, the differences among parental groups are concentrated on particular
facets of child rearing only, while other facets show no differences.
Thus, all three groups have common reactions to children's displays
of temper and insolence, requests for comfort, and requests for

---

*It is evident that replications are called for where urban-
rural differences in values are investigated. Until these studies
are done, one cannot really decipher what is meant by the term
"typical."

TABLE 5.2

Significant Effects in the Comparison of American and French American Working-Class Parents

Value Dimensions

Comparisons	1) Help Withholding (np = 58.6)	2) Siding with Baby vs. Child (np = 42.7)	3a) Temper Control (np = 30.0)	3b) Social Temper Control (np = 41.6)	4) Insolence Control (np = 25.0)	5) Attention Denial (np = 75.0)	6) Comfort Withholding (np = 41.6)	7) Autonomy Control (np = 58.3)	8) Guest Restriction (np = 62.5)	9) Siding with Guest vs. Child (np = 42.7)	10) Perceived Sex-Role Differences	11) Expected Sex-Role Differences
G	15.13	–	–	–	–	4.90	–	–	–	–	–	–
X	6.54	–	–	4.13	–	–	–	–	–	–	–	–
P	–	–	–	4.95	–	–	–	–	–	–	8.01	–
GX	6.29	–	–	–	–	–	–	–	–	–	–	–
GP	–	–	–	–	–	–	–	–	–	–	–	8.43
XP	–	–	–	–	–	–	–	–	–	–	–	–
GXP	–	–	–	–	–	–	–	–	–	–	–	–

Note: Entries are significant F values; those underlined are beyond the .01 level of confidence, the others are beyond the .05 level.
Source: Compiled by the authors.

116

TABLE 5.3

Significant Effects in the Comparisons of American, French American, and French Canadian Working-Class Parents

Value Dimensions

Comparisons	1) Help Withholding (np = 58.6)	2) Siding with Baby vs. Child (np = 42.7)	3a) Temper Control (np = 30.0)	3b) Social Temper Control (np = 41.6)	4) Insolence Control (np = 25.0)	5) Attention Denial (np = 75.0)	6) Comfort Withholding (np = 41.6)	7) Autonomy Control (np = 58.3)	8) Guest Restriction (np = 62.5)	9) Siding with Guest vs. Child (np = 42.7)	10) Perceived Sex-Role Differences	11) Expected Sex-Role Differences
G	6.61	—	—	—	—	5.25	—	—	—	—	—	—
X	—	—	—	6.69	—	—	—	—	—	5.84	—	—
P	—	—	—	—	—	—	—	—	—	—	10.86	—
GX	3.60	—	—	—	—	—	—	—	—	—	3.50	—
GP	—	—	—	5.65	—	—	—	—	—	—	—	—
XP	—	—	—	8.72	—	—	—	—	—	4.61	—	—
GXP	—	—	—	—	—	—	—	—	—	—	—	—

Note: Entries are significant F values; those underlined are beyond the .01 level of confidence, the others are beyond the .05 level.
Source: Compiled by the authors.

117

autonomy and guest privileges. The contrasts that do emerge, then, should be considered within this broad context of basically similar orientations toward children. It could be that these three parental groups share many features of some common North American working-class view of how children should be brought up, even though, as we shall see, the groups do differ in distinctive and intriguing ways.

Parental-Group Contrasts

There are two instances—help withholding and attention denial—where significant differences among parental groups emerge, and these appear in both the two-group (Table 5.2) and the three-group (Table 5.3) comparisons. In the case of help withholding ($p < .01$), we find that the means for all three groups fall below the neutral point (A = 49.58, FC = 43.81, and FA = 37.68), signifying that all three groups of parents generally give help to their children when it is requested. Of interest is the fact that the distinctive group is the FA parents, for they are the most ready to extend help, more ready in fact, than one would expect, whether one takes as a reference point their FC ancestry as represented by our FC sample or their national setting as represented by our A sample of parents. One wonders whether FA working-class parents, relative to As or FCs, may feel a greater need to support their children through gestures of helping because of their minority status and cultural isolation in the U.S. setting.

The groups also differ in their modes of coping with children's bids for attention. The A parents, as a group, tend to cater to the child's need for attention much more so that the FC and FA parents (Newman-Keuls test, $p < .01$). In their reactions to attention-getting ploys, then, the FA working-class parents are more like their FC and less like their A equivalents.

There are also parental group differences that emerge in interactions with sex of child or sex of parent. The first of these is depicted in Figure 5.2, which shows an interesting contrast between A parents and each of the French groups in modes of handling requests for help ($p < .05$). The A parents treat boys and girls differently and in the process show a bias against girls in the sense that help-seeking girls are less likely to be catered to than help-seeking boys. There is no such bias evident for either FC or FA parents, who are relatively more consistent than As in their treatment of boys and girls. Thus, in this case we find the FA working-class parents behaving more like FCs than As.

FIGURE 5.2

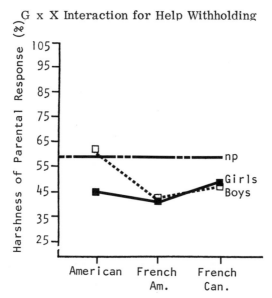

G x X Interaction for Help Withholding

Source: Constructed by the authors.

There is a different outcome on the sex-role perception scale,
depicted in Figure 5.3, for here parents' perceptions of the similarity or difference of boys and girls depend first, on whether they have
a son or daughter and second, on their ethnic or national background.
In general, FC, A, and FA parents of girls have essentially similar
perceptions of sex-role differentiations, whereas parents of boys,
depending upon their ethnic background, have quite different perceptions. Thus, A parents of boys perceive many more sex-role differences than do A parents of girls. The trend is just the opposite
for FC parents since parents of girls perceive more sex-role difference than do parents of boys. (This could be an example of A parents
of boys and FC parents of girls seeing what they want to see, as if,
for some reason, it were especially important for working-class A
boys not to be girlish and for working-class FC girls not to be boyish.) What is of special interest is the relatively balanced perceptions of FA working-class parents; in their case, parents of boys
and parents of girls have essentially similar perceptions of how boys
and girls behave. Our speculation is that the FA working-class parents, in this instance, present a type of mixture of FC and A outlooks on the sex-role comportment of boys and girls, making a type
of mid-way adjustment.

FIGURE 5.3

G x X Interaction for Perceived Sex-Role Differences

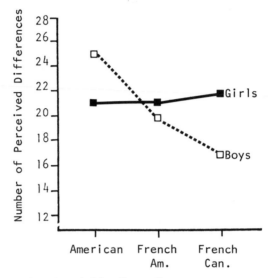

Source: Constructed by the authors.

The data for expected sex-role differences, depicted in Figure 5.4, take this line of analysis a step further. Because the GP interaction is significant only for the two-group (that is, A versus FA) comparison ($p < .01$), but not for the three-group comparison, brackets are placed around the FC plots in Figure 5.4. What we find is that FA mothers, relative to FA fathers, expect more boy-girl differences, while A mothers, relative to A fathers, expect fewer sex-role differences. These interesting differences suggest that it is FA working-class mothers and A working-class fathers who are more anxious or concerned about sex-role differentiations than their marital partners or, stated differently, that trends toward unisexism receive more encouragement from FA working-class fathers and A working-class mothers. Whatever the interpretation may be, it is interesting that when the basis of comparison is broadened to include all three groups, the FA-A differences are no longer distinctive enough to be statistically significant. Nonetheless, there is a suggestion in Figure 5.4 that the FA working-class parents are more like their FC than their A counterparts in their sex-role expectations.

FIGURE 5.4

G x P Interaction for Expected Sex-Role Differences

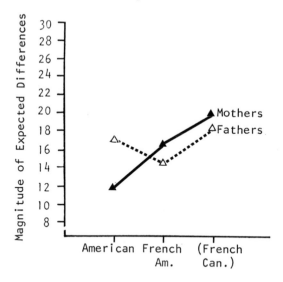

Source: Constructed by the authors.

Finally, there is a statistically significant GP interaction for the social temper episode ($p < .01$), depicted in Figure 5.5, and we have another instance of parental group differences related to mother-father differences in reactions. Consistent with the previous finding, we note that FC working-class mothers are more active than FC fathers in the control of their children's social temper outbursts. This FC working-class pattern stands in contrast to both the A pattern, where mothers are equally involved, or the FA pattern, where fathers are more involved than mothers in the control exerted on social temper. Thus, in this instance, the FA working-class families are more American than French Canadian because, like the As, the FA working-class mothers are relatively less active than FA fathers on this aspect of child rearing.

Parental Treatment of Boys versus Girls

We have already seen in the GX interactions some instances of differential parental treatment extended to boys in contrast to girls, differences that depend on the ethnic or national background of the

FIGURE 5.5

G x P Interaction for Social Temper Control

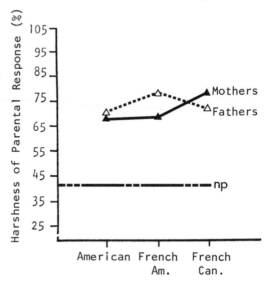

Source: Constructed by the authors.

parents. For example, we found that A working-class parents are more inclined to extend help to boys than to girls, whereas FC and FA working-class parents are more equitable in giving help. We also found that parents of boys and parents of girls have quite different perceptions of sex-role differentiations, depending on their ethnic-national background.

There are also instances here where the sex-of-child factor has a more generalized influence on the reactions of all three groups of parents. In fact there are three cases where girls are given harsher parental treatment than boys for what objectively is precisely the same misdemeanor. The first turns up on social temper displays where parents are harsher with girls than with boys ($p < .05$), and this holds for the two-group and three-group analyses, meaning that the FC, FA, and A parental groups all contribute to the bias against girls.

Similarly, on the child-guest dispute issue parents again are harsher on disputatious girls than on disputatious boys. This is so for the three-group (FA-A-FC) analysis, but not for the two-group (FA-A) analysis encompassing only the FA and A parents, meaning that the FA working-class parents are basically similar to their A

counterparts on the dispute issue, and it is the inclusion of the FC
group that produces the significant antigirl bias.

There is a similar bias reflected in the help giving issue, for
we find that parents are less likely to extend help to girls than to
boys. In this case, however, the difference emerges only in the
two-group analysis, but not in the three-group analysis, meaning
that for the help giving issue, FA working-class parents differ from
A parents, but this difference is eradicated by the inclusion of the
FC parents.

Two major trends stand out. First, girls are treated more
harshly than boys for what are objectively the same types and degrees of misbehavior. The message that these working-class parents seem to be transmitting is that, relative to boys, girls should
not be socially aggressive, nor should they be too dependent. Second,
FA working-class parents tend to adopt more of an American than a
French Canadian perspective on the social aggression matter, but
apparently not on the help giving matter.

Mothers versus Fathers as Socializers

We have already seen in the GP interactions that mothers and
fathers, depending upon their ethnic-national origin, have different
approaches to particular aspects of child rearing. Thus, FC
working-class mothers, relative to FC fathers, tend to take a more
active role in controlling a child's social temper displays, whereas
FA and A mothers tend to be less active than fathers in exerting control on social temper. Similarly, A fathers seem to be more concerned about sex-role differentiations than A mothers, whereas FA
fathers appear to be relatively less concerned about this issue than
FA mothers.

There are other instances of mother-father differences involving all three parental groups. Thus, fathers, relative to mothers,
tend to perceive more boy-girl differences in comportment ($p < .01$),
suggesting that in all three of our working-class samples, fathers
may be more concerned than mothers about modern trends toward
unisexism or the blurring of traditional sex roles. Two other pieces
of evidence support this interpretation, evidence that turns up in two
XP interactions, one for social temper control ($p < .01$), and the
other for the issue of a child-guest quarrel ($p < .05$). In both cases
fathers make greater distinctions between boys and girls than do
mothers, in the sense that fathers treat the social aggressiveness
of girls more harshly than that of boys, while mothers show no bias
one way or the other. These results indicate that A, FA, and FC
fathers show same-sex leniency in their reactions to social aggres-

sivity, which in turn suggests that in North American working-class homes, one parent—the father—through a bias against aggressive tendencies in girls, helps perpetuate and "shape" what he takes to be "appropriate" behavior for boys and for girls. By itself, the trend toward same-sex leniency is interesting because, in relation to other cultural samples of working-class parents who show cross-sex leniency, same-sex leniency may turn out to be mainly a North American characteristic, possibly a North American working-class characteristic. We will check on this possibility as we add other samples of parents in the chapters that follow.

SUMMARY AND CONCLUSIONS

When our comparison was restricted to FA and FC parents, we were tempted to conclude that basic French Canadian values may be deep and durable, since we had so many symptoms of the similarity of orientations of FA and FC parents showing up on a large number of our value dimensions. They even shared a bias against girls, both groups being harsher on a disputative or socially aggressive girl than an equivalently aggressive boy. When we included a three-way analysis with FA, FC, and A parents, we had to temper this conclusion somewhat, because the two French samples were in so many respects like American parents, suggesting to us that there may be widely shared, common, North American, working-class values that color FA as well as FC styles of child rearing.

There were, nonetheless, several very interesting differences between FA and FC parents that give one the impression that FA parents may be slowly drawn toward a style of child rearing found in the United States and away from a traditional style rooted in French Canada. For example, there were several signs of greater leniency among FA than FC parents: FA parents were less harsh in their responses to children's insolence and generally more prone to respond willingly and more immediately to children's requests and demands. On the matter of children's social temper displays, FA mothers, in particular, tended to let these forms of social aggression pass, as though they may be especially susceptible to the putative U.S. norm of "disciplined neglect" of children. FA fathers were more demanding than their wives on the social temper issue, suggesting to us the possibility that FA fathers, as "heads" of ethnically distinctive households in the United States, may be anxious to curtail their children's socially aggressive proclivities. Consistent with this idea of a drift toward U.S. value norms was the curious finding that FA parents were harsher with children who threatened to break a game than were the otherwise more demanding FC parents.

Why was it on this episode only, one that referred to the destruction of a game, that the FA parents dug their heels in? Could this be an inroad of U.S. materialism?

When the U.S. parent group was included in the analysis, we found that there are as many, or more, points of similarity in the reactions of these three groups of parents as there are points of contrast, suggesting to us that all three groups may be demonstrating the effects of a common conditioning to a general North American working-class system of values, or that, for some more basic reasons, all three make similar contributions to what we call a North American working-class style of interaction with children. For example, we found that all three groups have essentially similar reactions to children's temper and insolence outbursts, to children's requests for comfort, and to children's bids for autonomy.

Against this background of common reactions, we find a series of contrasts among the three groups that are both interesting and suggestive. First, on the issue of helping, there are parental-group differences in readiness to help, and it is the FA working-class parents who are the most ready, making them the distinctive group of the three. Our speculation here is that FA working-class parents may, relative to their A or FC counterparts, feel a greater need to support and assist their children because of the family's status as an ethnic minority group in the United States and the feeling of cultural isolation they may endure. Second, the parent groups differ in their styles of managing children's bids for attention, and in this case the distinctive group is the A working-class parents, who, relative to the two French groups, are more inclined to indulge children who seek attention. In this case, then, the FA parents are more FC than A in their reactions.

Various interactions involving the ethnicity or nationality of the parent groups were statistically significant, and two of these involved group by sex-of-child contrasts. On the help issue it was the A parents who were again distinctive because they reacted differently to boys and girls, being less likely to extend help to girls who ask for help than to boys. Neither French group showed such a bias, both groups treating boys and girls essentially alike on the help issue. This constitutes another instance where the FA working-class parents react more like their FC than their A counterparts.

There are also interesting parental group by sex-of-child contrasts in sex-role perceptions, and in this case we speculated that A parents of boys and FC parents of girls may exaggerate boy-girl differences in comportment because it could be particularly important in the working-class United States for boys not to be girlish, just as it may be important in working-class French Canada for girls not to be boyish. In this instance, the FA parents, whether parents of girls or parents of boys, have a much more balanced perception of the comportment of boys and girls, making them, in this respect, neither A nor FC in their outlooks.

With regard to parents' sex-role expectations, we find some evidence that FA mothers expect more boy-girl differences than do FA fathers, making them more like their FC than their A equivalents in this respect as well. There are also father-mother differences among the three groups on the social temper issue, and in this case the FC mothers are more active in controlling social temper outbursts than FC fathers, making this FC pattern different from both the A pattern (where mothers and fathers are equally active in controlling social temper) and the FA pattern (where fathers are more active than mothers). The trend, then, is for FA working-class families to be more like their A than their FC counterparts, since both the FA and A mothers are less active than fathers in discouraging social temper.

Parents of Boys versus Parents of Girls

There are other examples of differential treatment given boys and girls that generalize across groups. For instance, all three groups show harsher treatment to girls who display social temper than to boys. Similarly, when girls quarrel with a guest, they are treated more severely than are boys for exactly the same "crime," but in the quarrel-with-guest episode the trend suggests that it is the FC working-class parents who are especially harsh on girls relative to boys. Thus, in this case, the FA working-class parents are more American than French Canadian. Furthermore, on the help giving issue, we find that parents are generally more inclined to help boys than girls, and in this case the FA working-class parents are more French Canadian than American in their reactions. Overall, then, the evidence suggests that all three parental groups try to discourage girls from being socially aggressive and from being too dependent. It follows, of course, that in making girl-boy distinctions of this sort they are at the same time encouraging boys to be relatively more socially aggressive and relatively more dependent on parents. Finally, the FA working-class parents seem to take on more of a U.S. style (that is, less bias against girls) than an FC style (that is, more bias against girls) in handling social aggression, whereas on the help giving issue, the FAs are more French Canadian than American in their reactions.

Mothers versus Fathers

In addition to the mother-father differences that turned up in
the interactions, there are other more generalized mother-father
differences. For example, all three groups of fathers tend to perceive more boy-girl differences in behavior than do mothers, suggesting to us that fathers in these three-family groups may be more
concerned than mothers about contemporary tendencies to blur traditional sex-role distinctions. There is some independent support-
ing evidence for this interpretation, for we also discovered, on the
social temper control and the child-guest dispute matters, that these
working-class fathers react differently to boys and girls (actually,
react more harshly to socially aggressive girls than to socially aggressive boys) from working-class mothers who show no bias one
way or the other. We uncovered here an interesting case of same-
sex leniency on the part of the working-class fathers, for it is they
who show a bias that runs against girls and for boys. When our
cross-national analysis is carried further, this pattern of same-
sex leniency may end up being more a North American, and possibly
a working-class North American, tendency than a universal one. It
suggests that at least the working-class parents in North America,
be they FC, FA, or A, are trying to instill a sense of "appropriate"
comportment in their modes of bringing up daughters and sons.
Mothers and fathers, however, seem to have their own ideas as to
what is appropriate.

In conclusion, we have been able to capture a number of features of the child-rearing values of FA working-class parents by
comparing them with working-class FC and A parents. There are
no signs that their traditional values have been melted down in the
U.S. setting, if we take FC parents as a point of reference, for in
many instances our FA parents react more like FCs than As. There
are, nonetheless, certain signs of adjusting to the U.S. social setting, and these instances, where the FA parents approximate U.S.
styles of child rearing, can be regarded as attempts to make their
life in the United States functionally comfortable without losing a
deeper tradition and cultural identity.

6

CHILD-REARING VALUES IN FAMILIES
OF MIXED ETHNICITY:
A FRENCH AMERICAN MIXTURE

Still with the aim of tracking down Frenchness, in this chapter we examine the child-rearing values of parents in families of mixed ethnicity, specifically families situated in France and comprising a French father and an American mother. What effect, if any, would a cultural stranger, in the form of a non-French mother, have on the ways children in such families are treated? Would there be value adjustments because of the ethnic mixture, and who would make them, the mother, the father, or both?

These questions came to mind when we heard about a sizable group of American women living in the greater Paris region who had married French husbands and who were members of an association known as "American Wives of Europeans." Fortunately for us, a substantial number of these families had six-year-old children. In this chapter we will look into the values and attitudes of a sample of these parents, all from middle-class backgrounds—ten mothers of girls and their husbands and ten mothers of boys and their husbands. *
The parents were interviewed at home in the same fashion as those in our main French study already described. In terms of occupational level and education, the fathers were comparable in all respects to those of our middle-class French sample, which we will bring into the comparison. Our analysis, then, is based on two parental groups, one comprised of French husbands and American

---

*We are extremely grateful to Mme. Ellen Grandsard, a graduate student at the Université de Paris at the time, for contacting these families and conducting the interviews.

wives, which we will refer to as "Mixed-Ethnic" families, and the other of French husbands and French wives (our FF sample), which we will call "Same-Ethnic" families.

With more time, we might have been able to find matching mixed-ethnic families of French wives and American husbands living in the United States. That would have balanced and strengthened our study. And the mixed-ethnic families we have may not be all that representative, because the American women involved may be special, in the sense that they are particularly anxious to keep ties with their native land through membership in a special organization (that is, the Association of American Wives of Europeans). Nevertheless, we can with these groups at least begin to examine a series of important questions: Is the American mother really a foreign or strange cultural element in these families? Does her presence make an appreciable difference in the lives of the children (and the husbands) involved? Are these children treated differently from comparable youngsters in Same-Ethnic families? Would the French father in the Mixed-Ethnic family make adjustments because of the mother's cultural strangeness? Or would the wife be the main adjuster?

In the Mixed-Ethnic group, there were 20 couples made up of American wives and French husbands. The 20 couples in the Same-Ethnic group were French on both sides. Each group included ten mothers and ten fathers of girls and ten mothers and ten fathers of boys. The wives in both groups were highly educated, most having completed at least a bachelors degree, and their husbands' occupations and education clearly made them middle-class according to French or American standards. All families lived in or around Paris. The background characteristics of the two groups of parents are available in Table A 6.1.

The standard interviewing procedure was employed with one modification, namely that each parent reacted to either the French or English taped version of the child episodes, depending on which language he or she normally used in interaction with his/her child. Since coding procedures had been worked out for both languages, there was no difficulty in scoring and combining the French and English responses.

RESULTS

The findings are summarized in Table 6.1 and presented in detail in Table A 6.2. Considering first the pattern of significant contrasts, it is evident that there are very few differences between Same-Ethnic and Mixed-Ethnic families. Of the four significant

TABLE 6.1

Significant Effects in the Comparisons of Same-Ethnic and Mixed-Ethnic Families

Value Dimensions

Comparisons	1) Help Withholding (np = 58.6)	2) Siding with Baby vs. Child (np = 42.7)	3a) Temper Control (np = 30.0)	3b) Social Temper Control (np = 41.6)	4) Insolence Control (np = 25.0)	5) Attention Denial (np = 75.0)	6) Comfort Withholding (np = 41.6)	7) Autonomy Control (np = 58.3)	8) Guest Restriction (np = 62.5)	9) Siding with Guest vs. Child (np = 42.7)	10) Perceived Sex-Role Differences	11) Expected Sex-Role Differences
G	–	–	–	–	–	–	–	–	–	–	–	–
X	–	–	–	–	–	–	–	–	–	–	–	–
P	–	–	–	–	–	–	13.12	–	–	–	–	–
GX	–	–	–	–	–	–	–	–	–	–	–	–
GP	–	–	–	–	–	–	–	–	–	–	–	4.92
XP	–	–	–	–	8.59	–	–	–	–	–	–	–
GXP	–	–	–	–	14.00	–	–	–	–	–	–	–

Note: Entries are significant F values; those underlined are beyond the .01 level of confidence, the others are beyond the .05 level.
Source: Compiled by the authors.

130

differences that turned up, only two are attributable to the ethnicity of the husband and wife teams. Thus, the parents of the Mixed-Ethnic families differ from those of the Same-Ethnic in two distinctive ways only, and we shall examine these two contrasts shortly. The major point, however, is that apparently little has been changed in the interpersonal dynamics of the families that can be attributed to the Americanness of the mothers. The two contrasts that are traceable to the ethnic mixture become all the more interesting because they are so few.

Looking at the pattern of results, the similarities of the reactions of Mixed-Ethnic and Same-Ethnic parents stand out. When a child asks for <u>help</u> or <u>guest privileges</u>, both Mixed-Ethnic and Same-Ethnic parents comply. In a dispute between the child and a younger sibling both Mixed-Ethnic and Same-Ethnic groups <u>side with the baby</u> and against the child. When the child displays <u>temper</u>, <u>social temper</u>, or <u>insolence</u> both groups are severe in their reactions, whether the child's aggression is directed toward things or toward people. Similarly, when the child seeks <u>attention</u>, both groups fall near the neutral point on the scale, meaning that they do not give in to the child's pleas for attention. Both groups also tend to withhold <u>comfort</u> when it is requested; both are neutral to a child's request for <u>autonomy</u>; and both <u>side with the guest</u> and against the child when a child-guest dispute erupts. Furthermore, both groups have quite similar <u>perceptions</u> and <u>expectations</u> on the matter of <u>sex-roles</u>, meaning that they have similar expectations of how boys and girls should behave and similar perceptions of how boys and girls do behave.

Finally, there is a common tendency in both Same-Ethnic and Mixed-Ethnic families for fathers to be less <u>comforting</u> than mothers ($\underline{p} < .01$). Although in general both mothers and fathers extend comfort when the child requests it, the difference here is one of immediacy in compliance; French fathers apparently are inclined to leave comforting to mothers, whether the mothers are French-born or American-born.

Although there are no statistically significant differences between parental groups on any of our 11 scales, there are subtle and characteristic differences in <u>styles</u> of coping with a child's provocations that appear to us to be ethnically distinctive comparisons, even though they are not general enough to produce statistically reliable group differences (data available in Tables A 6.3 to A 6.9). Thus, when a child asks repeatedly for help, we find that at first (Table A 6.3) the Same-Ethnic parents are more inclined than the Mixed-Ethnic to refuse or ignore the child's request. However, if the child persists, the Same-Ethnic parents become progressively more inclined to urge the child to work things out on his or her own, whereas the Mixed-Ethnic parents become progressively more ready to comply with less and less hesitation.

A similar sequential change is noticeable when the dispute develops between child and baby (Tables A 6.5 and A 6.6). At first the Same-Ethnic parents tend to take the child's side and to work for a compromise, more so than the Mixed-Ethnic parents; but as the squabble shapes up, the Same-Ethnic parents, relative to the Mixed-Ethnic, move clearly to the baby's side in the dispute, are less inclined to seek compromises, and are more likely to threaten punishment. Later in the series of episodes when a dispute develops between the child and the guest, we note that the Same-Ethnic parents are by this time more ready than the Mixed-Ethnic to take the side of the guest right from the start of the squabble.

When the child is insolent (Tables A 6.7 and A 6.8), the Same-Ethnic parents are more severe than the Mixed-Ethnic in the sense of being more ready to punish or threaten punishment and less likely to divert, delay, or offer explanations. Overall, then, the Same-Ethnic, in contrast to the Mixed-Ethnic, parents make more charitable first responses to a child's annoying behavior, but as the behavior continues or progresses, they appear to have a shorter patience span, as though they were especially anxious to discourage a child from being a pest. When it is a question of insolence, however, they are relatively more severe than Mixed-Ethnic parents from the start.

With these points of similarity as background, the two statistically significant differences between parental groups stand out all the more prominently. Both instances involve interactions. Consider the GP interaction in Table 6.1 for expected sex-role differentiations ($p < .01$), plotted in Figure 6.1. Here we note that the American-born mothers are distinctive, relative to French-born mothers or fathers, in their expectations of how similar boys and girls should be. American-born mothers play down sex-role differences and expect instead quite similar comportment from boys and girls. The French husbands of these women, however, are apparently not influenced by the more unisex expectations of their wives, for their expectations are essentially the same as the husbands in the culturally intact French families.

The GXP interaction for insolence control ($p < .01$) complicates the picture in an interesting way. This interaction is plotted in Figure 6.2. Here we find a very clear cross-sex leniency pattern for the Same-Ethnic parents, but no signs of such a pattern for the

Mixed-Ethnic parents.* In Mixed-Ethnic families, both mothers and fathers treat insolent boys and girls in a similar manner.

FIGURE 6.1

G x P Interaction for Expected Sex-Role Differences

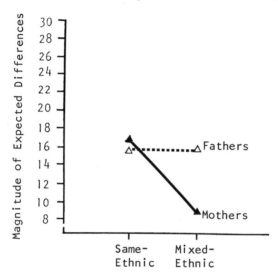

Source: Constructed by the authors.

There are three intriguing features to these contrasts. First, it seems that the American mothers are consistent in their beliefs about the essential similarity of boys and girls, as reflected in their score for expected expectations about sex-roles and in their manner of treating sons and daughters who are insolent. Second, the French husbands of these American women are apparently enticed into a new perspective of boys and girls, for compared to the French fathers in

---

*Note also that there is a significant ($p < .01$) XP interaction for insolence control that involves cross-sex leniency in the culturally intact families only; this XP trend is reflected in the GXP interaction now under consideration.

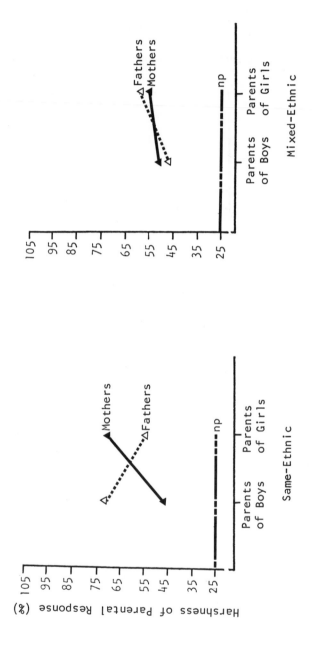

FIGURE 6.2

G x X x P Interaction for Insolence Control

Source: Constructed by the authors.

culturally intact families, they show none of the favoritism toward insolent daughters (and against equally insolent sons) that the Same-Ethnic fathers do. The point is that the presence of an American mother, a stranger in an otherwise French family, may have the effect of influencing the French husband so that he treats insolent sons and daughters in an equitable way.

The third feature is much more speculative: to the extent that the French husbands are influenced by their American wives on the matter of insolence control, they then forfeit an occasion where as fathers they could develop or maintain a special emotional relationship with their daughters, as the French fathers in the culturally intact families apparently do. It follows that the American mothers also make a forfeit—an apparently acceptable one in intact French families—where they as mothers could develop, through differential leniency, a special emotional relationship with their sons. This possibility could be interesting to pursue in follow-up research.

All told, then, this study throws some light—albeit of relatively low wattage—on the types of adjustments that marital partners are likely to make when they enter into particular cross-cultural marriages. The reasoning here is that our sample of American wives, who in the process of adjusting to the experience of a cross-cultural marriage and the rearing a child in France, have not lost all their individuality. They apparently hold distinctive views of what is expected of boys and girls who become insolent. What is intriguing is the possibility that in maintaining their distinctiveness, these women may have influenced their husbands and thereby affected an important feature of "normal" interpersonal relationships within the French family.

Of course it could well be that there are relatively few adjustments required when Americans and French join in cross-cultural marriages. Perhaps American women and their French husbands-to-be can forecast in the courtship period that there are few value conflicts likely to be encountered. Judging from our results, American women and French men who share a common middle-class background and decide to marry and settle in France apparently face surprisingly few value conflicts. If they do, they seem to make the necessary adjustments relatively early in the marriage, assuming that they stay married. This is not to say that there is necessarily anything special about American-French middle-class marriages, for the same degree of compatibility might be found in other ethnic mixtures when social class is kept constant. We would need comparable studies with other ethnic mixtures to test that possibility.

A FURTHER EXPLORATION OF VALUE
COMPATIBILITY: MIXED-ETHNICITY
VERSUS MIXED-CLASS

It is easy to talk about the compatibility of American and
French child-rearing values, but compatibility is such a relative
matter that we were forced to ask ourselves: compatible relative
to what? For example, would there be less value compatibility
were a French man to marry a French woman of a different social
class? Are cross-ethnic differences in values more or less pronounced than cross-class differences?

This question fascinated us, and we explored it by matching
up artificially the same French men who had actually married American women with another set of "wives," in this case French wives,
but ones from working-class backgrounds. For these purposes, we
used the working-class sample of French mothers from our main
French study. This purely artificial matchmaking is fun to do because it permits one to see what _might_ happen if cross-class marriages were actually to take place. Although the father-mother
matches are only statistical ones, all the parents involved are from
France, all have a six-year-old child and all are reacting to precisely the same child-centered episodes on our tapes. This manu-
factured parental group we will call the Mixed-Class group, and it
will be compared with the "Same-Class" group, which is the old
Same-Ethnic group of middle-class parents, renamed only.

We realize, of course, that the middle-class French fathers
we are including in the Mixed-Class group may not be the best possible choice for our purpose since they actually married American
women, and they seem to have been influenced by their cross-
cultural marital experience, judging by our comparisons of them
with French middle-class men who married middle-class French
women. On the other hand, they are a fair enough choice for our
purposes because they did enter into unconventional marriages and
because they were found to be generally very similar in their reactions to the Same-Ethnic middle-class French males. Except on
the issues of insolence control and sex-role differentiations, where
we suspect a value adjustment had taken place, these Mixed-Ethnic
middle-class French men, who are about to be matched up with
lower-class French women, are essentially French in their child-
rearing value orientations.

RESULTS

The comparisons of the Mixed-Class and the Same-Class
groups are summarized in Tables 6.2 and A 6.10. Note first that

TABLE 6.2

Significant Effects in the Comparisons of Same-Class versus Mixed-Class Families

Comparisons	Value Dimensions											
	1) Help Withholding (np = 58.6)	2) Siding with Baby vs. Child (np = 42.7)	3a) Temper Control (np = 30.0)	3b) Social Temper Control (np = 41.6)	4) Insolence Control (np = 25.0)	5) Attention Denial (np = 75.0)	6) Comfort Withholding (np = 41.6)	7) Autonomy Control (np = 58.3)	8) Guest Restriction (np = 62.5)	9) Siding with Guest vs. Child (np = 42.7)	10) Perceived Sex-Role Differences	11) Expected Sex-Role Differences
G	-	4.20	-	-	-	-	5.57	-	-	-	-	-
X	-	-	-	-	-	-	-	-	-	-	-	-
P	-	-	-	-	-	-	4.27	<u>9.70</u>	-	-	-	-
GX	-	-	-	-	-	-	-	-	-	-	4.14	4.21
GP	-	6.77	-	-	-	-	-	-	-	-	-	-
XP	-	-	-	-	-	-	-	-	-	-	-	-
GXP	-	-	-	-	<u>10.38</u>	-	-	-	-	-	-	-

Note: Entries are significant F values; those underlined are beyond the .01 level of confidence, the others are beyond the .05 level.
Source: Compiled by the authors.

137

there are six significant contrasts between Mixed-Class and Same-Class parental groups, and if we set aside the three involving insolence control and sex-role differentiations, for the reasons mentioned above, we still have more contrasts associated with social-class mixture than we had with ethnic mixtures. The contrasts in question are a group effect as well as significant GP interaction for the child-baby dispute and a group effect for requests for comfort, each significant at the .05 level of confidence. Thus, Mixed-Class parents are more severe in their treatment of children who quarrel with younger siblings and less comforting when comfort is requested than Same-Class parents are. The GP interaction (see Figure 6.3) means that the working-class mothers, because of their severity on the child-baby dispute issue, are clearly out of line with their "husbands" on the one hand and with the Same-Class parents on the other.

FIGURE 6.3

G x P Interaction for Siding with Baby versus Child

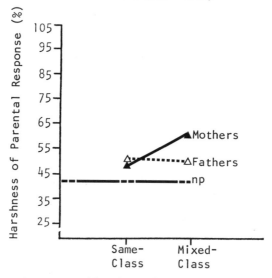

Source: Constructed by the authors.

The GXP interaction for insolence control ($p < .01$) plotted in Figure 6.4 tells us that the Mixed-Class fathers are out of line with the Same-Class fathers, but as we have already argued, this could be a consequence of the adjustments the Same-Class French men may have had to make to the child-rearing values of their real wives—middle-class American women. However, were we to shift the scores

FIGURE 6.4

G x X x P Interaction for Insolence Control

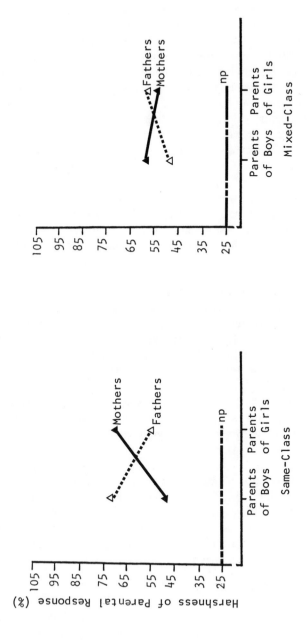

Source: Constructed by the authors.

for the working-class French mothers onto the graph for the Same-Class parents, we would have a clearer idea of the types of changes a mixed-class marriage might entail for a typical French middle-class male who just happened to marry a working-class French woman. In that case, the cross-sex leniency pattern for insolence control would be substantially modified, since the working-class mother would be much more equitable in her treatment of insolence, reacting the same whether the insolence came from a son or a daughter. The resulting one-sided cross-sex leniency might become a serious source of embarrassment for the father who would be seen as relatively less fair than his wife, since his tendency to favor the daughter would by comparison become too obvious. One wonders whether this would sit lightly on the psyche of the middle-class French male, or whether it would call for major adjustments between husband and wife.

In summary, what we have done in this chapter is merely scratch the surface of what happens in cases of mixed ethnic and mixed social-class marriages. First, we found surprisingly few instances of value clashes between partners of cross-cultural marriages involving American middle-class women and French middle-class men who were bringing up their children in France. The investigation, nonetheless, did reveal certain differences on fundamental issues, namely, divergent views on sex-role differentiations and differences in means of coping with children's insolence. There were also signs of adjustments being made to these differences, at least on the part of the French husbands. When we began to wonder just how much compatibility of values there actually was in mixed-ethnic marriages, we were led to the idea of comparing cross-ethnic marriages with cross-class marriages, but in this case the best we could do was artificially match up a set of French middle-class "fathers" with a set of French working-class "mothers" who were not actually married to one another. The results of this exercise suggested to us that there are likely to be at least as many and as serious value differences across social-class boundaries as there are across ethnic boundaries. This tentative conclusion is consonant with the generally powerful effects of social class that permeate all of our national group comparisons. But this has only been a pilot study, and the matters touched on deserve more careful study in follow-up investigations.

7

ANGLO FEATURES OF CHILD REARING: A COMPARISON OF ANGLO-CANADIAN, ANGLO-AMERICAN, AND ANGLO-ENGLISH PARENTS

As the investigation of Frenchness got underway, we naturally began to wonder about "Englishness" and the possible common denominators linking English Canadian parents, "old-stock" Anglo-Americans in the United States, and English parents in England. This is the focus of interest in the present chapter, and here for the first time, we have some points of view of social scientists to guide us.

According to the sociologist Seymour Lipset (1968), one should expect to find important value contrasts among various English-speaking groups. Lipset sees the English approach to education, for example, as elitist and the American approach as egalitarian. More generally, he believes that the Americans and the English would hold extreme positions on the issues of values with English Canadians being intermediary, on certain issues being closer to Americans and on others, closer to the English, depending on the particular value domain in question. If anything, the value patterns of English Canadians tend to be closer to those of Americans. Kasper Naegele (1968) came to a similar conclusion, arguing that Canada lies "between America and England" on value dimensions, selectively accepting and rejecting certain values endorsed by the English or by the Americans.

Taking these sociological characterizations of Englishness as guides, one might expect to find comparable differences in the child-rearing values of these three Anglo-Saxon parental groups. The questions that preoccupy us in this chapter, then, are the following: Would English Canadian parents react like their American counterparts in matters of child training, or would there be important contrasts? In terms of child-rearing values, would English Canadian parents hold an intermediary position between American and English parents, or would they be more similar to American than English parents? Or might they have evolved a distinctive Anglo-Canadian value system all of their own?

Our attempts to answer these questions start with a narrow, two-group comparison, involving our samples of English Canadian and American parents, and then we shift to a three-group comparison involving English parents from England. Ultimately, we try to evaluate the validity of Lipset's and Naegele's points of view.

PART I: ENGLISH CANADIAN VERSUS
"OLD-STOCK" AMERICAN PARENTS

Although English Canadian and "old-stock" American parents have a common cultural heritage in the sense that both are descendants of Anglo-Saxon immigrants to North America, we wonder, much as Lipset (1968) does, whether different life-styles and different value systems have evolved for these two groups. For example, the English Canadians, unlike the Americans, never developed a revolutionary tradition and have historically kept closer bonds with England. It has been argued that English Canadians may have been motivated to dissociate and protect themselves and their identity from their economically and socially powerful neighbor, and possibly as a consequence they may have developed quite different value systems. The Canadian historian Underhill (1962), for example, described the Canadians as the world's oldest "anti-Americans." Might some such need to remain distinctive have worked its way down to child-rearing values and practices?

The Sample of "Old-Stock" American Parents

Our sample of English Canadian (EC) parents has been described in full in Chapter 2. The sample of American parents (A) used in this comparison is a "composite" one in the sense that half of the interviews were conducted with parents living on the east coast of the United States (Providence, Rhode Island) and the other half on the west coast (San Diego, California). When analyzed statistically, there was, surprisingly, a near perfect overlap in the reactions of east and west coast parents.*

---

*Although we were delighted with this apparent homogeneity of values across the American continent, we make no real claims of that sort because here we were dealing with small subsamples

To be considered as an "old-stock" American family, both parents had to be American-born and from English-speaking homes, and at least three of the four grandparents also had to be American-born and English-speaking. The background characteristics of the old-stock American and English Canadian families are available in Table A 7.1. The numbers of years of schooling for the two middle-class samples are very similar, although the American working-class parents have over two more years of schooling than their Canadian counterparts. Nonetheless, the types of occupations are very similar both at the working-class and middle-class levels. The English Canadian families are all Protestants, whereas three of the 20 American middle-class families are Catholics and more than half (11 of 20) of the American working-class families are Catholics. This difference in religious background could be an important one, but we found relatively few old-stock working-class Americans who were Protestant, at least in the centers we worked with. Thus, some of the differences we will discuss may well be due as much to religious background as to nationality, and although we see this as a limitation on the comparability of the two parental groups, we also believe that the American sample is more representative than an all-Protestant sample would have been.

Procedure

The procedures followed in the American study were identical to those already described, except that the parents gave their responses orally and these were transcribed by the interviewers rather than written by the parents themselves. We made this change because by this time we were collecting data from various parts of the world where some working-class parents might have limited experience in reading and writing. Once this new procedure was adopted it was used with all parental groups studied thereafter, including the English parents.

The interviewers in both the San Diego and Providence settings were themselves Americans, thoroughly familiar with the settings and the life-styles of the residents.

---

from the east and west coasts. A whole new phase of research would be required to explore regional variations within nations or to establish within-nation homogeneity of values.

Results: Anglo-Canadian and
Anglo-American Parents

Our standard method of statistical analysis was applied for
the comparisons of Anglo-Canadian and Anglo-American parents.
Table 7.1 summarizes the statistical findings, and Table A 7.2
gives the means for each subgroup involved in the various comparisons.

Differences Attributable to Nationality

It came as a surprise to us to find so many differences between Anglo-Canadian and Anglo-American parents. Our stereotype was that these two parental groups were pretty much alike in
their orientations to children. Instead, the English Canadian parents turned out to be consistently harsher disciplinarians than their
American counterparts. On four discipline scales (child-baby dispute, temper control, social temper, and insolence control),
English Canadian parents reacted in a harsher, more punitive way
and with fewer gestures of understanding or willingness to take the
child's side. Although the English Canadian parents were not, as a
group, harsher on the child-guest dispute, those from working-
class backgrounds were significantly harsher disciplinarians than
their Anglo-American counterparts. There were, however, no national differences at the middle-class level (see Figure A 7.1).

A similar pattern turned up for insolence control in the sense
that social-class differences were more pronounced for English
Canadian than American families (see Figure A 7.2), and again both
groups of middle-class parents were relatively mild in their reactions to insolence displays compared to working-class parents, who
in both settings were more severe, and more so among English
Canadian than Anglo-American parents. In fact some 60 percent of
the English Canadian working-class parents reacted with some form
of nonphysical punishment to the child's display of insolence, for example, taking the game away or sending the child to his/her room.
English Canadian middle-class parents and American parents of
both social-class levels were more inclined to question, divert, or
ignore the insolent child (see Table A 7.3).

Anglo-American and Anglo-Canadian parents also differed in
their responses to a child's request for guest privileges. Although
both groups permit the child to have visitors, Canadian parents
were more likely than Americans to add qualifications, particularly
that the child and his visitor not disturb the routine of the home:
"Yes, if you play quietly," or "Yes, but in your room" (see Table
A 7.4).

TABLE 7.1

Significant Effects in the Comparisons of English and American Parents

Value Dimensions

Comparisons	1) Help Withholding (np = 58.6)	2) Siding with Baby vs. Child (np = 42.7)	3a) Temper Control (np = 30.0)	3b) Social Temper Control (np = 41.6)	4) Insolence Control (np = 25.0)	5) Attention Denial (np = 75.0)	6) Comfort Withholding (np = 41.6)	7) Autonomy Control (np = 58.3)	8) Guest Restriction (np = 62.5)	9) Siding with Guest vs. Child (np = 42.7)	10) Perceived Sex-Role Differences	11) Expected Sex-Role Differences
G	–	–	12.49	–	11.45	–	–	32.03	–	5.59	–	5.08
C	–	22.02	–	27.12	11.89	–	–	–	–	14.43	25.53	6.41
X	6.64	–	–	–	–	–	–	–	–	–	–	9.32
P	–	–	–	–	–	–	–	–	–	–	13.15	3.98
GC	8.26	–	–	–	–	–	–	9.20	–	–	–	–
GX	–	–	–	–	–	–	–	–	–	–	–	–
CX	–	–	–	–	–	–	–	–	–	–	6.81	–
GP	8.90	–	–	–	–	–	9.53	–	–	–	–	–
CP	–	–	–	–	–	–	–	–	–	–	–	–
XP	–	–	–	–	–	4.95	–	–	–	7.62	–	–
GCX	–	–	–	–	–	–	–	–	–	–	–	–
GCP	–	–	–	–	–	–	–	–	–	–	–	–
GXP	–	–	–	–	–	–	–	–	–	–	–	–
CXP	–	–	–	–	–	–	–	–	–	–	–	–
GCXP	–	–	–	–	–	–	–	–	–	–	–	–

Note: Entries are significant F values; those underlined are beyond the .01 level of confidence, the others are beyond the .05 level.

Source: Compiled by the authors.

145

National differences were also involved in an interesting three-way interaction on the issue of autonomy control (see Figure 7.1). Whereas American and English Canadian mothers reacted alike to a boy's or a girl's requests for autonomy, American fathers showed same-sex leniency (being more permissive with boys than girls), while English Canadian fathers showed cross-sex leniency (being more permissive with girls than boys). Theoretically, the American pattern would encourage same-sex identification on this important issue of autonomy, while the English Canadian pattern would encourage cross-sex identification.

Finally, there was a striking national-group contrast in sex-role expectations: American parents of girls expect more sex-role differentiations than do American parents of boys, whereas English Canadian parents of boys expect more sex-role differences than do English Canadian parents of girls (see Figure 7.2). Apparently our American parents were particularly concerned lest girls lose their femininity, while our English Canadian parents were concerned lest boys lose their masculinity.

Social-Class Differences

Social-class background had a pervasive effect on the reactions of both American and Canadian parents. This is particularly evident on matters of discipline, for on each of our discipline scales (that is, child-baby dispute, child-guest quarrel, temper control, social temper, and insolence control) the working-class child, whether Anglo-American or Anglo-Canadian, was more likely to receive severe parental treatment than was the middle-class child. It is particularly interesting that social class seems to have as great an impact on American as on Canadian parents. In two instances (insolence control and siding with guest versus child), the social-class difference was less pronounced for the American than the English Canadian parents, but the general trend was still evident (see Figures A 7.1 and A 7.2). Our general interpretation of this trend is that working-class parents may be more concerned than middle-class parents about the social propriety of the child's behavior.

In addition to being more severe in matters of discipline, both groups of lower-class Anglo parents were more prone to control or restrict a child's bids for autonomy than were middle-class Anglo parents (see Table A 7.5).

Social class also colored Anglo parents' attitudes toward sex roles (see Figures 7.3 and 7.4). In both the American and English Canadian settings, working-class parents of boys perceived and expected more sex-role differentiations than did parents of girls, whereas middle-class parents of girls perceived and expected more sex-role differentiations. Our interpretation of this pattern is that

FIGURE 7.1

G x X x P Interaction for Autonomy Control

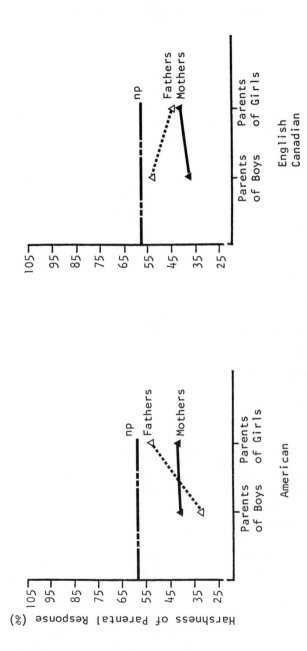

Source: Constructed by the authors.

147

FIGURE 7.2

G x X Interaction for Expected Sex-Role Differences

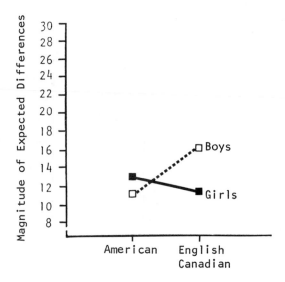

Source: Constructed by the authors.

there may be more concern among working-class parents about the possible erosion of the typical masculine profile of characteristics, whereas middle-class parents may be more concerned about a loss of feminine characteristics.

Parents of Boys versus Parents of Girls

There are other instances where our samples of Anglo-Canadian and Anglo-American parents reacted one way with sons and another way with daughters. For example, when a six-year-old boy, whether English Canadian or American, requests help, he was more likely to receive it, and receive it with more dispatch, than was his sister. Although, in general, both boys and girls can count on receiving parental help when it is requested, still our Anglo-North American parents seem more likely to delay, to urge self-help, or refuse to help when a girl makes the request (see Tables A 7.6, A 7.7, and A 7.8). Could this pattern mean that American and the English Canadian parents interpret a boy's request for help as being more urgent or of a more serious nature than that of a girl?

FIGURE 7.3

C x X Interaction for Perceived Sex-Role Differences

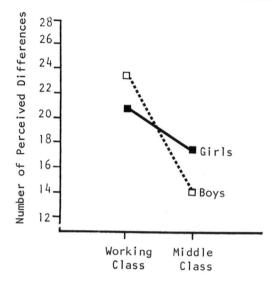

Source: Constructed by the authors.

This "favoritism" toward boys was also noticeable on the issue of a child-guest dispute, but in that instance Anglo fathers only favored sons, while Anglo mothers treated boys and girls essentially alike (see Figure A 7.3). Thus, Anglo-Canadian and Anglo-American fathers stand out because of their same-sex leniency on the issue of aggressivity directed toward a guest; they are relatively easy on sons but relatively harsh on daughters.

Differences between Fathers and Mothers

Perhaps the most intriguing is the differences in the roles played by fathers and mothers in these two Anglo settings. We found, for example, that fathers reacted differently than mothers on six scales: child-baby dispute, insolence control, attention denial, comfort withholding, where fathers were harsher in their reactions than mothers, and perceived and expected sex-role differences, where fathers perceived and expected more sex-role differentiations than did mothers.

Furthermore, on three scales (the child-guest dispute, comfort withholding, and autonomy control) we found that fathers and

FIGURE 7.4

C x X Interaction for Expected Sex-Role Differences

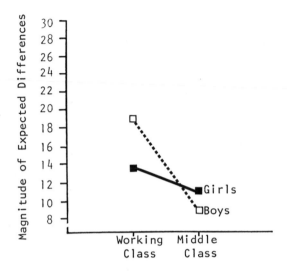

Source: Constructed by the authors.

mothers reacted in distinctively different ways to sons and to daughters. With regard to the child-guest dispute, both Anglo-American and Anglo-Canadian fathers were more lenient with sons than with daughters. For comfort withholding, both groups of Anglo fathers were generally harsher and less comforting than mothers, but in that case both parents displayed cross-sex leniency—mothers giving more comfort to sons than to daughters and fathers giving more comfort to daughters than to sons (see Figure 7.5).

As already noted, on the autonomy control issue, fathers reacted in different ways to sons and to daughters, whereas mothers tended to treat both boys and girls alike (see Figure 7.1). But there were also important differences between the reactions of Anglo-Canadian and Anglo-American fathers toward autonomy gestures: whereas English Canadian fathers were harsher than English Canadian mothers with both sons and daughters, they were particularly harsh with sons, tending toward cross-sex leniency. In contrast, Anglo-American fathers, relative to Anglo-American mothers, were more permissive with sons than with daughters, showing, in other words, a pattern of same-sex leniency. Thus, although Anglo fathers may be harsher and more punitive than Anglo mothers, we have

FIGURE 7.5

X x P Interaction for Comfort Withholding

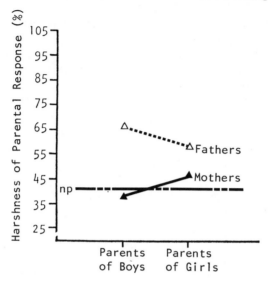

Source: Constructed by the authors.

encountered two instances where mothers are harsher than fathers: both Anglo-Canadian and Anglo-American fathers showed greater permissiveness toward sons in the child-guest dispute episode, and Anglo-American fathers showed more permissiveness toward sons' requests for autonomy.

Summary of Anglo-Canadian and Anglo-American Parental Reactions

Our purpose in this section was to investigate the pervasiveness of "Anglo" child-rearing values by comparing two North American groups of parents with Anglo-Saxon heritages—English Canadians and old-stock Americans. We wondered whether these two groups would show essentially similar attitudes toward child rearing, suggesting thereby a common bond of "Englishness" in their attitudes, or whether each group would have a distinctive pattern of reactions, suggesting thereby that national setting and all that it implies had taken dominance over common ancestry.

The results of our study, as expected, indicate the complexity of the question posed, for there are a number of sharp contrasts between Anglo-American and Anglo-Canadian parents in their orientations toward child rearing, but there are also many orientations they appear to share. In general, English Canadian parents distinguish themselves as being harsher disciplinarians, requiring their children to show more control over their aggressivity or temper directed toward younger siblings, toward peers, or toward things, and not permitting as much insolence directed toward parents. They also make more stipulations about how their children should behave when a guest is asked over to play. These contrasts between the Anglo-Canadian and the Anglo-American families jibe well with Naegele's (1968) description of Canada and his belief that "in contrast to America, Canada is a country of greater caution, reserve, and restraint."

We also found that social-class contrasts in matters of discipline, although pronounced for both groups, were more striking in Anglo-Canadian than in Anglo-American families. There were clear national differences in the importance of social class on the issues of insolence and child-guest quarreling. The fact that social-class differences are more pronounced in our samples of Anglo-Canadian parents is consistent with Lipset's (1968) argument that Canadians may be more "elitist" than Americans, implying that social-class differences should be less sharp in the United States than in Canada.

Finally, there were two other, more complex and subtle differences between Anglo-American and Anglo-Canadian parents. On the autonomy issue, both groups of Anglo mothers are generally more permissive than Anglo fathers, whether the child in question is a son or daughter. The interesting contrast is between the two groups of fathers, the Anglo-American fathers being more permissive with sons than with daughters, displaying thereby a same-sex bias, while the Anglo-Canadian fathers show a cross-sex bias. Then, on the issue of sex-role differentiations, we found that for Anglo-Americans it is the parents of girls who expect greater sex-role differences while for Anglo-Canadians it is the parents of boys who have the higher expectations. This contrast suggests to us that Anglo-Americans may be particularly concerned about maintaining the conventional nature of the sex-role identity of girls, while Anglo-Canadians are relatively more concerned about the sex-role identity of boys. Why girls in one case and boys in the other remains an intriguing question for further study.

There was an equally interesting series of results wherein our two samples of North American Anglo parents were essentially alike. For example, working-class parents, whether Anglo-Canadian or Anglo-American, are harsher disciplinarians than middle-class parents, even though we noticed on two issues (insolence and the child-guest dispute) that these social-class differences were more pronounced for our Anglo-Canadian than our Anglo-American parents. Aside from discipline, the working-class parents in both countries also perceive and expect more sex-role differentiations than do middle-class parents. Apparently, working-class North American Anglo parents want no ambiguity about the sex-role identity of their children.

We also found a common trend for fathers to be harsher socializers than mothers. In Anglo-American as well as Anglo-Canadian families, the six-year-old can apparently expect more attention and comfort from mother than from father, as well as less severe punishment when insolent toward parents or aggressive toward a younger sibling. North American Anglo mothers, then, appear to play a more lenient parental role than fathers, and it is also mothers who have less extreme sex-role expectations.

Incidentally, on the matter of sex-role differentiations, we found that working-class parents in both national settings perceive and expect greater differentiation in the behavior of boys and girls than do middle-class parents, suggesting that North American Anglo working-class parents may be relatively more concerned lest traditional sex-role identities be obliterated or attenuated by, for example, a societal trend toward unisexism. Furthermore, these working-class parents show a greater concern about boys losing their male identity, while our middle-class parents are relatively more concerned about girls losing their female identity. Although these interesting social-class differences hold for both Anglo-American and Anglo-Canadian settings, it is also true, as we have just mentioned, that our Anglo-American parents, with their relatively stronger concern for the sex-role identity of girls, project more of a middle-class outlook while our Anglo-Canadian parents, with their greater concern about boys' sex-role identity, project more of a working-class perspective on the sex-role issue.

Finally, both Anglo-American and Anglo-Canadian parents have common ways of reacting to sons and daughters. Thus, mothers in both settings contrast with fathers, in that mothers expect and perceive fewer sex-role differentiations. Not only do mothers expect boys and girls to be more alike in their behavior, but they also treat boys and girls in a more consistent manner, as on the autonomy and the child-guest dispute issues. However, when a child asks for comfort, mothers do not display the same degree of equalitarianism since they are more comforting toward sons than daughters. And when a child asks for help, both mothers and fathers favor sons over daughters. Clearly, there are intrafamily dynamics at work here that hold across the Canadian-American frontier, making our Canadian and American Anglo families alike in fascinating ways.

In summary, the major outcomes are the following:

1. Our sample of Anglo-Canadian parents contrasts sharply with Anglo-Americans by being harsher disciplinarians.

2. For both national samples, socioeconomic background has a common, pervasive influence on parents' attitudes toward discipline matters, although the contrast between working- and middle-class parents is more pronounced for our Anglo-Canadian than our Anglo-American parents.

3. For both national samples, a common mother-father contrast was found, with mothers being less harsh disciplinarians, more prone to give attention or comfort, less vigilant and less concerned about sex-role differentiations, and generally more consistent in how they treat boys and girls, except for the issue of comfort giving where mothers favor boys over girls.

4. For both national samples, we found a tendency for parents to favor boys over girls on the help giving issue.

5. There are common views as well on the sex-role issue, for in the Anglo-Canadian, as well as the Anglo-American setting, the two subgroups most vigilant and concerned about sex-role differentiations are the middle-class parents of girls and the working-class parents of boys. Overall though, the working-class parents in both settings are more vigilant and concerned than are the middle-class parents.

To this point, the findings do not permit us to say much about the existence of a distinctively Anglo-Saxon system of child-rearing values. Although we have uncovered a rich set of examples where Anglo-American and Anglo-Canadian parents show essentially similar orientations toward child rearing, we are certainly not sure that these represent values common to all Anglo-Saxons or to Anglo-Saxons exclusively. For example, we might find that these patterns hold for North American parents of various other ethnic origins. In other words, we need to go much further in order to have anything definite to say about an Anglo style of child rearing. In the next section we take our study one step further as we broaden our base of comparison by the inclusion of a third Anglo group of parents, this one from England. This addition will at least permit us to test Lipset's (1968) model of Anglo-Saxon value patterns, for he proposes that on value matters Americans are very different from English people, and that Canadians fall somewhere between the Americans and the English. Have Anglo-Canadian parents remained closer, in terms of child-rearing values, to England than America, or have

they developed a distinctive pattern of socialization values that is
neither English nor American ?

PART II: ENGLISH CANADIAN, OLD-STOCK
AMERICAN, AND ENGLISH PARENTS

Our purpose here is to compare the child-rearing values of
three national groups of parents all sharing an Anglo-Saxon heritage:
English Canadians, "old-stock" Americans, and English. Our hope
is that this three-way comparison will help us determine whether
there are common values shared by all three Anglo-Saxon groups.
The questions we have in mind are the following: Which child-
rearing attitudes, if any, are shared by all three samples of Anglo-
Saxon parents ? Which of these values are typically North American ?
Which, if any, are distinctively Anglo-American, Anglo-Canadian,
or English?

The English Sample

A sample of 40 English families was gathered in the metropolitan London area using our standard selection and interviewing procedures. To qualify as an "English" family, both parents had to be
born and raised in England (not Scotland, Wales, or Ireland), and
all grandparents but one had to be English (thus, one of the four
could be Scottish, Welsh, or Irish in origin). English-born Jewish
or immigrant families were not included in the sample. The background information for the 20 English working-class and the 20
English middle-class families is given in Table A 7.9. The compo-
sition of the English sample is in general quite comparable to that of
the English Canadian and Anglo-American samples, with certain
contrasts, nonetheless, apparent. With regard to scholarity, we
note that at the working-class level the English parents like the
English Canadians have somewhat less time in school than Anglo-
Americans, but at the middle-class level all three national groups
have essentially the same number of years of schooling. There are
generally more working mothers in our English samples, and, in
the English Canadian sample, the number of children per family is
slightly higher. These contrasts, mostly small in nature, may well
reflect real variations in styles of schooling and family life in the
three national settings. We did not pay specific attention to religion,
and, as a consequence, all of our English Canadian parents are
Protestant, whereas there are minorities of Catholic families in both
the American and British samples, somewhat more in the working-
class than the middle-class subgroups.

A new tape with the voice of an English-accented child living in London was made up specifically for the interviews with the British parents.

Results: Anglo-American, Anglo-Canadian, and Anglo-English Parents

The reactions of the three Anglo-Saxon parental groups are compared in Tables 7.2 and A 7.10.

Differences Attributable to Nationality

We note in Table 7.2 that significant national-group differences of one sort or another turned up on seven of the 12 scales, and on three other scales, national background interacted with some other factor. An interesting trend is evident if we simply consider the rank positions of the three groups on these ten scales: The English Canadian parents are generally the harshest disciplinarians, more so than either the American or the English parents, and this is particularly apparent on the temper, insolence, and guest privilege issues. There is no consistent pattern for the latter two groups, for in some instances the American parents are harsher while in other instances the English parents are harsher. Table 7.3 gives the means and ranks for the seven scales where significant group differences occurred.

The English parents contrast with both North American groups on the autonomy control issue, for they encourage autonomy less than either the Anglo-American or the Anglo-Canadian parents. Furthermore, and this was a surprise, the middle-class English parents are less prone to encourage autonomy than are the working-class parents. This group by social-class interaction, depicted in Figure 7.6 (page 159), is the first of a number of cases which show that socioeconomic background has a quite different effect in England than in English Canada or Anglo-America. The implications of this distinctive English pattern will be considered when we examine the full range of social-class differences.

Our three groups of Anglo parents also differ on the insolence issue, and in this case, the social-class background factor plays a role again. For instance, with our English samples, we find that both working- and middle-class parents are less harsh than comparable groups of Anglo-American parents in their reactions to an insolent child, although in this instance the middle-class parents for both national groups are less punitive than the working-class parents. In contrast, for English Canadians the social-class difference is much greater because of the relatively severe attitude of the English Canadian working-class parents. Thus, all three groups of Anglo, middle-class parents have similar degrees of punitiveness with an

TABLE 7.2

Significant Effects in the Comparisons of American, English Canadian, and English Parents

Value Dimensions

Comparisons	1) Help Withholding (np = 58.6)	2) Siding with Baby vs. Child (np = 42.7)	3a) Temper Control (np = 30.0)	3b) Social Temper Control (np = 41.6)	4) Insolence Control (np = 25.0)	5) Attention Denial (np = 75.0)	6) Comfort Withholding (np = 41.6)	7) Autonomy Control (np = 58.3)	8) Guest Restriction (np = 62.5)	9) Siding with Guest vs. Child (np = 42.7)	10) Perceived Sex-Role Differences	11) Expected Sex-Role Differences
G	–	4.55	17.53	5.47	20.85	–	–	17.51	10.74	7.31	–	–
C	–	47.29	11.77	46.32	44.09	–	–	8.38	–	32.60	36.70	16.75
X	6.62	–	–	–	–	–	–	–	–	7.92	–	–
P	–	7.22	–	–	6.52	7.87	7.51	–	–	4.30	17.97	8.37
GC	5.08	–	–	–	5.40	–	–	4.52	–	–	–	–
GX	–	–	–	–	–	–	–	–	–	–	–	–
CX	–	–	–	–	–	–	–	–	–	–	8.60	7.28
GP	4.57	4.72	–	–	–	–	6.10	–	–	–	–	5.09
CP	–	–	–	–	–	–	–	–	–	9.28	–	–
XP	–	–	–	–	–	–	–	–	–	–	–	–
GCX	–	–	–	–	–	–	–	–	–	–	–	–
GCP	–	–	–	–	–	–	–	–	–	–	–	–
GXP	–	–	–	–	–	–	–	–	–	–	–	–
CXP	–	–	–	–	–	–	–	–	–	–	–	–
GCXP	–	–	–	–	–	–	–	–	–	–	–	–

Note: Entries are significant F values; those underlined are beyond the .01 level of confidence, the others are beyond the .05 level.

Source: Compiled by the authors.

157

TABLE 7.3

Significant Ethnic Group Differences, Means and Rank Orders
(from Lenient to Harsh) for English Canadian,
Anglo-American, and English Parents*

	American		English Canadian		English	
Scale	Mean	Rank	Mean	Rank	Mean	Rank
Siding with Baby versus Child (neutral point = 42.70)	44.92	(1)	51.29	(3)	47.49	(2)
Temper Control (neutral point = 30.0)	55.77	(2)	65.25	(3)	43.50	(1)
Social Temper Control (neutral point = 41.60)	63.02	(2)	68.93	(3)	60.22	(1)
Insolence Control (neutral point = 25.00)	60.11	(2)	68.60	(3)	50.31	(1)
Autonomy Control (neutral point = 58.30)	42.29	(1)	44.57	(2)	68.34	(3)
Guest Restriction (neutral point = 62.50)	35.00	(1)	49.69	(3)	38.56	(2)
Siding with Guest versus Child (neutral point = 42.70)	58.75	(2)	61.41	(3)	53.94	(1)

*Connected means are significantly different:
_____ Newman Keuls Test of comparison is significant at p < .05.
═════════ Newman Keuls Test of comparison is significant at p < .01.
Source: Compiled by the authors.

FIGURE 7.6

G x C Interaction for Autonomy Control

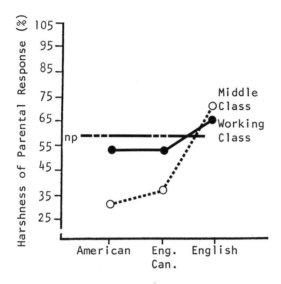

Source: Constructed by the authors.

insolent six-year-old child, while at the working-class level, the
English Canadian parents stand out because they take a much harsher attitude (see Figure 7.7).

The English parents are more lenient than the Anglo-Americans on four issues calling for discipline: temper, social temper,
insolence, and a child-guest dispute. On closer analysis, we find
that it is not that the English parents take sides with the child in
these cases, but that they use a generally milder form of discipline.
For example, when we consider parents' reactions to insolence, we
note that English parents almost never react with punishment to an
insolent statement and only occasionally do they turn to threats of
punishment. Instead they rely on reprimands or attempts to divert
the child. This relatively controlled reaction of the English parents
stands in sharp contrast with that of English Canadian parents,
particularly working-class parents, who typically either punish or
threaten to punish the insolent child. What distinguished the working-
class from the middle-class parents in all three national settings is
the tendency of middle-class parents to try to divert the child (for
example, in response to the child calling his/her parent stupid) or to
explain their refusals (for example, not to let the child cross the
street alone).

FIGURE 7.7

G x C Interaction for Insolence Control

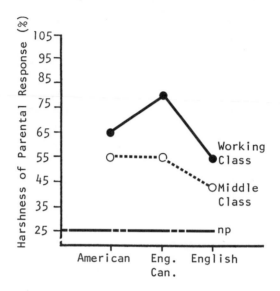

Source: Constructed by the authors.

The Anglo-American parents are somewhat more lenient than the English parents on the child-baby dispute and the guest privilege issues. On the child-baby dispute issue there are interesting differences between fathers and mothers in England and in North America, as depicted in Figure 7.8. Although the English Canadian parents are harsher than the Anglo-Americans, in both English Canadian and Anglo-American families, fathers are not as lenient as mothers, whereas English fathers stand out as particularly lenient, relative to North American fathers and even to English mothers.

With regard to guest privileges, the English and Anglo-American parents are about equally permissive, both more so than the English Canadian parents, who place many more restrictions on how the child should behave with his/her guest.

With regard to helping, there are two important interactions that imply differences in the ways our three Anglo-Saxon groups react to requests for help. In the first case (see Figure 7.9), we find that American and Anglo-Canadian working-class parents are less helpful than middle-class parents, whereas in England, the reverse holds in the sense that working-class parents are more prone than their middle-class counterparts to extend help. In the second

FIGURE 7.8

G x P Interaction for Siding with Baby versus Child

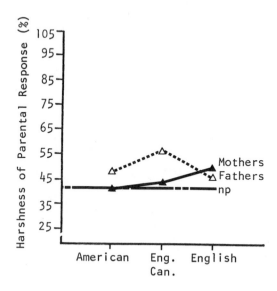

Source: Constructed by the authors.

case (see Figure 7.10), it appears that a six-year-old receives different amounts of help from father and mother depending on the national setting. In the Anglo-American family fathers are the more helpful; in the English Canadian family fathers and mothers are equally helpful; and in the English family mothers are more helpful.

There are also important pattern differences on the comfort withholding issue (Figure 7.11, page 164) since in both the Anglo-American and Anglo-Canadian families mothers are relatively more comforting than fathers, whereas in the English families fathers are relatively more comforting than mothers. These differences in style are seen, for example, in the parental reactions to the child's statement "Mummy/Daddy, it hurts." In this instance, Anglo-American and Anglo-Canadian fathers tend more often to react simply with an interested statement while mothers more often give immediate comfort, whereas English fathers are more comforting than English mothers.

Finally, there are national group differences in sex-role expectations, and these depend on whether the parents have a son or a daughter (see Figure 7.12, page 165). In the two-group comparisons

FIGURE 7.9

G x C Interaction for Help Withholding

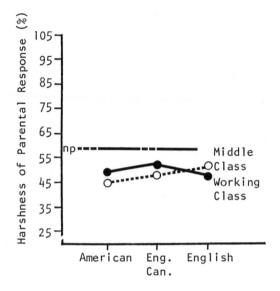

Source: Constructed by the authors.

described earlier in the chapter, we noticed that English Canadian parents of boys tend to perceive more sex-role differences than do English Canadian parents of girls, whereas the reverse pattern holds for Anglo-American parents. Here we find that English parents have a pattern quite similar to that of the Americans in that expectations of sex-role differentiations are particularly pronounced for parents of girls. Thus, in terms of sex-role expectations, the Anglo-American and English patterns are alike, both of them contrasting with that of the Anglo-Canadians.

Differences Attributable to Social-Class Background

On all scales related to discipline (siding with baby versus child, temper control, social temper, insolence control, and siding with guest versus child), we find, as was the case with other national comparisons, that working-class parents in all three of our Anglo-Saxon samples are harsher and more demanding in their reactions than are middle-class parents. For the aid scales, however, there are very interesting national and social-class differences. For instance, the English, Anglo-Canadian, and Anglo-American working-

FIGURE 7.10

G x P Interaction for Help Withholding

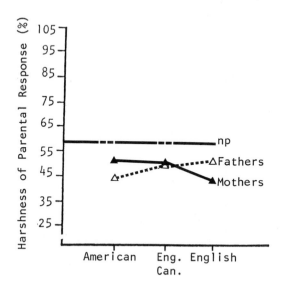

Source: Constructed by the authors.

and middle-class parents are essentially alike in their overall readiness to extend help and assistance to their six-year-olds, whereas the English working-class parents are more inclined than the middle-class parents to give help and assistance. The English pattern is distinctive, then, in that working-class parents are clearly more demanding than middle-class parents on discipline matters, at the same time as they are more ready to help on matters calling for parental aid.

Similarly, the English working-class parents are more ready than the middle-class to encourage their children on the autonomy issue. This is of special interest because it stands in striking contrast to the Anglo-American and Anglo-Canadian patterns, wherein working-class parents are relatively more restrictive in their response to a child's bid for autonomy.

Social-class differences in perceived and expected sex-role differences are just as evident in this comparison of our three Anglo-Saxon groups (see Figures 7.13 and 7.14, pages 166 and 167) as they were in the two-group comparison described earlier. There is, then, an important common pattern holding for all three Anglo groups: a tendency among working-class, relative to middle-class, parents to

FIGURE 7.11

G x P Interaction for Comfort Withholding

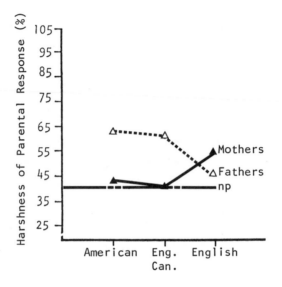

Source: Constructed by the authors.

perceive and expect more sex-role differentiations. There is also an interesting implication here: working-class parents of boys perceive and expect more sex-role differentiations than do working-class parents of girls, whereas middle-class parents of girls are relatively more "sensitive" to sex-role differences than are middle-class parents of boys.

Differences between Parents of Boys and Girls

There are two instances where all three Anglo-Saxon groups react differently with sons than with daughters. When a six-year-old boy requests help, he is more likely to receive it than is his sister, and when a child-guest dispute develops, a boy is less harshly treated than is a daughter. Furthermore, on the child-guest dispute issue, fathers in all three settings tend to show same-sex leniency, while mothers treat sons and daughters essentially alike. This interesting case of a father-son bias holding for all three Anglo groups is depicted in Figure 7.15 (page 168).

FIGURE 7.12

G x X Interaction for Expected Sex-Role Differences

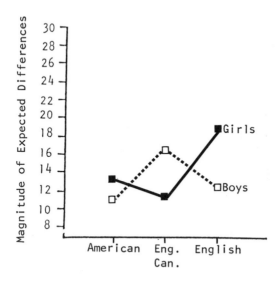

Source: Constructed by the authors.

Differences between Fathers and Mothers

In the previous section we found relatively large differences between Anglo-American and Anglo-Canadian families in the roles played by fathers and mothers, and these are still evident, although less pronounced, in this three-way comparison. The sex-of-parent factor was significant on a series of scales (siding with baby versus child, insolence control, attention denial, comfort withholding, siding with guest versus child, perceived and expected sex-role differentiations), but the roles played by mothers and fathers are different from one subset of scales to another. For instance, Anglo-Saxon fathers in all three settings expect and perceive more sex-role differentiations than do others. On other scales, however, there are important national-group variations. Thus, the relatively harsh reactions of Anglo-American and Anglo-Canadian fathers, as compared to mothers, are not always evident for the English families. In our sample of English families, the father sometimes reacts more harshly than the mother, as in the case of insolence and attention seeking, but he is less severe than the English mother on the child-baby dispute and comfort issues (see Figures 7.8 and 7.11).

FIGURE 7.13

C x X Interaction for Perceived Sex-Role Differences

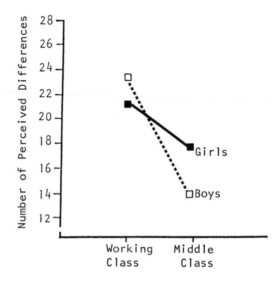

Source: Constructed by the authors.

On the child-guest dispute issue, however, we find a common mother-father difference involving all three Anglo-Saxon groups; this difference was not strong enough to be statistically significant in the two-group comparison. Thus, when all three national groups are considered, the Anglo mother is the harsher disciplinarian, putting her foot down harder than the Anglo father when a child-guest dispute erupts. And on this issue as well, the Anglo mothers in all three settings treat sons and daughters more equitably than do Anglo fathers, who again show same-sex leniency.

SUMMARY AND CONCLUSIONS

In this chapter we have examined and compared the child-rearing attitudes of three major Anglo-Saxon groups of parents: Anglo-Americans, Anglo-Canadians, and Anglos from England. We broke the analysis into two parts, first comparing the two North American groups of parents and then comparing all three. A number of intriguing findings came to light.

FIGURE 7.14

C x X Interaction for Expected Sex-Role Differences

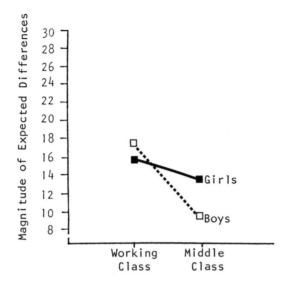

Source: Constructed by the authors.

First of all, differences attributable to the nationality of parents were numerous, suggesting that for almost every aspect of
child training included in our investigation, at least one of the three
parental groups had a distinctive approach to child rearing. The
English Canadian parents emerge as the harshest disciplinarians,
much more so than either the Anglo-American or the English parents
who show similar degrees of leniency with their six-year-old children. Thus, compared with Anglo-American and English parents,
the English Canadians are more severe and more punitive socializers
in the sense that they are less prone to side with the child in child-
baby or child-guest disputes, less prone to grant guest privileges,
and more prone to sanction a child who displays temper or insolence.
Harshness, however, does not color all aspects of Anglo-Canadian
child training, for on the autonomy issue, our two North American
parental groups are more inclined to encourage, while our sample
of English parents are much more inclined to discourage, a six-
year-old's gestures toward independence. These results are generally consistent with McClelland's (1961) findings in his cross-
national survey of motive systems, wherein English Canadians and

FIGURE 7.15

X x P Interaction for Siding with Guest versus Child

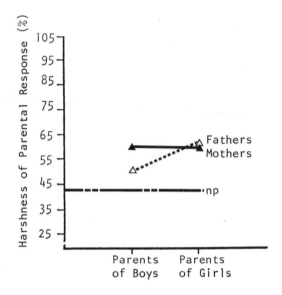

Source: Constructed by the authors.

Americans have higher indexes of achievement relative to the English, who in turn score higher on affiliation. On the other hand, our results are less consistent with the models presented by Naegele (1968) and Lipset (1968). They argue that, in terms of various social values, the United States and England would likely place at extremes, with Canada falling somewhere in between. This is clearly not the case for our findings on the permissive-punitive dimension. On the autonomy issue, however, the Anglo-Canadians do fall somewhere between the Americans and the English, although actually much closer to the Americans. Other results suggest that the Anglo-Canadian and the Anglo-American parents have a number of values in common which stand in contrast with those of British parents, suggesting that Anglo-Canadians may be evolving a set of values of their own, as in the case of discipline, although still drawing on American values as a reference source. For example, the two North American Anglo groups are distinctively different from the English on the help giving and autonomy issues, and this is so because social class seems to have a special twist in England, in that the English working-class parents are more inclined than the middle-

class parents to be helpful and more inclined to encourage autonomy.
There were no working-class-middle-class differences on these
dimensions for our Anglo-American and Anglo-Canadian parents.
This tendency among the English working-class parents to support
children's bids for independence is interesting because it holds out
hope for the working class to the extent that their values might
promote social mobility and provide them with a chance to catch
up with the middle class. Still, on discipline matters, the British
working-class parents are essentially like their North American
counterparts: in all three settings, the working-class parents are
clearly harsher disciplinarians than the middle-class parents.

There is another interesting way in which our sample of
English parents differs from both Anglo-Americans and Anglo-
Canadians. On a number of scales (namely, siding with baby
versus child, insolence control, attention denial, and comfort withholding), we find that in both Anglo-American and Anglo-Canadian
families the father is systematically a harsher disciplinarian and
generally less nurturant than the mother. In English families, on
the other hand, the father proves to be more prone to comfort than
the mother and less severe when a child-baby dispute occurs. At
the same time the English father is more punitive than the mother
toward insolence and less responsive to a child's requests for help
or for attention. This contrast suggests that in Anglo-American
and Anglo-Canadian families, the roles played by fathers and
mothers differentiate on the general issue of who should be harsh
and who lenient, whereas in English families the roles played by
mothers and fathers are less fixed and more likely to vary, in
terms of harshness and leniency, according to the value dimension
involved.

Nonetheless, there is one value dimension where all three of
our groups of Anglo-Saxon mothers take the more severe disciplinarian role, and this is the issue of a child-guest dispute. Apparently, Anglo mothers take it as their responsibility to see that
the child, when interacting with a visitor, behaves in a socially
acceptable way. Furthermore, on this issue, Anglo fathers and
mothers have a common harsh attitude toward daughters, whereas
the fathers are more lenient with sons.

Finally, we have found that our three groups of Anglo-Saxon
parents have fairly similar sex-role perceptions and expectations.
Working-class parents in all three settings expect and perceive
more sex-role differences than do their middle-class counterparts.
Fathers perceive and expect more sex-appropriate behavior than
do mothers. At the working-class level, parents of sons seem
more concerned about sex-role differentiations than do parents of
daughters, whereas at the middle-class level, parents of daughters
are more concerned than parents of sons.

In summary, we started this phase of our investigation with the aim of finding Anglo-Saxon patterns of child-rearing values, and we have found a number of instances where common value orientations are apparently involved:

1. In general, our three groups of Anglo-Saxon parents extend help when it is requested; they give only moderate amounts of attention and comfort when the child claims a slight injury; they grant the child guest privileges; and they discipline a child who is aggressive toward a younger sibling or a same-age friend, or one who displays temper or insolence.
2. All three sets of Anglo-Saxon parents also share common sex-role expectations and perceptions of sex-role differences.
3. In all three Anglo settings, parents from lower socioeconomic backgrounds have harsher, more punitive reactions in matters of discipline than do parents from middle-class backgrounds.
4. In all three settings, Anglo parents tend to be less severe in disciplining sons and more willing to help sons than daughters.

Although basically similar, we are far from sure that these common orientations toward child rearing are distinctively "English" or "Anglo," for, as we have seen in earlier chapters, many of the same patterns of reactions characterize groups with other than an Anglo-Saxon heritage. But even if we assume that these are stable underlying dimensions of Anglo-Saxon value systems, they must be viewed in conjunction with the fascinating differences among the three groups that were also uncovered in this study. We found, for instance, that the English Canadian parents are distinctive because they are generally harsher disciplinarians than either the Anglo-American or the English parents. We also found greater socioeconomic differences in parental reactions in Anglo-Canada than in Anglo-America or Anglo-England.

We found as well that the English parents are similar to the Anglo-Americans and different from Anglo-Canadians in terms of overall degrees of harshness and leniency; at the same time they were distinctively different from both the Anglo-American and the Anglo-Canadian parents in a number of ways. For instance, in contrast to our samples of North American Anglo parents, the English parents do not encourage gestures of independence from their six-year-old children; English working-class parents are more compliant and encouraging than middle-class parents on requests for help and autonomy; in our English families the roles played by mothers and fathers are more variable and unpredictable as far as leniency and harshness are concerned.

In a nutshell, it isn't that easy to find basic Anglo-Saxon modes of child rearing, nor is it easy to place in order the child-rearing values of American, English, and English Canadian parents.

8

THE BELGIAN STUDY

This chapter is meant to be a companion piece to the Canadian study, the one that started us on the search for Frenchness and Englishness. Here we begin another search: this time from Belgium where, as in Canada, two ethnolinguistic groups—the Walloons and the Flemings—have had to adjust to one another's presence as comembers of a single nation for generations. It is this bicultural-bilingual feature of Belgium and Canada and the ways each attempts to protect ethnic diversity within its borders that make them of special interest.

In Belgium as in Canada, ethnolinguistic background and social status are linked. The Walloon areas of the country, rich in coal and heavy industries, have enjoyed economic superiority over the more agricultural Flemish regions from medieval times. Since World War II, however, things have changed: new industries have developed in the Flemish regions while the importance of coal in the Walloon areas has diminished. Consequently, by the late 1960s the overall socioeconomic position of the Dutch Belgian population had equaled or surpassed that of the French Belgians.* This relatively recent reversal in status of the two Belgian groups and the "minorisation" of the French Belgians (Rens 1965) has as yet no parallel in the Canadian setting.

Our sample of DB parents was taken in the city of Oostende (Ostend in English) located on Belgium's North Sea coast. Oostende

---

*For convenience we will refer to the Walloons as French Belgians (FB) and the Flemings as Dutch Belgians (DB).

is almost entirely Flemish-speaking and is surrounded by other
Flemish towns and villages. Our sample of FB parents came from
Liége, a French-speaking city near the eastern border of the country. Liége is approximately 15 miles from the nearest Flemish-
speaking town, making it as uniformly French as Oostende is Flemish. Liége is also equally close to German-speaking populations;
in fact it is the most northern French-speaking city in Western
Europe. Thus, Oostende and Liége are both essentially unilingual
cities, and both are close to frontiers of contrasting ethnolinguistic
groups.

Although both groups are nominally Catholic, fewer FBs are
actively identified with the Catholic faith. In fact, only six of our
40 FB families gave their religion as Catholic; the rest either left
the question about religion blank or wrote in the word "none."

We will be dealing here with samples of both working-class
and middle-class parents, one set DB, the other FB. The background information for each of these groups is given in Table A 8.1.
It happened that there was some overlap between the educational
levels of the FB working- and middle-class parents, and this means
that other criteria (such as the amount of technical training demanded by an occupation or the residence district of the family
home) were used in making the judgment about a family's social-
class standing.

In planning the Belgian study, we decided to insert one new
issue into our taped child-parent episodes. The new item is the
child saying, "Hey, when are we going to eat?" Our guess was that
this incident might provoke parents because it challenges the dinner
hour, which is said to be much more sacred in Belgium than in
North America. Unfortunately, the Canadian and American studies
were too far along to have the same item included. The "eating
item" was inserted immediately after the child-baby quarrel and
before the child's request to cross the street to play. A separate
analysis was carried out for the parental replies to this question.

RESULTS: FRENCH BELGIAN AND
DUTCH BELGIAN PARENTS

The major outcomes of the Belgian study are summarized in
Tables 8.1 and A 8.2. At first glance we find again that social class
stands out as the most important source of influence on parental responses. In fact social class is involved in ten of the 18 statistically
significant main effects or interactions. Still, ethnicity also has
important effects as do the sex of child and the sex of parent.

TABLE 8.1

Significant Effects in the Comparisons of French and Dutch Belgian (Walloon and Flemish) Parents

Value Dimensions

Comparisons	1) Help Withholding (np = 58.6)	2) Siding with Baby vs. Child (np = 42.7)	3a) Temper Control (np = 30.0)	3b) Social Temper Control (np = 41.6)	4) Insolence Control (np = 25.0)	5) Attention Denial (np = 75.0)	6) Comfort Withholding (np = 41.6)	7) Autonomy Control (np = 58.3)	8) Guest Restriction (np = 62.5)	9) Siding with Guest vs. Child (np = 42.7)	10) Perceived Sex-Role Differences	11) Expected Sex-Role Differences
G	–	11.40	10.05	9.65	–	–	–	–	–	–	6.66	–
C	–	–	10.30	6.57	5.09	–	–	–	–	–	–	17.53
X	–	4.20	–	–	–	–	–	–	4.63	–	–	–
P	–	–	–	–	–	–	–	–	–	–	–	–
GC	–	–	–	–	–	–	–	–	–	–	–	–
GX	–	–	–	–	–	–	–	–	–	–	–	–
CX	–	–	13.13	–	–	–	–	–	–	6.31	6.89	–
GP	5.35	–	–	–	–	–	–	–	–	–	–	–
CP	–	–	–	–	–	–	–	–	–	–	–	–
XP	–	–	–	–	5.02	–	–	–	–	–	–	–
GCX	–	–	–	–	–	–	–	–	–	–	–	–
GCP	–	–	–	–	–	–	–	–	–	–	5.70	–
GXP	–	–	–	–	–	–	–	–	5.09	–	–	–
CXP	–	–	–	–	–	–	–	–	–	–	–	–
GCXP	–	–	–	–	–	–	–	–	–	–	–	–

Note: Entries are significant F values; those underlined are at the .01 level of confidence, the others are at the .05 level.
Source: Compiled by the authors.

174

Differences Related to Ethnicity

A clear ethnic contrast shows up on the discipline items (siding with baby versus child, temper control, social temper control, insolence control, and siding with guest versus child), and in most instances, FB parents are generally harsher disciplinarians than DB parents, the FB-DB differences reaching statistical significance in three cases: a child-baby dispute ($p < .01$), a child-guest dispute ($p < .01$), and temper displays ($p < .01$). Apparently FB parents have a much lower boiling point for a child's social aggressiveness or temper outbursts.

FB and DB parents have different approaches to discipline. Although both FB and DB parents are inclined to intervene directly when provoked by the child—by taking sides in a squabble or by stopping, reprimanding, threatening, or punishing—DB parents are, nonetheless, much more likely to let such incidents pass, either by ignoring them or making noncommittal comments (see Table A 8.3). Our suspicion is that DB parents view children's aggressive impulses more as normal and self-regulatory and less as threats to the systems of authority and affection within the family. Although DB children may get away with more of this sort of behavior than do their FB peers, it might be that the DB parents' "laissez-faire" approach pays off and, in time, reduces the occurrence of aggressiveness.

A second ethnic group difference turns up on the insolence control scale, but the picture is complicated by the influences of sex of child. Thus, as is shown in Figure 8.1, when a Belgian child is insolent to a parent, the harshness of the parental reaction depends on the child's sex, the social class of the family, and the ethnic group involved. In FB families, working-class parents are slightly harsher than middle-class parents, and boys in general are treated with somewhat more severity than girls, but neither the social class nor the sex difference is pronounced. In DB families, however, social-class and sex differences are more striking: DB working-class parents are particularly harsh on insolent boys while DB middle-class parents are particularly harsh on insolent girls.

There is, in fact, a general tendency for DB parents to make sharper distinctions than their FB counterparts between boys and girls and between the mother/father roles. For example, although both DB and FB parents are generally ready to give help when requested, the mother/father difference in degree of helpfulness is more pronounced in DB than in FB families, as though DB parents attributed greater significance to sex, in this case, sex of parents (see Figure A 8.1). Other examples of the DB tendency to emphasize the sex of child or sex of parent are evident in Figures 8.1, 8.2,

FIGURE 8.1

G x C x X Interaction for Insolence Control

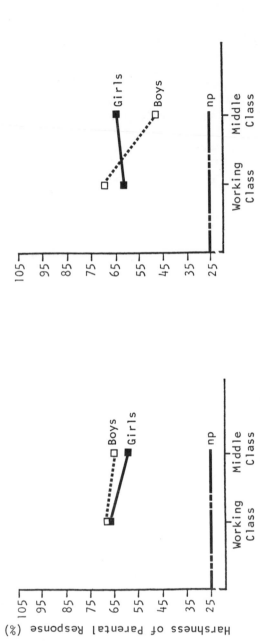

Source: Constructed by the authors.

FIGURE 8.2

G x X x P Interaction for Parental Responses to the Item: "Hey, when are we going to eat?"

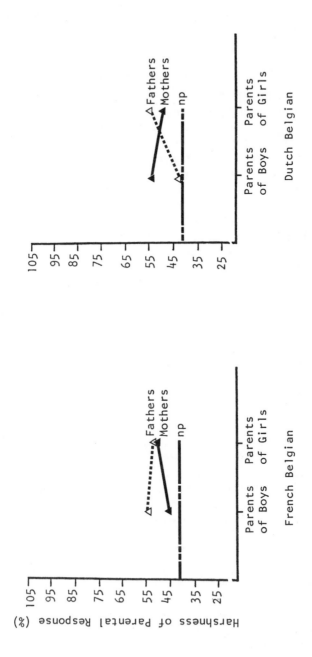

Source: Constructed by the authors.

and 8.5. For instance, the parental responses to the child's question: "Hey, when are we gonna eat?" are depicted in Figure 8.2, and when compared to their FB counterparts, the DB mothers and fathers play quite different roles and they discriminate more between sons and daughters in their modes of reacting. Furthermore, the DB parents show same-sex leniency (in the sense that mothers are more indulgent of daughters and fathers are more indulgent of sons), while FB parents show cross-sex leniency and again the DB same-sex leniency pattern is more pronounced.

If, as it seems, the DB parents are more sensitive to the sex of the child and to their own sex, is this sensitivity reflected in the data on sex roles? In other words, do the DB parents expect more sex-role differentiation than FB parents, and do they also perceive more instances of sex-role differentiation? There is no clear answer here, for there are no group differences in sex-role expectations (see Table 8.1), and yet, with regard to sex-role perceptions, the DB parents perceive fewer sex-role differences than FB parents ($p < .05$). For DB parents, then, there is a discrepancy between their expectations and perceptions, and this could reflect a desire on their part for greater sex-role differentiations.

But there is more to this issue because, as is clear in Figure 8.5, social class and sex of child interact with ethnicity in a fascinating way. For FB parents, social class has little effect on sex-role perceptions, and the tendency for parents of girls to have lower perception scores is about the same for middle- and working-class parents. In sharp contrast, the sex-role perceptions of DB parents are high or low depending upon the social class of the family and the sex of the child in question. This, then, constitutes another example where DB parents are much more sensitive than FB parents to the sex of the child in question, and this sensitivity is linked in some unexplained manner with social-class background. Clearly it would be interesting to explore this topic further in follow-up research.

So far, then, we have uncovered two major differences in the child-rearing values of DB and FB parents: DB parents exert much less control over their children's antisocial or aggressive impulses than FB parents do; DB parents are consistently more variable in their modes of reacting to children than are FB parents, and the variability is determined in large measure by the sex of the child in question and by the sex of the parent who is doing the reacting. We have also touched on a third major contrast in DB and FB child-rearing values—the relatively greater influence of social-class background on the reactions of DB than FB parents.

Differences Related to Social Class

Working-class parents, FB or DB, are generally harsher than middle-class parents in their reactions to a child's temper displays, whether the temper is directed toward parents (insolence), toward things (temper), or toward a sibling or a peer (social temper). However, this social-class difference in severity of reaction in the face of a child's aggressiveness is only one feature of the Belgian results. Nested within these social-class differences are other extremely interesting patterns.

The most prominent of these is a curious social class by sex of child "cross-over" pattern wherein middle-class parents are harsher in the intensity of their socialization on girls than on boys, while working-class parents are harsher on boys than on girls. The cross-over shows up clearly on two issues: temper display (Figure 8.3) and a child-guest dispute (Figure 8.4). What is more, the cross-over pattern is much more characteristic of DB than FB parents, as is clear not only on the insolence (Figure 8.1) and sex-role perception issues (Figure 8.5), but in general on most issues.

FIGURE 8.3

C x X Interaction for Temper Control

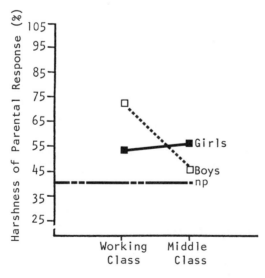

Source: Constructed by the authors.

FIGURE 8.4

C x X Interaction for Siding with Guest versus Child

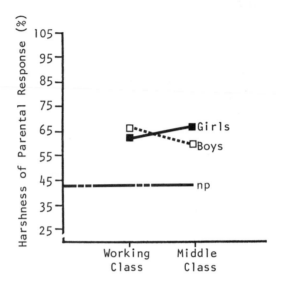

Source: Constructed by the authors.

It so happens that of all the nations included in our survey, Belgium has the most complex patterns of results, and fascinating as these patterns are, we are not able, with the information from this one study, to explain them in any comprehensive way. But perhaps the questions raised here may stimulate further research that will provide good answers. Why, for instance, should social class and sex of child be linked as they seem to be for our Belgian respondents, so that working-class parents single out boys for especially harsh treatment when they are insolent, temper bound, or aggressive, and middle-class parents, for the same types of provocation, show a comparable bias against girls? Why should this link between social class and sex of child be so much more pronounced in DB than in FB families? Could it be that the recent change in the socioeconomic status of DBs and FBs, mentioned earlier, is at work here? If the DBs have moved up in social status relative to FBs, perhaps they are simply displaying their lack of experience with their new social standing, and the DB middle-class parents, in particular, may be simply overplaying the middle-class role. Slipping down in status for the FBs may have reduced the

FIGURE 8.5

G x C x X Interaction for Perceived Sex-Role Differences

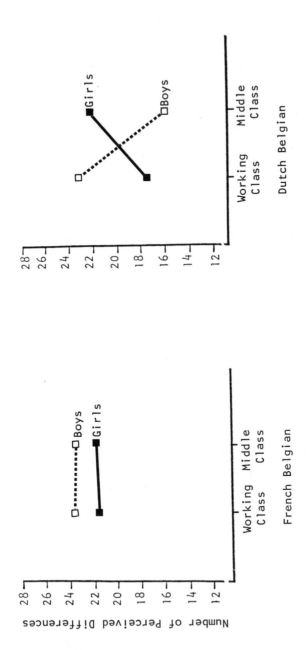

Source: Constructed by the authors.

importance of social-class differences since the whole ethnic group
may be preoccupied with adjusting to a new "minority" position.

It could also be that DB working-class parents are particularly concerned about the aggressive comportment of their sons because sons may be regarded either as more difficult to socialize
than girls or as more important to socialize. In other words, DB
working-class parents may be concerned about signs of antisocial
behavior in their sons because they know from experience that constraint and obedience are necessary traits for success in the
working-class world. Or perhaps it is that DB working-class parents are sensitive about their group's recently enhanced status, and
they count on boys, in particular, to help maintain whatever gains
have been made.

Why then would DB middle-class parents focus more on girls
than boys in the sense of being more severe with the antisocial comportment of girls and more vigilant of the sex-role behavior of
girls? Our speculation is that middle-class parents may be more
concerned about the unruly, aggressive behavior of girls because it
could reflect badly on their middle-class status, whereas aggressiveness in boys could be a useful trait for those who are expected to
help maintain the middle-class standing.

Differences Related to Sex of Child and Sex of Parent

As we have already noted, in our Belgian study the influences
of sex of child and sex of parent are generally linked with ethnic
background or social class. There is, in fact, only one significant
difference that is unambiguously related to sex of child—the child-
baby dispute issue—and here we find Belgian parents, whether DB
or FB, more harsh with girls than with boys. Apparently, quarreling with an infant is seen as unladylike and unbecoming to future
mothers. We have seen this type of differential socialization of
girls and boys, especially on mother-related issues, in various
other national studies already discussed, so it is not a distinctively
Belgian characteristic.

There is also only one significant main effect involving sex of
parent, and this is for the guest privilege issue where fathers,
whether DB or FB, tend to be less willing than mothers to grant
children such privileges. However, sex of child and social class
are also involved in the guest privilege issue in that the father-
mother difference in leniency is determined mainly by working-
class parents of girls (Figure 8.6). Thus, working-class mothers
in Belgium seem to be particularly lenient with their daughters' requests to invite visitors into the home. Since we have already seen

FIGURE 8.6

C x X x P Interaction for Guest Restrictions

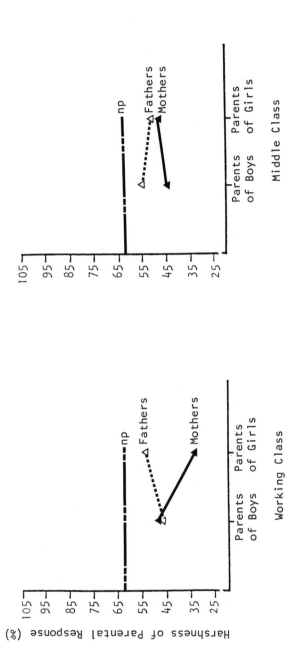

Source: Constructed by the authors.

183

(in Figure 8.4) that working-class girls are treated less harshly
than boys when they quarrel with guests, the finding that these
girls are also encouraged more to have guests come into the home
suggests that Belgian working-class mothers place special value on
training daughters to be sociable.

SUMMARY AND CONCLUSIONS

Belgium is of particular interest to us because there, as in
Canada, national unity depends so much on the collaboration of distinctive ethnolinguistic groups. We wondered at the start if social
contrasts as numerous and important as those found in the Canadian
study would turn up in bicultural-bilingual Belgium. As it happened,
we found as many social contrasts, involving social class as well as
ethnicity, and what is more, the complexity and number of factors
underlying these social contrasts were greater in Belgium than in
Canada.

In brief, we found three major differences in the child-rearing
values of Flemish (DB) and Walloon (FB) parents. First, relative
to DB parents, FB parents show a much greater concern with children's antisocial impulses. At both the middle- and working-class
levels, FB parents are clearly harsher disciplinarians when a child
is aggressive either toward a sibling, a playmate, or toward things,
such as a toy, and FB boys are reacted to somewhat more harshly
than FB girls for the same types of misbehavior. Again, one wonders if this relatively greater harshness among FB parents is attributable in part to the "minorization" process (see Rens 1965
and Phillipart 1967) the Walloons in Belgium are actually experiencing?

Second, DB parents are generally much more variable than FB
parents in their modes of reacting to children, and the variability is
mainly due to the gender of the parent and the child in interaction,
that is, whether it is a mother or a father reacting to a son or to a
daughter. Thus, DB parents emerge as extremely sensitive to the
fact that they are playing a parental role as a mother or a father and
that they are interacting with a son or a daughter. Here, too, we
wonder about the possible historical roots of this contrast. One possibility is that the DBs, descendants of an agricultural and fishing
tradition, expect sharper role differentiations between men and
women. In contrast, FB parents have for over two centuries seen
men and women play essentially similar roles in the coal mining
industry, and they could socialize their children with this expectation of male-female equivalence in mind.

Third, DB parents are caught up in a fascinating "cross-over"
pattern in which middle-class parents are harsher on girls than on

boys, while working-class parents are harsher on boys than on girls. This social class by sex of child cross-over trend turns up on a series of issues: the temper display, the child-guest dispute, and the display of insolence, and the same trend is seen in parents' sex-role perceptions. Perhaps this trend also has an historical link with the fragility of the DBs' recently acquired middle-class status. The reasoning would be that girls may be looked on as being more responsible for maintaining the new status position, thus, the greater emphasis placed on their socialization.

There were, of course, many commonalities running through the analysis where the FB-DB distinction vanishes. Thus, FB and DB parents have essentially similar reactions to a child who seeks attention, comfort, and autonomy. They also have similar sex-role expectations. Both ethnic groups are harsher on a daughter who quarrels with a younger sibling than on a son who is equally quarrelsome, making social aggression unladylike in the eyes of both groups. And, finally, both FB and DB working-class parents seem to place special value on training their daughters to be sociable.

The ethnic contrasts and similarities that we found here may well have deep social-psychological significance, and even though we cannot adequately explain them with the data from this one study, questions raised may stimulate follow-up investigations. It would be particularly worthwhile to explore carefully the pronounced ethnic group contrasts we found between FB and DB parents in levels of severity of socialization and in degrees of concern with the sex roles of parents and children. Perhaps on further study they will turn out to be pure instances of ethnic or "cultural" differences that distinguish the two main Belgian groups, one linked with a French tradition, the other with a Flemish-Dutch tradition.

9

ITALIAN APPROACHES TO CHILD REARING

In this and the following three chapters we present what we have come to call the "old-country" studies because groups of parents living in the old countries—Italy, Greece, Portugal, or Japan—are included in the comparisons. In this chapter, we start with parents currently living in Italy, and these we compare with North American parents of similar social-class backgrounds, as well as with old-country parents who immigrated from Italy to North America. With this research design, we are able to examine changes in child-rearing values that take place presumably as a consequence of leaving the homeland and settling in North America. But we will be just as interested in examples of resistance to change and in examples of mixtures of old-country and new-country child-rearing values.

In planning the homeland studies, we were far from sure that our simple procedures, with their sometimes rigid and cumbersome statistical accompaniments, would permit each nation's own styles of child rearing to show through. Now that the analyses are behind us, we are convinced that our procedures do capture each ethnic group's distinctive values. In fact, we were very pleasantly surprised and encouraged by the outcomes. At the same time, however, we realize that only small parts of the much more complex total are being picked up by our procedures and that many of the more subtle features may have been missed entirely.

Thus, in this chapter we focus our attention on Italian child-rearing attitudes and what happens to them in a North American context like Montreal. We are interested in Italians, as an ethnic group and as individuals, because they seem to be skilled at maintaining their own ways of life within their families and their own communities at the same time as they integrate smoothly into modern American and Canadian societies. Italians, like most immigrants, however, are targets of criticism no matter how well they cope with the bi-cultural demands placed on them. They are often damned because their old-country ways, such as "sticking together" or "gibber-jabbering in their own language," hold them back from being "fully Canadian" or "fully American." Immigrants, of course, realize that they have to regulate how much they are to be influenced by the host nation's styles of life, but in the process, the influence works in both directions because immigrants also make their own marks on the host nation's society. For example, Italian Canadians have earned a reputation for hard work and ingenuity in the construction industry in Toronto and Montreal; their musicians and artists are bringing new ideas to the arts in Canada; and their scholars and professionals, although less numerous, are considered outstanding contributors to their fields of specialization.

It is because Italian immigrants seem to be playing distinctive roles of all sorts in Canadian and American societies that one becomes inquisitive about their value systems, and child-rearing values are as good a place to start as any. How do Italians bring up their children? In our attempts to answer this question, we start with Italian homeland parents and compare their reactions to our taped episodes with the reactions of English Canadian parents. This lays the groundwork for talking about changes and resistances to change in values when we turn later to Italian immigrant parents who are rearing their children in Canada.

A DESCRIPTION OF THE ITALIAN HOMELAND PARENTS

In Italy, as in each of the other nations included in our survey, parents were contacted through the schools their children attended. The samples we worked with are described in Table A 9.1 along with the English Canadian samples already discussed in Chapter 2. We find certain differences: the Italian Homeland (IH) middle-class fathers have somewhat more schooling (some one-and-one-half years more) than their EC counterparts, and there are somewhat more professional than business-managerial occupations represented in the IH middle-class sample. The IH middle-class families also have fewer children (on the average 2 versus 3.4 for the EC middle-class group) and there are more working mothers in the IH middle-class sample (11 versus 2). Most of these differences seem inconsequential to us, except for two possible confounding factors: the greater number of IH middle-class working mothers, and the fact that all the IH parents are nominally Catholic, while all the EC parents are nominally Protestant.

Differences also appear when we compare the working-class samples: the IH working-class families have fewer children on the average (2.5 versus 3.3 for the EC working-class sample); they have more working mothers (5 versus 2); and the IH working-class mothers have less schooling than their EC counterparts (6.9 versus 9.3 years). There is a better match with respect to occupations than there was for the middle-class comparison.

All of the Italian parents lived in Rome or its immediate suburbs, and the interviews were conducted in the parents' homes by Italian graduate students who were specialists in child psychology. Since our Canadian parents were all from the Montreal metropolitan area, the samples are similar as well in terms of urbanism.

PART I: RESULTS—ITALIAN HOMELAND AND ENGLISH CANADIAN PARENTS

The relevant statistical comparisons are summarized in Tables 9.1 and A 9.2. From just a glance, it is evident that there are many statistically significant national-group differences, many social-class differences, and many instances where social class interacts with national background. Our discussion starts with the national group contrasts.

National-Group Contrasts

The Aid Episodes

As we examined the numerous differences between IH and EC parents in Table 9.1, we noted that they fall nicely into two sets, one comprising the "aid" episodes, the other, the "discipline" episodes. The "aid" episodes include the child's requests for help, for attention, for comfort, and for guest privileges. With regard to the help issue, we find that the IH parents are much more ready to give help than are their EC counterparts ($p < .01$). This is a clear ethnic contrast, uncluttered by interactions with other variables.*

---

*For all comparisons except those involving Italian parents, the help withholding scale incorporates parental responses to four different statements: "Mommy/Daddy, come look at my puzzle"; "Mommy/Daddy, help me"; "Does this piece go here"; and "Mommy/Daddy, get me another puzzle." In the Italian version there was a

TABLE 9.1

Significant Effects in the Comparisons of English Canadian and Italian Homeland Parents

Value Dimensions

Comparisons	1) Help Withholding[1] (np = 67.7)	2) Siding with Baby vs. Child (np = 42.7)	3a) Temper Control (np = 30.0)	3b) Social Temper Control (np = 41.6)	4) Insolence Control (np = 25.0)	5) Attention Denial (np = 75.0)	6) Comfort Withholding (np = 41.6)	7) Autonomy Control (np = 58.3)	8) Guest Restriction (np = 62.5)	9) Siding with Guest vs. Child (np = 42.7)	10) Perceived Sex-Role Differences	11) Expected Sex-Role Differences
G	29.90	7.20	53.78	–	57.79	4.78	–	9.07	50.06	–	–	4.27
C	–	19.82	8.86	16.48	45.96	–	–	7.72	–	–	20.31	24.83
X	–	–	–	–	–	–	–	–	–	5.84	–	–
P	–	7.42	4.43	15.67	4.63	–	8.06	–	–	–	6.59	6.89
GC	–	21.81	–	–	–	–	–	–	–	8.54	–	–
GX	–	–	–	–	–	–	–	–	–	–	–	–
CX	–	11.04	–	–	–	–	–	–	–	–	–	6.90
GP	–	–	–	–	–	–	–	–	–	–	–	–
CP	–	–	–	–	–	–	–	–	7.84	–	–	–
XP	–	–	–	–	–	–	5.82	–	–	–	–	–
GCX	–	–	–	–	–	–	–	–	–	–	–	–
GCP	–	–	–	–	–	–	–	–	–	–	–	–
GXP	–	–	–	–	–	–	–	–	–	–	–	–
CXP	–	–	–	–	–	–	–	–	–	–	–	–
GCXP	–	–	–	–	–	–	–	–	–	–	–	–

Note: Entries are significant F values; those underlined are beyond the .01 level of confidence, the others are beyond the .05 level.

[1] Values given for help withholding in the Italian comparisons are based on one less question than for other analyses. Therefore, the means and neutral point are different.

Source: Compiled by the authors.

189

The difference is based on contrasting strategies used by parents. For example, nearly all IH parents give complete and immediate help when it is requested, while EC parents much more often delay or qualify in some other way their expressions of help.

When a child seeks attention, however, the IH parents are less inclined than EC parents to comply ($p < .05$), although both groups clearly discourage attention seeking. This difference also seems to reflect an ethnic contrast since again there are no social-class variations or other forms of interaction involved.

On the comfort issue, the IH and EC parents are essentially alike, both groups being intent on discouraging children from being sissies or cry babies. In this case there are two important qualifications to be considered: a mother-father difference ($p < .01$) in which fathers (both IH and EC) are less inclined than mothers to extend comfort, and a three-way interaction ($p < .05$) which implies that IH and EC parents have distinctive reactions to children's requests for comfort depending upon the social-class background of the family and upon the sex of the child involved. This interaction is depicted in Figure 9.1 which highlights the contrast: EC working-class parents favor sons over daughters on the comfort issue while EC middle-class parents favor daughters over sons. For IH parents the pattern is reversed: IH working-class parents favor the comfort requests of daughters, while IH middle-class parents favor the comfort requests of sons. In other words, there appear to be differences in the amount of sympathy parents show toward children of one sex or the other, depending upon the social-class background and cultural setting involved. Perhaps this means that IH working-class parents have sympathy for the plight of daughters, as though being female in the working class calls for some type of parental compensation. Or, it could be that IH working-class parents tend to withhold expressions of comfort for sons because they feel that working-class boys have to become tough-skinned. These speculations are meant only to suggest the possible value of further research on this interesting matter. With the data on hand, we have no means of explaining these results.

---

translation error in the last statement: the Italian word for buy was introduced instead of the word for get or give. Consequently, we have constructed a special help withholding scale for this chapter, omitting the fourth question. The mean scores for this modified scale are included in all tables. The EC and FC means for this variable differ from the corresponding means presented in earlier comparisons, and the neutral point (67.7) is also different.

FIGURE 9.1

G x C x X Interaction for Comfort Withholding

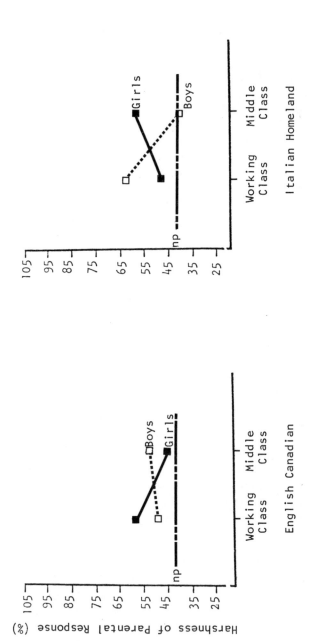

Source: Constructed by the authors.

With regard to guest privileges, we find that IH parents are much more lenient than EC parents ($p < .01$), in the sense that IH parents are much more willing to permit playmates into the house. Again, there are no social-class or interaction effects to complicate what appears to be another strong cultural contrast in parental values. In addition, both cultural groups contribute to a common two-way interaction (Figure A 9.1, $p < .01$), wherein working-class fathers in the two cultural settings are more inclined than working-class mothers to encourage the visits of playmates, whereas middle-class fathers are less encouraging than middle-class mothers on the issue of playmate visits.

What might this pattern signify? If it represented social-class differences in the presentability of homes, why wouldn't fathers and mothers from working-class homes both show the same reluctance to have neighbors' children in as guests? If it represents simply a contrast between middle-class mothers and fathers, perhaps middle-class mothers consider playmates as aids in entertaining their children or teaching them how to be sociable, while middle-class fathers see playmates more as annoyances or pests. Although this is an isolated instance, it still would be instructive to explore its meaning in more detail in future research.

In summary, when we consider the total set of aid episodes and use EC parents as a point of reference, we find two examples of distinctively Italian manners of reacting: IH parents are very much inclined to comply with their six-year-olds' requests for help and their requests to have playmates into the house for visits. These stand out as major cultural contrasts, and they are not diminished or qualified by subgroup differences in social-class background. Apparently, Italians and English Canadians conceive of their roles as parents somewhat differently, the former apparently see it as more natural to help children when help is requested, while the latter seem to regard requests for help more as occasions to train children in patience and self-reliance. Similarly, IH parents seem to regard visits of playmates more as occasions for their children to learn to be sociable and feel themselves part of a community group, whereas EC parents react more as though such visits were an annoyance or an impingement on the privacy of the home.

There is no evidence that IH parents are generally more lenient toward requests for aid. On the contrary, they are harsher than their EC counterparts toward children's demands for attention, and they are as discouraging as EC parents toward children's requests for comfort. In other words, our IH parents are selectively lenient on the help and guest privilege issues only, maintaining relatively stringent standards when children clamor for attention or for comfort.

The Discipline Episodes

The items that typically call for one type of discipline or another are the child-baby dispute, the temper, social temper and
insolence outbursts, and the child-guest quarrel. Whereas social
class had no effect on the IH-EC differences for the aid episodes,
it has a marked effect on each of the discipline episodes. For example, on the child-baby dispute matter, the IH parents are significantly harsher on the child than are EC parents ($p < .01$), even
though both parental groups discourage between-sibling fighting. The
important point, however, is that there are very important social-
class differences for the EC sample of parents, but hardly any for
the IH parents. Thus, in Figure 9.2 there are large working-class-
middle-class divergences in the reactions of EC parents compared
to essentially similar reactions on the part of working- and middle-
class IH parents. In other words, both subsets of IH parents react
rather harshly against child-baby disputes, whereas subgroups of
EC parents take either a harsh position (the case of the EC working-
class parents) or a relatively lenient stance (the case of the EC
middle-class parents). Note that it is the EC middle-class parents
who are much more inclined to take a "psychological" approach to
between-sibling quarrels, either overlooking such incidents or dis-
tracting the aggressive child.

On the child-baby dispute issue, there is another sense in
which IH parents show relatively more consensus than EC parents.
This is depicted in Figure A 9.2 which represents a significant interaction ($p < .01$), wherein IH mothers and fathers have a much more
unified approach toward an aggressive child than do EC parents, because the EC mothers are more prone to overlook the dispute than
are EC fathers.

Similar trends appear for temper and insolence. In both cases
the IH parents are significantly ($p < .01$) more lenient than their EC
counterparts, implying that children in IH families are given more
freedom to vent aggression by means of temper and insolence.
Since our temper episode deals with temper directed toward material
objects, it is possible that material things may be more highly
valued by EC than IH parents, consonant with the stereotype of the
materialistic North American. Or it could be that IH parents permit
their children to use things as a convenient outlet for aggression.
This trend does not hold for the social temper or child-guest dispute
matters, however, for in these instances the IH and EC parents are
equally severe, both group means falling well above the neutral
points.

What is most important, however, are the consistently large
social-class differences between our EC and IH samples. For example, although EC parents are generally much harsher than their

FIGURE 9.2

G x C Interaction for Siding with Baby versus Child

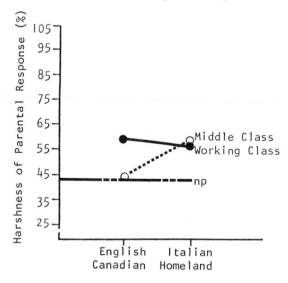

Source: Constructed by the authors.

IH counterparts on temper displays (Figure A 9.3), EC middle-
class parents are much more lenient than EC working-class parents.
On the other hand, IH parents of both social-class levels have a
common, and in this case, a more lenient, reaction (Figure A 9.3).
Similar social-class differences turn up for social temper (Figure
A 9.4), insolence (Figure A 9.5), and child-guest disputes (Figure
A 9.6). Thus, the same pattern of social-class differences appears
for each of the discipline issues.

All told, this analysis of attitudes toward discipline provides
us with an interesting contrast in the child-rearing values of IH and
EC parents. It turns out that the IH parents are relatively harsher
than their EC counterparts on the child-baby dispute matter, equally
harsh on the social temper and child-guest dispute issues, and decidedly more lenient on the temper and insolence issues. Relative
to EC parents, our sample of IH parents have an interesting style of
channeling their children's aggressivity, forbidding it to be directed
to siblings or other peers, but permitting relatively more of it to
flow toward material things and parents. Between-sibling squabbles
appear to be particularly disconcerting to IH parents, while material
things and parents seem to be more legitimate avenues for expressing

frustrations. Whether used consciously or not, the IH parents may have evolved an effective child-training procedure whereby they legitimize certain forms of aggression, thereby making other parental demands for compliance more tolerable and more acceptable.

We also discovered a consistent pattern of social-class contrasts between IH and EC parents on the discipline episodes. There is much greater consensus among working- and middle-class IH subgroups of parents than among EC subgroups. Apparently, in Italy there are generalized norms for disciplining children that cut across social-class boundaries, whereas in English Canada, working-class parents are consistently more harsh and demanding on discipline matters than middle-class parents. In fact the EC middle-class parents are lenient to the point of ignoring or overlooking children's provocations.

The Autonomy Episode

The IH parents are much more restrictive than their EC counterparts with regard to children's bids for autonomy ($p < .01$). In fact the mean for the IH parents falls above the neutral point, while the EC mean is below the neutral point. Although there is a strong social-class effect ($p < .01$), indicating that working-class parents are typically more restrictive than middle-class parents, the social-class differences in this case are as marked for IH as for EC groups. We may well have hit on a powerful cultural difference here, and, interestingly, there is some research support for it. Rosen (1959), working with various second-generation ethnic groups in the United States, asked mothers to state the age when they expected their children to "do things on their own" or "make decisions on their own," and so on. He found that Italian American mothers expected such signs of autonomy to appear at a much later age than did Greek American, Negro, Jewish, or Anglo-Protestant mothers. In other words, the Italian American mothers delayed independence training relative to these other North American ethnic groups.

The Sex-Role Issue

In terms of our measure of perceived sex-role differences, the IH and EC parents have essentially similar perceptions of how much boys and girls differ in their comportment. However, the IH parents have significantly higher expectations about sex-role differentiations ($p < .05$). Thus, relative to their EC counterparts, the IH parents likely experience more discrepancy between their expectations and their observations of sex-roles. This suggests that EC parents may be relatively content with the sex-role comportment of their children, while IH parents may see more signs of unisexism than they want to see. Why, one might ask, wouldn't the IH parents be prompted to bring their expectations and perceptions more into line? This question would be worth separate study. It could be that by keeping their expectations high, they feel that they still exert some degree of control over further social movements that might reduce sex-role differentiations even more.

The sex-role issue, then, provides another instance of national differences in child-rearing values, one of potential interest in its own right. At the same time, we have uncovered several features of sex-role expectations and perceptions that cut across national boundaries. For example, working-class parents, whether IH or EC, expect and perceive more signs of sex-role differentiation than do middle-class parents ($p < .01$). This, in fact, seems to be a very general social-class difference, suggesting to us that there may be a universally greater concern among lower social-class parents about the potential blurring or eradication of sex-role identities. In contrast, middle-class parents seem generally less concerned, and one wonders whether they may even encourage a reduction in the sharpness of sex-role boundaries. Similarly, we find that fathers, both IH and EC, expect and perceive more sex-role differentiations than do mothers ($p < .05$, in each case), suggesting that here, too, there may be a generally greater concern on the part of fathers about trends toward unisexism. Perhaps mothers deemphasize sex-role differentiations, either consciously or unconsciously, as a means of reducing status differences between males and females in the societies we are dealing with in this investigation.

Finally, we uncovered an isolated case where social class and sex of child both influence sex-role expectations ($p < .05$). In Figure 9.3 we see that working-class parents, whether IH or EC, have relatively higher sex-role expectations for boys, while middle-class parents have relatively higher sex-role expectations for girls. This suggests that working-class parents may be particularly concerned about boys losing their sex-role identity, as though masculinity was essential for survival in the lower social-class strata, while middle-class parents are relatively more concerned lest girls lose their femininity, as though femininity in some way characterized higher social status. It follows that working-class parents would be relatively less concerned if their daughters got masculinized in the process, just as middle-class parents would be less concerned if their sons got feminized! Other speculations also come to mind. For instance, perhaps these trends reflect actual tendencies in the two societies for middle-class girls to become more masculine—possibly because girls recognize that prestige and power are more associated with maleness than femaleness—and this prompts corrective measures on the part of middle-class parents, especially

FIGURE 9.3

C x X Interaction for Expected Sex-Role Differences

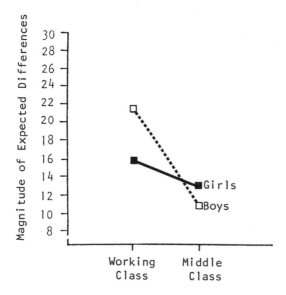

Source: Constructed by the authors.

middle-class fathers who might be sensitive to this new source of competition, whereas middle-class mothers might be more under-standing and sympathetic with such a drift toward masculinity. Similarly, it could be that working-class boys in the two societies associate maleness more with unrewarding and frustrating work and femaleness more with stability and responsibility in directing the family. On this basis, the working-class boys might choose to shift toward the feminine role and thereby worry their parents, particu-larly their fathers, who realize how difficult it would be for a male to succeed in the working class if he were not as much of a man as possible. But it should be clear that these speculations, based on a single instance of CX interaction, are meant only to sensitize the reader to what could be investigated in follow-up research.

SUMMARY AND CONCLUSIONS: PART I

In comparing IH and EC parents' attitudes toward child rear-ing, we found a whole network of contrasts that pattern themselves into two distinct sets, one comprising instances where a child asks for aid or assistance, the other, where a child misbehaves in such a fashion that some form of parental discipline is likely to follow. On the aid episodes we found two ways in which IH parents were distinctively different from their EC counterparts: they were much more ready to comply with a child's request for help and with a child's request to have playmates come into the home for visits. We argued that these cultural contrasts, unaffected by variations in social class, likely reflect differences in the ways IH and EC parents conceive of their roles as parents, IH parents seeing it as appropriate and natural to comply with a child's requests for help and to institute an open-door policy with regard to the visits of playmates, while EC parents see it as appropriate to hold back on gestures of help and on guest privileges. If EC parents look on these issues as occasions to inculcate self-sufficiency and self-entertainment, IH parents let these particular issues pass with relatively little constraint and search out others to use for purposes of character building.

However, there was no general tendency for IH parents to be more lenient than EC parents on matters related to aid. Instead, they were selectively lenient on the help and guest privilege matters, but not on the attention and comfort matters. Thus, IH youngsters were discouraged from becoming pests or sissies to the same extent as their EC counterparts.

On matters calling for discipline, IH parents are harsher socializers than the EC parents on the child-baby dispute issue, and equally harsh on displays of social temper and child-guest quarreling. Still, they are much more lenient than EC parents on displays of temper and insolence. In view of this pattern of differences, we argued that the distinctive feature of IH child-rearing values is the way parents channel a child's aggressive impulses, blocking them when they are directed to siblings or peers, but legitimizing them when directed toward material things or toward parents. Whether conscious or not, this particular form of channeling aggression might have developed as an effective means of socializing children, in the sense that giving legitimacy to certain outlets for aggression could make the taboos placed on other outlets more tolerable.

The discipline episodes also revealed a very strong and consistent pattern of social-class differences between IH and EC parents, and contrary to what might be expected, social class in our results plays a greater role in English Canada than in Italy. On each of the discipline items, the working- and middle-class IH parents shared a common view of how naughty children should be treated, whereas in EC families there were pronounced social-class differences between the more demanding working-class parents and the much more permissive middle-class parents. Whereas in Italy there seems to be culture-wide norms for disciplining children, in English Canada there appear to be class-specific norms. With regard to fostering independence in children, the IH parents seem much more restrictive than their EC counterparts, tending to discourage gestures of autonomy much more than EC parents. When children made gestures for autonomy, working-class parents, whether IH or EC, were more restrictive than were middle-class parents. Since social class did not play a role in this case, the observed difference in willingness to grant independence to children seems to be a genuine national or cultural contrast between IH and EC parents.

Finally, on our measures of sex-role differentiation, we found that IH parents expect more boy-girl differences in behavior than do EC parents, although both groups have essentially common perceptions of sex-role differentiations. Thus, IH parents, relative to ECs, may experience a greater discrepancy between what they expect and what they perceive on the matter of sex roles. We speculated that the IH parents may not be prompted to bring their perceptions and expectations into line because the maintenance of higher expectations may function to reduce further drifts toward unisexism.

Over and above national contrasts on the sex-role issue, there were numerous instances where IH and EC parents had essentially similar outlooks on sex-role comportment. For example, working-class parents, whether IH or EC, expect and perceive more boy-girl differences in behavior than do middle-class parents; this is especially pronounced for working-class parents of boys, much less so for middle-class parents of girls. Similarly, fathers, both IH and EC, expect and perceive more sex-role differences than do mothers. We speculated about the meaning of these social-class and mother-father contrasts, for they have turned up in several other national studies already discussed in earlier chapters. Might there, for instance, be a universal tendency for those lower in social-status positions to be particularly concerned about the erosion of sex-role identities, especially the identity of boys? For sure, working-class boys have to be masculine and tough if they are to survive. Similarly, fathers may be especially concerned about drifts toward unisexism, because in this more or less male-dominated world they stand to lose power if the male-female distinction is blurred. But why is it that working-class IH and EC parents seem more concerned lest boys lose their masculine identity, while middle-class parents are more concerned lest girls lose their feminine identity? Certain speculations were offered for this question and others like it, with the aim of pointing out the need for further detailed research on the fascinating issue of sex-role identities.

PART II: A COMPARISON OF ITALIAN IMMIGRANT
AND ITALIAN HOMELAND PARENTS

The distinctively Italian approaches to child rearing that we
uncovered in the IH-EC comparisons can serve as important reference points as we now compare a group of Italian parents who never
left Italy with a group of Italian parents who, although born and
raised in Italy, have immigrated to Canada and started their own
families there. This comparison of Italian Homeland (IH) and
Italian Immigrant (II) parents provides us with an opportunity to
tease out changes in child-rearing values resulting from immigration and to life experiences in a new social setting. But, as mentioned earlier, we will be just as interested in instances of value
persistence or resistance to change. A word of clarification is
called for here, for it is presumptuous for us to use the terms
"change" and "persistence" when we are working only with similarities and dissimilarities of value profiles of two separate groups of
parents. Actually, we are working on the presumption that our immigrant and homeland parental groups would have identical values
had the former not left the old country and come to North America.
We want the reader to be clear about our definitions of "change" and
"persistence" of values.

A Description of the Italian Immigrant Sample

Because there are many more working-class than middle-
class Italians who immigrate to Canada, we restricted our attention
to working-class parents only. The basic background information
on the Italian Immigrant parents is presented in Table A 9.3 which
can be compared with that for Italian Homelanders already described
in Table A 9.1.
All of our Italian Immigrant parents were born in central
Italy, the great majority coming from the areas of Lazio, the region including Rome, and Marches, a region on the Adriatic en-
circling the city of Ancona. Although the immigrant sample was not
drawn from Rome exclusively as was the case for the homeland
sample, it does represent areas of Italy equivalent to Rome in
terms of industrial development and degree of urbanization.
The immigrant parents had been Canadian residents for a
period of 15 to 16 years on the average, and at the time they were
interviewed, all were living in Montreal. There is a large and co-
hesive Italian community in Montreal (approximately 94,000 native-
speakers), and in spite of the relatively long period of time spent in
Canada, the immigrant parents had maintained strong ties to Italy.

For example, all families spoke Italian in the home; three-quarters subscribed to Italian language newspapers; in all but six of the 20 families, one or both parents had returned to Italy at least once; and all but four families maintain regular contact with relatives still in Italy.

Although the average educational level of the immigrants (about six-and-a-half years) was lower than that of the Italian Homelanders (about eight-and-a-half years), the positions they held were comparable to those of the homelanders. For those immigrants holding "blue-collar, skilled" jobs, their work represents a step up from their fathers' occupational status; all but one had fathers who were unskilled laborers or small farmers in Italy. In a sense, then, the immigrant families have started to fulfill the dream they likely had as they left their homeland, for, with the exception of six women and two men who had left "to marry" in Canada, and one man who said he immigrated to "find adventure," the majority of the Italian Immigrants said they had come to Canada to improve their standard of living.

PART II: RESULTS—VALUES THAT CHANGE
AND VALUES THAT PERSIST

The statistical comparisons of the II and IH working-class parents are presented in Tables 9.2 and A 9.4. A quick overview of these results suggests that in leaving Italy for Canada, certain child-rearing values change, while other basically Italian values persist. We also find instances of value persistence in the form of a number of sex-of-parent effects (the P row in Table 9.2) which indicate that Italian mothers and fathers, whether II or IH, play different or complementary roles in the socialization of their children.

Instances of Value Persistence

When children request help, the II parents are significantly more compliant than their IH counterparts ($p < .05$). This difference is noteworthy because we have already found in the previous section that the IH parents were significantly more compliant than EC parents on the help-request issue. As we see it, immigration and life experiences in Canada may have the effect of exaggerating a characteristically Italian tendency to give immediate and direct help to children when help is requested. Rather than shifting to the relatively less helpful EC pattern, the II parents seemed to have become more Italian than Italians in Italy in their readiness to help.

TABLE 9.2

Significant Effects in the Comparisons of Italian Immigrant and Italian Homeland Working-Class Parents

Value Dimensions

Comparisons	1) Help Withholding[1] (np = 67.7)	2) Siding with Baby vs. Child (np = 42.7)	3a) Temper Control (np = 30.0)	3b) Social Temper Control (np = 41.6)	4) Insolence Control (np = 25.0)	5) Attention Denial (np = 75.0)	6) Comfort Withholding (np = 41.6)	7) Autonomy Control (np = 58.3)	8) Guest Restriction (np = 62.5)	9) Siding with Guest vs. Child (np = 42.7)	10) Perceived Sex-Role Differences	11) Expected Sex-Role Differences
G	6.97	–	23.87	–	11.16	–	–	–	–	–	–	8.51
X	–	–	–	–	–	–	–	–	–	9.30	–	–
P	7.74	5.54	–	4.56	–	–	5.02	–	–	–	9.84	–
GX	–	–	–	–	–	–	–	–	–	–	–	–
GP	–	–	–	–	–	–	–	–	–	–	–	–
XP	–	–	–	–	–	–	–	6.76	4.63	–	–	–
GXP	–	–	–	–	–	–	–	4.15	–	–	8.12	–

Note: Entries are significant F values; those underlined are beyond the .01 level of confidence, the others are beyond the .05 level.
[1] Values given for help withholding in the Italian comparisons are based on one less question than for the other analyses. Therefore, the means and neutral point are different.
Source: Compiled by the authors.

When faced with a child-baby dispute, the II and IH parents
have similar reactions, and since the IH parents were more severe
than EC parents on this feature of socialization, it seems that
within-family aggression of this sort is as salient and important an
issue for II as for IH parents. In this case then we have a clear example of what we think of as value persistence.

The same can be said about the management of children's demands for attention: the II and IH mean scores are very similar,
and since the IH parents have been found to be significantly more
severe than their EC counterparts on demands for attention, this
Italian tendency to discourage children from demanding attention
seems to hold up for II parents in Canada.

We find value persistence as well on the guest privilege issue,
for again the reactions of II and IH parents are alike, meaning that
the Italian tendency to encourage children to invite guests in to play
is as characteristic of II as it is of IH parents, and both groups
stand in contrast to the much more restrictive EC parents.

Another example of value stability turns up in the sex of child
comparisons. On the child-guest dispute issue, girls in both II and
IH families are treated more harshly than boys for what is objectively the same misdemeanor ($p < .01$). Interestingly, the same example of parental bias occurred in the IH-EC analysis suggesting to us
that all three parental groups—II, IH, and EC—share a common in-
clination to come down particularly hard on girls who quarrel with
playmates. The important point here is that both IH and II parents
contribute to this bias against daughters, meaning that there is no
value change involved. But we should add that this value hasn't
really been seriously challenged since EC parents share the same
bias; perhaps in other national settings where no such bias against
girls existed this value would have changed.

There are no differences either in the ways II and IH fathers
and mothers play their distinctive parental roles. We have several
examples of this form of value persistence on the issues of: help
withholding ($p < .01$); child-baby dispute ($p < .05$); social temper
($p < .05$); and comfort withholding ($p < .05$). Thus, Italian fathers,
whether IH or II, are softer or more lenient than Italian mothers
in their reactions to requests for help, child-baby disputes, and
social temper outbursts, but harsher than mothers on requests for
comfort. Since there are no complicating interaction effects involved, these represent to us four important examples of value persistence, in the sense that Italian fathers and mothers fulfill their
parental roles in the same distinctive ways in Italy as in Canada.

Finally, there is one other interesting example of value persistence that appears on the guest restriction issue, depicted in
Figure A 9.7. Note that the characteristically Italian tendency to

encourage children to have guests into the house is marked by
cross-sex leniency, that is, fathers are particularly permissive
toward daughters' requests for guest privileges, while mothers are
particularly lenient toward sons' requests. Whatever it is that
prompts this cross-sex bias, the main point is that it is as characteristic of IH as it is of II parents. In brief, there is no change
in the basically Italian mode of dealing with guest privileges.

Instances of Value Change

Changes in values occur on the temper and insolence issues
and on parents' sex-role expectations, and each of these changes is
clearly in the direction of English Canadian values. For instance,
in the previous section we found IH parents to be significantly more
lenient than their EC counterparts on temper and insolence displays;
they also had significantly higher sex-role expectations than did EC
parents. Now we find that II parents are also significantly less lenient than their IH counterparts on temper and insolence displays,
and they have significantly lower sex-role expectations than do IH
parents. Apparently, then, the II parents have shifted away from
IH parents and toward Anglo-Canadian parents on each of these
issues.

There are two other cases of value change, autonomy ($p < .05$)
being one and perceived sex-role differentiations ($p < .01$) the other,
and these turn up in three-way interactions. The comparisons for
the autonomy issue are depicted in Figure 9.4 where we find a quite
different form of mother-child relationship in II than in IH families.
For II parents, there is clearly same-sex leniency shown with
fathers favoring sons and mothers daughters, whereas in IH families there is much more mother-father consensus on how to deal
with bids for autonomy. One gets the impression that II parents
become sensitive to the much greater tendency among English
Canadians to encourage independence in six-year-olds, and in at-
tempting to adjust to a new and quite different norm, they make a
partial adjustment only, selectively encouraging the independence
gestures of like-sexed children. Perhaps the like-sexed pattern
derives from a feeling on the part of parents that they understand
and trust the way the same-sexed child thinks and behaves. Of
course our data base is too limited to go much further with this possibility; the best we can do is suggest that some such change may
well be underway for II parents as a consequence of immigration to
Canada.

The change involved in perceived sex-role differences is much
more complex and obscure (see Figure 9.5). The II-IH contrast in

FIGURE 9.4

G x X x P Interaction for Autonomy Control

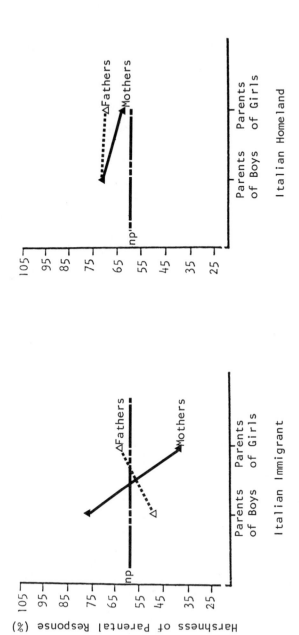

Source: Constructed by the authors.

205

FIGURE 9.5

G x X x P Interaction for Perceived Sex-Role Differences

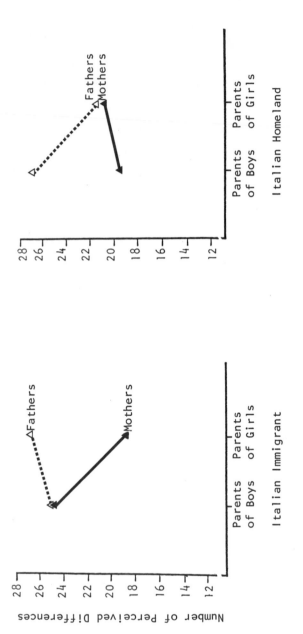

Source: Constructed by the authors.

this case revolves around mother-father differences in perceptions, which, in turn, are related to the sex of the child involved. In IH families, parents of girls have essentially similar sex-role perceptions, while parents of boys diverge in their perceptions, fathers of boys seeing more evidence of sex-role differentiations than do mothers of boys. In II families, however, parents of boys have essentially similar sex-role perceptions, while fathers of girls see more sex-role differentiation than do mothers of girls. Thus, Italian fathers, whether IH or II, seem to be more satisfied with the degree of sex-role differentiation they perceive than are Italian mothers, and this fact is reflected in a significant ($p < .01$) mother-father difference. The intriguing point, however, is that, if we take the mothers' perceptions as a point of reference, fathers are overly optimistic about the sex-role issue, and they may see what they want to see.

But why is there such a pronounced difference between II and IH parents in their sex-role perceptions? Why, in other words, do IH mothers and fathers of boys have such different sex-role perceptions, and why do II mothers and fathers of girls have similar differences in perceptions? Our speculation is that parental divergences in sex-role perceptions reflect basic concerns about children losing sex-role identity. It could be that there is more concern—and thus more reason for perceptual distortions to take place—about the sex-role identity of IH sons in Italy and about the sex-role identity of II daughters in Canada. Unfortunately, we can't take this line of thought any further, nor can we even speculate as to why this should be so. Of course, this form of perceptual discordance between parents may have a more factual basis. Thus, it could be that in Italy boys go out of their way to present themselves differently to fathers and to mothers, being more masculine with their fathers and more feminine with their mothers, while in Canada II girls may be particularly inclined to play up their femininity with their fathers more so than with their mothers. But at this stage of our work, it is a mystery to us why this should be so.

PART II: SUMMARY AND CONCLUSIONS

Our aim in this section was to explore the stability of child-rearing values of Italian parents who, through immigration, have started a new way of life in Canada. Although we had to limit our analysis to working-class II and IH parents only, the exploration was extremely fruitful because we were able to find numerous examples of both value stability and value change. We were also able to pinpoint which values are more likely to give way to assimilation before others. Knowing about the sequence of value changes gives one a better understanding of how immigrants adjust to a new society.

In the first place, we found interesting instances of value persistence rather than change. For example, relative to Anglo-Canadians who tend to hold back on giving help to their children, Italian Homeland parents are inclined to comply fully and immediately with children's requests for help. This tendency to be helpful holds as well for II parents, meaning that there is no shift in the direction of EC values. Instead, the II parents are even more inclined than the IH parents to give help. We see this as an exaggeration of the help-giving attitude on the part of Italian immigrant parents, and the exaggeration could be functional to the extent that it enhances within-family bonds of solidarity, which would be especially important in working-class immigrant families. Other basically Italian attitudes hold up as well: Italian parents in both Canada and Italy take a strong stand against aggression directed toward siblings or toward peers, and they are also relatively severe on children who clamor for attention. On the other hand, II parents, like their counterparts in Italy, maintain an open-door policy on guest privileges, making both groups distinctively different from the much more restrictive EC parents. It is doubly interesting to note that both II and IH parents show cross-sex leniency on the guest privilege issue—mothers favor sons who ask to have guests in to play, while fathers favor daughters.

There is no change either in the basically Italian tendency to discourage children's bids for autonomy, meaning that both II and IH working-class parents tend to hold back on this form of early independence training. This Italian tendency to delay independence training has been documented by Rosen (1959) in his research on various ethnic groups in the United States.

Nor are their changes in the ways Italian mothers and fathers complement one another as parents. Thus, in II as in IH families, fathers are more ready than mothers to give help, to overlook a child-baby dispute, and to be lenient on social temper outbursts. Italian fathers, though, are less likely than mothers to comfort a child.

In many respects, then, Italian immigrant parents in the Canadian setting remain pretty much Italian in their ways of relating to children. In other respects, however, they change, and usually the change is unambiguously in the direction of EC ways of relating to children. For instance, the Italian leniency on temper outbursts and insolence changes in the Canadian scene in the sense that II parents seem to shift from IH to EC ways of dealing with these types of aggression. It could well be that these features of

Italian child rearing are modified because they would otherwise be too public and, thus, noticeably out of place in the EC setting. Similarly, the more pronounced sex-role expectations of Italian Homeland parents give way in the Canadian context so that the sex-role expectations of II parents become very similar to those of EC parents. Again, this may mean that II parents feel that, for the sake of their children's comfort in the Canadian society, they cannot maintain unrealistic expectations with regard to sex-role differentiations.

There is also an important change in the attitudes of Italian parents toward children's requests for autonomy, although, as mentioned above, the overall degree of autonomy does not change. Whereas in IH families mothers and fathers both discourage the autonomy bids of six-year-olds, in II families there are unmistakeable signs of disagreement between mothers and fathers which take the form of same-sex leniency. Thus, II fathers favor sons over daughters on requests for autonomy, while II mothers favor daughters over sons. Our speculation is that as this value feature starts to change toward the much more supportive EC norm, the change creates a tension in II families, manifesting itself in the same-sex leniency split. It is as though each parent adjusts by making a partial change only, and each chooses the same-sex child as the agent of change because that child is seen as closer, more understanding, and more likely to make the change responsibly.

Although we can only speculate in our attempts at explanation, the examples of value change and value persistence we refer to here are actually extremely prominent ones in the statistical sense. Because this is so, follow-up research on the basic issues involved would likely be very worthwhile and productive.

PART III: A COMPARISON OF ITALIAN
IMMIGRANT, ENGLISH CANADIAN, AND
FRENCH CANADIAN PARENTS

In this final section we go one step further with our analysis. So far, we have compared the child-rearing values of Italian Homeland parents with those of Anglo-Canadians, and then we followed, so to speak, a group of working-class Italian immigrants to Canada to see how much the experiences of immigration and living in Canada as young parents impinged on and modified the basic Italian orientations toward child rearing they presumably brought with them. Thus, we had a fairly good idea of the possible mismatches between Italian and Anglo-Canadian values and what value adjustments might be expected from Italian immigrants to Canada. We had taken Anglo-

Canadians as our Canadian reference group because we believed
that Italian immigrants viewed Canada mainly as a subregion of
North America, not easily distinguished from the United States.
Even in the mainly French province of Quebec, Italian immigrants
seem to orient themselves and their families toward English Canadian institutions for the most part, expecting that their children
will be educated in English-language schools so that they can ulti-
mately take on responsible roles in English-speaking North America.
But we were far from sure about all this and wondered whether this
apparent orientation toward English Canada told the whole story.
Might there not be just as important links, through religion and
European background, with French Canadians? And might not the
Italian immigrant to Quebec, whether consciously or not, take
French Canadians as an equally significant reference group?

Our purpose in this section is to relate the child-training
values of Italian Immigrant parents to those of a broader range of
Canadians, including French Canadians as well as English Canadians.
As we shall see, broadening the perspective in this way opens up a
whole new range of possibilities just as it does in the next chapter
where we examine the consequences of immigrating from Greece to
Canada. The process of immigrating takes on a special significance
because we were dealing with particular peoples (Italians and
Greeks) as the immigrants and both English and French Canadians
as the representatives of the host nation. Although the process may
be the same in both cases, as it turns out, it is a quite different
Canada and a quite different Montreal for Italian immigrants from
what it is for Greek immigrants.

PART III: RESULTS—A COMPARISON OF
ITALIAN IMMIGRANT, ENGLISH CANADIAN,
AND FRENCH CANADIAN PARENTS

The statistical information is presented in Tables 9.3 and
A 9.5. In this case we are comparing five different parental groups:
Italian Immigrants (II), French Canadian working-class (FCWC),
French Canadian middle-class (FCMC), English Canadian working-
class (ECWC), and English Canadian middle-class (ECMC). We
have already described the backgrounds of the Canadian groups in
Chapter 2 and the Italian Immigrant group in Part II of this chapter.
In general, the three working-class groups—II, EC, and FC—are
well matched, although we were unable to equate them perfectly.
Thus, the II parents have less schooling than the Canadians (a difference of some two years); the II parents have somewhat fewer
children (one less child on the average); and there are more II

TABLE 9.3

Significant Effects in the Comparisons of Italian Immigrant Working-Class, English Canadian Working-Class and Middle-Class, and French Canadian Working-Class and Middle-Class Parents

Value Dimensions

Comparisons	1) Help Withholding[1] (np = 67.7)	2) Siding with Baby vs. Child (np = 42.7)	3a) Temper Control (np = 30.0)	3b) Social Temper Control (np = 41.6)	4) Insolence Control (np = 25.0)	5) Attention Denial (np = 75.0)	6) Comfort Withholding (np = 41.6)	7) Autonomy Control (np = 58.3)	8) Guest Restriction (np = 62.5)	9) Siding with Guest vs. Child (np = 42.7)	10) Perceived Sex-Role Differences	11) Expected Sex-Role Differences
G	10.85	10.38	3.79	11.37	17.03	–	–	3.09	14.03	11.54	6.80	5.86
X	–	–	–	9.00	–	–	–	–	–	10.13	–	–
P	12.45	–	–	–	–	6.83	6.68	–	–	–	6.45	–
GX	–	–	–	–	–	–	–	–	–	–	–	3.01
GP	–	4.75	–	–	–	–	–	–	–	–	2.99	–
XP	6.06	–	–	–	–	–	–	–	–	–	–	–
GXP	–	–	–	–	–	–	–	5.01	–	–	–	–

Note: Entries are significant F values; those underlined are beyond the .01 level of confidence, the others are beyond the .05 level. [1] Values given for help withholding in the Italian comparisons are based on one less question than for the other analyses. Therefore the means and neutral point are different.

Source: Compiled by the authors.

working mothers (11 versus 0 and 2 for FC and EC parents, respectively). The two groups, however, differ in religious affiliation: the EC parents are all Protestants while the FC and II parents are all Catholics.

The group-by-group comparisons summarized in Table 9.4
were tested for significance with the Newman-Keuls statistic. Note
that there are a large number of group differences; in fact, there
are differences between one group and another on all scales but two.
The interesting question, however, is whether it is the II parents
who figure most frequently in these differences, in other words, we
want to know if the II parents stand out as the odd group, relative to
the two Canadian comparison groups.

Parental Group Comparisons

Help Withholding

Although all five parental groups tend to offer help to their
six-year-olds when it is requested, the II parents turn out to be the
most helpful group, significantly more so than any of the Canadian
comparison groups. On the issue of helping, then, the II parents
are particularly lenient and distinctively different from Canadian
parents, be they English Canadian or French Canadian, middle-
class or working-class.

The Child-Baby Dispute

On this issue, all five parental groups take sides against a
six-year-old who becomes involved in a quarrel with a younger sibling, but the II parents turn out to be no more harsh in their reactions than any other Canadian group, except that they are significantly more severe than the very lenient ECMC parents. With respect to their manner of coping with sibling quarrels, then, the II
parents overlap with both FC and EC working-class parents and,
interestingly enough, with FC middle-class parents as well.

Temper Control

In this case, all group means fall above the neutral point, and
the distinctive parental group is the ECWC, the most severe of all
on the temper control issue. The II parents, even though they stand
relatively high on the scale, close to the FC and EC working-class
groups, are not significantly different from any of the comparison
groups. Thus, the II parents, relative to the Canadian comparison
groups, are as typical as can be in their reactions to a child's temper outburst.

TABLE 9.4

Significant Ethnic Group Differences for the Analyses of Variance[1,2]

Scale	Significant Differences

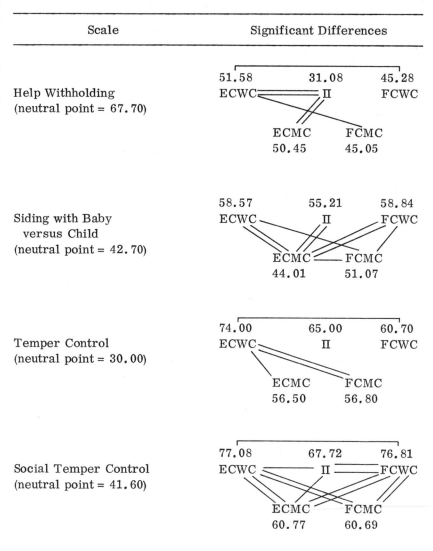

Help Withholding
(neutral point = 67.70)

51.58   31.08   45.28
ECWC — II — FCWC
ECMC   FCMC
50.45   45.05

Siding with Baby versus Child
(neutral point = 42.70)

58.57   55.21   58.84
ECWC — II — FCWC
ECMC — FCMC
44.01   51.07

Temper Control
(neutral point = 30.00)

74.00   65.00   60.70
ECWC — II — FCWC
ECMC — FCMC
56.50   56.80

Social Temper Control
(neutral point = 41.60)

77.08   67.72   76.81
ECWC — II — FCWC
ECMC — FCMC
60.77   60.69

(continued)

Table 9.4, continued

Scale	Significant Differences

Insolence Control
(neutral point = 25.00)

```
      81.67          68.96          71.67
      ECWC ═══════════ II ═══════════ FCWC
                  ECMC        FCMC
                  55.53       52.65
```


Attention Denial
(neutral point = 75.00)

(F test not significant)

```
      80.40          86.25          88.24
      ECWC            II            FCWC

                  ECMC        FCMC
                  83.75       81.67
```


Comfort Withholding
(neutral point = 41.60)

(F test not significant)

```
      54.60          56.26          52.10
      ECWC            II            FCWC

                  ECMC        FCMC
                  50.02       48.07
```


Autonomy Control
(neutral point = 58.30)

(Newman Keuls test showed
no comparisons significant)

```
      52.91          54.57          51.66
      ECWC            II            FCWC

                  ECMC        FCMC
                  36.24       38.33
```


Guest Restriction
(neutral point = 62.50)

```
      52.13          26.87          38.75
      ECWC ═══════════ II ─────────── FCWC
                  ECMC ═══════ FCMC
                  46.25       31.25
```

Scale	Significant Differences

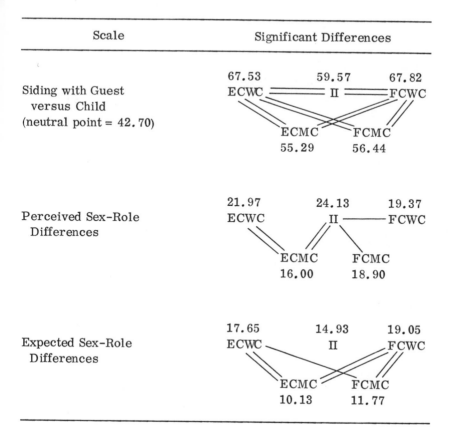

Siding with Guest versus Child (neutral point = 42.70)

67.53 59.57 67.82
ECWC ═══ II ═══ FCWC
ECMC   FCMC
55.29 56.44

Perceived Sex-Role Differences

21.97 24.13 19.37
ECWC II ——— FCWC
ECMC FCMC
16.00 18.90

Expected Sex-Role Differences

17.65 14.93 19.05
ECWC II FCWC
ECMC FCMC
10.13 11.77

[1]Entries represent group means where a higher mean indicates a harsher response or for perceived and expected sex-role differences, a perception or expectation of greater boy/girl differences.

[2]Connected means are significantly different:

Newman Keuls Test of comparison is significant at $\underline{p} < .05$.

Newman Keuls Test of comparison is significant at $\underline{p} < .01$.

Source: Compiled by the authors.

Social Temper

When it is a question of a child's social temper, all parental groups express their displeasure, but the II parents are significantly different from all other groups, except, the FCMC, in that they are less harsh in their reactions to social temper than the two Canadian working-class samples, but significantly more harsh than the ECMC parents. In their style of dealing with social temper, then, the II parents are most like FCMC parents.

Insolence

In the case of insolence control, the mean score for the II parents again falls at the center of the spread of scores, making them significantly more harsh than the ECWC group. Accordingly, on the issue of insolence, the II parents react most like the FCWC parents, providing us with another sample where II parents are more like FC than EC parents.

However, if we examine specific reactions to the insolence items, we find that the II parents have a distinctive mode of reacting which is all the more interesting because we know that, relative to IH parents, the II parents have changed from a very lenient reaction to insolence to one more like that of Canadian parents. We find that II parents, especially II mothers, are extremely upset when their six-year-olds call them "stupid." Rather than relying on reprimands, threats, and nonphysical punishments, as Canadian parents do, they are more inclined to react with direct physical punishment (see Tables A 9.6 and A 9.7).

Attention and Comfort Seeking

All five parental groups tend to discourage children from demanding attention or comfort, and there are no significant differences between or among groups in the severity or leniency of reactions. Although the mean scores for the II parents fall near the harsh pole on both the attention and comfort scales, the statistical analysis indicates that the II parents are in no way distinctive.

Autonomy

All parental groups encourage autonomy to one degree or another, but in this case again there are no significant differences between or among any of the mean scores. Even though the mean for the II parents is the highest of all, the statistical analysis indicates that, as a group, the II parents are no more severe on children's autonomy bids than any of the Canadian comparison groups.

Guest Privileges

Although all five groups encourage their children to have guests in to play, there is still a large spread of scores, ranging from the two EC groups (the ECMC and the ECWC), who tend to qualify and limit their approvals, to the more lenient II and FCMC groups, who comply without qualifications. In this case, then, the II parents are the most receptive to children's requests for guest privileges, and they are closest to the FCMC in this regard. This example constitutes another instance where II and FC parents, especially the FCMC, display similar modes of reacting to children.

Child-Guest Dispute

All five groups tend to take sides against the child in a child-baby dispute, and again the mean score for the II parents falls in the center of the distribution of scores, making them significantly less harsh than either the EC or FC working-class groups, but essentially similar to the two Canadian middle-class groups. With regard to between-sibling aggressivity, then, the II parents have more of a Canadian middle-class than working-class perspective.

Perceptions of Sex-Role Differences

In the case of sex-role perceptions, there is a large spread of scores, ranging from a low for the ECMC parents to a high for the II parents. In terms of their perceptions of sex-role differences, then, the II parents are extreme, overlapping only with the ECWC parents.

Expected and Perceived Sex-Role Differentiations

Here the scores range from a low for the two Canadian middle-class groups to a high for the two working-class groups. The mean score for the II parents falls clearly in the center of the distribution, not different statistically from any other comparison group. Apparently, in changing from the high level of sex-role expectations characteristic of Italian Homelanders, the II parents have adjusted their expectations in such a way that they jibe nicely with the many variations to be found in Canada. Still, there is an interesting discrepancy between the sex-role perceptions and the sex-role expectations of II parents. Relative to the other groups, they are not at all extreme in what they expect of boys and girls, and yet they perceive more instances of boy-girl differences in conduct than do any of the other parental groups. For instance, compared to the FCWC parents, who tend to expect more sex-role differences than they perceive, the II parents perceive more sex-role differences than they expect. Thus, it could well be that the FCWC parents are disappointed by what they perceive, whereas the II parents are likely more surprised than disappointed.

Parental Group Contrasts Seen through Interactions

There are four other contrasts between parental groups which turn up in interactions, and these help us locate with somewhat more precision the value systems of II parents relative to those of the Canadian comparison groups.

The first involves a mother-father difference on the child-baby dispute issue (the GP interaction depicted in Figure 9.6), indicating that II parents are much more like FCWC than ECWC parents in their reactions. This is so because in both II and FCWC families, mothers take a harsher stand than fathers in curbing between-sibling disputes, whereas in EC families, whether working-class or middle-class, fathers are the harsher disciplinarians on this particular issue.

The second instance is a mother-father difference in sex-role perceptions (see Figure 9.7). In this case the FCMC parents are distinctive because they are the only group in which mothers perceive more sex-role differences than do fathers. This means that the II parents are much like the ECWC and the FCWC parents in the sense that for all three working-class groups, fathers have higher sex-role perception scores than do mothers. In terms of the magnitude of the father-mother differences, the II parents are more similar to FCWC than to ECWC parents.

The third example is a daughter-son difference in sex-role expectations (Figure 9.8), and here the ECWC is the distinctive group because of the extremely high sex-role expectations that ECWC parents have of boys. For the II parents and all other comparison groups, parents of boys have relatively lower sex-role expectations than parents of girls. Thus, the II pattern is more FC than EC in makeup, and also more middle-class than working-class.

Finally there is a complex three-factor interaction for autonomy control depicted in Figure 9.9. The major trend here is the same-sex leniency shown by all three working-class groups, II parents included. Thus, the working-class fathers encourage more the independence moves of sons than of daughters, while working-class mothers encourage more the independence bids of daughters than of sons. In middle-class families, whether EC or FC, both parents tend to show more encouragement toward daughters than toward sons. In this case, then, the II parents display a working-class style of dealing with children's autonomy bids, and in this regard they are especially close to the FCWC parents.

FIGURE 9.6

G x P Interaction for Siding with Baby versus Child

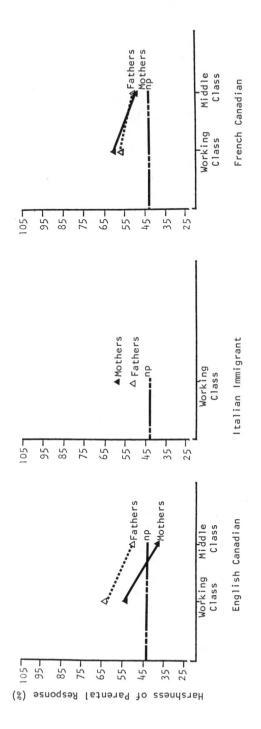

Source: Constructed by the authors.

219

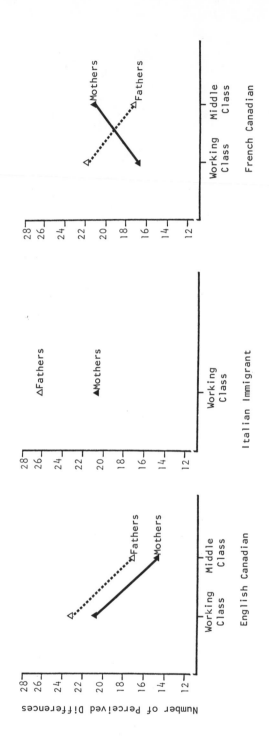

FIGURE 9.7

G x P Interaction for Perceived Sex-Role Differences

Source: Constructed by the authors.

220

FIGURE 9.8

G x X Interaction for Expected Sex-Role Differences

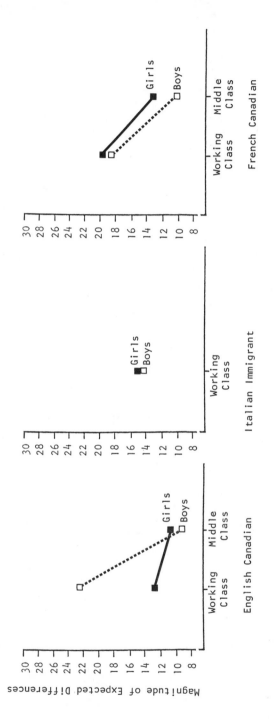

Source: Constructed by the authors.

221

FIGURE 9.9

G x X x P Interaction for Autonomy Control

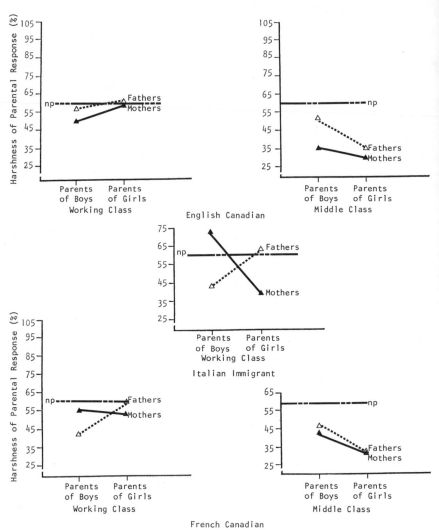

Source: Constructed by the authors.

Cross-Group Similarities

Finally, there are several interesting general trends that hold for all five comparison groups, II parents included. These involve daughter-son and mother-father differences.

Differences in Treatment of Daughters and Sons

For all five parental groups, girls are treated more harshly than boys when they display social temper or enter into a child-guest dispute (both significant at the $p < .01$ level). Thus, all parental groups, with the II parents contributing to this bias against girls as much as any of the Canadian comparison groups, discourage girls from being socially aggressive, which means as well that all groups tend, relatively, to encourage boys to display the same degrees of social aggressivity.

Mother-Father Differences in Reactions

What emerges is that mothers are generally harsher than fathers on the help issue ($p < .01$), and again the II parents contribute as much to this trend as any other group. There is, however, a significant interaction on the help issue (depicted in Figure A 9. 8), revealing the same-sex leniency pattern again, with mothers more inclined to help daughters than sons and fathers more inclined to help sons than daughters. Again the II parents contribute to this trend as much as any other comparison group. Thus, on the issue of help giving, mothers are generally more helpful than fathers, although mothers favor daughters and fathers favor sons.

In contrast, on the attention and the comfort issues fathers are harsher than mothers, and here, too, the II parents contribute to the general trend as much as any of the Canadian comparison groups. Fathers also tend to perceive more sex-role differences in behavior than do mothers, the only exception being the FCMC parents.

PART III: SUMMARY AND CONCLUSIONS

In this section we examined more details of the child-training values of II parents by comparing their approaches to child rearing with those of various groups of Canadian parents with whom they could have direct or indirect contact. What is striking about this analysis is that although many parental group differences turned up, the II parents are not that different from one Canadian parental group or another. The similarities between the II parents and one or another of the Canadian comparison groups are summarized, scale by scale, in Table 9.5. Several general trends show through. First, there is only one scale, that of help withholding, where II parents <u>do not</u> overlap with <u>at least</u> any of the Canadian groups. In other words, except for their extreme lenience in help giving, the II parents are similar to at least one other Canadian comparison group. In the second place, in their modes of reacting to children, the II parents are as similar to middle-class Canadian parents as they are to working-class Canadian parents. The total similarity count is 15 for middle-class and 14 for working-class. Third, the II parents overlap more often with FC parents (16 instances) than with EC parents (13 instances), and they overlap most with FCMC parents (9 instances) and least with ECMC parents (6 instances). In fact, the II parents overlap with FCMC parents on all issues except three: <u>help withholding</u> (where they are distinctively different from all comparison groups), <u>insolence control</u> (where they are closer to FCWC parents in terms of general harshness, but different from all Canadian groups in their heavy use of physical discipline), and <u>the perception of sex-role differences</u> (where they are distinctively different from all comparison groups but one).

TABLE 9.5

Summary of Similarities between Canadian
and Italian Immigrant Parents*

| | Group | | | |
Scale	ECWC	FCWC	ECMC	FCMC
Help withholding				
Siding with baby versus child	X	X		X
Temper control	X	X	X	X
Social temper control				X
Insolence control		X		
Attention denial	X	X	X	X
Comfort withholding	X	X	X	X
Autonomy control	X	X	X	X
Guest restriction				X
Siding with guest versus child			X	X
Perceived sex-role differences	X			
Expected sex-role differences	X	X	X	X
Total number of similarities	7	7	6	9

*An X indicates similarity or overlap of patterns of reactions and is based on lack of a statistically significant difference between the II parents and the comparison group in question.
<u>Source</u>: Compiled by the authors.

The II parents apparently come to Canada with training and skills that mark them as working-class, but the substance of their value orientations in the Canadian context turns out to be as much or more middle-class than working-class in nature. This close alignment with Canadian middle-class values is likely due in part to changes and adjustments in the values of II parents that take place as a consequence of immigration and life experiences in Canada, and in part to similarities that exist between middle-class Canadian values and basic Italian values which are maintained by II parents in Canada. Nonetheless, another possibility suggests itself: in making a break with the homeland and deciding to settle elsewhere, the Italian immigrant may, with the aim of advancing socially, make a double break with the past, a physical one with the homeland as place of residence, and a psychological one with the socioeconomic position held in the homeland. Regardless of the validity of this line of argument, our results indicate clearly that II parents can be comfortable with the child-rearing values of middle-class Canadian parents. In particular, they should be as comfortable, or more so, with FC as with EC child-rearing values. They may, in fact, be in a position to utilize the value systems of both EC and FC societies, and thereby make their adjustment to the new world easier and more comfortable. Although derived from our analyses, these specula- tions should be viewed simply as suggestions for further research, but they do draw attention to the potentially important role that value compatibility can play in the adjustment of immigrants to a new land.

One of the group comparisons was of special interest because it revealed a discrepancy between what II parents expect and what they perceive with respect to the sex-role differentiations of their children. It turns out that the II parents do not expect as much dif- ferentiation between boy-behavior and girl-behavior as they seem to encounter in their experiences with boys and girls. Thus, relative to the various Canadian comparison groups, the II parents give the impression of being surprised that boys and girls behave as differ- ently as they do. In sharp contrast, the FCWC parents expect more sex-role differences than they actually perceive, possibly making them more concerned or upset by the mismatch between what is ex- pected and what transpires.

In addition to the group-by-group comparisons, a number of interactions were statistically significant, indicating that the paren- tal groups differed in other complex and subtle ways. In these cases, too, we find that the II parents are never really out of place relative to the comparison groups, and again they are generally closer to FC than to EC parents in their child-rearing orientations. For example, on the issue of a child-baby dispute, the EC pattern, including both ECWC and ECMC parents, indicates that fathers are harsher than mothers in sanctioning within-family squabbling of this sort. The FC pattern is quite different, for FC mothers are either as harsh as or harsher than fathers on the child-baby dispute matter. The point of special interest is that the II pattern is definitely more FC, especially FCWC, than EC since II mothers are decidedly more demanding than II fathers on the issue of a child-baby quarrel. Furthermore, the II parents turn out to be more similar to FCWC than to ECWC parents in their perceptions of sex-role differences, in the sense that both II and FCWC fathers perceive many more sex-role differences than do their wives. In other words, fathers in both II and FCWC families appear to be more vigilant or more sensitive than mothers about the sex-role identities of their children.

Other interactions indicated that in their expectations of sex-role differences the II parents are more similar to FC than to EC parents. For example, in II and FC families, parents of girls expect more sex-role differences than do parents of boys. The opposite trend appears for the ECWC group since it is the ECWC parents of boys who expect more sex-role differences. Our guess is that II and FC parents, for some unknown reason, are more concerned about girls losing their feminine identity, while EC parents are concerned lest boys lose their masculine identity. Although the data suggest something like this, we have no way of explaining or interpreting the differences that turned up.

With regard to autonomy, the II parents fit the general working-class pattern, characterized by same-sex leniency: fathers are more inclined to encourage independence in sons than in daughters, while mothers are more inclined to encourage the independence in daughters than in sons. However, in middle-class families, whether EC or FC, both parents are more restrictive toward sons than toward daughters who bid for independence. On the autonomy issue, then, the II families are more working-class in orientation, and somewhat more FC than EC. Apparently all three working-class groups, EC, FC, and II, are more bothered than middle-class parents are about the child's desire to act on his/her own. Our guess here is that the II parents, like other European-based groups we have studied, may have their own special concerns about the social contacts a child makes when on his/her own, especially social contacts that take the child away from parental supervision.

Finally, there were several cross-national trends uncovered in this analysis, that is, trends that characterize all five parental groups, Canadians as well as Italian immigrants. We found, for example, that the II parents show the same bias against girls as the Canadian comparison groups do: in particular, all parental groups are harsher on socially aggressive girls than on socially aggressive boys. Apart from their overall distinctiveness in willingness to extend help, the II parents are otherwise like the Canadian groups, in that mothers in all groups are more ready to help than are fathers. Furthermore, all parental groups show same-sex favoritism in their willingness to extend help. The II fathers are also similar to Canadian fathers in their tendencies to be harsher than mothers on children's bids for attention or for comfort. And finally, II parents are like Canadians in the sense that fathers in all cases tend to perceive more sex-role differences than do mothers.

In brief, this analysis has permitted us to view the child-rearing values of II parents in relation to those of various Canadian-born parental groups. Over and above the distinctive features of the II value system that emerged, perhaps the most important outcome is the finding that the values of II parents overlap as much or more with those of FC parents as they do with those of EC parents. This means that there are no grounds for II parents to feel self-conscious or uncomfortable about their ways of bringing up children in the Canadian society. On the contrary, they have the advantage of being able to draw on numerous patterns of value overlaps as a means of relating to both of Canada's major ethnic groups, French Canadians as well as English Canadians. The findings also suggest that their range of comfort is potentially very broad since their child-rearing values are, from the Canadian perspective, as much middle-class as working-class in nature.

HIGHLIGHTS OF THE ITALIAN STUDY

In Part I when we compared Italian Homeland and English Canadian parents, we found one set of differences on the "aid" scales and another on the "discipline" scales. It turned out that Italian Homeland parents were much more ready than Anglo-Canadians to give their children help when requested and much more compliant on guest privileges. To us, these strong and unambiguous national differences reflect basic contrasts in the ways the two groups interpret their roles as parents, as though EC parents consider help giving and guest visits more as issues to be used to inculcate self-sufficiency and self-entertainment, while IH parents see helpfulness as a way of developing close affectional ties within the family and guest visits as a way of strengthening a closer sense of community or extended family. It is not the case that IH parents are more lenient across the board, for they are as harsh as EC parents when a child clamors for attention or for comfort. Thus, children in both groups are discouraged from being pesty or soft-skinned.

When it comes to discipline, however, the IH parents are in certain respects harsher disciplinarians, as in the case of child-baby disputes. But, they are selectively harsh, suggesting to us that their purpose is to channel or direct the child's impulses in distinctive ways, blocking aggression directed toward siblings or peers, but letting it pass more freely toward material things and toward parents themselves. There is, then, more selectivity in the use of discipline among IH than EC parents, and the distinctive IH modes of channeling a child's aggressivity—giving relatively more legitimacy to certain forms—may at the same time highlight the more forbidden forms.

Interestingly, differences in the social-class backgrounds of parents played a more substantial role in the reactions of EC than IH parents. In Italy, then, there seem to be social rules about treating naughtiness that are more pervasive than in Anglo-Canada, where working-class parents take a much more severe stance than middle-class parents, who seem more prone to treat misbehavior with more reserve and "psychological" understanding.

On our measure of independence training, the IH parents are generally more restrictive and protective than their EC counterparts, and this emerges as another unambiguous national contrast in values.

There was an equally interesting contrast in the attitudes of IH and EC parents toward sex-roles: IH parents expect more sex-role differentiations than they perceive, suggesting that IH parents may maintain this discrepancy because it could help stave off further obliteration of the sex roles. But there were a number of cross-national similarities on the sex-role matter that complicate this cultural contrast. Thus, working-class parents, whether IH or EC, expect and perceive more sex-role differences than do middle-class parents, and fathers, both IH and EC, expect and perceive more differences than do mothers. Since we have encountered these same trends in so many other national settings, we wonder whether there may be universal tendencies among lower-status parents to be more concerned about the erosion of male-female differences in behavior. Perhaps males are particularly concerned about the obliteration of sex-role differences, for in this essentially male-privileged world, they may stand to lose power. But why is it that working-class parents, IH or EC, seem more concerned about boys losing their male identity, while middle-class parents from both cultures seem more concerned about girls maintaining their femininity? These questions, which emerge directly from the results of our study, strike us as fascinating topics for further research.

In Part II where we were particularly interested in value changes and resistances to change, we compared the reactions of

Italian Homeland and Italian Immigrant parents, restricting ourselves to comparable groups of working-class parents from each
setting. Interestingly, there were numerous examples of both value
change and value persistence, throwing a good deal of new light on
the problems immigrants face in trying to adjust to a new society.
The instances of resistance to change are especially instructive.
On the help giving issue, the II parents are as distinctively Italian
as the IH parents; if anything, more so. Rather than moving toward
the less helpful EC norm, the II parents seem to exaggerate help
giving beyond that of the IH parents, and this exaggeration, we
reasoned, could survive in the New World because it would likely
increase within-family solidarity which could be particularly comforting to working-class immigrant families. Distinctively Italian
values hold up as well on other issues: II parents take just as
forceful a position against child-baby or child-guest fighting as IH
parents do, and they are just as harsh as IH parents on children
who seek parental attention. II parents also maintain as liberal and
as receptive a policy on guest visiting as do the IH parents. In addition, we found cross-sex leniency to prevail for both IH and II parents on the guest privilege issue, meaning that for both Italian
groups, mothers are more favorable to sons who request guest
privileges than to daughters, while fathers are more favorable to
daughters than to sons.

The distinctively Italian reluctance to encourage independence,
which we found in the earlier IH-EC comparisons, holds up as well
for the II parents. This clear-cut contrast between Italian and
Anglo-Canadian parents on such a theoretically important matter
as independence training has been documented by other researchers
studying Italians in America.

There are no changes either in the ways Italian fathers and
mothers play their separate or complementary roles in the socialization of their six-year-olds. For example, Italian fathers,
whether IH or II, are more helpful than Italian mothers, less harsh
on child-baby quarrels or social temper outbursts, but harsher than
Italian mothers on the comfort issue.

For us as researchers, it is exciting to learn that Italian immigrant parents retain so much of their Italianness in the Canadian
scene and to be able to discover which features of values show this
resistance to change. Just as interesting, though, is the discovery
of particular values that show the influence of life in the new setting.
Most evident are changes in the "old-country" tendency to let children aggress through temper displays and insolence. These clearly
change in the direction of EC parental norms, and this may be so
because insolence or destructiveness might, if made public enough,
stand out in Canada as extremely odd ways for children to behave.

Italian immigrant parents also temper their sex-role expectations, bringing them in line with the expectations of EC parents. Apparently, II parents feel that they should, for the social comfort of their children in Canada, make these adjustments to local norms.

Finally, we see the beginnings of a change in the Italian attitude of discouraging children's bids for independence, even though, as mentioned above, the overall attitude does not change. What happens is that II mothers and fathers disagree in their approaches to a child's requests for autonomy and the disagreement shows up in the form of same-sex leniency: II fathers favor sons who request autonomy over daughters, while II mothers favor daughters over sons. We argued that the beginnings of change in this important value domain may cause tension in II families, which could manifest itself in this interesting form of disagreement. Might it be that most changes in child-rearing values evolve through a stage of disagreement of this sort? But why would the change be characterized by same-sex leniency? Do parents think of the same-sex-child as a more responsible agent of change?

In Part III we were able to get another perspective on the values of II parents. We needed to go further if we wanted to have a good idea just how distinctive or odd the child-rearing values of Italian immigrants are in the eyes of members of the host community. As it turned out, on all of our value dimensions except one, the II values overlap with those of at least one of the Canadian comparison groups. The one exception was the help giving dimension, and here the lenient II parents remain distinctive. Furthermore, although the II parents come from working-class backgrounds in Italy and work at the "working-class" occupational levels here in Canada, their child-rearing values are in general as similar to those of middle-class Canadians as they are to those of working-class Canadians. What is more, in terms of child-rearing values, the II parents are more similar to FCs than to ECs. The value overlap, in fact, is most pronounced with FC middle-class parents, for II parents are similar to FCMC parents on all value dimensions except three: help giving (in which case the II parents are the most willing to help of all groups), insolence control (where they are distinctive because of their surprisingly strong tendency to use physical punishment), and the perception of sex-role differences (where they have distinctively higher scores than the Canadians). The particularly close similarity with FC parents may reflect the influence of religious values since both the II and FC parents are Catholic while the EC parents are Protestant. But there may be more to it than religion. The close alignment with middle-class Canadian values may signify that those Italians who immigrate separate themselves from Italy in two respects, physically from the homeland as place of residence and psychologically from the socioeconomic status they held in the homeland. In other words, they may have arrived in Canada with aspirations toward middle-class standards and norms that could help them move up to middle-class occupational levels in Canada.

There were other signs, derived from interactions, of a greater alignment of II parents with FC than with EC parents. On the child-baby dispute issue, II and FC patterns are much more alike in that mothers in both cases are equally as severe as fathers; this is not so for EC families. With respect to sex roles, II parents are much like FC working-class parents, in that fathers in both cases seem more vigilant and more preoccupied with sex-role differences than are mothers. Furthermore, in both II and FC families, parents of girls have greater sex-role expectations than do parents of boys, while in EC families the reverse is true. Thus, II and FC parents seem more concerned about their daughters losing femininity, while EC parents seem more concerned about sons losing masculinity.

On the autonomy issue, the II parents are like both the FC and EC working-class parents in that they are much more likely than middle-class parents to discourage bids for autonomy, as though they were concerned about a child venturing out on his or her own where parental supervision is more difficult to maintain. Interestingly, the pattern for all three working-class groups—II, FC, and EC—is characterized by same-sex leniency. Perhaps parents believe that a same-sexed child is ready for independence earlier than the opposite-sexed child?

Finally, we uncovered an interesting series of examples where all five parental groups, Canadians as well as Italian immigrants, have similar reactions. These include: (a) a cross-national tendency for parents to be harsher with girls who show signs of social aggressivity than with boys; (b) a general tendency for mothers to be more ready than fathers to give help, which is strengthened by a cross-national trend of same-sex leniency that helps determine which child gets more help; (c) a general tendency for fathers to be more severe than mothers, with children who clamor for attention or comfort; and (d) a general tendency for fathers to perceive more instances of boy-girl differences in behavior than do mothers. The important point to keep in mind with regard to these cross-national trends, is that the orientations of the II parents are in no sense odd or distinctive.

In brief, we feel we have gained a new perspective of Italian immigrant parents when we see them in relation to various groups of native-born Canadians. We have been able to tease out certain distinctive characteristics of the II parents' values, and this has been both interesting and instructive for us. Equally instructive, is the finding that the child-rearing values of II parents overlap in so many ways with those of native-born Canadians. Part of this overlap is traceable to value adjustments made by II parents since leaving the old country, while part is due to basic similarities between old-country and new-country ways of treating children. What is exciting about this is that II parents seem to have evolved a set of values that permits them to make comfortable and compatible social contacts with all sorts of Canadians—French or English, working-class or middle-class.

10

GREEK APPROACHES TO CHILD REARING

There were several reasons for wanting Greece represented in our sample of national groups, aside from the fact that Western-style conceptions of society began there. Today Greece is an active center for behavioral research, providing us with rich, cross-national information on the social psychology of Greek people (for example, Triandis, Vassiliou, and Nassiakou 1968; Triandis et al. 1972; Triandis and Triandis 1969). In addition, large numbers of Greek people have come and are still coming to North America to settle.

We selected Canada rather than the United States as our North American reference group because Canada is presently one of the most active receiving nations for immigrants in the world and because immigrants to Canada have a choice of two societies to refer to, one English-based, the other French-based. Greek immigrants to the province of Quebec typically align themselves and their families, through choice of residence site and school district, more with the English Canadian than the French Canadian society, but as we shall see, they have to adjust as well to many aspects of the French Canadian world around them.

As in the Italian study, we start with Greek homeland parents, each having a six-year-old child, and we compare their approaches to child rearing with those of English Canadian parents of similar social class and educational backgrounds. The orienting question is: How do the Greek and the Anglo-Canadian approaches to child rearing compare? Do they have basically different conceptions of parenthood and childhood, or are there overlaps of perspective that might cushion the adjustments of immigrants? Then we examine what happens to Greek immigrants who have settled in Canada and started their own families. Here we ask ourselves: Do Greek immigrants

remain Greek, or do they adjust and modify their child-rearing
values? If so, are the changes in the direction of French Canadian
or English Canadian norms?

A DESCRIPTION OF THE GREEK HOMELAND PARENTS

The Greek Homeland (GH) parents all lived in or close to the
city of Athens. Samples of working-class and middle-class families were drawn; their background characteristics are given in
Table A 10.1, and these can be compared with similar data for our
English Canadian samples, presented in Table A 2.1. The working-
class groups are well matched in terms of fathers' occupations, although Greek fathers and mothers have slightly less education than
their Canadian counterparts. At the middle-class level, the educational differences are more pronounced, averaging two and a half
years of schooling. The occupations are also different since most
of the Canadians are in business-managerial positions while most
of the Greeks are in white-collar positions. Our Greek informants
thought that this difference was representative of young, middle-
class Greek families because in Greece managerial positions are
normally attained through seniority while in Canada such positions
are often available to men still in their thirties.

PART I: A COMPARISON OF GREEK AND
ENGLISH CANADIAN PARENTS

National-Group Comparisons

The large number of statistically significant contrasts between
EC and GH parents summarized in Tables 10.1 and A 10.2 point to
fundamental differences in child-rearing approaches. Our interpretation of these differences—and here we may well reveal a North
American bias—is that EC parents are more intent than GH parents
to develop self-reliance and resourcefulness in their children. We
say this because we found that EC parents were more inclined than
GH parents to withhold gestures of helping, were less likely to get
involved in child-baby disputes, were less likely to encourage guest
privileges (which could make a child dependent on playmates as
sources of entertainment), and were more likely to encourage a
child's bids for autonomy. At the same time, EC parents were less
inclined than GH parents to let outbursts of temper or insolence
pass without sanctions of some sort. Thus, by way of contrast, the
GH parents emerge as those who encourage more dependence on

TABLE 10.1

Significant Effects in the Comparisons of English Canadian and Greek Homeland Parents

Value Dimensions

Comparisons	1) Help Withholding (np = 58.6)	2) Siding with Baby vs. Child (np = 42.7)	3a) Temper Control (np = 30.0)	3b) Social Temper Control (np = 41.6)	4) Insolence Control (np = 25.0)	5) Attention Denial (np = 75.0)	6) Comfort Withholding (np = 41.6)	7) Autonomy Control (np = 58.3)	8) Guest Restriction (np = 62.5)	9) Siding with Guest vs. Child (np = 42.7)	10) Perceived Sex-Role Differences	11) Expected Sex-Role Differences
G	40.00	9.49	6.20	–	29.35	–	–	22.48	38.29	–	8.84	15.96
C	–	22.28	8.84	14.55	42.77	4.28	–	–	–	14.78	6.26	17.93
X	–	–	–	–	–	7.32	–	–	–	–	–	–
P	–	5.55	–	–	–	–	–	–	–	–	6.00	–
GC	–	18.14	–	10.36	15.00	–	–	–	5.45	6.31	4.79	–
GX	–	–	–	–	–	–	–	–	–	9.04	–	7.93
CX	–	–	–	–	–	–	–	–	–	7.81	–	4.88
GP	–	13.84	–	–	4.62	–	6.37	–	–	–	–	–
CP	–	–	–	–	–	–	–	–	6.27	–	–	6.64
XP	–	–	–	–	–	–	–	–	–	–	–	–
GCX	–	–	–	–	–	–	–	–	–	–	–	–
GCP	–	–	–	–	–	–	4.30	–	–	–	–	–
GXP	–	–	–	–	–	–	–	–	–	–	–	–
CXP	–	–	–	–	–	–	–	–	–	–	–	–
GCXP	–	–	–	–	–	–	–	–	–	–	–	6.74

Note: Entries are significant F values; those underlined are beyond the .01 level of confidence, the others are beyond the .05 level.
Source: Compiled by the authors.

235

parents, and the parent role becomes more that of an indulgent
guardian in GH than EC families. This description, incidentally,
jibes well with that of Triandis and Triandis (1969) who argue that
"within the family, the (Greek) child is indulged, protected and
constantly loved and petted" (p. 34) .

The fact that GH parents tolerate relatively more insolence
and temper displays is intriguing to us, for, from our North American perspectives, such displays "naturally" provoke harsh parental
reactions. On reflection, however, we see that there could be much
value in the GH approach, for in letting insolence and temper pass
without applying heavyweight punishment, the GH parents protect
themselves from being aggressive models in the eyes of their children, and in the long run their approach could effectively reduce
children's temper and insolence tendencies. Furthermore, they
might be able to make good use of the fact that they were the brunt
of the child's insolence and temper outbursts, especially if the child
felt guilty because of her/his aggressiveness.

The EC-GH contrasts are attributable more to certain subgroups of parents than others. Thus, on the insolence issue, the
EC working-class parents are particularly harsh, whereas for the
GH parents, social class has little effect (Figure A 10.1). Furthermore EC fathers are particularly severe, which contrasts with the
Greek pattern where GH fathers are less severe than GH mothers
(Figure A 10.2). For guest privileges, EC working-class parents
are more restrictive than EC middle-class parents, which is the
reverse of the GH pattern (Figure 10.1). Finally, on the child-baby
dispute issue, the EC mothers stand out as the most lenient subgroup of all (Figure A 10.3).

Social-Class Background Effects

Social-class background affects parents' reactions to children
in very similar ways in English Canadian and Greek Homeland settings, even though social class has a somewhat greater influence on
EC than GH parents (see Figures A 10.1; A 10.5; and A 10.7). However, in both settings, working-class parents are consistently more
punitive and severe than middle-class parents, a finding noted in
most (but not all) of the other national comparisons discussed in
other chapters. There are, in fact, five instances where this generalized social-class difference shows through, and all five are
episodes calling for discipline: the child-baby and child-guest disputes, temper, social temper, and insolence. We, again, interpret
this trend to mean that working-class parents may be particularly
concerned or anxious when children fail to control aggression and

FIGURE 10.1

G x C Interaction for Guest Restrictions

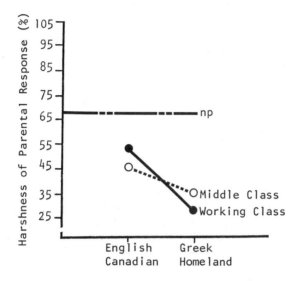

Source: Constructed by the authors.

emotions, because they may see servility and self-control as requirements of working-class status. To the extent that they are
sensitive to unchecked aggressivity, we would expect working-class
parents to react more harshly to such episodes, realizing, too,
that they would be presenting their children with more aggressive
parental models. In contrast, the less concerned middle-class parents would present their children with more patient, "cool" parental
models.

Social-class background also affects parents' reactions when
the child asks to have a guest in to play, and its effects are different in English Canada and Greece (see Figure 10.1). Thus, EC
working-class parents are less compliant toward guest privileges
than EC middle-class parents, whereas GH working-class parents
are more compliant than GH middle-class parents. This interplay
of ethnicity and social class on the matter of guests is interesting
even though we are unable to explain why certain subgroups—the
EC middle class and the GH working class—are more receptive to
the visits of playmates than others.

Treatment Given Sons and Daughters

Both EC and GH parents are harsher on girls than on boys when the child seeks <u>attention</u>, and since we have found the same trend in several other national comparisons already described, we begin to wonder why it has cross-national generality. In contrast, there is an important national-group difference on the <u>child-guest dispute</u> issue, since EC girls are treated more harshly than EC boys while GH girls are treated less harshly than GH boys (see Figure A 10.6). The implication is that masculine aggressivity is taken more lightly by EC than GH parents.

Mother-Father Comparisons

For one subset of episodes, mothers and fathers, whether EC or GH, differ in their reactions to children in an interesting way: fathers are more severe than mothers when children disturb the peace and quiet of the home with <u>child-baby disputes</u> or <u>requests for attention</u>, but are less severe than mothers when a commotion arises because of a <u>child-guest</u> dispute. Thus, socialization responsibilities seem to pass from mothers to fathers, depending upon the episode, for example, a child-sibling quarrel versus a child-guest quarrel. In order to minimize parental wrath, then, children in both settings would have to learn to regulate behavior and misbehavior according to which parent was present.

The statistical interactions indicate that there are more instances of mother-father differences in EC than in GH families. For example, EC fathers are more severe than EC mothers on child-baby disputes and comfort requests, whereas GH parents are more alike in their reactions. There is also somewhat more mother involvement, possibly more mother domination, in the child-rearing process in Greece than in English Canada (see Figures 10.2; 10.3; A 10.2; and A 10.3). Finally, on the guest privilege issue, middle-class fathers, both EC and GH, are more inclined to encourage their children to rely on themselves for entertainment, whereas middle-class mothers seem more inclined to encourage guest visits (see Figure 10.4).

Sex-Role Perceptions and Expectations

EC and GH parents have basically different views on how similar boys and girls should be and how similar they actually are. For instance, GH parents expect greater differentiation in the

FIGURE 10.2

G x P Interaction for Comfort Withholding

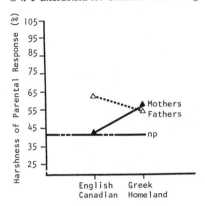

Source: Constructed by the authors.

FIGURE 10.3

G x C x P Interaction for Comfort Withholding

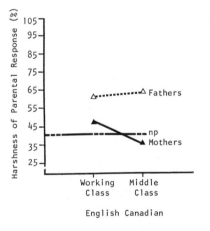

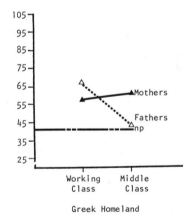

English Canadian

Greek Homeland

Source: Constructed by the authors.

239

FIGURE 10.4

C x P Interaction for Guest Restrictions

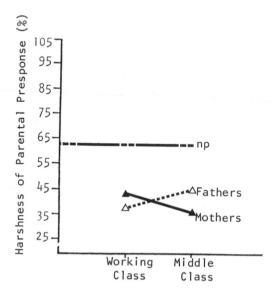

Source: Constructed by the authors.

conduct of boys and girls, and they notice more instances of sex-specific forms of comportment than do EC parents. This interesting national difference could mean many things. Perhaps boys and girls actually do maintain sex-role identities more in Greece than in English Canada. Or perhaps parents see pretty much what they want to see; since GH parents expect greater sex-role differentiation than EC parents, their perceptions may be influenced by their expectations.

We also found that social-class background affects parents' perceptions of sex-role differences, and it is the middle-class parents, especially the EC middle class, who perceive relatively few instances of boy-girl differences in comportment. Furthermore, fathers perceive more sex-role differences than mothers, suggesting that in these two cultural settings fathers may be more attentive than mothers to the sex-role identities of their children and possibly more worried that these identities might become blurred (see Figure A 10.7).

Finally, we found that parents' sex-role expectations are colored by a combination of factors—ethnicity, social class, sex of child, and sex of parents (see Figures 10.5; 10.6; A 10.8; and A 10.9). For instance, GH parents have generally higher sex-role expectations than EC parents do, but it is the EC middle-class parents, EC mothers in particular, who contributed most to this EC-GH difference because their sex-role expectations are curiously low. Our speculation is that trends toward unisexism in English Canada might well be a middle-class phenomenon, sustained by middle-class parents, especially mothers. Consonant with this notion is the finding that EC fathers seem more concerned than mothers about the sex-role identities of their children, while in GH families mothers are as concerned as fathers.

FIGURE 10.5

G x X Interaction for Expected Sex-Role Differences

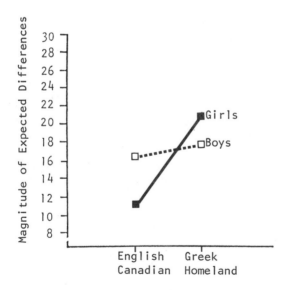

Source: Constructed by the authors.

FIGURE 10.6

G x C x X x P Interaction for Expected Sex-Role Differences

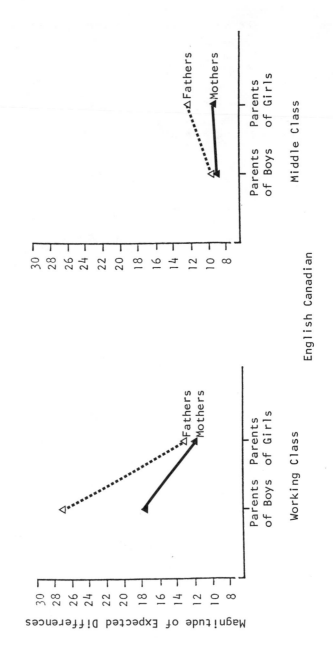

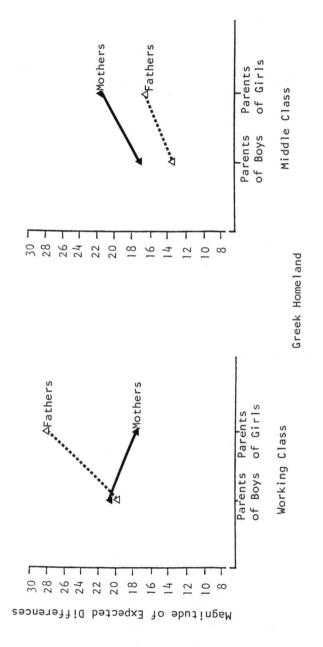

Magnitude of Expected Differences

Parents Parents
of Boys of Girls

Working Class

Parents Parents
of Boys of Girls

Middle Class

Greek Homeland

Source: Constructed by the authors.

243

What is more, EC parents seem particularly concerned about the sex-role identity of girls. This national-group difference is especially clear at the working-class level. The impression we get from this pattern is that a concern of EC working-class fathers of boys revolves around the possibility that their sons might drift away from masculine conduct, as though these fathers believe that to survive in the working-class milieu in Canada, sons must be masculine. Daughters, in contrast, should not be too "feminine" or "dainty." GH working-class fathers, interestingly enough, seem to be concerned about daughters drifting away from traditional feminine norms of conduct, and they are relatively less concerned about their sons' sex-role identity, perhaps because in Greece a working-class son has few real chances of drifting away from thoroughly masculine roles.

Working-class GH mothers seem to place much less emphasis on this issue than fathers do, as though a change of the traditional female role would not be all that unpleasant to contemplate. Instead, it is the middle-class GH mothers who are particularly concerned about the sex-role identity of daughters, making them the more conservative subgroup and the ones who might be called on to combat a change of status for women, a movement that might well emanate from the working class.

PART II: A COMPARISON OF GREEK IMMIGRANT
AND GREEK HOMELAND PARENTS

After determining certain basic differences in child-rearing values, we wondered whether Greek child-rearing values would change when Greek adults immigrated to Canada and started their families there. Would the move from Greece to Canada radically change the immigrant's system of child-rearing values? Which values might be especially vulnerable to the change and which might be especially resistant to change? These questions directed our thinking in this section where we compare two groups of working-class parents, one from Greece (the GH working-class parents already described) and the other Greek Immigrant (GI) parents living in Montreal.

A Description of the Greek Immigrant Parents

The Greek immigrant working-class families were interviewed in Montreal by two Greek-Canadian interviewers. The sample comprised husband and wife pairs, both members born in Greece, with an average of ten years of residence in Canada, and with a six-year-old Canadian-born child. Their background characteristics are given in Table A 10.3, and these can be compared with comparable data for the GH parents, given in Table A 10.1. The occupations for the two working-class samples had, on the average, about a year less education than their counterparts still living in Greece. However, in terms of general demographic characteristics, the two samples are well balanced.

PART II: RESULTS—GREEK IMMIGRANTS
AND GREEKS AT HOME

The statistical results for these comparisons are presented in Tables 10.2 and A 10.4, and in Figures 10.7 and 10.8. Note first that there are very few differences in the reactions of GH and GI parents and, thus, few symptoms of "change" on the part of the GI parents that can be attributed to their Canadian experiences. Of the five statistically significant entries in the tables, only three reflect differences between GH and GI families. The other two—indicating that mothers are harsher than fathers on the child-guest dispute issues and that fathers have higher sex-role perception scores than mothers—hold for Greeks at home as well as for Greeks in Canada.

What then are the three GH-GI contrasts? First, there is a group difference on the child-guest dispute issue, and in this case it turns out that GI parents are less severe than GH parents in their reactions to this sort of social aggressivity. If we assume that the difference represents a change toward more leniency on the part of GI parents as they become acculturated to Canada, one wonders what the nature of this change might be. It does not represent a drift toward EC working-class norms, for the EC working-class parents are as severe as the GH parents on the child-guest dispute issue (see Table A 10.2). However, it could represent a drift toward Canadian middle-class norms, for both EC and FC middle-class parents are relatively lenient on most discipline issues and on this issue in particular (see Table 2.4 in Chapter 2). It could be, then, that our GI parents, indisputably working class, take middle-class Canadian parents as their frame of reference on this particular issue. Because the disciplining of children is often a very public event, immigrants have many occasions to learn that "proper" parents refrain from public displays of discipline, in contrast to "ordinary" folk who are more inclined to punish children right out in the open.

TABLE 10.2

Significant Effects in the Comparisons of Greek Immigrant and Greek Homeland Working–Class Parents

Value Dimensions

Comparisons	1) Help Withholding (np = 58.6)	2) Siding with Baby vs. Child (np = 42.7)	3a) Temper Control (np = 30.0)	3b) Social Temper Control (np = 41.6)	4) Insolence Control (np = 25.0)	5) Attention Denial (np = 75.0)	6) Comfort Withholding (np = 41.6)	7) Autonomy Control (np = 58.3)	8) Guest Restriction (np = 62.5)	9) Siding with Guest vs. Child (np = 42.7)	10) Perceived Sex-Role Differences	11) Expected Sex-Role Differences
G	—	—	—	—	—	—	—	—	—	4.55	—	—
X	—	—	—	—	—	—	—	—	—	—	—	—
P	—	—	—	—	—	—	—	—	—	<u>7.83</u>	<u>19.86</u>	—
GX	—	—	—	—	—	4.22	—	—	—	—	—	—
GP	—	—	—	—	—	—	—	—	—	—	—	—
XP	—	—	—	—	—	—	—	—	—	—	—	—
GXP	—	—	—	—	—	—	—	—	—	—	—	<u>7.95</u>

Note: Entries are significant F values; those underlined are at the .01 level of confidence, the others are at the .05 level.
Source: Compiled by the authors.

246

FIGURE 10.7

G x X Interaction for Attention Denial

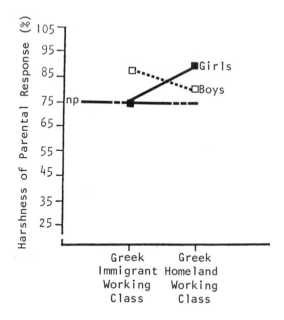

Source: Constructed by the authors.

There is also a change on the <u>attention denial</u> scale, but it is difficult to explain. In Figure 10.7 we find that in GI families, attention-seeking <u>boys</u> are treated more severely than attention-seeking girls, while in GH families, attention-seeking <u>girls</u> are treated more harshly than attention-seeking boys. If this reflects a change on the part of GI parents, it is not a drift toward a Canadian norm, for neither EC nor FC parents show a similar pattern (see Table 2.4, Chapter 2). Both EC and FC parents are harsher on attention-seeking <u>girls</u> than on attention-seeking boys. Thus, this "change" in the GI pattern remains a mystery for us.

We have better luck in interpreting the complex pattern for <u>sex-role expectancy</u> scores, depicted in Figure 10.11. The major contrast is between the sex-role expectations of mothers and fathers: GH fathers of girls have higher sex-role expectations than GH mothers of girls, while GH mothers of boys have higher sex-role expectations than do GH fathers of boys. The pattern is reversed for GI parents, since GI mothers of girls have higher sex-role expectations than GI fathers of girls, while GI fathers of boys have

FIGURE 10.8

G x X x P Interaction for Expected Sex-Role Differences

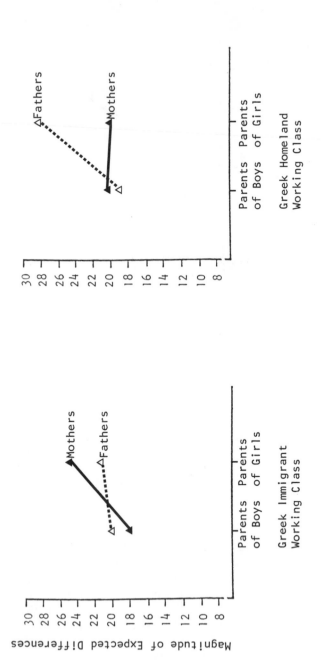

Source: Constructed by the authors.

higher sex-role expectations than GI mothers of boys. This distinctive GI pattern, which reflects a concern for the sex-role identity of the same-sex child, does not match the corresponding EC patterns, either EC working class or middle class, but, interestingly enough, it matches very well the FC patterns, both working class and middle class. In other words, the sex-role expectations of GI mothers and fathers are definitely different from those of GH parents, but surprisingly similar to those of FC mothers and fathers. Apparently, then, there are two particular issues—sex-role expectations and the management of disputes with a guest—that are the first to give way to influences of the Canadian setting. On balance, though, there really are very few signs of value change reflected here, which means that the GI parents have remained, at least up to this point in their residence in Canada, pretty much Greek in their orientations toward children.

This is not the first example we have encountered of immigrants holding on to their distinctive homeland styles of child rearing. For instance, in an earlier chapter we found that French Canadian immigrants to the United States also stayed surprisingly French Canadian in their approaches to children, although they too showed subtle signs of beginning to adjust their values in an American direction. This is also the case for Japanese immigrants to Canada, as we shall see in Chapter 12. Nevertheless, in the present case, we have uncovered a few clues as to how Greek immigrants to Canada make very subtle adjustments to the Canadian society that surrounds them. What is intriguing is that, in the few instances where there seems to be a change in values, the GI parents seem to be modeling more on Canadian middle-class than working-class child-rearing values and on FC values as much as or more than on EC values. Thus, GI parents are less punitive than GH parents in their treatment of social aggressiveness, and the direction of the change is toward the relatively more lenient EC and FC middle-class parents. And then there is a shift in the sex-role expectations of GI parents away from a GH pattern toward a FC rather than an EC pattern. The pattern itself is fascinating because it turns out that GI and FC mothers have particularly high sex-role expectations for their daughters, while GI and FC fathers have particularly high sex-role expectations for their sons. All told, then, GI families are apparently susceptible to influences from both EC and FC societies, and particularly from the middle-class strata of these societies.

PART III: A COMPARISON OF GREEK IMMIGRANT,
ENGLISH CANADIAN, AND FRENCH CANADIAN PARENTS

Although we have found relatively few differences between the
GH and GI working-class groups of parents in their orientations toward children and, therefore, few signs of value change, important
questions still remain. Which Canadian society—the French or the
English—is more like the Greek society in terms of child-rearing
values? How different are the child-rearing values of Greek working-
class immigrants from those of Canadian middle-class parents?
Might there be a particularly favorable route toward social adjustment and upward mobility available in Canada to Greek immigrants?

With these questions in mind, we will explore in this section
various degrees of value compatibility by comparing the child-
rearing values of GI parents with those of English and French Canadian parents of both working- and middle-class status. Five groups
are involved: Greek immigrant parents of working-class background
(GI), English Canadian working-class parents (ECWC), French
Canadian working-class parents (FCWC), English Canadian middle-
class parents (ECMC), and French Canadian middle-class parents
(FCMC). When the background characteristics of all five groups
are compared, we find that hardly any of the working-class parents
had completed high school, which means that all three working-class
groups of fathers had the same disadvantage in the Montreal job
market. Most held skilled or unskilled blue-collar positions. The
two middle-class samples stand in sharp contrast both educationally
and occupationally, so that, on the basis of demographic characteristics, there is no reason to expect the child-rearing values of GI
parents to overlap with those of either EC or FC middle-class parents.

PART III: RESULTS—GREEK PARENTS VERSUS
ENGLISH AND FRENCH CANADIAN PARENTS

From the statistical information given in Tables 10.3 and
A 10.5, one sees immediately that there are very many group differences. In fact, group differences of one sort or another appear
on all but two scales, attention denial and comfort withholding, and
in both cases, all five groups tend to withhold the attention and comfort sought by the child. Otherwise, there are significant differences involving at least two of the five parental groups for every
other scale, and these are diagramed in Table A 10.6.

TABLE 10.3

Significant Effects in the Comparisons of English Canadian Working- and Middle-Class, French Canadian Working- and Middle-Class, and Greek Immigrant Parents

Value Dimensions

Comparisons	1) Help Withholding (np = 58.6)	2) Siding with Baby vs. Child (np = 42.7)	3a) Temper Control (np = 30.0)	3b) Social Temper Control (np = 41.6)	4) Insolence Control (np = 25.0)	5) Attention Denial (np = 75.0)	6) Comfort Withholding (np = 41.6)	7) Autonomy Control (np = 58.3)	8) Guest Restriction (np = 62.5)	9) Siding with Guest vs. Child (np = 42.7)	10) Perceived Sex-Role Differences	11) Expected Sex-Role Differences
G	4.29	12.81	6.22	12.77	17.92	–	–	6.33	12.69	11.63	6.65	7.43
X	–	–	–	5.66	–	10.95	–	–	–	8.20	–	–
P	–	–	–	–	–	–	–	–	–	8.61	8.63	–
GX	–	–	–	–	–	–	–	–	–	–	–	2.80
GP	–	4.15	–	–	–	–	–	–	–	–	3.77	–
XP	–	–	–	5.52	–	–	–	–	–	–	–	–
GXP	–	–	–	–	–	–	–	–	–	–	–	–

Note: Entries are significant F values; those underlined are beyond the .01 level of confidence, the others are beyond the .05 level.
Source: Compiled by the authors.

251

Parental Reactions to Children's Requests for Help

Although all five groups of parents tend to give aid when the child requests it, the amount and immediacy of the help given varies from group to group. GI and FC parents tend to be fairly indulgent, whereas EC parents, both working and middle class, are less generous with their aid. Although the GI parents, the most lenient group of all, are more like FC than EC parents, there is no evidence of an adjustment of GI values to an FC form of help giving, because the help-giving tendency of GI parents is no different from that of their working-class countrymen still in Greece. Instead, what we have is evidence for a value overlap between French Canadian and Greek parents, GI or GH, rather than a value change.

When we examine the actual reactions of parents to the child's requests for help, we find that the strategies of the GI parents are qualitatively different from those of Canadian parents (see Tables A 10.7 to A 10.9). In general, GI parents tend more to give direct and immediate help, whereas Canadian parents first delay, and when they finally comply, they offer only partial help while encouraging self-help.

Parental Reactions to the Child-Baby Squabble

All five parental groups take some disciplinary measure to control child-baby squabbles, but the harshness of the control measures varies greatly; for example, all three working-class groups, GI, EC, and FC, are significantly harsher than either the EC or the FC middle-class groups. In addition, the EC groups, both working and middle class, are distinctive because fathers are significantly harsher than mothers in disciplining the child, and there are no corresponding father-mother differences for the GI, the FCWC, or the FCMC groups (see Figure 10.9). Thus, on the child-baby dispute issue, the GI parents are more like FC parents, particularly FC working-class parents.

When we analyze parents' responses to the child-baby squabble, as in Table A 10.10, we find that for Canadian parents there is considerable variability in deciding when to intervene against the older child, while for GI parents, the child is perceived as wrong from the very beginning. The six-year-old Greek child may be indulged by his parents, but he is, nonetheless, expected to extend nurturance and tolerance to a younger sibling. Canadian parents may be less indulgent, but they do tolerate more aggressivity directed toward a younger sibling.

FIGURE 10.9

G x P Interaction for Siding with Baby versus Child

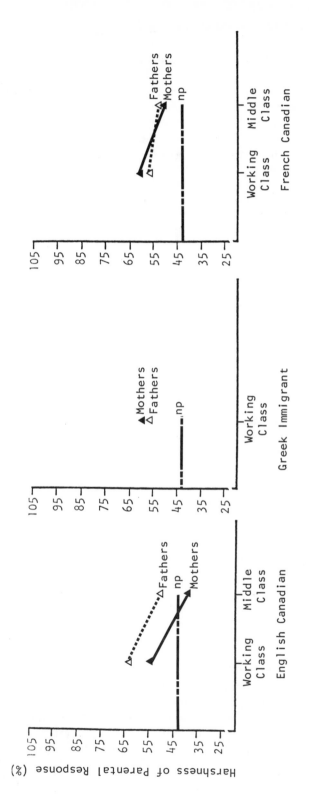

Source: Constructed by the authors.

Parental Reactions to Children's Temper Outbursts

Although all parental groups take steps to control temper outbursts, ECWC parents are more severe than any of the other groups.
The GI parents, the most lenient of all, are not statistically different from the FCWC, or either of the middle-class groups, nor, as
we saw in the last section, are they different from Greek Homeland
working-class parents. This, then, is a second instance where GI
parents react much like Canadian parents because of an overlap of
values of Canadian and Greek parents, Greeks living in Canada or
in Greece.

In Table A 10.11 we find that Canadian parents tend to respond
in kind by threatening the child ("You break it, and I'll warm your
bottom!" "If you do, it'll be the last game I buy you.") or by diverting the child, while GI parents use reprimands rather than counter-
threats: "You're a very bad child." "You shouldn't break toys."

Parental Reactions to Children's
Social Temper Displays

When the child's anger is directed toward a sibling or a playmate, parents in all five groups take steps to control the aggressive
impulses. GI parents, however, are significantly less harsh than
either the EC or FC working-class parents, making them much like
the mild-mannered EC and FC middle-class parents.

There are two interactions associated with social temper displays. The first tells us that GI parents, like Greek Homeland parents, make little distinction between boys and girls in handling
social temper, while Canadian parents are generally harsher with
girls. Once again, then, there is no evidence here of acculturation
on the part of the GI parents. Secondly, when a boy becomes socially aggressive, fathers generally are more tolerant than mothers,
whereas social aggressivity from girls generates no such mother-
father difference. This bias of fathers toward a son's aggressivity
holds for all five groups, including the GIs and the Greek Homeland
parents as well. Thus, there is again no evidence of value change
on the part of our GI parents.

When parents' reactions to the child's social aggressivity are
analyzed (see Tables A 10.12 and A 10.13), we again find that GI
parents typically use reprimands as their mode of control, while
Canadian parents use threats of punishment as well as reprimands.
Furthermore, the reactions of GI parents are essentially the same
whether the child's aggressivity is directed toward a sibling or a
guest, whereas EC and FC parents are more punitive when the child

threatens a guest than when he threatens a sibling. Perhaps this is a reflection of a more general Greek tendency to treat all ingroup members as family. According to Triandis and Triandis (1969), in Greece "the ingroup includes a person's relatives, friends, friends of friends, and guests. The outgroup is everyone else" (p. 33). Our Canadian parents, in contrast, seem to reflect a different outlook—that a guest is special and apart from family members.

Parental Reactions to Insolence

When the child's temper is directed toward the parents themselves, all parental groups take disciplinary steps, but the FC and EC working-class parents are much more harsh in their reactions than either the EC or the FC middle-class group or the GIs. Since the GI parents' scores on the insolence scale are almost identical to those of Greek Homeland working-class parents, what we have here is another instance of value overlap between Canadian middle-class and Greek working-class parents, rather than a shift toward Canadian middle-class norms.

Tables A 10.14 and A 10.15 break down parents' reactions to insolence, and we find that GI parents react to insolence mainly with reprimands; EC and FC working-class parents use more punishments and threats along with reprimands; and EC and FC middle-class parents are more inclined to divert the child. Incidentally, name calling ("You're stupid, Mommy/Daddy") provokes harsher reactions than a challenge to authority ("I'm gonna go anyway!"), for all five groups of parents.

Parental Reactions to the Child's
Requests for Autonomy

When a six-year-old makes a bid for independence ("It's not raining now, can I go across the street and play?"), the GI parents, as a group, discourage the child, whereas all four Canadian groups give one degree of encouragement or another. Still the GI parents are closer to EC and FC working-class parents (who tend to limit autonomy) than to EC and FC middle-class parents (who are much more encouraging). Since the GI and Greek Homeland parents are essentially the same in their reactions to autonomy, the GI group in this case did not change their values even though they are quite far off Canadian middle-class norms. In other words, in this instance they show a working-class tendency to restrict autonomy bids.

Parental Reactions to Requests for Guest Privileges

With more or less enthusiasm, all five parental groups comply with a child's request for guest privileges, and the GI parents
are clearly the most enthusiastic of all, followed closely by the
FCMC group (Table A 10.16). In contrast, the ECMC, ECWC, and
FCWC groups qualify their compliance with numerous cautions and
reminders about how children should behave with a visitor. Again,
there are no signs of a shift in the values of GI parents toward the
FCMC open-door policy because Greek Homeland parents are
equally hospitable (see Table 10.2).

Sex-Role Differentiations

GI parents have the highest sex-role perception score, meaning that of all groups they perceive more differences in the comportment of boys and girls. Since they are essentially like the
Greek Homeland parents in this respect, there is no evidence for
value change reflected here. Compared to the various Canadian
groups, their sex-role perceptions are most like those of ECWC
parents and least like those of the two middle-class groups (see
Table A 10.6 and Figure 10.10).
        The results are similar for sex-role expectations: GI parents
score highest, but again they are not essentially different from
Greek Homeland parents, and, thus, there is no value change indicated. Their sex-role expectations are more in line with those of
working-class than middle-class Canadian parents (see Table
A 10.6), and in their underlying structure, closer to those of FC
than EC parents (see Figure 10.11).
        Since GI parents, relative to ECs and FCs, expect quite dif-
ferent standards of conduct from boys, as compared to girls, and
since GI boys and girls apparently conform to these expectations,
we wondered if GI parents actually exaggerate son-daughter differences in their modes of interacting with children. To explore this
possibility, we computed "girl-boy difference scores" for each
group, subtracting the mean harshness-leniency score for parents
of boys from the comparable score for parents of girls. The absolute values were summed over the ten scales, so that the larger the
score, the greater the distinction parents make between sons and
daughters. From high to low, these were: ECMC = 68.37; ECWC
= 65.37; GIWC = 55.20; FCWC = 53.81; and FCMC = 49.46. What
this means is that the GI parents who are particularly prone to expect and perceive differences in the comportment of boys and girls,
are not at all inclined to react differentially to boys and girls. In

FIGURE 10.10

G x P Interaction for Perceived Sex-Role Differences

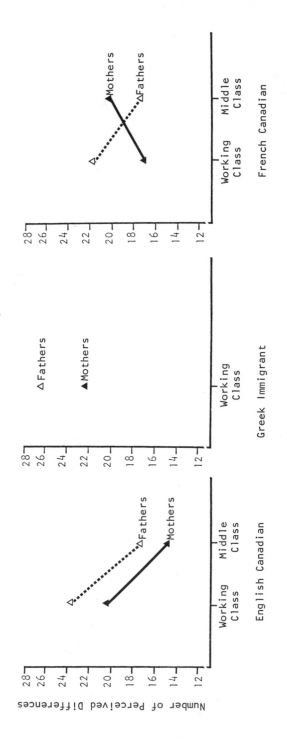

Source: Constructed by the authors.

FIGURE 10.11

G x X Interaction for Expected Sex-Role Differences

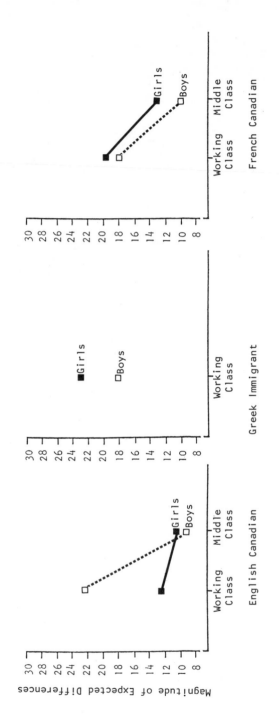

Source: Constructed by the authors.

fact, the GI parents are much more egalitarian in their approach to children than are either of the two EC groups, who by their reactions, seem to place more emphasis on sex-role differences. Furthermore, GI parents line up much closer to FC than EC working-class parents in this analysis.

To explore further these group differences in the emphasis placed on sex-roles, we calculated corresponding "mother-father difference scores," summed over the ten scales, indicating how similar mothers and fathers in each group are in their reactions to children. These scores are: ECMC = 84.44; ECWC = 72.80; GIWC = 59.57; FCWC = 53.91; and FCMC = 35.72. What this means is that GI parents present a very unified front, as mothers and fathers, to their children, much more so than the EC parents who play quite distinctive roles as mothers and fathers. Furthermore, the GI parents again line up much closer to FC than EC working-class parents in this analysis.

Overall, then, GI parents tend to expect relatively sharp sex-role differentiations, and perhaps because their expectations are matched closely by their perceptions of sex-role differences, they are able to react equitably to sons and daughters and to present a common, unified front in dealing with their children's misbehaviors and requests. Apparently, GI parents do not have to "shape" the behavior of boys and girls differentially in order to promote distinctive sex-role identities in their children; these identities appear to develop as expected. If parents don't do the shaping, we are now left with an intriguing question: What are the factors in Greek society that promote and assure distinctive sex-role identities among children?

GREEK APPROACHES TO CHILD
REARING: AN OVERVIEW

According to Triandis, the Greek child is "indulged, protected, and constantly loved and petted." This description of the Greek child led us to expect various contrasts between Greek and Canadian parents' child-rearing orientations, especially contrasts on matters of nurturance and discipline. We did indeed find national group differences touching on both nurturance and discipline and, interestingly enough, many of these are clearly in line with Triandis' views.

In certain respects, Greek and Canadian parents have very similar orientations. For instance, they both tend to hold back when a child clamors for comfort or attention. In other respects, however, they have quite different approaches to child rearing: they react quite differently to a child's request for help, to a child's request to have a playmate come into the house to play, and to a child's attempts to do something on his or her own. With regard to repeated requests for help, Greek parents tend to comply more quickly and fully, from the first request on. Canadian parents, in contrast, are more inclined to delay acting on the request, giving only partial help and urging the child to work things out for himself or herself. As we see it, the Canadian norm seems to turn more around encouraging the child to be self-sufficient and independent, while the Greek norm turns more around satisfying the child's wants. This we believe may be an important national contrast in values.

There are also striking national contrasts in the ways parents respond to a child's request to have a playmate come into the house. For instance, when we compare working-class samples of Greek, English Canadian, and French Canadian parents, the Canadian parental groups tend to qualify their compliance with numerous reminders of how the child should behave with a guest, whereas Greek parents, homelanders or immigrants to Canada, simply agree to the request for guest privileges, with no qualifications. It is also true that Greek parents are much more willing to have playmates come into the home, and we believe this relatively liberal attitude may stem from a more general tendency in Greek society to treat guests and friends as family members (Triandis 1969). Thus, if we view our children's friends much as we view our own children, there should be no reason to qualify or otherwise restrict interactions between our children and their playmates.

Although Greek parents seem to have a much more hospitable and open-door attitude toward playmates, they are nonetheless much less likely than Canadian parents to permit their children to venture away from the home on their own. Thus, the greater freedom within the home enjoyed by Greek children apparently does not extend outside the home. Going across the street to play, for example, would likely involve too much freedom from adult supervision, and our feeling is that Greek parents place relatively greater value on keeping the child comfortable and happy at home, where he or she will be within the orbit of adult guidance and care.

Thus, in terms of obtaining direct and immediate help and in the freedom they enjoy with guest privileges, Greek children appear to be, as Triandis puts it, "pampered and indulged," relative to their Canadian counterparts. The degree of indulgence is even more striking when one examines parental approaches to discipline. We have found that Greek Immigrant parents are in general essentially like Greek Homeland parents in their reactions to discipline-provoking issues, and when compared with our Canadian-born groups, both groups of Greek parents are much less severe in their treatment of insolence, temper and social temper displays, and child-guest disputes. This much more lenient attitude, especially the tendency to let insolence and temper displays pass, without applying heavyweight sanctions, points to a fundamental difference in child-rearing values. What ends are served when parents absorb insolence and temper outbursts to this extent? Our thoughts on this are that, by letting insolence and temper outbursts pass, Greek parents may defuse aggressiveness and at the same time protect their children from adult models who are counter-aggressive and punitive. For all we psychologists know, this may be a time-honored technique that effectively reduces the aggressive impulses of children. Furthermore, it may also be that Greek parents feel, consciously or not, that in order to keep the children content with the restrictions imposed on them—for example, the curtailment of freedom in the domain of autonomy and independence—some safety valves for frustration must be provided. Perhaps insolence and temper outbursts are seen by Greek parents as this form of safety valve.

The leniency of Greek parents is, therefore, selective. Not only do Greek parents, relative to Canadians, restrict the independence gestures of children, but they also are as harsh as the Canadian parents or, in the case of Greek Homelanders, somewhat harsher, in their reactions to the child-baby dispute. Thus, relative to Canadians, Greek parents place a premium on the development of considerateness toward younger siblings. This feature of their values is also in the direction of peace and harmony within the home.

Our interests went beyond searching for distinctively Greek child-rearing values, for we focused as well on points of value overlap between Greek Immigrant and Canadian parents. We were particularly interested in determining which Canadian groups—French or English, middle class or working class—are most and least similar to Greek immigrants with respect to child-rearing orientations. By way of summary, we have compiled in Table 10.4 the instances where Greek Immigrant parents are more similar to one or another of these Canadian subgroups. We find that the child-rearing values of Greek Immigrant parents are more similar to Canadian middle-class than working-class parents, and more similar to French Canadian than English Canadian middle-class parents. This is so even though the Greek immigrants included in our sample are from thoroughly working-class backgrounds, and even though they characteristically align themselves more with the Anglophone than the Francophone community in Quebec. We also know that this greater similarity with middle-class French Canadian values is not attributable to shifts in values as a consequence of immigrating and settling in Quebec, for there were very few instances of values changing from old-country styles to Canadian styles anywhere in this analysis. Instead, most of the similarities seem to be instances of fundamental value overlaps between Greek and Canadian middle-class groups, particularly French Canadians. We have no sure explanation for these overlaps; they may represent deep and ancient similarities between Greek and old-country French approaches to children that were transported from Greece to France to French Canada generations ago, or they may reflect common adjustments made to the modern world by Greeks and French Canadians, based on common concerns with the family, the land, and the church.

TABLE 10.4

Instances of Value Overlap between Canadian
and Greek Immigrant Parents
(X indicates similarity)

| | Group | | | |
Scale	ECWC	ECMC	FCWC	FCMC
Help withholding			X	X
Siding with baby versus child	X*		X	
Temper control		X	X	X
Social temper control		X		X
Insolence control		X		X
Attention denial	X	X	X	X
Comfort withholding	X	X	X	X
Autonomy control	X		X	
Guest restriction				X
Siding with guest versus child		X		X
Perceived sex-role differences	X			
Expected sex-role differences	X*			
Total number of similarities	4*	6	7	8

*These similarities turned up for the main effect analysis but not for the interactions; consequently, they were not included in the total number of similarities between groups.
Source: Compiled by the authors.

Whatever the final explanation of these value overlaps may be, another interesting question has emerged: Why have Greek immigrants tended to prefer English Canadians to French Canadians as a reference group? This preference may well provide economic benefits and assurances in the North American scene, but these potential advantages of an Anglophone orientation might be bought at the price of value mismatches of various sorts. But perhaps mismatches help protect a group from too many outside influences. In fact, what this study has shown is that Greek Immigrant parents have been able, so far at least, to be as much Franco-Canadian as they are Anglo-Canadian in their approaches to child rearing while still staying as Greek as they apparently want to be.

This is not to say that there were no signs of acculturation showing through. Actually, in our comparisons of Greek Homeland and Greek Immigrant parents we did find subtle signs of shifts in values. For instance, the Greek Immigrant parents are less severe than Greek Homeland parents on children's social aggressiveness, and this may reflect a move toward the more "laissez-aller" tendency of Canadian middle-class parents who, as we described in Chapter 2, are prone to play down the importance of children's emotional outbursts. There is also some indication that Greek Immigrant parents have shifted their sex-role expectations in the direction of French Canadian norms, in particular, toward a greater concern for the sex-role identity of a same-sexed child. Although this trend is real enough in the statistical sense, it remains mysterious to us, for we have no way of explaining its meaning, either for Greek immigrants or for French Canadians. The main point, however, is that there are some signs of value shifts in the thinking of Greek Immigrant parents, and although only isolated cases, they may be the beginnings of deeper changes that will turn up in time or with other generations of Greek Canadians.

11

PORTUGUESE APPROACHES
TO CHILD REARING

For those who have followed the social development of communities in New England, there seem to be remarkable changes in
the self-views of American ethnic groups. For instance, 30 years
ago Portuguese-Americans in this region of the United States tended
to play down their ethnicity, giving the impression that they were
anxious to become as "American" as possible. In reality, quite
outside public view, they maintained close contact with one another
through church congregations and such community organizations as
Portuguese American Civic Clubs. They have apparently been suc-
cessful in keeping both the Portuguese and the American roots of
their heritage alive, for now that it is appropriate in America to
show one's ethnicity, it is commonplace to find well-attended Portuguese churches with services in Portuguese as well as English, a
flourishing system of civic clubs, bilingual elementary school programs, and Portuguese-American candidates being elected to political offices while others take on major responsibilities in public
affairs.

These developments are due in part to the perseverance of
long-term residents and in part to the active participation of large
numbers of new immigrants who enrich and strengthen established
Portuguese communities (see O. L. Mazzatenta 1975). Thus, Portuguese people and their homeland hold a fascination for anyone interested in America's multiethnic foundations.

In this chapter, our focus will be on Portuguese parents and
their child-rearing values. We start by comparing our "old-stock"
American parents with Portuguese Homeland parents, and then we
compare Portuguese Homeland and Portuguese Immigrant parents—
those who have emigrated from Portugal to the United States where

264

they are currently bringing up their own families. The questions that orient us here are the same as those we asked in the Italian and Greek studies: What is distinctive about Portuguese child-rearing values? Which features of these values are particularly vulnerable to change as a consequence of experiences in the United States, and which are particularly resistant to change?

A DESCRIPTION OF THE PORTUGUESE
HOMELAND PARENTS

All of our Portuguese Homeland (PH) parents came from Lisbon and its surroundings (Table A 11.1) and were compared with our sample of "old-stock" American (A) parents (Table A 7.1). There are large differences, especially in years of schooling: A working-class fathers have some five or six more years of schooling than their PH working-class counterparts, and the difference is even more pronounced for mothers; also at the middle-class level there are educational differences favoring Americans. There are also more working mothers in the PH than the A middle-class samples. Our collaborators in Portugal suggest that there are basic differences in educational norms and standards in the two countries rather than differences in social-class standing; they assured us that the PH samples were in their opinion representative of working- and middle-class families in Portugal.

PART I: PORTUGUESE HOMELAND
AND AMERICAN PARENTS

Similarities

The basic statistical comparisons of Portuguese Homeland (PH) and American (A) parents are presented in Tables 11.1 and A 11.2. It is immediately evident that there are numerous statistically significant differences between PH and A parents, showing up as main effects or as interactions. There are, in fact, relatively few cases of value overlap between PH and A parents. It is only on the help giving and temper control issues that the A and PH parents react alike, both groups generally complying with the child's request for help, and both taking steps to control temper outbursts. Furthermore, both groups are more inclined to comply with a boy's than with a girl's requests for help; middle-class parents in both nations are more ready than working-class parents to extend help when it is requested; and fathers in both settings perceive more

TABLE 11.1

Significant Effects in the Comparisons of American and Portuguese Homeland Parents

Value Dimensions

Comparisons	1) Help Withholding (np = 58.6)	2) Siding with Baby vs. Child (np = 42.7)	3a) Temper Control (np = 30.0)	3b) Social Temper Control (np = 41.6)	4) Insolence Control (np = 25.0)	5) Attention Denial (np = 75.0)	6) Comfort Withholding (np = 41.6)	7) Autonomy Control (np = 58.3)	8) Guest Restriction (np = 62.5)	9) Siding with Guest vs. Child (np = 42.7)	10) Perceived Sex-Role Differences	11) Expected Sex-Role Differences
G	–	43.66	–	7.36	11.24	12.07	–	10.48	5.92	–	14.03	–
C	4.36	8.67	7.97	4.57	5.54	–	–	–	–	–	6.91	–
X	5.08	–	–	–	–	–	–	–	–	–	–	–
P	–	–	–	–	–	–	–	–	–	–	14.84	–
GC	–	14.75	–	7.30	–	–	–	4.71	–	–	–	–
GX	–	–	–	–	–	–	–	–	–	–	–	–
CX	–	–	–	–	–	–	–	–	–	–	–	–
GP	–	–	–	–	–	–	6.19	–	–	–	–	–
CP	–	–	–	–	–	–	–	–	–	–	–	4.53
XP	–	–	–	–	–	–	–	–	–	–	–	–
GCX	–	–	–	–	–	–	–	–	–	–	–	–
GCP	–	–	–	–	–	–	–	–	–	–	–	–
GXP	–	–	–	–	–	–	–	–	–	4.30	–	–
CXP	–	–	–	–	–	–	–	–	–	–	–	–
GCXP	–	–	–	–	–	–	–	–	–	–	–	–

Note: Entries are significant F values; those underlined are beyond the .01 level of confidence, the others are beyond the .05 level.

Source: Compiled by the authors.

266

sex-role differences than do mothers. With these few instances of value overlap as background, the numerous contrasts between PH and A parents stand out all the more clearly.

Differences

For 10 of the 12 scales, we found either straightforward national differences or differences involving national background in interaction with social class, sex of parent, and/or sex of child. National group differences which are unaffected by interactions show up on three scales only: insolence control, attention denial, and guest restrictions, indicating that A parents react much more harshly than PH parents to insolence, are more likely than PH parents to put limits on a child's guest privileges, but are much more inclined than PH parents to cater to a child who clamors for attention.

Social-class background has different effects on the child-rearing values of A and PH parents, and these show through clearly on three scales: the child-baby dispute, social temper control, and autonomy control (see Figures 11.1 through 11.3). In all three instances there are greater social-class differences among A than among PH parents, and it is the A middle-class parents who are especially lenient on these issues. As a consequence, the child-rearing orientations of PH parents, regardless of their social-class background, are more similar to working-class than to middle-class American values. PH parents are also more similar to working- than middle-class A parents on the autonomy issue (see Figure 11.3) in that they tend not to encourage a child's bid for independence. Since we have encountered this same trend in our Italian and Greek studies, it appears that parents in all three Mediterranean settings, when compared to North American parents, hold back on independence training.

Mother-Father Differences

There are also interesting mother-father differences in modes of reacting to children in Portugal and the United States, and these show up on two issues—comfort and sex-role expectations (see Figures 11.4 and 11.5). On the comfort issue, American mothers and fathers have quite different reactions, and fathers are more likely than mothers to withhold comfort. In contrast, PH mothers and fathers are essentially alike in their reactions to the child's comfort seeking. Thus, when "hurt" in an interplay with a sibling, the A child can expect a certain amount of comfort from mother, at least, whereas the PH child can expect little comfort from either parent.

FIGURE 11.1

G x C Interaction for Siding with Baby versus Child

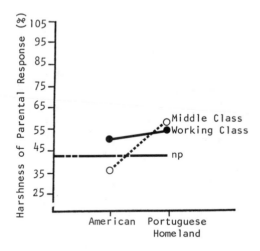

Source: Constructed by the authors.

FIGURE 11.2

G x C Interaction for Social Temper Control

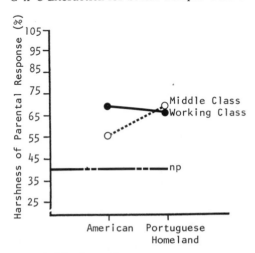

Source: Constructed by the authors.

268

FIGURE 11.3

G x C Interaction for Autonomy Control

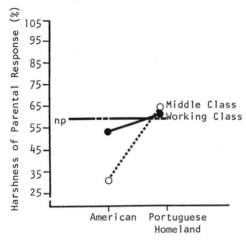

Source: Constructed by the authors.

FIGURE 11.4

G x P Interaction for Comfort Withholding

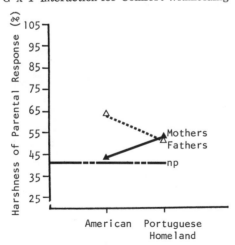

Source: Constructed by the authors.

FIGURE 11.5

G x P Interaction for Expected Sex-Role Differences

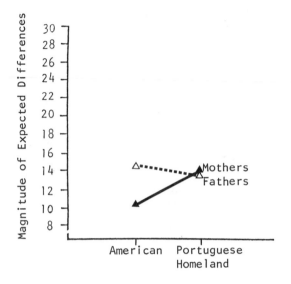

Source: Constructed by the authors.

A similar pattern shows up for parental sex-role expectations, and again there is a large father-mother contrast for A parents, with fathers having higher sex-role expectations than mothers, versus virtual consensus for PH mothers and fathers. Thus, in American families, the father seems more intent than the mother to discourage children from becoming comfort demanders, and he is also more anxious that boys be boys and girls be girls. In contrast, PH mothers and fathers have essentially similar reactions to both these issues, providing their children with a more unified parental set of standards.

Finally, there is a significant three-way interaction on the child-guest dispute issue which also points to distinctive patterns of mother-father differences in Portugal and the United States (see Figure 11.6). Here there is a clear A-PH contrast in the ways fathers and mothers react to sons and daughters when the latter become embroiled in a quarrel with a playmate. American parents in this instance show same-sex leniency, that is, fathers are more lenient with sons than with daughters. By contrast, there is little sex-linked bias one way or another for PH parents, except that, in general, mothers are somewhat harsher than fathers. There is,

FIGURE 11.6

G x X x P Interaction for Siding with Guest versus Child

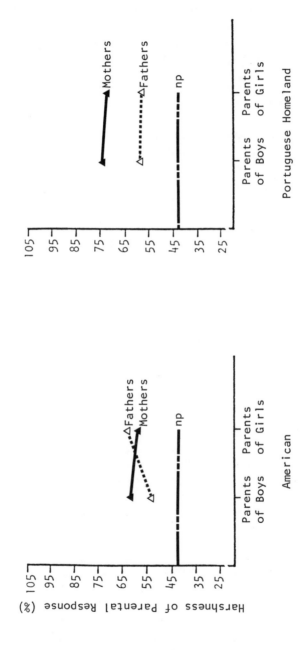

Source: Constructed by the authors.

then, further evidence here of a more unified mother-father approach to children in PH families, regardless of the child's sex,
while in A families there are clear signs of biases involving the
sex of the parent and the sex of the child.

PART I: SUMMARY AND CONCLUSIONS

This analysis tells us a good deal about PH in relation to A
parents. For all scales but two (temper control and help withholding), some form of value differences emerged between PH and A
parents. With respect to similarities, both groups of parents discourage displays of temper and both comply with children's requests
for help. On the help giving issue, both PH and A parents tend to
favor boys over girls, and in both nations, middle-class parents
are in general more ready to help than are working-class parents.

It is also true that middle-class parents, whether PH or A,
are generally less severe than working-class parents on issues
calling for discipline, and this we have found to be the case in
various other national groups already described. But if working-
class PH and A parents are harsher disciplinarians, they are not
harsher on nurturance-related issues, such as granting attention,
comfort, or guest privileges. In these instances working-class
parents are as nurturant as the middle class.

Similarities aside, the predominant feature of this analysis
is the large number of contrasts that were found between PH and A
parents. These contrasts form interesting patterns, for it is not
that one group is consistently more severe or more helpful than the
other, but that each group is selectively more severe or more helpful on particular issues. Thus, relative to their PH counterparts,
A parents are lenient on such issues as child-baby disputes, social
temper displays, and requests for autonomy, and the inference we
draw is that A parents use these episodes to train the child to work
problems out on his or her own. At the same time, A parents are
selectively harsh when it comes to a child's insolence or the possible abuse of guest privileges. Thus, relative to PH parents, A
parents seem to place greater value on developing self-sufficiency,
independence, and a healthy "respect" for parents.

The contrast is clear, for PH parents are relatively harsher
on social temper and social aggressiveness, they tend to discourage
the child's independence gestures, but they are definitely more
lenient on guest privileges and on insolence. Thus, relative to their
American counterparts, PH parents place greater value on controlling the potentially aggressive impulses of their children and on
supervising the child's social contacts, for example, by encouraging

playmates to come into the home, but discouraging the child from
venturing away from home. Still we are fascinated with the finding
that PH parents are at the same time particularly lenient on social
aggression directed toward parents in the form of insolence. From
the American perspective one wonders if PH parents purposely use
permissiveness on insolence as a means of gaining control over
children by playing on feelings of guilt and regret, or that by ignoring or otherwise "extinguishing" insolence, they "defuse" insolence
and make it an easily manageable escape vent for frustrations. It
could be that American parents are the ones who have a "hang-up"
on insolence.

There are also greater mother-father differences in modes
of reacting to children among A than among PH parents. For example, A fathers have greater sex-role expectations and are more
inclined to withhold comfort than A mothers, whereas PH mothers
and fathers have essentially similar reactions on these issues.

Social-class differences in modes of reacting to children are
more pronounced in A than in PH families, and this is due mainly
to the A middle-class parents who, as a subgroup, are distinctively
more lenient on the child-baby dispute, the social temper, and the
autonomy control issues. As a consequence, PH child-rearing
values overlap more with A working-class than A middle-class
parents.

Finally, on the child-guest dispute issue there is a marked
PH-A difference due to the fact that A parents show same-sex
leniency (fathers favoring sons, mothers daughters) while PH parents show no such sex-linked bias.

PART II: THE PORTUGUESE IMMIGRANT
TO THE UNITED STATES

It is evident from the results just reviewed that there are a
great many value contrasts between Portuguese Homeland and
American parents, and when thinking about Portuguese immigrants
to the United States, one can imagine the social pressures they
might encounter to adjust and change their values in the direction of
American norms. In this section we direct attention to Portuguese
immigrants (PI) who are bringing up their children in the United
States, and we will attempt to tease out examples of value change
and value resistance by comparing, first, the reactions of PI parents with both working-class and middle-class A parents. Although
our PI parents are from working-class backgrounds only, we still
want to determine whether they take American working-class or
American middle-class parents as the major reference group. This

matter is of particular interest to us because in earlier chapters we have found fascinating examples where working-class immigrants from Europe orient themselves as much or more toward middle-class North American values as toward working-class values.

A Description of the Portuguese Immigrant Sample

As in the Greek and Italian studies, we will be dealing here with working-class parents only. The background information for the PI parents is given in Table A 11.3 and that for PH parents in Table A 11.1. The two groups differ in several important respects. In the first place, the PI working-class parents all came from the Portuguese islands, particularly from the Azores. Because of the facts of Portuguese immigration, we could not find sufficient numbers of mainlanders who had immigrated to the United States. Although our Portuguese collaborators assured us that, in their opinion, there should be no basic differences in the child-rearing values of islanders and mainlanders, we unfortunately have no way of testing that opinion in this study. In addition to the island-mainland difference, the PI working-class parents also fall somewhat lower than their PH working-class counterparts in the occupational hierarchy, and they have had two years or so less education. Furthermore, more PI than PH mothers were employed outside the home. Thus, there are important background differences between our PI and PH samples that could well invalidate some of our conclusions about value changes. With these limitations in mind, we proceed on the assumption that the differences are basically minor, that we are dealing with essentially comparable groups of working-class Portuguese parents, one old-country residents and the other relatively recent immigrants to the United States. All of the PI parents currently live in southeastern New England, in and around Providence, Rhode Island, and New Bedford, Massachusetts.

PART II: PORTUGUESE HOMELAND VERSUS PORTUGUESE IMMIGRANT PARENTS

The statistical results for the PH-PI comparisons are presented in Tables 11.2 and A 11.4. First, there are relatively few differences to speak of, eight significant entries (Table 11.2) versus some 21 when PH and A parents are compared (Table 11.1). Thus, as might be expected, there seems to be a common set of child-rearing values linking PH and PI parents. However, all but one of

TABLE 11.2

Significant Effects in the Comparisons of Portuguese Immigrant
and Portuguese Homeland Working-Class Parents

Comparisons	Value Dimensions										
	1) Help Withholding (np = 58.6)	2) Siding with Baby vs. Child (np = 42.7)	3a) Temper Control (np = 30.0)	3b) Social Temper Control (np = 41.6)	4) Insolence Control (np = 25.0)	5) Attention Denial (np = 75.0)	6) Comfort Withholding (np = 41.6)	7) Autonomy Control (np = 58.3)	8) Guest Restriction (np = 62.5)	9) Siding with Guest vs. Child (np = 42.7)	10) Perceived Sex-Role Differences	11) Expected Sex-Role Differences
G	–	4.65	–	–	<u>21.29</u>	4.57	–	–	4.45	–	–	<u>7.68</u>
X	–	–	–	–	–	–	–	–	–	–	–	–
P	–	–	–	–	–	–	–	–	–	–	<u>8.41</u>	–
GX	–	–	–	–	–	–	–	–	5.68	–	–	–
GP	–	–	–	–	–	–	–	–	–	–	–	–
XP	–	–	–	–	–	–	–	–	–	–	–	–
GXP	–	–	–	–	–	–	–	6.17	–	–	–	–

Note: Entries are significant F values; those underlined are beyond the .01 level of confidence, the others are beyond the .05 level.
Source: Compiled by the authors.

275

the differences indicate that PI parents have changed their child-rearing orientations away from PH styles and toward American styles. These point-for-point shifts toward American child-rearing orientations are impressive. For instance, relative to their PH counterparts, PI parents are less harsh on the child-baby dispute and the attention demanding issues, but more harsh on insolence and more restrictive on guest privileges. There is, then, an interesting subset of values that changes in the American direction and an equally interesting subset—including help giving, temper, social temper, comfort, autonomy, child-guest dispute, and sex-role perceptions—that remains essentially Portuguese.

Still, not all the "changes" are in the direction of American norms. The case of sex-role expectations is interesting because even though the PI parents end up decidedly different from PH parents in their sex-role expectations (see Table A 11.4), they have not shifted closer to A parents. Instead, it seems that the American experience has amplified the sex-role issue for PI parents, increasing their expectations of boy-girl differentiations.

On the guest privilege matter there seem to be two features of Portuguese values that shift in the direction of American norms, one being the tendency already mentioned for PI parents to become more restrictive on guest privileges, and the second, a tendency for PI parents to restrict more the guest privileges of boys than those of girls, which is the reverse of the pattern for PH parents. This double shift on the part of PI parents is clearly in the direction of American norms, and in particular American working-class norms (see Figure 11.7).

The case of autonomy is interesting because it could be an example of overadjusting to American norms. What we find is that both mothers and fathers in PH families encourage more the autonomy gestures of girls than those of boys, meaning that PH fathers show cross-sex leniency on this issue, while PH mothers show same-sex leniency (see Figure 11.8). The PI-PH contrast is basically due to the PI mothers who show a very pronounced pattern of cross-sex leniency, the opposite of that for PH mothers. This striking difference could represent a value change on the part of PI mothers in the direction of the norm for working-class A mothers, but if so, the PI mothers seem to be overplaying the American role since they end up being even more biased toward the independence moves of boys than A mothers are. What is there in the experiences of PI mothers in America that would incline them to encourage sons who show signs of wanting independence but to discourage daughters who make similar overtures toward independence? Whatever the answer is, at least PI mothers seem to catch the idea that A parents favor boys in this way. But why would PI mothers be the ones to catch this American idea?

FIGURE 11.7

G x X Interaction for Guest Restrictions

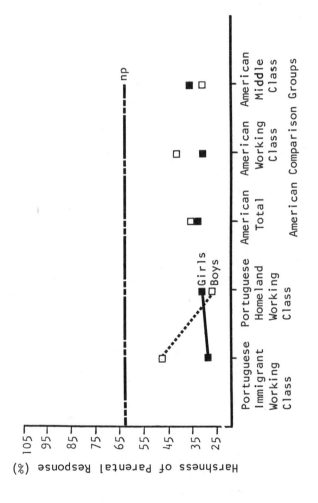

Source: Constructed by the authors.

FIGURE 11.8

G x X x P Interaction for Autonomy Control

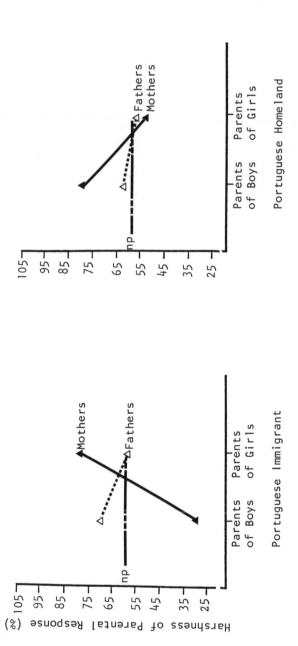

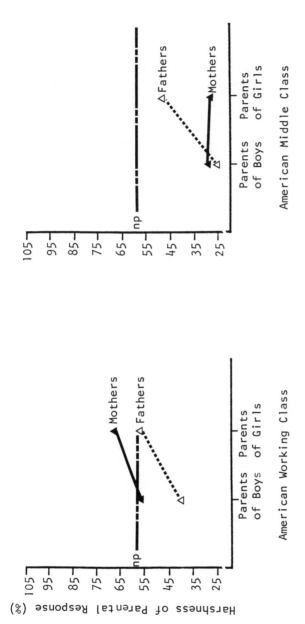

Harshness of Parental Response (%)

Parents   Parents
of Boys   of Girls

American Working Class

Parents   Parents
of Boys   of Girls

American Middle Class

Source: Constructed by the authors.

In summary, our aim in this section was to search for possible changes that might take place in the child-rearing values of Portuguese people who have immigrated and are now raising their families in the United States. The focus of the analysis was on a comparison of Portuguese immigrant parents and Portuguese homeland parents, both of working-class standing. The findings suggest that the immigrant parents do change certain of their child-rearing values toward American norms at the same time as they keep other values essentially unchanged. For example, PI parents were much more lenient than PH parents on child-baby disputes and on demands for attention, but they were harsher in their reactions to insolence and requests for guest privileges. They also seem to have adopted a more subtle feature of American child rearing in the case of guest privileges, for, in contrast to PH parents, they are more restrictive on sons' than on daughters' requests to have playmates into the home as guests. There is some indication, too, that PI mothers may have picked up another American working-class value on the autonomy issue, for, in contrast to PH parents, they are much more ready to grant autonomy to boys than to girls.

The shift in sex-role expectations is intriguing because, if anything, it seems to be a change away from American norms. In our attempts to explain this change, we are left with the speculation that bringing up children in the United States may enhance the salience of sex-role differentiations in the thinking of PI parents.

Instructive as value changes are, those instances where PI parents remain similar to PH parents are equally interesting and instructive, for they provide examples of value persistence in the face of the American experience. Actually, the value changes we have just highlighted form one subset of PI-PH differences, and these have to be viewed in the broader context of numerous examples of "no change." Although instances of no change are as instructive as instances of change, it is difficult to know whether we are dealing with real value resistance or simply natural compatibilities between PI and A working-class values. In other words, value change and value resistance are relative matters, and, if we had information on Portuguese immigrants to other national settings, what we refer to as value resistance in the United States might well become an example of value change, because the value was more challenged in the other setting. Similarly, values that change for Portuguese in the United States might not be affected at all in other settings. But this is a deeper research matter that calls for further study, and we are happy to have found some excellent examples of change and of no change for Portuguese immigrating to the United States.

PART III: PORTUGUESE IMMIGRANT, AMERICAN
WORKING-CLASS, AND AMERICAN MIDDLE-
CLASS PARENTS

Our purpose in this final section is to examine in somewhat
more detail the types of value changes that take place for PI parents living in the United States. At this point we pose essentially
the same question that we asked in the Italian and Greek studies:
Do PI parents, selected as they were to represent people from
working-class backgrounds, orient themselves more toward American working-class (AWC) or American middle-class (AMC) norms
of child rearing? This question becomes particularly interesting
when asked for the third time, because, unlike Greek and Italian
immigrant parents who seem to bring their child-rearing values
more in line with North American middle-class standards, Portuguese immigrant parents model more on American working-class
standards. In fact, we are ultimately left with a set of intriguing
questions about why PI parents are distinctively different from
Italian and Greek immigrant parents on this very matter.

Background Characteristics of the
Three Parental Groups

The relevant information on the three groups of parents is
available in Table A 11.3 for the PI parents and in Table A 7.1 for
the "old-stock" American middle-class and working-class parents.
The AWC parents had substantially more education than the PI parents (some eight years on the average), although both groups hold
similar occupations. The PI sample also had more working mothers
(13) than the A sample (5), and the PI parents have somewhat larger
families as well (3.3 children versus 2.4). The A sample includes
both Protestant and Catholic parents while the majority of PI parents
are Catholic. Thus, although our PI sample may represent typical
Portuguese immigrants to the United States, the match with our
American comparison groups is poor in terms of education, family
size, and number of working mothers. With some misgivings, then,
we proceed as though these sample differences were unimportant,
assuming that we have comparable samples of working-class parents,
one comprising immigrants from Portugal, the other old-stock
Americans.

PART III: RESULTS—PORTUGUESE IMMIGRANTS
VERSUS WORKING- AND MIDDLE-CLASS
AMERICANS

The statistical results for the three group comparisons are
presented in Tables 11.3 and A 11.5. The differences among parental groups are striking, for there is a general theme underlying
all seven of the among-group differences—the PI and AWC mean
scores in each case are very similar and both are different from
those for AMC parents. In other words, PI and AWC parents have
remarkably similar child-rearing orientations, and the odd group
is the AMC parents who stand out because of their leniency and
their "laissez-aller" attitudes.

Consider the child-baby dispute issue. We already know that
the PI parents have become more lenient than PH parents on this
issue; in this, they are very similar to AWC parents, but not as
lenient as AMC parents. With regard to insolence, the PI parents
have also become less lenient than the PH parents and actually more
severe than either the AMC or AWC parents, but again they fall
closer to AWC than AMC norms. On the sex-role expectation issue,
the PI parents have also changed to a more extreme position than
either of the American groups, and although they end up closer to
the AWC than the AMC parents, one can't conclude that the shift in
this case is toward American norms. Rather, as mentioned earlier,
something about their experiences as Portuguese immigrants to the
United States may have made the matter of children's sex roles particularly salient for PI parents. The main point, however, is that
on those value dimensions where changes occur, the PI parents tend
to change in the direction of working-class rather than middle-class
American values. There is a suggestion, too, that, in changing, PI
parents may overshoot the mark, as with insolence and sex-role
expectations, but even so, the resting state of the value is still
closer to American working-class than middle-class norms.

The four remaining contrasts in Tables 11.3 and A 11.5 are
cases where PI parents have not changed their child-rearing values
relative to PH parents, but where they, nonetheless, are closer to
working-class than middle-class American norms. The issues in
question here are: temper control, social temper control, autonomy,
and sex-role perceptions, and in each instance the PI scores are
essentially similar to those of AWC parents, both groups being
quite different from the relatively more lenient, less demanding
AMC parents.

The group difference on the comfort issue is special (see
Figure 11.9). Here, the PI parents stand out as different from both
American groups because PI fathers are more ready to extend

TABLE 11.3

Significant Effects in the Comparisons of Portuguese Immigrant Working-Class, American Working-Class, and American Middle-Class Parents

Value Dimensions

Comparisons	1) Help Withholding (np = 58.6)	2) Siding with Baby vs. Child (np = 42.7)	3a) Temper Control (np = 30.0)	3b) Social Temper Control (np = 41.6)	4) Insolence Control (np = 25.0)	5) Attention Denial (np = 75.0)	6) Comfort Withholding (np = 41.6)	7) Autonomy Control (np = 58.3)	8) Guest Restriction (np = 62.5)	9) Siding with Guest vs. Child (np = 42.7)	10) Perceived Sex-Role Differences	11) Expected Sex-Role Differences
G	–	10.17	6.38	5.33	5.68	–	–	6.76	–	–	5.43	7.19
X	7.42	–	–	–	–	–	–	–	–	–	–	–
P	5.58	–	–	–	–	–	–	–	–	–	11.29	8.99
GX	–	–	–	–	–	–	–	–	–	–	–	–
GP	–	–	–	–	–	–	7.38	–	–	–	–	–
XP	–	–	–	–	–	–	6.54	–	–	–	–	–
GXP	–	–	–	–	–	–	–	–	–	–	–	–

Note: Entries are significant F values; those underlined are beyond the .01 level of confidence, the others are beyond the .05 level.
Source: Compiled by the authors.

283

comfort than PI mothers, which is the reverse of the AWC and
AMC patterns. Interestingly, this PI pattern is remarkably similar to that for PH middle-class parents, but not to PH working-
class parents, suggesting that some changes in the child-rearing
values of Portuguese immigrants go in the direction of old-country
elites.

FIGURE 11.9

G x P Interaction for Comfort Withholding

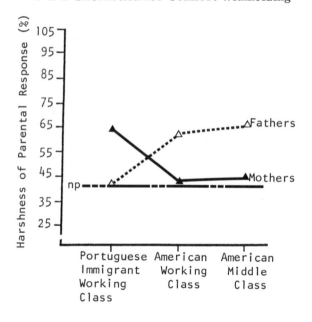

Source: Constructed by the authors.

In summary, from this analysis we find a consistent and unambiguous tendency for PI parents to be much more like AWC than
AMC parents in their child-rearing orientations. In cases where
they appear to have shifted their values toward American norms,
the shift is specifically toward working-class rather than middle-
class American standards. In cases where they have not shifted
values from homeland standards, they, nonetheless, are much more
like AWC than AMC parents in their reactions to children. These
two lines of evidence suggest that the PI parents may well have

modeled on American working-class norms and made adjustments
wherever at odds with AWC parents. Where their child-rearing
values—that they presumably brought with them from Portugal—are
in line with those of working-class American parents, there would
be no pressure for change.

All this seems reasonable enough. Why shouldn't immigrants
to a new setting take as reference people of comparable social-class
standing? We began to wonder about this very reasonable idea as
soon as we found that Italian and Greek immigrants apparently do
not take working-class North American norms as their points of reference, and this led us to more basic questions: Why is it that Portuguese immigrants differ in this regard from Italian and Greek immigrants? Why would one ethnic group set its sights at a lower
social-class level than another? Might this be a sign of a real "cultural" difference between Portuguese and Italians and Portuguese
and Greeks?

THE PORTUGUESE STUDY IN PERSPECTIVE

Once the similarities and contrasts in the child-rearing values
of Portuguese "homeland" and "old-stock" American parents were
isolated and analyzed, we "followed," so to speak, a group of young
adults who left Portugal and immigrated to the United States where
they had started their own families. By comparing these immigrant
parents with their counterparts in Portugal, we uncovered an interesting set of value "changes" that we assume are due to new life experiences in the United States. We also uncovered an equally impressive set of value "persistences." And then, by comparing Portuguese immigrant and American parents, we were able to determine
in more detail how the child-rearing values of Portuguese immigrants are influenced in the American setting.

Portuguese homeland parents turn out to have quite distinctive
orientations toward children. It is not that they are consistently
more or less harsh or lenient than American parents, for it all depends on the value dimension in question. Relative to American
parents, they are harsher in their reactions to outbursts of social
temper or aggressivity and more inclined to discourage independence gestures; at the same time they are more lenient on requests
for guest privileges and on displays of insolence. The contrast is
sharp, suggesting to us that Portuguese homeland parents are relatively more concerned with supervising and controlling the potentially aggressive impulses of their children—to the point of permitting aggression to be channeled toward parents in the form of insolence—and with supervising the children's social contacts—by

encouraging the visits of playmates into the home but discouraging their own child's ventures away from home. In comparison, American parents place more value on having children work out interpersonal squabbles on their own, on encouraging gestures of independence, and on limiting dependence on playmates; at the same time they demand "respect" for parents by reacting strongly against insolence. The Portuguese comparison is not the first where we have found this relatively strong North American reaction against insolence. Perhaps American and Canadian parents have a "hang-up" of sorts on insolence. But why do other national groups, like the Portuguese, let insolence pass with much less notice?

There were other contrasts. In two instances, Portuguese mothers and fathers react more in unison than do American mothers and fathers. American fathers are more inclined than their wives to withhold gestures of comfort and they expect more sex-role differentiations. There is no such parental diversity for the Portuguese families. Also, on a number of issues, there are sharper social-class differences in attitudes toward child rearing for Americans than Portuguese, due in large part to the extreme leniency of the American middle-class parents. As a consequence, the values of Portuguese parents are more in line with American working-class than American middle-class values. Finally, on the child-guest dispute issue, American parents show same-sex leniency while Portuguese show no such sex-linked bias.

Interestingly, we found very few instances here of value overlap. Still, both Portuguese and American parents discourage temper displays and both extend help when it is requested. Furthermore, on the help-giving issue, both are more helpful to boys than to girls, and in both nations, middle-class parents are not only more ready to help than working-class parents, but are generally more lenient. Other than these examples, we encountered mainly value contrasts.

In light of the number and the magnitude of the contrasts between Portuguese homeland and American parents, we were not surprised to find, in Part II, many instances of value "change" on the part of Portuguese immigrants, who were settled and now bringing up their families in the United States, and the changes were in most cases unmistakably in the direction of American values. Thus, Portuguese immigrant parents, compared to their counterparts in Portugal, are <u>more</u> lenient on child-baby disputes and on demands for attention, but <u>less</u> lenient on insolence and guest privileges. On these particular value dimensions, then, they apparently have been influenced by American norms. Furthermore, on the guest privilege issue, they are more restrictive with sons than daughters, but more lenient with sons than daughters on the autonomy issue. Here, too, they appeared to have moved toward American norms and away from old-country norms. On the sex-role expectation issue, they have also moved away from old-country norms, but it is difficult to judge if the change is really in the direction of American norms. If so, it is an overshoot. Our guess is that their experiences in America had oversensitized the Portuguese immigrant parents to the sex-role comportment of their children.

So the Portuguese immigrant parents change certain of their child-rearing attitudes in the direction of American norms. Certain other values, however, do not change. Thus, there are no signs of change on any of the following issues: help giving, temper, social temper, comfort, autonomy, child-guest disputes, and sex-role perceptions. In fact, with regard to sex-role perceptions, Portuguese immigrant fathers, like Portuguese homeland fathers, are more vigilant than mothers. And there are no such mother-father differences for American parents.

Once we had a good idea that there were value changes and that these were in the American direction, we, then, in the final section, examined the details of these changes by comparing the reactions of Portuguese immigrant parents with those of both working-class and middle-class American parents. This analysis was straightforward and unambiguous: when there are value changes, they are consistently in the direction of American working-class norms. Furthermore, in the cases where the values of Portuguese immigrant parents remain essentially unchanged, it so happens that these values were already clearly in line with those of American working-class parents. A simple rule, then, seems to guide Portuguese immigrant parents in their attempts to adjust to the American host society: in cases where one's own values are off the norms, modify values in the direction of the norms; where values are not at odds with local norms, hold fast. This would mean that the Portuguese immigrant parents have focused mainly on American working-class rather than middle-class norms, and reasonable as this may seem, it is fascinating to us that this was apparently not the strategy followed by Italian and Greek immigrant parents, who, although of the same socioeconomic background as the Portuguese immigrants, set their sights more on middle-class than working-class norms. Perhaps here we have uncovered a real "cultural" difference between the Portuguese immigrant on the one hand and the Italian and Greek immigrant on the other. And this difference would be well worth further study.

12

JAPANESE APPROACHES
TO CHILD REARING

In this chapter we shift our focus to Japan, the one non-Western nation included in our investigation. All along we wondered what sorts of value contrasts might emerge if a non-Western nation were introduced, and Japan seemed like a particularly interesting choice. While highly industrialized and thoroughly modern in today's world, Japan's centuries of cultural isolation may well have protected and kept alive certain aspects of a distinctive non-Western way of life. Since Canada has sizable Japanese-Canadian communities from the west coast to the east, we again chose Canada as the Western comparison nation.

As we did for each of the old-country studies, we begin by comparing Japanese homeland and English Canadian parents, which becomes our reference frame for describing the changes and the lack of changes in the values of Japanese immigrants who are bringing up their six-year-olds in Canada.

A DESCRIPTION OF THE JAPANESE
HOMELAND SAMPLE

Unlike the other "old-country" studies, that for Japan is based on the reactions of middle-class parents only. This is so because Canadian immigration policies favor middle- over working-class Japanese applicants, making it very difficult to find representative working-class subgroups. For the Canadian scene, then, middle-class Japanese immigrant families are more typical. Our analyses here are accordingly based on middle-class samples of Japanese Homeland, Japanese Immigrant, and English Canadian parents.

The Homeland parents all lived in a collective housing development near Tokyo. Because they were reluctant to have interviewers come to their homes, arrangements were made to meet them at a community kindergarten where the mothers were interviewed individually on weekdays and the fathers on Sundays. Because of this time lag, parents might have been prompted to discuss the interview, even though they were asked not to. In order to reduce the effects of possible discussion, we balanced the order in which parents were questioned, half of the fathers being interviewed before their wives and half after their wives.

Table A 12.1 gives the background characteristics of the Japanese Homeland (JH) groups.* Although most of JH fathers in the sample have university degrees, their average years of schooling is still about two years less than that of either the Japanese Immigrant (JI) or the English Canadian (EC) middle-class groups (see Table A 12.3). This difference may account for the somewhat smaller number of professionals in the JH group. Overall, however, the three parental groups are fairly well matched.

PART I: RESULTS—JAPANESE HOMELAND
VERSUS ENGLISH CANADIAN PARENTS

The statistical comparisons are presented in Tables 12.1 and A 12.2, and it is evident that there are numerous statistically significant contrasts. We will examine these JH-EC differences first and then turn to the ways in which both parental groups react alike.

Group Differences

There are eight statistically significant differences between JH and EC parents' modes of reacting to our taped episodes, and these form two coherent patterns. JH parents are significantly harsher than their EC counterparts on the help giving, child-baby dispute, and comfort giving issues, at the same time as they are significantly more lenient on the temper, insolence, and guest privileges issues. In addition, the JH parents both expect more

---

*The interview sheets in this case were designed and printed in Japan, and unfortunately certain standard background questions were omitted. Thus, we do not know the number of children per family nor the number of working mothers.

TABLE 12.1

Significant Effects in the Comparisons of English Canadian Middle-Class and Japanese Homeland Middle-Class Parents

Value Dimensions

Comparisons	1) Help Withholding (np = 58.6)	2) Siding with Baby vs. Child (np = 42.7)	3a) Temper Control (np = 30.0)	3b) Social Temper Control (np = 41.6)	4) Insolence Control (np = 25.0)	5) Attention Denial (np = 75.0)	6) Comfort Withholding (np = 41.6)	7) Autonomy Control (np = 58.3)	8) Guest Restriction (np = 62.5)	9) Siding with Guest vs. Child (np = 42.7)	10) Perceived Sex-Role Differences	11) Expected Sex-Role Differences
G	20.78	12.50	12.35	–	35.31	–	30.07	–	16.56	–	27.00	52.79
X	–	–	–	–	–	–	–	–	–	7.04	–	–
P	–	4.35	–	–	–	–	15.05	7.43	4.11	–	–	–
GX	4.62	–	4.44	–	–	5.57	–	–	–	–	6.59	5.43
GP	–	4.36	–	–	–	–	–	–	–	–	–	–
XP	–	–	–	–	–	–	–	–	–	–	–	–
GXP	–	–	–	5.52	–	–	–	–	–	–	–	–

Note: Entries are significant F values; those underlined are beyond the .01 level of confidence, the others are beyond the .05 level.
Source: Compiled by the authors.

290

and perceive more sex-role differentiations than do EC parents. There is, in other words, a zig-zag pattern here wherein JH parents, compared to their EC counterparts, are harsher in certain respects and more lenient in other respects. But rather than being haphazard, the differences seem to fall into meaningful and revealing clusters.

From a North American perspective, the JH parents might well appear to be inconsistent in their ways of treating children. For instance, compared to their EC counterparts, JH parents tend to withhold overt gestures of help and comfort and emphasize sex-role differences, appearing thereby to be more severe and harsh; at the same time they are relatively lenient in coping with temper and insolence outbursts as well as guest privileges, appearing thereby to be softer, less severe socializers than EC parents. But one could just as easily argue that EC parents are inconsistent, for they are relatively severe in their reactions to outbursts of temper and insolence, while at the same time letting child-baby quarrels pass with relatively little fuss. Rather than inconsistencies, what we most likely have here are differences in child-rearing goals and in strategies to reach these goals. As we see it, JH parents are particularly intent on making their children self-sufficient, and, thus, they discourage them from turning to others for help and comfort. They also seem particularly intent on fostering sociability since they are more prone than EC parents to encourage guest privileges. Aggression directed toward a younger sibling is clearly discouraged, but aggression channeled through insolence and through nonsocial temper outbursts is given relatively free rein, as though the JH parents work on the principle that children have to have some means of letting off steam, and that parents and things are more appropriate outlets than younger siblings. Furthermore, as we have argued in the Greek study, parents could make good use of the fact that insolence is not prohibited.

From a North American perspective, the aims of the EC middle-class parents are more familiar. EC children, relative to their JH counterparts, are more readily helped and comforted, are left more on their own to work out difficulties that arise in their encounters with younger siblings, and relatively little attention is given to the fact that they are boys or girls. EC children will not, however, be permitted to be nasty or mean with parents, or break things when frustrated, nor are they given free run of the home with regard to guest privileges.

Although less familiar to us, the goals of the JH middle-class parents are intriguing because they seem to reflect a totally different conception of child rearing. Included in this conception is a very pronounced set of expectations about how boys and girls should behave that differs fundamentally from North American norms. And apparently these sex-role norms are adhered to, because the JH parents have much higher sex-role perception scores than do their EC counterparts.

This difference in emphasis placed on sex-role differentiations is reflected in the different ways JH and EC parents react to sons and to daughters. There are, in fact, five instances where JH and EC parents react differently to boys and to girls: help withholding, temper control, attention control, perceived sex-role differentiations, and expected sex-role differentiations (see the GX interactions in Figures 12.1 to 12.5). What is interesting is that on the help, temper, and attention issues the EC middle-class parents are harsher on girls than on boys, while JH middle-class parents are harsher on boys than on girls. Furthermore, EC parents of girls expect and perceive more differences between boys and girls than is the case for EC parents of boys, whereas JH parents of boys expect and perceive more sex-role differentiations than do JH parents of girls. This important national-group contrast suggests that girls in EC middle-class families are the target of a systematic bias: they are less likely than their brothers to be helped or to receive attention; they are more severely treated for temper displays; and they are expected not to lose their feminine identity. In other terms, relative to her brother, the EC middle-class girl is encouraged to be more independent (that is, not to demand help or attention); to keep her emotions better under control (that is, not to display temper); and to distinguish herself in her comportment from boys. In contrast, the JH middle-class boy is the focus of the very same bias in the sense that he is expected to be more self-sufficient than his sister, to have his emotions better under control, and to distinguish himself from girlish modes of behavior. This strong and pervasive national difference in parent relationships with sons and daughters will be of major interest when we explore the value changes of Japanese immigrant parents.

There is also one instance where JH and EC parents differ in their roles as mothers and fathers, namely the child-baby dispute issue (see Figure 12.6). In this case we find that EC fathers are harsher than EC mothers on child-baby disputes, whereas JH fathers and mothers react in unison, both being equally harsh. On the matter of within-family squabbles, then, there is more divergence between mothers and fathers in EC middle-class families, fathers tending to come down hard, while mothers are more neutral, taking neither side in the dispute.

Finally, there is an interesting three-way interaction on the social temper matter, depicted in Figure 12.7. This means that on the social temper issue, JH middle-class parents display cross-sex

FIGURE 12.1

G x X Interaction for Help Withholding

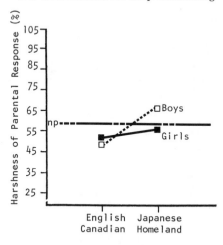

Middle Class

Source: Constructed by the authors.

FIGURE 12.2

G x X Interaction for Temper Control

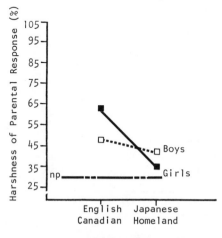

Middle Class

Source: Constructed by the authors.

293

FIGURE 12.3

G x X Interaction for Attention Denial

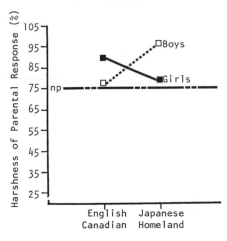

Source: Constructed by the authors.

FIGURE 12.4

G x X Interaction for Perceived Sex-Role Differences

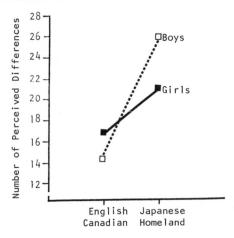

Source: Constructed by the authors.

294

FIGURE 12.5

G x X Interaction for Expected Sex-Role Differences

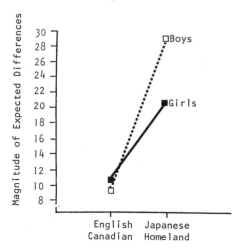

Source: Constructed by the authors.

FIGURE 12.6

G x P Interaction for Siding with Baby versus Child

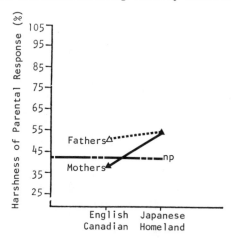

Source: Constructed by the authors.

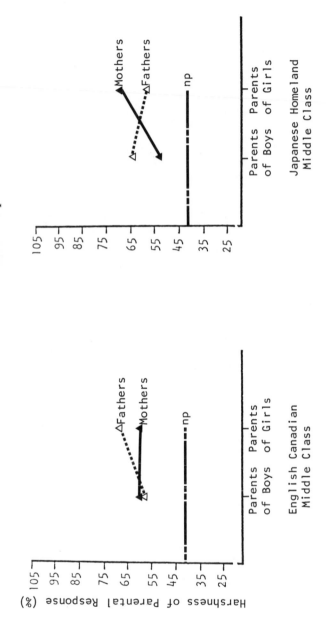

FIGURE 12.7

G x X x P Interaction for Social Temper

Source: Constructed by the authors.

leniency (fathers favoring daughters and mothers favoring sons), while EC middle-class parents show same-sex leniency, although actually it is only EC fathers who show a bias toward sons, whereas EC mothers show no bias one way or the other. Although interesting in itself, this is the only instance of same-sex or cross-sex leniency that emerged in the JH-EC comparisons, and the more salient contrast to keep in mind is that JH and EC parents, as separate mother-father teams, have their own distinctive ways of reacting to sons and to daughters.

Group Similarities

Because JH and EC middle-class parents have their own distinctive ways of reacting to sons and to daughters, there are few possibilities in the analysis for cross-national similarities to emerge. In fact, there is only one instance where JH and EC patterns overlap, and this is on the child-guest dispute issue where daughters, whether JH or EC, are treated more harshly than sons when a dispute with a guest develops. But this is an isolated case, and no similar trend is noticeable on any other issues (see the "sex of child" row in Table A 12.2). We emphasize this because in the analysis of Japanese immigrant parents, we will encounter an impressive number of cases where JI and EC parents share common biases toward sons or toward daughters, indicating that important changes take place in the values of Japanese parents when they migrate and start their families in Canada.

Even though JH and EC parents have quite distinctive modes of treating sons as compared to daughters, there are, nonetheless, four instances where they have essentially similar perspectives on how they should play their roles as mothers or fathers. The issues in question are: child-baby disputes, comfort withholding, autonomy control, and guest restrictions. In all four instances, fathers, whether JH or EC, react more harshly than mothers, as though in both settings it was accepted that fathers should not be bothered with quarrels, requests for comfort or autonomy, or with having playmates in the house. JH and EC mothers seem to have more patience, or perhaps it is that they have to have more patience.

The autonomy issue is of special interest because we find that mothers, both JH and EC, are more inclined than fathers to encourage their children's bids for independence. In light of the work of McClelland (1961) and Rosen (1959), this maternal encouragement of independence could have a favorable influence on the development of achievement motivation in JH and EC middle-class children. And since the trend is not limited to children of one sex or the other, this example of maternal encouragement could influence the achievement motivation of girls as well as boys in both societies.

PART I: SUMMARY AND CONCLUSIONS

This analysis has shown that JH and EC middle-class parents have quite different conceptions of child rearing, each group having a distinctive view of what it is to be a parent and what it is to be a child. In fact, there are very few instances here of common values shared by these two parental groups. Compared to their JH counterparts, EC middle-class parents are more ready to extend help and comfort to their six-year-old children, and, for issues like child-baby disputes, more prone to hold back and let their children work things out on their own. At the same time, however, EC middle-class parents are much harsher in their reactions to insolence, are more severe when children threaten to break things, and are less generous with regard to guest privileges. By contrast, JH middle-class parents are more intent on developing self-sufficiency and toughness in their six-year-olds, for they are less ready to respond to requests for help or comfort, and are more severe with instances of aggression directed toward a younger sibling. At the same time, they are more prone to overlook instances of aggression directed toward parents or toward material things, and are more lenient on the matter of guest privileges.

At a deeper level, EC middle-class parents, relative to their JH counterparts, show a bias against daughters in the sense that, in EC middle-class families, daughters are given less help and less attention than sons, are treated more harshly for temper displays, and are expected not to blur their sex-role identity. The contrast is sharp, for in JH middle-class families, sons are much more the target of parental concern: they are expected to be more self-sufficient than daughters, to keep their emotions better under control, and to maintain their sex-role identity. In brief, we have found an important set of examples here where JH and EC parents differ in what they expect of sons and of daughters, and hardly any cases where their perceptions of sons and daughters overlap.

There is, however, a good deal of similarity in the ways EC and JH middle-class parents conduct themselves as fathers or mothers. In both cultural settings, fathers react more harshly toward misdemeanors, and they are more negative and discouraging than mothers whenever the child makes requests for help, comfort, attention, or autonomy. Thus, in both EC and JH middle-class families, fathers are protected from being bothered by the everyday annoyances of children, but because the issue of autonomy is involved here, there could be a deeper significance to these mother-father differences. The fact that it is the mothers, both EC and JH, who are relatively more inclined to support children's bids for independence could be significant because it is now thought that maternal encouragement of independence has a particularly favorable influence on the development of children's achievement motivation. Our middle-class JH and EC children, then, may be particularly well prepared to reap the advantages of early training in independence that McClelland (1961) believes to contribute to achievement motivation, as well as the possible disadvantages that Rudin (1965) refers to.

PART II: JAPANESE IMMIGRANT PARENTS
IN ENGLISH CANADA

Would there be adjustive changes in the child-rearing values of Japanese parents who immigrate and start their families in Canada? There certainly is plenty of room for change, as we have just seen. Which values would be most easily modified, and which would more likely resist change? These are the questions of major interest to us in this section, where we introduce Japanese middle-class immigrant (JI) parents as the important comparison group.

A DESCRIPTION OF THE JAPANESE
IMMIGRANT PARENTS

According to the 1971 census of Canada, Toronto and Vancouver are the two major Canadian centers for Japanese immigration. We decided to draw our sample of Japanese immigrant parents from Toronto because we felt that our English Canadian comparison sample, drawn from Montreal, might be more like ECs in Toronto than ECs in Vancouver. Of course, proximity does not guarantee that ECs in these two cities are similar in terms of child-rearing values, but we will assume that our Montreal sample of EC parents is essentially like those that our JI parents interact with in Toronto.

Table A 12.3 presents the background characteristics of the JI and EC middle-class samples. The typical father in both groups has completed university education, and the typical mother has had some university experience; all fathers in both groups hold either professional or business-managerial type positions. The only notable difference between the two samples is the number of children per family—two, on the average, for the JI group, and three for the EC group.

PART II: RESULTS—JAPANESE IMMIGRANT
VERSUS ENGLISH CANADIAN PARENTS

The relevant statistical information is given in Tables 12.2
and A 12.4 for the comparison of JI and EC parents, and in Tables
12.3 and A 12.5 for a three-group comparison involving JH, JI, and
EC parents. The results from both the two-group and three-group
analyses indicate that many old-country child-rearing values hold
up in the North American setting, while others change.

As we examine specific value dimensions, we see that, much
like their homeland counterparts, the JI parents have much greater
sex-role expectations than EC parents, are more inclined to withhold overt gestures of help or comfort, and are systematically less
severe than EC parents in their treatment of temper and insolence
outbursts. They are also more ready than EC parents to grant their
children guest privileges. We take these similarities between JI
and JH parents to be indications that these features of Japanese-
style child-rearing values resist the acculturation influences of life
in Canada.

Equally impressive are the examples of change that take place
in Japanese-style values. When we compared JH and EC parents in
the previous section, we found that EC parents were harsher or more
demanding with daughters than with sons, whereas JH parents were
harsher or more demanding with sons than with daughters. In fact,
this tendency to treat sons and daughters differently showed up on
five separate scales. Since no such patterns emerge in the JI-EC
comparisons—all five interactions depicted in Figures 12.1 to 12.5
disappear—it follows that JI parents have become systematically
less focused on sons than their JH counterparts. In fact, EC and JI
girls in both families are treated more severely than boys when it is
a question of temper displays or disputes with a guest, and this
trend holds for most of the taped episodes. Thus, as the values of
JI parents shift in the direction of EC norms, they reflect as well
an EC bias against girls. For instance, both JI and EC parents
perceive aggression directed toward things (the temper episode) and
toward peers (the child-guest dispute) as unladylike. What is noteworthy is that, in the eyes of these same parents, the exact same
forms of aggression are much less unmanly. It seems, therefore,
that both JI and EC parents, consciously or not, attempt to shape
the characters of their sons and daughters along quite different lines.
Actually, one might have expected that JI parents would emphasize
this son-daughter difference more than EC parents because JI parents have much higher sex-role expectation scores than EC parents
do. But as it turns out, the JI and EC parents contribute equally to
this bias against the aggressivity of girls.

TABLE 12.2

Significant Effects in the Comparisons of English Canadian Middle-Class and Japanese Immigrant Middle-Class Parents

Value Dimensions

Comparisons	1) Help Withholding (np = 58.6)	2) Siding with Baby vs. Child (np = 42.7)	3a) Temper Control (np = 30.0)	3b) Social Temper Control (np = 41.6)	4) Insolence Control (np = 25.0)	5) Attention Denial (np = 75.0)	6) Comfort Withholding (np = 41.6)	7) Autonomy Control (np = 58.3)	8) Guest Restriction (np = 62.5)	9) Siding with Guest vs. Child (np = 42.7)	10) Perceived Sex-Role Differences	11) Expected Sex-Role Differences
G	<u>14.33</u>	–	<u>10.81</u>	–	<u>10.29</u>	–	<u>20.37</u>	–	5.67	–	–	<u>16.45</u>
X	–	7.30	<u>10.16</u>	–	–	6.35	6.99	4.85	–	5.51	–	–
P	–	–	–	–	–	–	–	–	<u>7.81</u>	–	–	–
GX	–	–	–	–	–	–	–	–	–	–	–	–
GP	–	–	–	–	–	–	–	<u>7.84</u>	–	–	–	–
XP	–	–	–	–	–	–	–	–	–	–	–	–
GXP	–	–	–	–	–	–	–	–	–	–	–	–

Note: Entries are significant F values; those underlined are beyond the .01 level of confidence, the others are beyond the .05 level.
Source: Compiled by the authors.

301

TABLE 12.3

Significant Effects in the Comparisons of English Canadian Middle-Class, Japanese Immigrant Middle-Class, and Japanese Homeland Middle-Class Parents

Value Dimensions

Comparisons	1) Help Withholding (np = 58.6)	2) Siding with Baby vs. Child (np = 42.7)	3a) Temper Control (np = 30.0)	3b) Social Temper Control (np = 41.6)	4) Insolence Control (np = 25.0)	5) Attention Denial (np = 75.0)	6) Comfort Withholding (np = 41.6)	7) Autonomy Control (np = 58.3)	8) Guest Restriction (np = 62.5)	9) Siding with Guest vs. Child (np = 42.7)	10) Perceived Sex-Role Differences	11) Expected Sex-Role Differences
G	10.59	7.30	9.20	–	18.38	–	16.19	–	9.60	–	8.30	22.99
X	–	–	5.23	–	–	–	–	–	–	10.08	–	3.56
P	–	5.02	–	–	–	6.45	13.23	–	7.88	–	–	–
GX	4.06	–	3.82	–	–	–	–	–	–	–	–	–
GP	–	–	–	–	–	–	–	5.51	–	–	–	–
XP	–	–	–	–	–	–	–	–	–	–	–	–
GXP	–	–	–	–	–	–	–	–	–	–	–	–

Note: Entries are significant F values; those underlined are beyond the .01 level of confidence, the others are beyond the .05 level.
Source: Compiled by the authors.

302

The bias, however, works the opposite way on the autonomy issue in which case boys are given less encouragement than girls to venture out on their own. Thus, for both EC and JI parents, proper girl-like behavior entails a personal control of temper, personal control over aggression, and a certain degree of independence from parents. Proper boy-like behavior, in contrast, entails greater freedom in the expression of temper, whether directed toward things or toward peers, coupled with a certain degree of dependence on parents.

Why is it that two such diverse groups of parents, one Japanese in origin, the other English Canadian, end up with this particular perspective on how sons and daughters should be brought up? If pushed to its extreme, a socialization policy wherein girls are encouraged more than boys to show restraint and control of aggression and to be independent, would produce a society of females who are rational and self-controlled, and of males who are relatively dependent and impulsive. Whether this is the intention, subconscious or not, of our EC and JI parents, there is nonetheless an inconsistency on the part of EC parents, because they expect few boy-girl differences in comportment at the same time as they seem to train their sons and daughters along quite different, sex-specific lines. This inconsistency could contribute to sex-role conflicts for EC young people. By comparison JI parents are more consistent, for their sex-role expectations and their ways of treating children both lead toward sex-role differentiations.

The JI and EC parents are also very much alike in the ways they play their roles as mothers and fathers, but since the JH and EC parents were also much alike in these respects, there are no signs here of change in values on the part of JI parents. All told, there are four instances where fathers, both JI and EC, are more severe than mothers with their children, namely the child-baby dispute, attention, comfort, and guest privileges issues. Although in each instance JI and EC fathers are harsher than JI and EC mothers, there is no general trend for the mothers to be more lenient than the fathers. Instead, father-mother differences emerge on a select subset of issues only, suggesting that in both JI and EC middle-class families, fathers are expected to be more demanding than mothers on particular matters, namely, child-baby disputes and requests for attention, comfort, and guest privileges.

With the information available to us from this investigation, we have no way of determining why this particular combination of episodes emerges as a set, nor why this set discriminates between mother and father roles for both JI and EC parents. One possibility is that both groups of fathers are particularly intent on discouraging their children from becoming demanders or pests. Such a proposition is partially consistent with one other piece of information available, namely the fact that EC fathers are also more severe than EC mothers on the <u>autonomy</u> issue (see Figure 12.8). However, this is not the case for JI fathers, who are actually less severe than JI mothers on autonomy requests. Apparently, then, EC fathers are guided by the principle that children should not be demanders, whereas JI fathers are guided by some more complex set of principles.

FIGURE 12.8

G x P Interaction for Autonomy Control

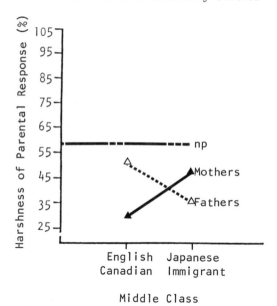

Middle Class

Source: Constructed by the authors.

Figure 12.8 also indicates that in EC middle-class families, mothers are more inclined than fathers to encourage gestures of autonomy, which is the reverse of the JI middle-class pattern. This finding brings us back to work on achievement motivation and the contention that, in cases where mothers rather than fathers take the more active role in independence training, the greater the chances are that children will be motivated toward achievement. This means that the EC middle-class family should be a more propitious training ground for achievement motivation than the JI middle-class family, and interestingly, McClelland's cross-national indexes of achievement do place English Canada much higher than Japan (see McClelland 1961, pp. 461-63).

THE JAPANESE STUDY: AN OVERVIEW

Our aims in this final old-country study were threefold: to identify attitudes toward child rearing, to compare Japanese and English Canadian child-rearing attitudes, and to search for changes that might take place in such attitudes when Japanese parents immigrate to Canada and start their own families in a North American setting. With these purposes in mind, we collected and compared three samples of middle-class parents, one of native Japanese living in Japan, a second of immigrants from Japan now living in Canada, and a third of native English Canadians.

Evidence for Value Stability

First, we found that Japanese homeland and immigrant parents are in many respects very much alike in their child-rearing values, so much so that there are numerous sharp contrasts between English Canadian and Japanese (old-country as well as immigrant) values. In fact, when viewed from a North American perspective, one gets the impression that Japanese parents are inconsistent in their approaches to children. Compared to their EC counterparts, they withhold gestures of help and comfort, leaving the impression that they are harsh socializers; at the same time they let temper and insolence outbursts pass with relatively little fuss, and show lenience toward children's requests for guest privileges. On second thought, however, one begins to wonder which group is the more inconsistent or whether either group actually is inconsistent, for it is just as true that EC parents blow hot and cold, being harsh on temper and insolence but tender on requests for help and comfort. And one could easily argue that, by overlooking displays of temper and insolence and holding back on gestures of help and comfort, Japanese parents are eminently consistent if their aim is to foster self-reliance and independence. What stands out is the fact that JH and JI parents present essentially the same pattern of reactions on an interesting subset of issues, and on that subset they are distinctively different from the EC comparison group. Thus, relative to their EC counterparts, Japanese middle-class parents, those at home as well as those in Canada, place more stress on self-reliance, on the ability to take the bumps of life without whimpering, on being sociable, and on differentiating sex-role modes of conduct. They also give their children more freedom to vent aggression through temper and insolence displays. The important point here is that these contrasts in Japanese and English Canadian child-rearing orientations hold as well for Japanese immigrant parents as for Japanese homelanders.

There is a second example of what appears to be value stability or resistance to change, but in this case the pattern displayed by both JH and JI parents just happened to be like that of EC parents. Thus, there was no real test in the Canadian setting of the durability of the values involved. The example in question is the tendency for JH and JI fathers to be more demanding socializers than mothers on a series of issues, ranging from child-baby disputes to guest privileges. The fact that both JI and JH fathers are harsher socializers than their wives does not constitute a real case of value resistance since there was no need for JI parents to change in order to be in style with EC parents, who show the same tendency. Some other setting could well elicit changes on the very same issue.

The two groups of Japanese parents also expect more sex-role differentiations than English Canadian parents do, and one wonders what effect this greater stress placed on sex-role identities might have on JI families who find themselves in a Canadian setting where the norms for sex roles are much more relaxed. Although conflicts could develop within JI families around this issue, our guess is that JI parents would likely let their children work out their own solutions to the sex-role issue, since they place great stress on self-reliance and independence in their child-rearing attitudes.

Evidence for Value Changes

By shifting our focus from JH to JI middle-class parents and comparing both with English Canadian parents, we were able to isolate a number of intriguing changes in Japanese child-rearing values that seem to be attributable to the life experiences of JI parents in Canada. We inferred that a change took place if the JI parents reacted in a substantially different manner from their JH counterparts when each group was compared with EC middle-class parents. In the first place, the JI parents are less severe than their JH counterparts on the child-baby dispute issue, and the shift is clearly in the direction of EC value norms. They also change their perspectives about sex-role differences, bringing them more in line with those of EC parents. At a deeper level, changes show up in the ways JI parents, relative to their JH counterparts, react to sons and to daughters. Whereas JH parents are generally harsher and more demanding on sons than on daughters, the JI parents show no such bias against sons. Rather they are much more like EC parents in the distinctions they make between sons and daughters. Actually, in certain instances they appear to have adopted the EC tendency to be harsher on daughters than on sons. Thus, relative to Japanese homelanders, the JI parents end up with a totally different conception of how parents should relate to sons and to daughters.

We also noted that other Japanese-style values change, but not necessarily in line with EC values. The case in point is the decrease noted in the amount of maternal encouragement JI parents give to a child's bids for autonomy. This represents a change, as we define it, but it is not an example of a shift toward EC values. This example suggests that deeper forms of value changes can take place for immigrants, deeper in the sense that the change need not be limited to simple adjustments to the host nation's norms.

Japanese Parents in the Canadian Context

As we come to the end of our Japanese study, we begin to see various features of the value profile of JI parents and how these features mesh with those of the English Canadian profile. Certain features, as we have shown, are basically Japanese in nature, while others are residues of value shifts in the direction of Canadian value norms. Although important differences between JI and EC parents remain, as with sex-role expectations, there are also fascinating similarities that should help in the overall adjustment process. One interesting example is the similarity in the ways both parental groups react to boys and to girls. In both JI and EC middle-class families, girls are, in general, treated more harshly than boys, and in certain instances, the trend is quite pronounced. For example, both JI and EC girls are discouraged more than boys are from losing their tempers or quarreling with a guest. Thus, both groups of parents seem to insist that girls restrain themselves on such issues, while boys are given greater freedom to express temper and aggression. At the same time, both JI and EC girls are given more encouragement than boys to be independent. It seems then that both groups of parents want to shape boys and girls along sex-distinctive lines, and what is fascinating is that both groups have a common view of what constitutes appropriate sex-role behavior. Girls apparently should be more rational and self-controlled relative to boys, who in turn should be more emotive and expressive.

JI and EC middle-class parents are also very much alike in the ways they play their roles as mothers and fathers. Thus, in both JI and EC families, fathers are harsher than mothers in their reactions to children who quarrel with a younger sibling, who ask for attention or comfort, or who request guest privileges. It is not that the fathers are generally harsher, but only so on a subset of issues.

Finally, on the autonomy issue, JI and EC values diverge again in an interesting way. In EC families, mothers encourage autonomy bids more than fathers, whereas in JI families, mothers are less encouraging than fathers. According to McClelland and Rosen, maternal encouragement of independence is more effective than paternal encouragement in the development of achievement motivation, which would make EC middle-class families a more effective training ground for achievement motivation. But we have to be cautious with this interpretation, because we also have strong indications in our findings that JI parents, as a team, place great stress on developing independent and self-reliant children. Clearly, more research is needed to explain these discrepancies and to determine just which traits of character are given high priority in the Japanese immigrants' scheme of child rearing.

MAJOR TRENDS IN THE VALUE ADJUSTMENTS
OF IMMIGRANT PARENTS

Since this is the last of the four old-country studies, we were prompted to search through all four for general types of value adjustments that might characterize all immigrant groups who leave their homelands and start their families in the New World. A sample of four immigrant groups is small enough, and since one of the four, Japan, includes only middle-class parents, our base for exploring general trends is all the smaller. General trends, however, do emerge. For example, all four groups adjust their values to one extent or another, and the changes are nearly always in the direction of host-nation norms. Yet all four maintain at least some features of old-country value styles.

Still, each of our four examples has its own distinctive mode of adjusting, and there are clear differences in the depth and breadth of the value adjustments made. For instance, our Portuguese parents are relatively "large" adjusters compared to the Japanese and Italians who are "small" adjusters, even when full consideration is given to the room available for adjustment, which was done by using homeland and host-nation child-rearing value styles as frames of reference. In terms of depth of change, our Japanese parents make important adjustments of a very subtle sort, compared to the Portuguese who make adjustments of a more predictable sort. When adjustments are made, certain groups become less severe on particular value dimensions and more severe on others (for example, the Portuguese), while other groups change only in the direction of more leniency (for example, the Japanese and Greeks) or in the direction of less leniency (for example, the Italians).

Of the four groups, the Portuguese immigrant parents stand out as the most susceptible to acculturation influences. Except for those instances where there are basic value overlaps, and thus no room for change, they are the most prone to adjust old-country values, and their value malleability shows itself in bi-directional adjustments, that is, they become more demanding or severe on particular value dimensions and less demanding on others, but always in the direction of host-nation norms. Certain features of the Portuguese old-country values persist: Portuguese immigrant parents remain harsher in their reactions to social temper; they are less prone to encourage autonomy gestures; and fathers remain less conciliatory than mothers in their reactions to requests for comfort and more vigilant than mothers with respect to sex-role differences. But otherwise, values adjust toward American norms in that Portuguese immigrant parents become more lenient on requests for attention, more lenient on child-baby disputes, less lenient with sons who are insolent, less lenient with daughters who ask for guest privileges, and less demanding of sex-role differences.

The Japanese, Greek, and Italian immigrant groups are relatively less malleable, and each keeps numerous features of the distinctive child-rearing style of the homeland. The Japanese immigrant parents stay Japanese on a solid set of dimensions; like their homeland counterparts, they remain harsher than the host-nation parents on requests for help and comfort; they remain softer on insolence, temper, and guest privileges; and they maintain a high expectation of sex-role differences. Where value changes occur, they are all in the direction of greater liberality, in the sense that Japanese immigrant parents become less harsh on child-baby disputes, less vigilant in their sex-role perceptions, and less focused and severe on sons than on daughters—and in each case the adjustment is in line with host-nation values. This last mentioned aspect of value change is extensive and deep, and it could be due to the fact that the Japanese immigrant parents were from middle-class backgrounds only, and perhaps middle-class value changes take this more subtle form.

Greek immigrants to Canada can count on a number of value overlaps with the host nation's norms which make immigration somewhat easier and more comfortable. But there is still much room for value adjustment, and the fact that few adjustments are made means that the Greek immigrant parents remain, in various respects, essentially Greek. They remain softer than Canadians on insolence, temper, social temper, and child-guest disputes and harsher on autonomy requests. Values that change in the direction of host-nation norms are illustrated by the fact that our Greek immigrant parents become less severe than Greek homelanders on child-baby disputes, they reduce their sex-role expectations, bringing them in line with those of Canadians, and they show signs of shifting to a pattern of same-sex leniency, also a Canadian characteristic.

Italian immigrant parents make relatively few value adjustments, even though there is much room for change, and the changes are all in the direction of leniency. Overall, they stay basically Italian: they remain softer than host-nation parents on the help and guest privilege issues, harsher on the attention, the child-baby and the child-guest dispute issues, and less encouraging on the autonomy issue. They maintain the distinctive, old-country ways of playing their roles as mothers and fathers, and they keep a cross-sex leniency pattern on guest privileges. The value adjustments they do make are clearly in the direction of host-nation norms, for they become less lenient on insolence and temper outbursts, and they reduce their sex-role expectations. They also show signs of becoming more liberal on the autonomy issue to the extent that mothers and fathers disagree on autonomy, which is not the case for Italian homeland parents.

There are several general trends that emerge here. The first is an adaptation in parental sex-role expectations. The Greek, Italian, and Portuguese parents each adjust their sex-role expectations down to North American levels, while the Japanese parents do essentially the same, but in a less obvious way: they reduce their sex-role perceptions and change radically their modes of treating sons and daughters, in both instances becoming much like host-nation parents. What is interesting here is that the agents of these changes could very likely be the children of immigrant parents, who, through social contacts in the new setting, are in the best position to draw attention to the fact that changes are called for in the way old-country people view sex roles.

The second general trend is a change in old-country ways of treating sons as compared to daughters, and in this instance, too, children are likely the agents who activate the change or bring the need for change to parents' attention. For three groups, adjustments are made that bring distinctively foreign attitudes toward sons and daughters into line: Japanese immigrant parents shift from oversocializing sons to the Canadian tendency of oversocializing daughters; Greek parents shift to the Canadian same-sex leniency pattern on particular dimensions; and Portuguese parents become more lenient with sons who are insolent and more lenient with daughters who ask for guest privileges, both in the direction of

American norms. It is only the Italian immigrant parents who do not show similar value adjustments.

The third trend is a general reduction in the harshness of old-country responses to child-baby quarreling, and we wonder if children may not be the instrumental agents in effecting this change as well. Greek, Portuguese, and Japanese immigrant groups are all less demanding on this issue than their homeland counterparts, becoming thereby more like host-nation parents. Again, the exception is the Italians who stay stubbornly Italian in this respect, and again refrain from a value shift that would make them more lenient.

One might also expect that adjustments would be made in the lenient attitude several immigrant groups have toward insolence. Too much softness on insolence might well become a public sign of immigrant status that would meet with social disapproval. Italian and Portuguese immigrant groups do adjust by becoming more severe on insolence, but Japanese and Greek groups do not, as though for them this feature of old-country values was still, for some reason, essential.

There are other value changes and resistances to change that might be anticipated. One might expect changes on the autonomy issue, for example, since North Americans are said to place relatively greater emphasis on early independence training. In fact, three of our four homeland groups are much less prone than the host-nation parents to encourage autonomy gestures, the fourth being the middle-class Japanese, who were already as liberal as the host-nation parents on autonomy. However, the other three groups—the Italian, Greek, and Portuguese immigrant parents— had plenty of room to change, but none did, which suggests that they were either not able or not willing to make such an adjustment in their values.

In summary, what we find in this analysis of value adjustments is that the children of immigrants, through social contacts in the new national setting, are the likely major agents of value change. It is the children who are best placed to find mismatches between the values of their parents and those of host-nation parents, and they are also well placed to relay those discrepancies to parents who, we presume, are anxious to make their children's social adjustment as easy as possible. Immigrant parents, it seems, make value adjustments with their children clearly in mind. They apparently begin by tempering and bringing into line old-country sex-role expectations, and then they make as many adjustments as they can "afford" in their actual modes of behaving with children— for example, modifying their ways of treating sons as compared to daughters or their styles of playing the roles of mother and father.

Some, like our Portuguese parents, can apparently afford to make many adjustments, while others, like our Italian and Japanese parents, can afford few changes because they seem much more intent on keeping the basic outlines of their distinctively Italian and Japanese child-rearing styles. We find this exploration of great interest, and it would be exciting to go further in follow-up studies with a larger sample of immigrant groups, a broader sample of host nations, and a more comprehensive set of value dimensions.

13

CHILD-REARING VALUES:
IN PERSPECTIVE

With the globe-trotting behind us, we try in this final chapter
to bring the pieces together and get some perspective on the whole
investigation. We began innocently enough in Chapter 2 by focusing
on the child-rearing values of French-speaking and English-speaking
Canadian parents, and as we explored the similarities and differences between these two groups, we began to wonder what was
"French" about French Canadians and "English" about English
Canadians. This line of questioning ultimately prompted us to explore the supposedly distinctive characteristics of various national
groups in Europe, North America, and even the Far East. Even
though we have found the globe-trotting instructive and exciting, we
realized from the start that there was no logical end to the number
of nations one might incorporate in such an investigation. Nor were
we directed by some overall theoretical plan. Rather, we simply
followed our own interests, starting with an examination of "Frenchness" in child-rearing values which led to a comparative study of
French Canadian, French French, French Belgian, and Franco-
American parents, as well as those involved in French-American
mixed marriages. Then we explored "Englishness" in a comparable
way by comparing the child-rearing values of English Canadian,
English English, and Anglo-American parents. Then, since we had
focused sharply on the French-English bicultural fact in Canada, we
did the same in bicultural Belgium by comparing the child-rearing
values of Flemish and Walloon parents, providing thereby an important comparison piece for the Canadian study.

But Canada is much more than bicultural, for it derives its
identity as much from the multiculturality of its people today as
from the biculturality of its founders. Accordingly, we extended

our investigation to immigrant groups—Greek, Italian, Portuguese, and Japanese couples who have immigrated to Canada or the United States and who are now starting their own families in the North American scene. In order to see what changes take place in child-rearing values as a consequence of immigration, we also included comparable "homeland" groups of young parents living in Greece, Italy, Portugal, and Japan, and this permitted us to trace changes in values from homeland to the New World, and, by comparing the values of immigrant and host-nation parents, to pinpoint examples of resistance to change.

The first way we will try to get perspective on this broad-ranged study is to bring ten homeland groups together into one over-all comparison. The earlier chapters dealt with two-nation or at most three-nation comparisons, and now we want to broaden the comparison base by looking at ten national groups at one time. To us this seems necessary because our selection of national groups, haphazard as it may be, happens to be a collection of this world's centers of civilization, each group being, in fact, a distinctive variation on the human condition. We want to examine these ten centers of humanity on a wider screen, to see which general trends, if any, run through, and which features, if any, still stand out as distinctive when the line of regard has been extended to this degree.

Once we have brought the ten homeland groups into compari-son and ferreted out examples of cross-nationally common and cross-nationally distinctive child-rearing values, we then try to trace the psychological roots of these common and distinctive values. This we do by relating the results derived from our approach to child-rearing values to those derived from a quite different and in-dependent cross-national approach to values, David McClelland's investigation of motive systems. Whatever links turn up between our findings and McClelland's should deepen our understanding of why parents interact as they do with children and what impact par-ents' styles of interacting have on the developing child. Finally, we try to demonstrate the potential usefulness of our approach to child-rearing values by extending the approach to teacher-pupil re-lationships. In this demonstration, we focus on the matches and mismatches of the child-rearing values of parents and teachers and the impact these alignments or misalignments of values can have on the child at school and on the education process itself.

A TEN-NATION PERSPECTIVE

As we anticipated in the introductory chapter, many of those features that stood out as different and distinctive in the two- or three-nation comparisons, already described in earlier chapters, level off or fade away on the wider screen. But what is fascinating to us is that not all narrow-screen contrasts fade away on the wide screen. Some distinctive national characteristics hold up even in this ten-nation comparison, and, what is just as important, some surprisingly stable cross-national trends stand out in sharper relief.

The parental groups we will be dealing with here are: American, English Canadian, French Canadian, English, French, French Belgian, Dutch Belgian, Italian, Greek, and Portuguese. In each case, we have full information on both working- and middle-class subgroups of parents. Our mode of analysis will be the same as in earlier chapters, based this time on a series of 10 x 2 x 2 x 2 analyses of variance covering ten national groups. The significant outcomes from these analyses are summarized in Table 13.1 (the mean scores for each subgroup available in Table A 13.1).

The statistical complexity here is much greater than in earlier chapters. In fact, the complexity seems to increase geometrically as the number of groups included increases. In order not to get lost in this complexity, we will follow through the standard analyses, as before, but give more attention here to general patterns of results than to the many details and the many group-by-group comparisons one could pursue. In addition, we will make use of three separate means of organizing the findings: ranking national groups in terms of relative leniency or harshness; comparing groups with respect to the neutral points of our scales; and distinguishing between aid and discipline scales as we compare national and social-class subgroups.

The rankings presented in Tables 13.2, 13.3, and 13.4 place in order each social-class subgroup of parents from each nation, running from most harsh or most demanding to least. Separate rankings are given for the "aid" scales, the "discipline" scales, and for the perceived and expected sex-role scales. These help one see the setting-to-setting differences that are traceable to national background and to social class. In other words, they provide an overview of how parents from a particular social background in a particular national setting compare with parents from a similar social background in another setting.

The neutral points provide a slightly different perspective. As indicated earlier, the neutral point for any particular scale is the dividing line above which a parent tries to exert control or constraint on the child's behavior. For example, the neutral point of 41.6 on the comfort withholding scale is the dividing line between giving and refusing comfort to the child; for the insolence control scale the neutral point of 25.0 is the break between tolerating insolence and trying to limit it. The summary of the analysis of neutral points is presented in Table 13.5.

TABLE 13.1

Significant Effects in the Ten-Nation Comparison

Value Dimensions

Comparisons	1) Help Withholding (np = 67.8)	2) Siding with Baby vs. Child (np = 42.7)	3a) Temper Control (np = 30.0)	3b) Social Temper Control (np = 41.6)	4) Insolence Control (np = 25.0)	5) Attention Denial (np = 75.0)	6) Comfort Withholding (np = 41.6)	7) Autonomy Control (np = 58.3)	8) Guest Restriction (np = 62.5)	9) Siding with Guest vs. Child (np = 42.7)	10) Perceived Sex-Role Differences	11) Expected Sex-Role Differences
G	8.61	13.33 / 52.67	9.35 / 29.25	6.87 / 60.49	12.18 / 59.38	3.03	2.27 / 9.56	9.33 / 12.02	15.27	4.15 / 11.77	6.23 / 26.87	6.18 / 54.50
C	–	–	–	–	–	–	–	–	–	–	–	–
X	–	–	–	–	–	–	–	–	–	–	–	–
P	5.68	5.26	–	3.73	3.39	10.83	9.37	–	–	4.65	16.93	–
GC	2.15	–	–	4.08	–	–	–	–	–	10.57	2.42	–
GX	–	–	–	–	–	–	–	–	–	4.19	–	–
GP	–	2.84	–	–	–	–	2.18	–	–	–	–	2.45
CX	–	–	–	–	4.96	–	–	–	–	–	–	–
CP	–	5.55	–	–	–	–	–	–	–	–	5.32	4.43
XP	–	–	–	–	–	–	–	–	–	–	–	4.45
GCX	–	–	–	–	–	–	–	–	–	–	–	–
GCP	–	–	–	–	–	–	–	–	–	–	–	–
GXP	–	–	–	–	–	–	–	–	–	–	–	–
CXP	–	–	–	–	–	–	–	–	–	–	–	–
GCXP	–	–	–	–	–	–	–	–	–	–	–	–

Note: Entries are significant F values; those underlined are beyond the .01 level of confidence, the others are beyond the .05 level.

Source: Compiled by the authors.

316

TABLE 13.2

National Social-Class Subgroups Ranked According to Harshness of Reactions on Aid Scales[1]

Aid Scales

National Groups	Help Withholding WC	Help Withholding MC	Attention Denial WC	Attention Denial MC	Comfort Withholding WC	Comfort Withholding MC	Autonomy Control WC	Autonomy Control MC	Guest Restrictions WC	Guest Restrictions MC	Median Aid Ranking WC	Median Aid Ranking MC	Composite Rank Order Medians[2] for Aid WC	Composite Rank Order Medians[2] for Aid MC
Americans	5	6	10	9	8	3	8	10	7	7	8	7	9.5	8
English Canadians	3	3	7	4	6	7	9	9	1	3	6	4	5.5	3
French Canadians	7	8	2	6	10	8	10	8	4.5	8	7	8	8	10
English	9	2	8	3	9	9	6	1	6	4	8	3	9.5	2
French	2	1	4	10	1	2	1	5	4.5	6	2	5	1	5
French Belgians	1	4	9	7	2	5	2	6	3	2	2.5	5	2	5
Dutch Belgians	4	5	5	5	3	1	4	2	2	1	3.8	2	3	1
Italians	10	9	1	2	5	6	5	7	10	9	5.3	7	4	8
Greeks	8	10	6	8	4	4	3	3	9	5	6	5	5.5	5
Portuguese	6	7	3	1	7	10	7	4	8	10	6.8	7	7	8

[1] National social-class subgroups are rank ordered within columns. The lower the rank the harsher the overall parental reaction. A national social-class subgroup ranked 1 on a given scale is the harshest, while a national social-class subgroup ranked 10 is the most lenient or most conciliatory.

[2] The composite rank order represents the ordering of the median ranks of each subgroup on the aid scales.

Source: Compiled by the authors.

TABLE 13.3

National Social-Class Subgroups Ranked According to Harshness of Reactions on Discipline Scales[1]

National Groups	Siding with Baby versus Child		Temper Control		Social Temper Control		Insolence Control		Siding with Guest versus Child		Median Discipline Ranking		Composite Rank Order for Discipline Medians[2]	
	WC	MC	WC	MC	WC	MC	WC	MC	WC	MC	WC	MC	WC	MC
American	9	10	6	6	7	9	5	5	6	7	6.3	7	6.5	8
English Canadian	4	9	1	2.5	2	7	1	4	2	9	1.8	7	1	8
French Canadian	3	7	5	1	3	8	2	6	1	8	2.8	7	3	8
English	10	8	9	9	9	10	8	9	7	10	8.8	9.3	9	10
French	1	6	4	7	5	6	6	1	9	6	5	6	5	6
French Belgian	2	1	2	4	1	1	3	2	3	1	2.3	1.9	2	1
Dutch Belgian	7	5	8	8	4	5	4	3	4	4	4.9	5.3	4	5
Italian	8	4	10	10	10	4	9	10	8	2	9	4.3	10	4
Greek	6	3	7	5	6	3	7	7	5	3	6.3	3.9	6.5	3
Portuguese	5	2	3	2.5	8	2	10	8	10	5	8	2.5	8	2

[1]National social-class subgroups are rank ordered within columns. The lower the rank the harsher the overall parental reaction. A national social-class subgroup ranked 1 on a given scale is the harshest, while a national social-class subgroup ranked 10 is the most lenient or most conciliatory.

[2]The composite rank order represents the ordering of the median ranks of each subgroup on the discipline scales.

TABLE 13.4

National Social-Class Subgroups Ranked According
to the Number of Sex-Role Differences
Expected and Perceived

| | Scales | | | |
| | Expected Sex-Role Differences | | Perceived Sex-Role Differences | |
National Groups	WC	MC	WC	MC
American	9	10	4.5	8.5
English Canadian	7	9	8	7
French Canadian	6	8	10	6
English	8	5	7	10
French	3	3	4.5	4
French Belgian	1	4	3	2
Dutch Belgian	4	2	9	5
Italian	5	7	6	8.5
Greek	2	1	2	3
Portuguese	10	6	1	1

Note: National social-class subgroups are rank ordered
within columns according to the number of sex-role differences
expected or perceived. A national subgroup ranked 1 perceived
or expects the most differences in behavior between boys and
girls. A national subgroup ranked 10 perceived or expects the
fewest differences.

Source: Compiled by the authors.

319

TABLE 13.5

Positions of National-Group Means Relative to the Neutral Points of the Aid and Discipline Scales

Scales	American		English Canadian		French Canadian		English		French		French Belgian		Dutch Belgian		Italian		Greek		Portuguese	
	WC	MC	WC	MC	WC	MC	WC	MC	WC	MC	WC	MC	WC	MC	WC	MC	WC	MC	WC	MC
Aid Scales																				
Help Withholding (np = 67.8)	+	+	+	+	+	+	+	+	+	+	+	+	+	+	+	+	+	+	+	+
Attention Denial (np = 75.0)	+	0	-	-	-	-	+	-	+	+	+	+	+	-	+	-	+	-	+	-
Comfort Withholding (np = 41.6)	-	-	-	-	-	-	-	-	-	-	-	-	-	-	-	-	-	-	-	-
Autonomy Control (np = 58.3)	+	+	+	+	+	+	-	-	-	-	-	-	-	-	-	-	-	-	-	-
Guest Restriction (np = 62.5)	+	+	+	+	+	+	+	+	+	+	+	+	+	+	+	+	+	+	+	+
Discipline Scales																				
Insolence Control (np = 25.0)	-	-	-	-	-	-	-	-	-	-	-	-	-	-	-	-	-	-	-	-
Siding with Baby (np = 42.7)	-	+	-	-	-	-	-	-	-	-	-	-	-	-	-	-	-	-	-	-
Siding with Guest (np = 42.7)	-	-	-	-	-	-	-	-	-	-	-	-	-	-	-	-	-	-	-	-
Temper Control (np = 30.0)	-	-	-	-	-	-	-	-	-	-	-	-	-	-	-	-	-	-	-	-
Social Temper Control (np = 41.6)	-	-	-	-	-	-	-	-	-	-	-	-	-	-	-	-	-	-	-	-

Note: A minus sign indicates that the mean lies above the neutral point, for example, more toward the severe pole, while a plus sign indicates that the mean lies below the neutral point, for example, more toward the lenient pole. A zero signifies that the mean lies on the neutral point. The help withholding scale is based on three questions only because of a translation problem with the Italian sample (see Chapter 9).

Source: Compiled by the authors.

We have referred to aid and discipline scales in earlier chapters. It will be recalled that what we mean by aid scales are instances where the child in our tape recordings requests something from a parent, be it help, attention, comfort, autonomy, or guest privileges. The five discipline scales are instances where the child misbehaves and where parental intervention is called for, as in aggressivity directed toward a younger sibling, or a same-age friend, displays of temper toward things, or insolence. Thus, the distinction between aid and discipline scales is not based on intercorrelations, but simply on the fact that in one case the child instigates parental reaction by a request of some sort, while in the other case the child instigates a reaction from the parent by not conforming to societal rules. By considering the two types of scales separately and by calculating composite rank orders (Rokeach 1973), we are able to compare national and social-class groups in terms of their overall readiness to aid their children on the one hand and to discipline them on the other.

The analyses to follow then are based on our standard statistical analyses, supplemented by these three means of organizing the findings from the various comparisons.

THE EFFECTS OF NATIONAL BACKGROUND AND SOCIAL CLASS ON CHILD-REARING VALUES

From just a rapid inspection of Table 13.1, it is clear that national background and social class, both alone and in interaction, have pervasive and strong influences on parents' child-rearing values. In fact, significant differences among national groups of parents turned up on all of our scales, including those dealing with sex roles. Similarly, differences resulting from social class appeared on all but three scales—help withholding, attention denial, and guest restrictions.

Consider first the effects of social-class background. It is striking to find that for most of the aspects of child-rearing values touched on in our study, working-class parents are harsher and more demanding socializers than are their middle-class counterparts. Still, the amount of difference between working-class and middle-class parents varies from setting to setting and from value dimension to value dimension. In some cases there are no class differences and in certain few instances, middle-class parents turn out to be more demanding than working-class parents. Overall, though, this broad-ranged analysis has turned up a powerful "general trend," running across the ten national settings, indicating that parents from lower socioeconomic backgrounds tend to be more severe and demanding with their six-year-old children than parents from middle-class backgrounds.

There are limits to the generality of this trend, however, for in six cases (Figures 13.1 through 13.6) there are noteworthy interactions between social class and national origin. It is these interactions that force us to switch from the general to the specific, and we are immediately reminded that if there weren't exceptions of this sort, the world would be much less interesting than it actually is. As we review the outcomes for each of our value dimensions, these exceptions will come to light, along with features of the more general trend.

Parents' Reactions to Requests for Help

In all ten national settings, parents of both social-class backgrounds are prone to extend help to a six-year-old child when help is requested. However, in all national settings but two, middle-class parents are more helpful than working-class parents (see Figure 13.1). The interesting exceptions here are England and France: the French and the English middle-class parents are less helpful than their working-class counterparts, and compared to middle-class parents in the other nations, they are also generally less helpful. The French working-class parents are also severe on the help issue relative to their social-class equivalents in other national settings. In contrast, the English working-class parents are very helpful, ranking close to the Greek and Italian parents as one of the three most helpful of all working-class subgroups. In Greece and in Italy, however, helpfulness is also very pronounced among middle-class parents as well.

In our three North American settings (the United States, English Canada, and French Canada), social-class differences on help giving are small, whereas in our European nations, social-class differences in attitudes toward helping are generally much larger.

These trends emerge for the help giving issue: (1) Italian and Greek parents, whether from working- or middle-class backgrounds, are particularly responsive to their six-year-olds' requests for help; (2) in fact, all three of our Mediterranean samples, Portugal included, are more helpful than parents from West European settings; (3) in general, middle-class parents are more ready to extend help than working-class parents, but our French and English parents are exceptions to the general trend since French parents, whether working or middle class, are distinctively less helpful, whether compared to English middle-class parents or to other

FIGURE 13.1

G x C Interaction for Help Witholding

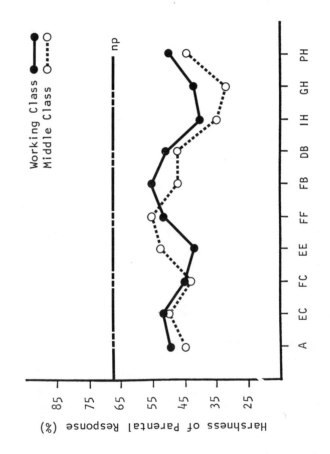

Source: Constructed by the authors.

national working-class subgroups; (4) for our three North American samples of parents there is less difference between social-class subgroups than is the case for our European samples.

Parents' Reactions to Bids for Attention

There are no social-class differences in parental responses to the six-year-old's bids for attention, and in general parents in most national settings tend to reject or ignore such bids. There are, however, three interesting exceptions to these general trends: American parents, whether of working- or middle-class standing, are particularly responsive to a child's demand for attention (see Table 13.5) as are French middle-class parents and French Belgian working-class parents.

Parents' Reactions to Requests for Comfort

When a six-year-old asks for comfort, it is more likely to be forthcoming in middle-class than in working-class families, and this is so in all ten of our national settings. Relative to the other settings, French Canadian and English parents stand out as the most comforting, whereas the French French and the Dutch Belgian parents are the least conciliatory, in that they tend either to refuse or ignore the child's requests for comfort.

Parents' Reactions to Requests for Autonomy

In general, middle-class parents grant their six-year-olds more autonomy than do working-class parents. But there are interesting national differences here. For example, in England, Dutch Belgium, and Portugal, middle-class parents are less prone than working-class parents to grant autonomy, whereas in Greece there is little difference in the reactions of working- and middle-class parents to requests for autonomy.

In this case, too, there is a definite difference between North American and European parents in their modes of coping with autonomy requests. American, English Canadian, and French Canadian parents were generally more permissive than all seven European parental groups, which is in line with the putative permissiveness of North American in contrast to European parents.

Parents' Reactions to Requests for Guest Privileges

Social class has little to do with the guest privilege issue.
Still there are important national group differences here. For example, Belgian parents, both Dutch and French, and English Canadians are much less willing to grant guest privileges than are the
parents in our Mediterranean countries, those in the United States,
or those in French Canada.

Parents' Reactions to Child-Baby Disputes

For eight national groups out of ten, working-class parents
display a harsher attitude than their middle-class counterparts when
the six-year-old child starts a quarrel with a younger sibling. The
two exceptions to this general trend are Italy and Portugal where
the social-class subgroups are essentially alike. There is in fact
an interesting pattern display in Figure 13.2 indicating that social-
class differences in reaction to child-baby disputes are fairly large
for the three North American samples or for France and England,
less so for the two Belgian samples, and almost nonexistent for the
three Mediterranean samples. Thus, even though American parents,
in general, are very lenient on this issue, the American middle-
class parents are particularly inclined to take the child's side in the
dispute. In fact we find in Table 13.5 that theirs is the only mean
score falling below the neutral point on the scale. Among the
working-class subsamples, the French French and the French Belgian parents are the most severe, while the American and the
English parents are the most lenient. However, in France there is
a large social-class difference, whereas in French Belgium the
middle-class parents are essentially as harsh as the working-class.
Overall, then, harshness toward a child-baby dispute seems to be
the marked characteristic of our Francophone working-class parents,
while leniency is the marked characteristic of our three Anglophone
middle-class subgroups. Finally, we have found large social-class
differences in reactions to a child-baby dispute for our North American samples of parents, less pronounced class differences for our
West European samples, and practically none for our Mediterranean
parental groups.

Parents' Reactions to Temper Displays

When a child displays temper, there is a universally strong
social-class difference in parent reactions: in all ten national

FIGURE 13.2

G x C Interaction for Child-Baby Dispute

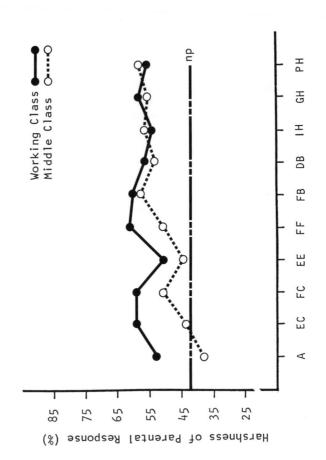

Source: Constructed by the authors.

settings, working-class parents responded more harshly than middle-class parents. Although no group tolerates temper outbursts, there are, nonetheless, large national differences in the modes of controlling temper. For example, English Canadian, French Belgian, and Portuguese parents either threaten or punish a child who shows temper, while Italian, English, and Dutch Belgian parents tend more to ignore the outburst or redirect the child's attention.

Parents' Reactions to Social Temper Displays

When the temper outburst is directed toward another person— a younger sibling or a same-age friend—social class no longer has so uniform an influence. For instance, English parents of both social classes still rank among the most lenient on social temper displays, whereas Italian middle-class parents become as harsh as their working-class counterparts on this issue, and compared with other middle-class subgroups, they no longer rank among the more permissive. Similarly, French Canadian middle-class parents, who were relatively severe on the temper scale, react in a rather lenient way when it is a question of social temper. French Belgian parents of both social classes still rank among the harshest and most punitive of all in this instance, whereas English Canadian middle-class and Portuguese working-class parents are relatively lenient on the social temper issue. In other words, there are distinct changes in the way different national subgroups of parents react, as attention switches from temper directed toward things to temper directed toward persons.

There is more to say about social temper, however, for here we encountered another significant national group by social-class interaction (see Figure 13.3), which is similar in important ways to that for the child-baby dispute issue. Again we find large social-class differences for our three North American groups and for the English, whereas social-class differences are less pronounced for the West European groups, and very small for the three Mediterranean groups. In other words, when a six-year-old displays social temper, working-class parents in our three North American settings and in England react harshly, while middle-class parents in North America are relatively permissive in their attitudes. This stands in sharp contrast to the Mediterranean nations where social-class differences are minimal.

FIGURE 13.3

G x C Interaction for Social Temper Control

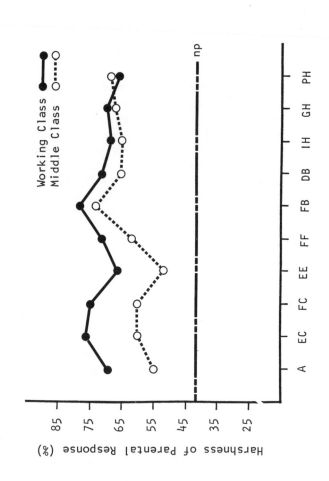

Source: Constructed by the authors.

Parents' Reactions to Insolence

Insolence from a six-year-old is not tolerated in any of the ten national settings. However, there are important differences from one national and social-class group to another, making this the third discipline scale where national background and social class interact significantly (see Figure 13.4). Thus, it is generally true that working-class parents are harsher disciplinarians than their middle-class counterparts, except in France where, if anything, the opposite holds. However, the three Mediterranean national groups are much more lenient on insolence than they were on other discipline scales, falling close to the generally lenient English parents in this instance. In the three North American settings, the social-class differences are again very pronounced, with the middle-class parents being much more lenient than working-class parents, especially so for the two Canadian groups. In the three West European nations, middle-class parents have a particularly harsh attitude toward insolence. France stands out because the French middle-class parents are more demanding on this issue than any of their middle-class counterparts in other settings, and in this instance even more demanding than the working-class French parents.

Parents' Reactions to a Child-Guest Dispute

When the issue is a squabble between a six-year-old and a same-age visitor to the home, we again find a relatively large social-class difference for our American, English Canadian, French Canadian, and English parents, while social-class distinctions are essentially nonexistent in the other settings, whether West European or Mediterranean (see Figure 13.5). It is also true that the three North American middle-class subgroups, along with the English, are tolerant on the child-guest dispute issue relative to our other middle-class subgroups, and the contrast with the more demanding working-class parents is sharp in these four settings. In the West European and Mediterranean settings, there are no such social-class differences in reactions; in some nations, the middle-class parents are the more tolerant, while in others (for example, Portugal, Italy, and French Belgium) the working-class parents are the more tolerant.

Parents' Sex-Role Perceptions

Again, there was a significant national group by social-class interaction in parents' perceptions of sex-role differences (see

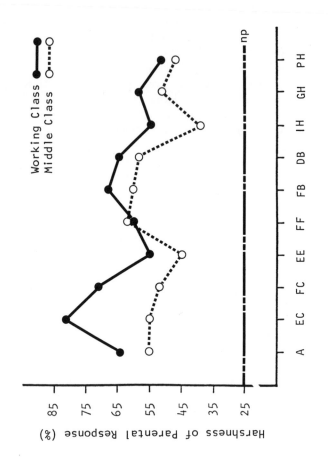

FIGURE 13.4

G x C Interaction for Insolence Control

Source: Constructed by the authors.

FIGURE 13.5

G x C Interaction for Child-Guest Dispute

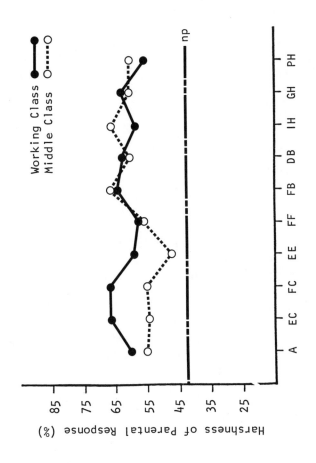

Source: Constructed by the authors.

Figure 13.6). In this case, though, the pattern of outcomes is quite different from that for the discipline scales. Although in general, working-class parents perceive more sex-role differences than middle-class parents, there are large national variations in the influence of social class on sex-role perceptions. For four parental groups—the American, English Canadian, English, and Italian—social-class differences are large compared with the remaining groups, for whom such differences are either much smaller, or, as in the case of the French Belgians, absent.

In terms of rankings, the Portuguese, Greek, and French Belgian parents have the highest sex-role perceptions, and since in these three cases there are few working- middle-class differences, there appear to be strong nationwide norms in Portugal, Greece, and French Belgium for boys and girls to maintain distinctive forms of comportment.

Parents' Sex-Role Expectations

In the case of the parents' sex-role expectations there is no nation by social-class interaction, and this is so because in all settings except Portugal, working-class parents have higher sex-role expectations than their middle-class counterparts. There is, in other words, a strong cross-national trend for social-class subgroups to have distinctive sex-role expectations, with working-class parents expecting more boy-girl differences. Why Portugal is an exception to this trend is an interesting question to be explored.

Furthermore, our ten groups of parents differ in the magnitude of their sex-role expectations. Greek, French, French Belgian, and Dutch Belgian parents have the highest sex-role expectations, whereas American, English Canadian, and Portuguese parents have the lowest.

Similarly, there are interesting differences among national groups in the sex-role expectations parents have for boys as compared to girls. This significant interaction is discussed below in the context of other "sex-of-child" contrasts.

In summary, several clear trends run through this series of comparisons, and the trends themselves interact in instructive ways. What fascinates us most is that there are no universal trends but rather regional patterns of child-rearing orientations, such as those for North American parents that differ from West European parents, who differ in turn from Mediterranean parents. These regional patterns override and cut across clusters of nations linked by language and ethnicity, such as "French" people living in France, Belgium, and Canada. We do not find, in other words, a cross-national French

FIGURE 13.6

G x C Interaction for Perceived Sex-Role Differences

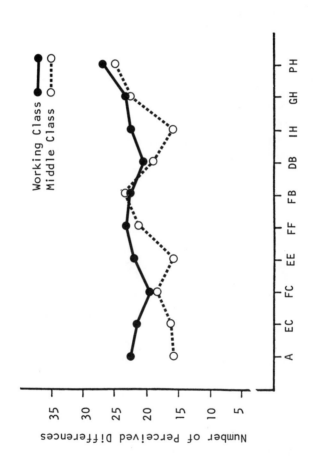

Source: Constructed by the authors.

style of child-rearing values. Nor is there a clear "English" cluster encompassing Anglo-Americans, Anglo-Canadians, and English parents. Instead, French Canadian parents, for example, typically fall into a North American regional grouping of common modes of reacting to children.

One particularly revealing trend is the interplay between national background and social-class standing. One's social-class standing has more pronounced effects on child-rearing values for certain national groups of parents than for others. Furthermore the effects of social class change as we switch attention from "aid" type issues to "discipline" type issues. On the aid scales—those where a child requests something from parents—social class has little effect on the reactions of North American parents but a prominent effect on the reactions of European parents. The particular effect, however, is not always in the direction of middle-class parents being more ready to extend help or aid. In fact, in England and France we find that working-class parents are relatively more ready than middle-class parents to extend aid.

Discipline issues break out as a separate category of parent-child interactions, for parents who were lenient on requests for aid are not comparably lenient in their reactions to provocations of one sort or another. The social class dynamics underlying these two categories of parent-child interactions seem to be fundamentally different. Thus, distinctive patterns of reactions emerge for our four discipline scales, and, in general, social-class differences in modes of disciplining a troublesome six-year-old child are fairly large in North America and in Great Britain, less so in West European settings, and hardly evident at all in Mediterranean settings.

Overall, then, the child-rearing values of parents differ not only in degrees of harshness or leniency from one national setting to another, but also in the ways these values express themselves on aid and discipline issues and in the ways social-class background affects the values. For certain clusters of nations, social-class differences in parental severity on discipline matters are prominent, as for our three North American nations and England, whereas social-class background has little impact on the use of discipline in our Mediterranean nations where child-rearing norms appear to permeate all social strata. For our West European nations, the role played by social-class background varies from one nation to another, thereby setting this region off from North America and the Mediterranean with respect to the influence of social class on child-rearing values.

COMPARISONS OF THE CHILD-REARING
VALUES OF MOTHERS AND FATHERS

There were important differences in the reactions of mothers and fathers, and some of these are general trends while others are specific to particular national groups of parents. The general trends are fascinating: fathers in general are more helpful than mothers and also more lenient than mothers in coping with a six-year-old's displays of social temper or disputes with a guest. On the other hand, mothers are generally more prone than fathers to comply with bids for attention, and they are also more perceptive of sex-role differences than are fathers. These strike us as examples of cross-national patterns of complementarity between parents, wherein fathers are the relatively more lenient socializers in particular domains of interaction, but harsher socializers in other domains. These trends are fascinating because they suggest that there may be certain characteristics of maternal and paternal comportment that hold across many nations and possibly universally, wherein fathers are more helpful and more ready to let social aggressivity pass, while mothers are more responsive to attention bids and more perceptive of and possibly more concerned about sex-role differentiations. Of course it could be that children, in general, expect fathers and mothers to behave in particular ways and, through their expectations, help define maternal and paternal roles.

Apart from these general trends, there are a number of interesting interactions involving sex of parent and national group as depicted in Figures 13.7 and 13.8. Thus, mothers are more comforting than fathers in our American, English Canadian, French, Dutch Belgian, French Belgian, and Italian families, while fathers are more comforting than mothers in our French Canadian, English, Greek, and Portuguese families. However, the instances where fathers are more comforting are less pronounced than those where mothers are the more comforting. Furthermore, it is the American and English Canadian mothers who are especially prone to extend comfort, whereas it is the French, Dutch Belgian, and French Belgian fathers who are especially prone to withhold comfort.

Again, on the child-baby dispute issue there is a second national group by sex-of-parent interaction (see Figure 13.8), which shows us that for our American and English Canadian parents there is also a large mother-father contrast, and again the American and English Canadian mothers are less harsh than their husbands when confronted with a child-baby quarrel. The general trend for the other national groups is that both parents react more or less alike on this issue, although French and Belgian fathers are somewhat harsher than their wives, whereas French Canadian mothers and those from the three Mediterranean settings are somewhat harsher than their husbands.

FIGURE 13.7

G x P Interaction for Comfort Withholding

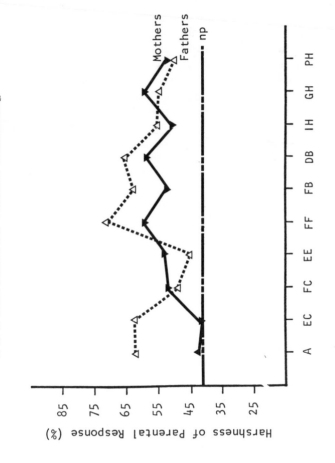

Source: Constructed by the authors.

FIGURE 13.8

G x P Interaction for Child-Baby Dispute

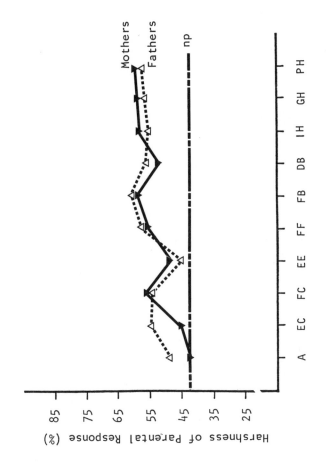

Source: Constructed by the authors.

In two instances mother-father differences in reactions are dependent upon social-class background, one being the child-baby dispute issue, the other, sex-role expectations. These two interactions are depicted in Figures 13.9 and 13.10, and they tell us that when confronted with a child-baby dispute, working-class mothers are generally harsher than their husbands, whereas middle-class mothers are more lenient than their husbands. With regard to sex-role expectations, mother-father differences in expectations are much more pronounced in working-class families, and it is the fathers who have particularly strong sex-role expectations. Thus, social class has a pervasive effect on the ways mothers and fathers deal with sibling quarrels, just as it also affects how mothers and fathers react to trends toward unisexism in children's comportment.

VALUE DIFFERENCES IN THE REARING OF SONS AND DAUGHTERS

Although not numerous, there are several interesting differences in the ways parents react to sons and to daughters. First, for the child-guest dispute issue, there is a cross-national tendency to be more permissive with disputative sons than with disputative daughters. However, on closer inspection we find that this trend holds only for one set of national groups but not for the other. This statistically significant interaction involving national group and sex of child is depicted in Figure 13.11, and it tells us that on the child-guest dispute issue, sons are treated more leniently than daughters in our American, French Canadian, English, Italian, and Greek families, whereas the bias favors daughters in our English Canadian, French, Dutch Belgian, French Belgian, and Portuguese families. Apparently, there are different norms about this form of children's aggressivity, and it is intriguing to us that certain national groups adopt the norm that disputes among peers are less appropriate for daughters than for sons, while other national groups adopt the opposite norm.

Finally, there are three cross-national trends wherein sons and daughters are treated differently depending upon the social-class background of the family (Figures 13.12, 13.13, and 13.14). The first has to do with insolence, where we find that in middle-class families insolent daughters are treated more harshly than insolent sons, whereas in working-class families insolent sons are treated more harshly than insolent daughters (Figure 13.12). The two other examples pertain to sex-role expectations and sex-role perceptions: middle-class parents of daughters both expect and perceive more signs of sex-role differentiation than do middle-class parents of sons,

FIGURE 13.9

C x P Interaction for Child–Baby Dispute

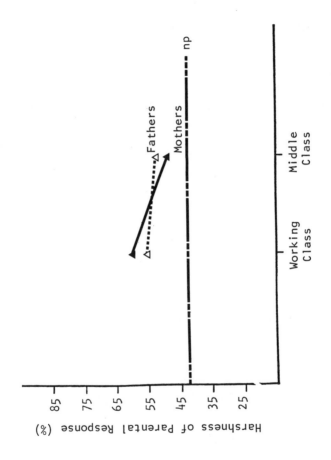

Source: Constructed by the authors.

FIGURE 13.10

C x P Interaction for Sex-Role Expectations

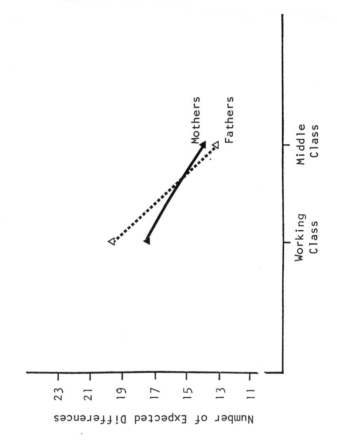

Source: Constructed by the authors.

FIGURE 13.11

G x X Interaction for Sex-Role Expectations

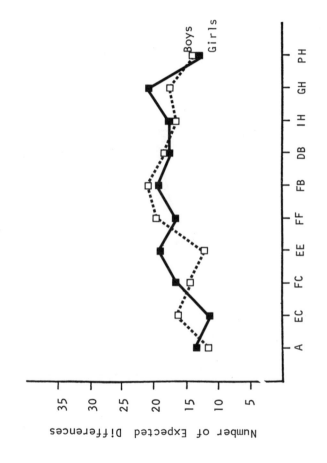

Source: Constructed by the authors.

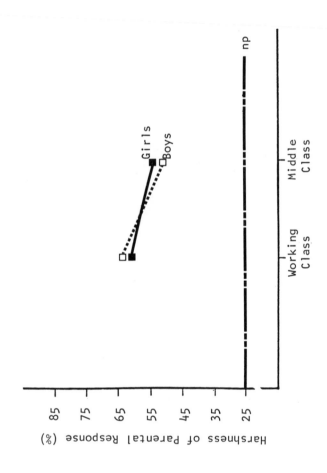

FIGURE 13.12

C x X Interaction for Insolence Control

FIGURE 13.13

C x X Interaction for Sex-Role Perceptions

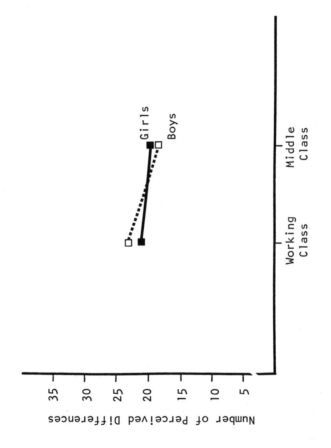

Source: Constructed by the authors.

FIGURE 13.14

C x X Interaction for Sex-Role Expectations

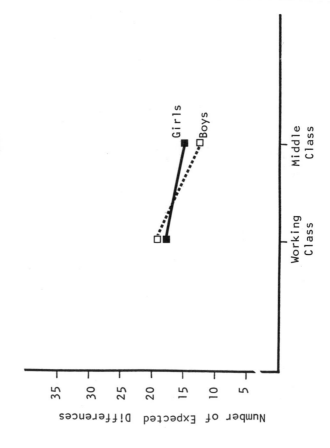

Source: Constructed by the authors.

344

whereas the reverse is true for working-class parents, that is, working-class parents of sons both expect and perceive more sex-role differentiations than do working-class parents of daughters (Figures 13.13 and 13.14). This trend, which is contributed to by all ten of our national groups, suggests that middle-class parents are generally more concerned about their daughters maintaining femininity than they are about their sons maintaining masculinity; working-class parents have a quite different set of concerns—that their sons stay masculine rather than their daughters stay feminine. This pervasive trend merits further investigation.

Note that, for each social-class subgroup, there is a consistency between the subgroup's treatment of insolence and its concerns about sex-role differentiations: the middle-class parents discourage girls from being insolent, as though it were not ladylike, while the working-class parents encourage girls to be insolent, as though, in the working class, girls have to be able to fight and stand up for their rights.

DISTINCTIVE NATIONAL APPROACHES TO CHILD REARING: A TEN-NATION PERSPECTIVE

By way of conclusion, we present here a nation-by-nation review of the distinctive emphases each national group of parents places on child rearing. By focusing on what is distinctive about each parental group's approach, we go beyond the more general trends that hold for most or all national groups and try instead to highlight the unique features of each group. As we proceed, however, it should be kept in mind that what is distinctive or unique in a ten-nation comparison might not hold up if we were to increase the size of the sample of comparison nations, or if we were to include in our sample more exotic world settings. Also, as we proceed we should expect that certain features of parental behavior that were distinctive in earlier comparisons—where a national group was compared with one or two others—will not hold up as distinctive since our perspective now includes ten nations. Thus, the distinctive national characteristics reviewed here should be seen as complementary to those already discussed in earlier chapters where the perspective was narrower.

In these summaries, we emphasize degrees of leniency or severity on aid, discipline, and sex-role issues, using the composite ranks in Tables 13.2 and 13.3 as a guide, and we give attention to social-class background, sex of parent, and sex of child where these factors contribute to distinctive national trends. We also draw attention to national group placements with reference to the neutral points of particular scales (Table 13.5).

The American Parents

As a group, our American parents stand out as permissive and lenient relative to the other nine parental groups. Furthermore, their leniency is seen at both social-class levels and is reflected in a wide range of value issues, including both aid and discipline matters. We find, for instance, that of all ten groups the American parents are most often on the lenient side of the neutral point (see Table 13.5). Whereas all parental groups tend to extend help and guest privileges to a six-year-old, our American parents distinguish themselves by also catering to the child's requests for attention, which is not the case in any of the other settings. Furthermore, our American parents also cater to the child's bids for autonomy. Leniency on autonomy, however, seems to be a North American value and not characteristic of any of our European samples. Thus, for aid-related issues, those where the child requests something or some privilege, American parents contrast with our other groups by their willingness to comply with the child's requests for help, guest privileges, attention, and autonomy. The basic child-rearing value that seems to mediate these gestures of compliance is a desire on the parents' part to have the child see the adult world as supportive, cooperative, and composed of friends rather than taskmasters. For the American child, asking usually leads to receiving.

A very similar picture emerges for discipline issues, for again the American parents stand out as particularly lenient. For instance, although all ten parental groups fall on the restrictive side of the neutral points of all discipline scales—thereby stopping the six-year-old child who misbehaves—the American middle-class parents take the child's side on the child-baby dispute, suggesting that on this issue American parents are the most willing to give the child opportunities to test the limits of disciplinary rules.

The American parents are also distinctive because of the way social-class variations affect their approaches to child rearing. Social-class differences are comparatively large, especially on matters of discipline. For instance, American middle-class parents are consistently less harsh disciplinarians than their working-class counterparts, and these class differences are large. On the aid scales, social-class contrasts are much smaller, and in one case (the attention issue) the working-class parents are somewhat more prone to give attention. Our American parents, then, stand out because of marked social-class differences on discipline matters, with working-class parents being the harsher disciplinarians, while on matters of aid, the social-class contrast disappears.

Another distinctive feature of the American families is the effect social-class background has on sex-role expectations and perceptions. Compared to other parental groups, American parents of both social classes have relatively low sex-role expectations, meaning that neither subgroup expects large boy-girl differences in comportment. Middle-class American parents also have relatively low sex-role perceptions so that they neither expect nor perceive sex-role contrasts, whereas American working-class parents perceive more sex-role contrasts than they expect. There is then a discrepancy between what the American working-class parents expect and what they perceive in the sex-role comportment of their children, as though for them children are overemphasizing sex-role contrasts.

There are also mother-father and son-daughter differences that help characterize American families. American mothers are more ready than American fathers to comfort a six-year-old and to minimize child-baby disputes. The same mother-father differences appear as well in English Canadian families, setting these two national groups off from the others. Finally, on the child-guest dispute, sons are treated more leniently than daughters in American families, suggesting that sons are encouraged to be aggressive with peers relative to girls who, for the same provocation, are more severely socialized.

The English Canadian Parents

Our English Canadian parents stand out as relatively severe and demanding in the ten-nation comparison and clearly as the most demanding of the three North American parental groups. The way this harshness is shown, however, varies with the social-class background of the parents. The English Canadian working-class parents rank as the harshest of all ten working-class subgroups on matters of discipline (composite rank order = 1), but are more lenient on the aid scales, ranking near the average (composite rank order = 5.5). In contrast, the English Canadian middle-class parents rank among the most lenient groups on the discipline issues (composite rank order = 8), but as relatively harsh on the aid issues (composite rank order = 3). In general, social-class contrasts are large for Anglo-Canadian parents on matters of discipline and on the issue of granting the child autonomy, but are less pronounced on the other aid issues, for example, extending help, or giving attention, comfort, or guest privileges. What happens on the aid issues, then, is that the working-class parents are relatively more lenient than they are on discipline matters, while the middle-class parents are relatively less lenient. Apparently, there are strong social-class norms in English Canada that affect parents' modes of disciplining and granting aid to children.

On certain issues, though, they are North American, in the sense that they are similar to Americans and different from Europeans. For instance, like our American parents, they grant the six-year-old autonomy (that is, like the Americans, they also fall above the neutral point on that scale), and on the sex-role issue, they also have relatively low sex-role expectations and sex-role perceptions.

English Canadian parents are also distinctive in their harshness on the temper displays, particularly temper directed toward things rather than people. On this matter, the English Canadian working class are the most severe of all ten working-class subgroups, and the middle class, too, are among the three most severe middle-class subgroups. Why so much attention is given to materialistic in contrast to social forms of temper displays in Canada is interesting. This is not an American tendency because our American parents are not particularly severe on the nonsocial temper control matter, whereas both English Canadian and French Canadian middle-class parents are. Temper control aside, middle-class English Canadian parents otherwise fall more toward the lenient pole on matters of discipline, while working-class English Canadian parents fall clearly near the severe pole. On the aid issues, both working- and middle-class English Canadian parents tend to withhold help and guest privileges relative to other national groups, whereas they are very compliant, and thus very North American, toward a child's requests for autonomy.

As mentioned, English Canadian mothers are more ready than English Canadian fathers to extend comfort and to minimize child-baby disputes; and in these instances they are like American mothers. Finally, on the child-guest quarrel, daughters are treated more leniently than sons in English-Canadian families.

The French Canadian Parents

In terms of leniency-harshness, our French Canadian parents are very similar to Anglo-Canadian parents on the discipline issues, but different from them on the aid issues. As with Anglo-Canadians, social-class variations are large on matters of discipline, but of much less importance on aid matters. Thus, the French Canadian middle-class parents rank as very lenient on both discipline and aid issues. The working-class subgroup ranks among the most harsh on discipline, but, unlike their Anglo-Canadian counterparts, relatively lenient on aid matters. Interestingly, the French Canadian middle-class parents are comparatively harsh only in response to nonsocial temper outbursts, the same feature that distinguished the middle-class

Anglo-Canadian subgroup. There appears to be a distinctively Canadian middle-class reaction to a child's threat to break things; both French and English middle-class subgroups react with relative severity in this instance.

On the sex-role issue, the French Canadian parents are also similar to Anglo-Canadians, since both groups have low expectations of sex-role differentiations, and in both cases, sex-role perceptions are generally in line with expectations.

In French Canadian families, fathers are more prone than mothers to extend comfort to a six-year-old, making them different from both American and Anglo-Canadian fathers, and on the child-guest dispute issue, sons are treated more leniently than daughters, making the French Canadian parents more like the American than the Anglo-Canadian parents.

Overall, the French Canadian, English Canadian, and American parents form a North American set. Although they differ from each other in distinctive ways in the degrees of harshness or leniency displayed in their approaches to child rearing, they are alike in so many ways that the three groups form a sharp contrast with our European samples. For example, in contrast to European parents, they are much more prone to grant the six-year-old autonomy. Then, in each of the three North American settings, there is a sharp difference in approach to matters of discipline, depending upon the social-class background of the family: middle-class North American parents are much more permissive and lenient than working-class parents when the child's behavior calls for discipline. In fact, North American middle-class parents prefer to divert, distract, or at the most scold rather than threaten or actually punish a child who misbehaves. Social class is less important on aid issues for North American families. Finally, parents in North America have relatively low sex-role expectations—they tend toward unisexism—and their perceptions of sex-role differences are generally in line with their expectations.

The English Parents

One distinctive characteristic of the English parents is that they are very lenient on matters of discipline, and this holds for both social-class subgroups (composite ranks are 9 and 10 respectively for working-class and middle-class). As in North America, the social-class differences for our English families are fairly large, and, as is generally the case, the middle-class parents are more lenient than the working-class. What is particularly interesting— and this constitutes a second distinctive feature of the English parents—

is that on the aid scales, the typical social-class trend is reversed, in the sense that the working-class parents are more ready than their middle-class counterparts to extend help, attention, autonomy, and guest privileges to the six-year-old child. This interesting reversal means that on matters of aid, English working-class families rank as extremely compliant (composite rank is 9.5), whereas English middle-class families rank among the least compliant (composite rank is 2). It would be valuable now to explore in detail why English parents differentiate discipline and aid issues as sharply as they do, and why the middle-class subgroup is comparatively lenient in the case of discipline (much as we have found in other national settings) but, contrary to the general cross-national trend, comparatively reluctant to extend aid to the six-year-old.

Consistent with their overall leniency, the English parents also de-emphasize sex-role differences, ranking generally toward the low pole on both the sex-role expectation and sex-role perception scales. That is, relative to our other national groups, they neither expect nor perceive marked sex-role differentiations. Nonetheless, the English middle-class parents perceive fewer sex-role differences than they expect, suggesting that they, relative to the other middle-class subgroups, may be surprised, if not bothered, by the degree of unisexism they encounter in their environments.

Finally, English fathers are more ready than English mothers to give comfort to a six-year-old, making them different from American and English Canadian parents, and on the child-guest dispute issue, they, like Americans but unlike English Canadians, treat sons more leniently than daughters.

The French Parents

The French parents have their own ways of being distinctive in their child-rearing orientations. In matters of discipline, they rank near the average of our ten groups in their degree of leniency-harshness, but there is a good deal of variation. For instance, the French working-class parents are the most severe of all working-class subgroups on the child-baby dispute issue, but one of the least severe on the child-guest dispute issue. Similarly, the French middle-class parents who are otherwise average on the leniency-harshness dimensions are the most severe of all on the insolence issue. In that instance, they do not hesitate to use punishment as their form of reaction. Thus, the French middle-class parents tolerate a good deal of social misbehavior, except for insolence, in which case they are not only harsher than middle-class parents in our nine settings, but also harsher than their working-class counterparts from France.

The French working-class parents stand out as the least compliant of all working-class subgroups on the aid issues (composite rank is 1), and although the French middle-class subgroup ranks as relatively more compliant on the aid issues, their overall rank hides several distinctive characteristics. For instance, the French middle-class parents are extremely negative to a child's requests for help or comfort (ranking among the least compliant); they are the most ready to comply with the child's bids for attention, more so than any other national parental group, including the Americans. They are, in fact, the only group whose mean score on the attention scale falls on the lenient side of the neutral point (see Table A 13.1).

The typical social-class pattern—where middle-class subgroups are generally more lenient or less harsh than working-class parents—is not at all clear in France. For instance, the typical pattern reverses for the help and insolence issues and essentially disappears on the perceived sex-role scale. In general, French parents of both social-class backgrounds have relatively high sex-role expectations, and their perceptions are in line with their expectations.

In sum, our French parents turn out to be averagely harsh in matters of discipline, with a unique social-class twist wherein the middle-class subgroup is particularly severe in its reactions to insolence. The typical social-class pattern shows through on some aid issues but reverses on the matters of extending help, where the French working-class parents are the more helpful. The French middle-class parents, who are so severe on insolence, are surprisingly willing to comply with a six-year-old's clamors for attention.

In France we find on the comfort matter that mothers are much more comforting than fathers, making the French pattern more like the American and English Canadian but different from the French Canadian and English. On the child-guest dispute issue, daughters in France are treated more leniently than sons, more like the English Canadian pattern than the American, French Canadian, and English patterns.

The French Belgian Parents

Of all ten parental groups included in our study, the Walloon parents turn out to be the most severe and least compliant. The French Belgian parents of both social-class backgrounds are relatively severe on all discipline scales: the middle-class parents are the most severe of all ten middle-class subgroups, and the working-class parents, after the English Canadians, are the second most demanding of all working-class subgroups. Social-class differences in degree of harshness are present, but compared to our North

American groups, they are small, and in general they fit the typical social-class pattern except for the child-guest dispute issue where the Walloon middle-class parents are as demanding as their working-class compatriots. Thus, neither social-class subgroup tolerates child-guest squabbles.

The French Belgian working-class parents also show little leniency on the aid issues, ranking second only to the French working class parents, the least compliant of all. In contrast, the middle-class parents are somewhat less harsh on aid than on discipline matters, ranking near the average among the ten middle-class subgroups. Still, on the guest privilege issue, they, along with the Dutch Belgian parents, are the least compliant middle-class subgroup.

Interestingly, the Walloon working-class parents, who are otherwise noncompliant on the aid issues, are one of the two groups most ready to give attention, the other being the French middle-class parents. The point of interest is that these two subgroups of parents are both particularly noncompliant on the help and comfort issues but very compliant on the attention issue. This interesting pattern suggests that parents who turn a cold shoulder to requests for comfort and help but who respond to requests for attention are not necessarily inconsistent or distant with their children; their comportment may fit into a general socialization tactic.

French Belgian working-class parents also have the highest sex-role expectation score, meaning that they expect sharp boy-girl differences in comportment, and their perceptions of sex-role differences are generally in line with their expectations. As is typical for most national settings the middle-class subgroup has less extreme sex-role expectations, and yet they, too, relative to the other middle-class subgroups, have relatively high sex-role expectations.

On the comfort issue, French Belgian mothers are more ready than fathers to comfort, and, in fact, the French Belgian and Dutch Belgian fathers are the least comforting of all groups in our study. On the child-guest dispute issue, daughters in French Belgian families are treated more leniently than sons.

The Dutch Belgian Parents

Although not as extreme as the French Belgians, the Flemish parents also rank as harsh socializers in the ten-nation comparison. However, their demandingness shows up more on aid than discipline issues. The rank orders on the discipline scales are respectively 4 and 5 for Dutch Belgian working- and middle-class families, but 3 and 1 on the aid scales. On two discipline scales—siding with baby versus child and temper control—the Dutch Belgian parents rank as rather permissive.

The typical social-class pattern is apparent for the discipline scales, but generally less so for the aid scales. Overall, the Dutch Belgian parents are relatively harsher in their noncompliance on aid matters than in their methods of controlling misbehavior. Thus, Dutch Belgian middle-class parents rank as the harshest of all middle-class subgroups on the aid scales, and this is so because they tend to refuse to comfort the six-year-old, to grant autonomy, or to grant guest privileges. However, they are less severe when it comes to giving help or attention. Apparently, we have another sign here of a particular socialization tactic, distinctive to Dutch Belgian parents, wherein comfort and autonomy requests are discouraged, while help and attention requests are treated more sympathetically.

The Dutch Belgian parents have generally high sex-role expectations, although they perceive relatively few signs of sex-role differentiations, suggesting that they may be upset about the current trends toward unisexism that they see around them.

As mentioned, the Dutch Belgian and French Belgian fathers are much less inclined than their wives to extend comfort to a six-year-old; they are the least compliant of all fathers on this issue. Like the French Belgians, the Dutch Belgian parents also treat daughters more leniently than sons when they become involved in a child-guest dispute.

The Italian Parents

What is distinctive about our Italian parents is that they, relative to our other nine national samples, have markedly different modes of reacting to discipline as compared to aid issues, and their modes of reacting are clearly related to their social-class standing. Thus, it is difficult to place either of our Italian subgroups of parents on a simple leniency-severity dimension, for it turns out that the working-class subgroup is extremely lenient on discipline matters (composite rank of 10), but toward the severe pole on aid matters (composite rank of 4). The middle-class parents are relatively severe on discipline matters (rank of 4), but lenient on aid matters (rank of 8). There are apparently two quite separate patterns of child-rearing values in Italy, one tied to each social-class stratum. As a consequence, the typical social-class differences in leniency-harshness are not consistent from scale to scale; instead they vary markedly or reverse depending upon the issue in question.

There are, nonetheless, several child-rearing values that cut across social-class lines. For instance, both subgroups are extremely lenient on temper and insolence outbursts; they are compliant to requests for help and for guest privileges, more so than any other group included in our ten-nation comparison. At the same time, both subgroups are among the most noncompliant to the child's bids for attention, making them quite distinct from our French and Belgian groups, for instance.

On the sex-role topic, the Italian parents rank near the average relative to the nine other national groups in terms of sex-role expectations and perceptions. Furthermore, their perceptions of sex-role differences are in line with their expectations of how boys and girls should behave.

Italian mothers are more comforting than Italian fathers, a pattern that contrasts with that for our Greek and Portuguese parents, the other two Mediterranean groups. On the child-guest dispute issue, sons are treated more leniently than daughters in our Italian families, a pattern similar to that of the Greek families but different from that of the Portuguese.

The Greek Parents

In the ten-nation comparison, our Greek parents are near the average in leniency-severity for both discipline and aid issues. There is, however, a set of features that characterizes both social-class subgroups: both are relatively lenient on insolence, both tend to comply with requests for help and attention, but both are relatively noncompliant on the autonomy issue. The pattern is unique. They are like Italian parents in their leniency on insolence, for example, but different from Italians in their greater compliance with attention demands; and they are different from French parents on both counts.

The typical middle-class-working-class differences in leniency-severity do not hold for our Greek samples. Social-class differences are generally small for the discipline matters but more pronounced for the aid issues. Greek middle-class parents, relative to other middle-class subgroups, rank as severe socializers of social aggressivity (child-baby and child-guest disputes and social temper outbursts), and they are close to the working-class parents on severity of discipline, essentially because the Greek working-class parents are relatively lenient compared to other working-class subgroups. On the aid issues, the Greek middle-class parents are more conciliatory than the working-class parents, except on the guest privilege matter where they are more restrictive.

The Greek parents have extremely high sex-role expectations, ranking 2 and 1 for working- and middle-class subgroups, respectively, and apparently boys and girls behave as expected since the parental perceptions are in line with expectations. Fathers are more comforting than mothers in our Greek families, a pattern like that of the

Portuguese but different from that of the Italians. On the child-guest dispute issue, Greek sons are treated more leniently than daughters, a pattern like that of the Italians but different from that of the Portuguese.

The Portuguese Parents

There are several characteristics that distinguish the Portuguese parents: both social-class subgroups tolerate a great deal of insolence (composite ranks are 10 and 8, respectively, for working- and middle-class subgroups), both groups encourage guest privileges (ranks 8 and 10), they tend to extend help (ranks 6 and 7), while at the same time they discourage temper displays (ranks 3 and 2.5) and demands for attention (ranks 3 and 1). Although these characteristics hold for both social groups, thereby describing unique features of all Portuguese parents, still there are important differences between the child-rearing orientations of working- and middle-class subgroups. On discipline matters, the middle-class parents are one of the most severe of all middle-class subgroups (composite rank 2), while the working-class parents are one of the most lenient (composite rank 8). On aid matters, however, both middle- and working-class subgroups are very compliant (composite ranks 8 and 7, respectively).

The distinctively harsh reaction to discipline by the Portuguese middle-class parents stands out as does a reversal of the typical pattern of social-class differences on leniency. In fact, the Portuguese middle-class parents score nearer the severity pole on all discipline scales except insolence. Similarly, on the aid scales, the middle-class parents are less compliant than the working-class on the attention and autonomy scales. In fact, the Portuguese middle-class parents fit the typical pattern only on the help, comfort, and guest privileges issues, where they are more ready to aid than are the working-class parents.

Broader patterns now become apparent (see Table A 13.1). We see, for example, that all three Mediterranean groups are extremely lenient on insolence, all three (with the exception of the middle-class Greek parents) encourage their children to have guests into the home, and all three are very ready to comply with requests for help. At the same time, the Portuguese parents are like the Italians, but different from Greeks, in their severe reactions to bids for attention and in their more compliant approach to requests for autonomy. The Portuguese parents stand out as different from both Italians and Greeks by the harsh position they adopt on temper outbursts.

The Portuguese parents also present a distinctive point of view on the sex-role issue. They tend to have relatively low sex-role expectations—in fact, the working-class subgroup has the lowest score of all, reflecting an expectation of unisexism. At the same time, both groups rank 1 within their respective subgroups for sex-role perceptions, meaning that they perceive in their environment a great deal of differentiation in the comportment of boys and girls. To see more sex-role differences than one expects may be less upsetting than the reverse would be, but still it is puzzling to find such a great discrepancy between expectations and perceptions on the part of our Portuguese parents. It could be an important sign of changes to come in sex-role comportment.

On the comfort issue, Portuguese fathers are more comforting than mothers, a pattern like that of the Greeks but different from that of the Italians, while on the child-guest dispute issue, Portuguese daughters are treated more leniently than sons, a pattern different from that of both Italians and Greeks.

MOTIVATIONAL ROOTS OF CHILD-REARING VALUES

How might one begin to explain the striking nation-to-nation differences in child-rearing values that we have just reviewed? As a first step, we might try to relate these differences to independent sources of information about the same samples of nations. It would be wonderful to be able to choose among a number of cross-national investigations for such a purpose, but unfortunately, the field of cross-national psychology is too new to provide us with a wide choice. The study we will rely on here as our comparison source is McClelland and colleagues' on national differences in types and degrees of social motivation (1961 and 1975). It is one of the few comprehensive projects available, but rich as it is in its implications, there is no way to judge in advance how relevant it is for our purposes. Perhaps cross-national indexes of Witkin and Berry's "field dependence" or of Bronfenbrenner's "studied neglect" would be more relevant, but multinational data of these sorts are not available. Thus, we think of our use of McClelland's work in this context more as an example of the type of integration we will be able to make as more cross-national data become available.

That is not to say that McClelland's research should not be pertinent, because it does provide us with information on a wide array of motive systems that vary in relative importance from nation to nation, and some of these differences in motives should be related to some of the differences we have found in child-rearing values. We would be presumptuous, however, to attempt to predict just how they would be related to each of our child-rearing dimensions.

As we started our search for relationships, one limitation became clear: the nations we selected for our study would not necessarily cover the wide span of national differences in motives that McClelland has discovered in his survey of some 60 to 70 nations. In several instances, the particular ten nations we have surveyed fall very close to one another in terms of the much broader range of information McClelland presents with his much larger and more diversified sample.*

McClelland has developed procedures for determining how much each particular motive permeates the thinking of an individual or a societal group of individuals. He argues that certain nations or cultural groups place greater emphasis on certain motives and less emphasis on others, and that this starts in early childhood. Depending upon which motives are stressed, nations establish quite different "standards" or "expectations" with respect to achievement, affiliation, power, and so on.

The motive systems that McClelland concentrated on are: achievement, power, affiliation, other-directedness, and activity inhibition. Each of these he defined in a technical manner, but, in general, the definitions are very close to the commonsense meanings of the terms. Thus, by "need for achievement" he means a desire to compete and do well against standards of excellence, or more generally, an "inner concern" with achievement that might become the dominant motive for a certain national group.

Need Power is defined "as a concern with the control of the means of influencing" people (McClelland 1961, p. 167), which would show itself in "emotional reactions to a dominance situation, for example, pleasure in winning or anger in losing an argument, . . . wanting to avoid weakness . . . disputing a position . . . demanding or forcing something." The need also expresses itself in preoccupation with superior-subordinate relationships.

Need Affiliation is basically an interest in friendly interpersonal relationships, with desires "to be liked, accepted or forgiven." Thus,

---

*For example, our ten nations are all relatively low (in standard score terms) in achievement, most falling near McClelland's midpoint. None is really high; the highest is France with a standard score of .51, compared to Argentina and Turkey in McClelland's tables with scores of 1.84 and 2.16. Similarly, there is little range of scores for power, all ten of our nations being relatively low, and for affiliation we have no really low scores. Our range of scores, however, was better for the other-directedness and activity inhibition indexes.

"a high need for affiliation indicates a concern in fantasy and in action for warm, close relationships with other people" (1961, p. 150).

Incidentally, by analyzing the themes occurring in children's readers in a large number of nations, McClelland was able to develop statistical indexes of the frequency and importance of each theme, and with these, to explore the intercorrelations of motive systems. Thus, affiliation and power were found to be negatively correlated, and McClelland reasoned that it is apparently "difficult to want to order people about (power) and to like them and want to be approved by them (affiliation) at one and the same time" (1961, p. 203). Similarly, power was found to be unrelated to achievement.

Other-Directedness has a special meaning. It is derived from the early work of David Riesman (1950) who drew attention to what he saw as a change in American society, a move away from the importance placed on "traditionalistic norms" as guides for proper conduct to a heavier reliance on the actions and opinions of others as models of what is correct and appropriate. McClelland expands this notion by contrasting tradition-bound societies, where "a near exclusive loyalty to kin group, or to a set of other-worldly religious goals" (1961, p. 193), could become a handicap to economic and social development, in contrast to societies who use the mass media or other sources of interpersonal norms of behavior as a behavioral guide, permitting the "authority of tradition" to be replaced by a new voice of authority—other people and other people's behavior. For parents, the other-directed orientation shifts the emphasis away from tradition and what is expected of parents, to the mass media which become important guides because they show and tell parents what others are doing.

This contrast between tradition-directed and other-directed societies is fascinating for us, especially when we find that two of the groups in our study, Italy and Portugal, stand extremely high in their affiliative rankings but extremely low in their degree of other-directedness. This suggests that for Italians and Portuguese, affiliation is limited to the traditional family group, with only a minimal influence from others outside the family. By way of contrast, English and Japanese parents, two other groups in our sample, rank relatively high on both affiliation and other-directedness, implying that in England and Japan the boundaries of social influence are much more extensive.

Activity Inhibition is thought of as an index of restraint or control. In the analysis of children's readers, it is measured by the number of times the word "not" appears. Readers have many more "not" references in certain societies than in others, and this presumably reflects societal differences in preoccupation with the teaching of personal restraint or control (McClelland 1975, p. 66). This factor, which is particularly relevant to the variations we have found in parental leniency or harshness, has proven in McClelland's recent work to be extremely important when combined with other motive states. For instance, imperialistic forms of power seem to be based on national values that stress the development of power at the expense of affiliation within the framework of high levels of activity inhibition. Basically, this index reflects "a heightened need for discipline and control" (McClelland 1975, p. 309).

As a reference source for these various motives, McClelland has provided a systematic count of the frequency of each of these themes found in samples of children's readers, those books used in the early elementary grades of public schools in each of the nations included in his survey. Data were available for readers from different time periods, and we decided to base our correlations on the analysis of readers in popular use in and around 1950 since that date fits well the age of elementary schooling for the majority of parents in our study. Thus, we presume that our parent groups would likely have been in the orbit of influence of the particular pattern of motives considered important in their society at that time. Judging from McClelland's research, the analysis of the thematic content of children's readers has extensive sociopsychological and politicoeconomic implications for the societies involved. Accordingly, we will relate our findings with his, in an attempt to throw light on the basic psychosocial factors that underlie the nation-to-nation and social-class-to-social-class variations in the child-rearing values we have encountered in our study.

In Table 13.6, rank 1 is assigned to that nation, among the ten, with the highest score for a particular motive system (for example, France for achievement, French Belgium tied with Italy for power, and so on), and 10 is assigned the nation with the lowest score. Thus, among the ten nations for which we have data, France has the highest index for achievement, Italy has the highest index for affiliation, and so on. The national variations in these various motive systems are presented in Table 13.7 in the form of ranks. Actually, ten of the nations included in our child-rearing study were also included in McClelland's study; unfortunately, McClelland does not have data on Dutch Belgians.

Table 13.8 presents the nation-by-nation rankings on each of our various child-rearing dimensions, with rank 1 assigned to the parental group that was most demanding or most harsh, relatively, in its treatment of children on any particular dimension. Thus, when a child asks for help, the French sample of middle-class parents is least cooperative and the Greek sample is the most compliant. When we average across dimensions, we arrive at an "overall harshness" rank, and here we find a range, for the middle-class samples,

TABLE 13.6

National Ranks on McClelland's Motivation Indexes*

National Group	Achievement	Power	Affiliation	Other-Directedness	Activity Inhibition
American	4	4	7	2	2
English Canadian	2.5	3	4.5	6	6
French Canadian	6	10	9	–	–
English	7	5	2	1	1
French	1	8	10	7	7
French Belgian	10	1.5	8	5	9
Italian	8	1.5	1	9	5
Greek	2.5	7	6	4	4
Portuguese	5	9	3	8	8
Japanese	9	6	4.5	3	3

*Rank 1 is assigned to the nation with the highest index of a particular motive as reflected in the themes of its children's readers. Thus the lower the rank (nearer rank 1) the greater the emphasis given to that motive system, in that national setting, and the higher the rank (nearer rank 10), the less the emphasis given to that motive in that national setting.

Source: Compiled by the authors.

TABLE 13.7

National Rankings on Child-Rearing Dimensions*

	Aid Dimensions					Discipline Dimensions						Sex-Role Emphasis	
	Help	Attention	Comfort	Guest Privileges	Autonomy	Dispute with Guest	Insolence	Dispute with Baby	Social Temper	Temper	Overall Harshness Rank	Expected S-R Differences	Perceived S-R Differences
National Middle-Class Subgroups													
American	5	9	3	6	10	7	4	10	9	6	10	10	8.5
English Canadian	3	5	7	2	8	9	3	9	6	2	5	9	7
French Canadian	7	6	8	7	7	8	5	7	7	1	7	8	6
English	2	4	9	3	1	10	8	8	10	8	8	5	10
French	1	10	2	5	4	5	1	6	5	7	2	3	5
French Belgian	4	7	5	1	5	1	2	1	1	4	1	4	4
Italian	8	3	6	8	6	2	9	4	4	10	6	7	8.5
Greek	9	8	4	4	2	3	6	3	3	5	4	2	3
Portuguese	6	1	10	9.5	3	4	7	2	2	3	3	6	1
Japanese	–	2	1	9.5	9	6	10	5	8	9	9	1	2
National Working-Class Subgroups													
American	4	9	7	6	7	5	4	8	6	6	7	8	4.5
English Canadian	3	7	5	1	8	2	1	4	2	1	2	6	8
French Canadian	6	3	9	3.5	9	1	2	3	3	5	4	5	9
English	8	8	8	5	5	6	7	9	8	8	9	7	7
French	2	5	1	3.5	1	8	5	1	4	4	3	3	4.5
French Belgian	1	1	2	2	2	3	3	2	1	2	1	1	3
Italian	9	2	4	9	4	7	8	7	9	9	8	4	6
Greek	7	6	3	8	3	4	6	6	5	7	5	2	2
Portuguese	5	4	6	7	6	9	9	5	7	3	6	9	1

*Ranks run upwards, with 1 indicating the group most severe on a particular dimension (or for the sex-role issue, the group most likely to expect or perceive sex-role differences) to 10, indicating the group most lenient. There are ten nations for which we have middle-class samples of parents, but only nine for which we have working-class samples.

Source: Compiled by the authors.

TABLE 13.8

Correlations between McClelland's Motive Systems and Our Child-Rearing Dimensions*

Motive Systems	(n)	Aid Dimensions					Discipline Dimensions					Sex-Role Emphasis	
		Help	Attention	Comfort	Guest Privileges	Autonomy	Dispute with Guest	Insolence	Dispute with Baby	Social Temper	Temper	Expected S-R Differences	Perceived S-R Differences
Achievement	(10) MC	+.20	-.53*	+.08	+.18	+.11	-.26	+.48*	-.38	-.04	+.29	-.17	-.02
	(9) WC	+.27	-.54*	+.23	+.10	0.00	-.10	+.18	+.27	+.17	+.23	-.08	+.09
Power	(10) MC	+.07	+.39	+.15	+.24	-.24	+.24	+.02	-.01	+.07	-.36	-.19	-.45*
	(9) WC	+.08	+.70*	+.35	+.11	+.25	+.11	+.10	-.21	+.01	-.05	+.29	-.04
Affiliation	(10) MC	-.25	+.77*	-.43	-.28	+.19	-.05	-.77*	+.06	-.09	-.43	-.08	-.21
	(9) WC	-.68*	-.12	-.25	-.53*	-.15	-.33	-.60*	-.73*	-.72*	-.43	-.40	0.00
Other-Directedness	(9) MC	+.21	-.22	+.25	+.25	-.02	-.57*	-.13	-.43	-.65*	-.13	+.15	-.28
	(8) WC	-.02	-.69*	-.43	+.24	-.14	+.45	+.33	-.48	+.12	-.12	-.02	-.15
Activity-Inhibition	(9) MC	-.07	-.02	+.18	+.12	-.08	-.63*	-.53*	-.63*	-.85*	-.53*	-.05	-.51*
	(8) WC	-.64*	-.79*	-.62*	-.33	-.52*	+.07	-.14	-.86*	-.55*	-.69*	-.31	-.43

*Entries are values for Spearman's rank-order correlations (rho). Because of the exploratory nature of this phase of our work, we will draw attention to correlations falling at the p < .10 level of confidence as well as those reaching the conventional .05 and .01 confidence levels. Significance levels vary in relation to the number (n) of nations involved: with n = 10, the rho must be at least .44 for the .10 level of confidence, .55 for the .05 level, and .73 for the .01 level; with n = 9 the corresponding minima are: .46, .58, and .77; and with n = 8, they are: .52, .62, and .81.

The positive sign before a correlation means that the more parents were themselves raised in an atmosphere that empha-sized a particular motive system, the harsher or more demanding they tend to be with their own children on a particular aid or discipline dimension. A negative sign means the opposite, that is, the more a motive was stressed in the parents' childhood, the more lenient they are with their own children on a particular dimension.

Source: Compiled by the authors.

from the French Belgians, the most severe overall, to the Japanese, the most lenient, and for the working-class samples, from the French Belgians, again the most demanding, to the English, the least demanding.

The information in Tables 13.6 and 13.7 are brought together in Table 13.8 in the form of rank-order correlations. When positive, the correlation indicates that the more a particular motive was stressed in the early lives of parents from a specified national setting, the more lenient those parents were on a particular child-rearing dimension. Thus, in Table 13.8 the significant negative correlations of achievement and attention (-.53 and -.54) signify that parents who themselves were raised in a society where relatively great emphasis was placed on achievement (such as France, English Canada, and Greece in our samples), are relatively more lenient with their own children's demands for attention. Thus, the negative sign before a correlation signifies that a high rank on one of McClelland's indexes is associated with a low rank on one of our dimensions. Because this is only an exploratory study, we will discuss not only correlations that meet conventional levels of statistical significance but also those that reach the .10 significance level only.

Although there are several alternatives open to us in interpreting these correlations, we will assume that parents try to foster in their children those values that best characterize their own life-styles, presuming that the parents' life-styles in turn have been colored by the values stressed in their own upbringing. Thus, we will argue that parents who have had achievement-related values emphasized in their upbringing will be more comfortable with, and thus encourage, achievement-related comportment in their children. Parents need not, however, be conscious of their biases.

Correlations with Achievement

There are three noteworthy correlations between the achievement scores and two of our child-rearing dimensions—two with attention (rho = -.53 and -.54) and one with insolence (+.48)—that we will try to explain. The theory of achievement motivation would lead us to expect that achievement-oriented parents might well want their children to seek out attention in the sense of singling themselves out. In terms of the specific episode used to measure attention seeking in our study—the child complains that the baby has hurt him by stepping on his hand—achievement-oriented parents might not want anyone, even a younger sibling, to walk all over their child! The two negative correlations with our attention measure indicate that the higher the achievement orientation of the parental group, the more lenient they are with their children's attention seeking. This seems consistent with theoretical expectations, but the correlation between achievement and insolence control scores (rho = +.48) must be integrated. Apparently there are limits as to how far children can go in singling themselves out. When they, through insolence outbursts, try to push parents around, the more achievement-oriented parents are more severe on insolence, while the less achievement-oriented parents are more lenient on insolence. Note, however, that this correlation holds only for our middle-class subgroups.

Of course, it could well be that any three correlations out of the 24 computed could turn up significant by chance only. Our working assumption, however, is that the relationships reflected here are other than chance affairs. Thus, although there are few signs here of the influence of achievement on our parental child-rearing values, the three instances of such an influence are theoretically consistent and interesting.

Correlations with Power

In this case, only two significant correlations emerged, one between power and attention, holding for the working-class only (+.70), and one between power and sex-role perceptions (-.45).

The first correlation suggests that power-oriented parents do not expect or want their children to be sissies or whimperers on the attention issue. Thus, the more power-oriented they are, the more they discourage children from using attention-getting ploys (rho = +.70). The correlation between power and sex-role perceptions suggests that the more power-oriented the parental group, the more insistent they are that girls be as prepared as boys for a power-dominated world. In other words, in the views of such parents, traditional femininity could be dysfunctional. Our reasoning here is that the negative correlation on the sex-role matter means that power-oriented parents make little distinction between boys and girls in their sex-role perceptions. Again, although these two correlations do have a consistency with the theory of power, it is clear that we have very few signs in our data of the influence of power on the child-rearing values of our parental groups.

Correlations with Affiliation

In their modes of socializing children, affiliation-minded parents would be expected to promote a different set of values, and our data suggest that the social-class backgrounds of parents play a determining role as to which values are stressed. Affiliation-oriented parents from working-class origins seem to be anxious to help their children (rho = -.68), and to encourage friendliness through guest privileges (-.53); they are also lenient with outbursts of social temper (-.72), disputes with a younger sibling (-.73), and insolence (-.60). This lenience on discipline matters suggests that the more affiliative the parents are, the more careful they are not to present a model of counteraggressiveness on discipline matters, as though they were consciously trying to minimize such episodes, letting them pass without commotion.

Affiliation-oriented parents of middle-class backgrounds seem to take a different approach. First, they discourage attention demanding (+.77), as though such a habit could spoil close friendly interpersonal relationships, but, much like their working-class counterparts, they also let insolence outbursts pass with little counteraggressiveness (-.77). These correlations also are consistent with the theory of affiliation, and, what is particularly encouraging for us, this index generates a larger number of correlates with various of our child-rearing dimensions.

Correlations with Other-Directedness

According to theory, other-directed parents would be expected to neglect tradition as a guide in child rearing and turn more to outside sources—other people or mass media. There are three significant correlations between other-directedness and our child-rearing dimensions, and these are specific to particular social-class subgroups. They indicate that other-directed parents from working-class backgrounds tend to be lenient with attention demanding (rho = -.69), offering relatively little resistance to such ploys. In contrast, other-directed parents from middle-class backgrounds tend to be lenient with social temper (-.65) and with child-guest disputes (-.57). These correlations are consistent with the notion that other-directedness may inhibit parents from reacting spontaneously to children's outbursts, as though they do not have clear standards of their own as to how one should curb children's tendencies to be pests or to be socially aggressive. Even though they are consistent in this sense, we again have very few correlations that relate our value dimensions to this parental characteristic.

Correlations with Activity Inhibition

By contrast, there are a large number of correlations between activity inhibition and our child-rearing dimensions, and these are marked by important social-class differences. The theory would predict that parents who are characterized with a high degree of activity inhibition would try to develop personal control in their children, as in themselves. The correlations suggest that activity-inhibited parents are especially lenient, and lenient on a number of dimensions. One gets the impression, in fact, that they don't have to be harsh or punitive with their children, either because the children are generally more self-controlled, or, in instances where a child does cut up or act out, these parents can reestablish control by staying at the reminder or at most the reprimand stage on our leniency-severity scale.

For our working-class subgroups, the more activity inhibited the parental group, the more lenient and compliant they are on both aid and discipline matters. For example, they are especially prone to give help (-.64), attention (-.79), comfort (-.62), and autonomy (-.52), and when discipline is called for—as in displays of social temper (-.55), disputes with a younger sibling (-.86), or temper (-.69)—they are particularly easygoing and nonpunitive. Activity-inhibited parents from middle-class backgrounds show no such tendencies toward leniency on aid dimensions, and this social-class contrast is very sharp. But on all discipline dimensions they, too, are strikingly nonpunitive and easygoing. Apparently, they can keep control without moving to punitive extremes. The activity-inhibited middle-class parents also tend to de-emphasize sex-role differences.

There is, then, a pervasive relationship between activity inhibition and leniency on our child-rearing dimensions, a leniency that touches both aid and discipline matters for our working-class subsamples of parents, but only the discipline matters for our middle-class parents. In this instance we have found an important root of parental leniency on our child-rearing dimensions, namely, the degree of activity inhibition or personal control that these parents experienced in their own early socialization.

In summary, our purpose here was to relate the nation-to-nation variations in parents' child-rearing attitudes found in our own study to other cross-national information on value systems. With this end in mind, we turned to McClelland's research on motive systems and brought our work and his into contact via simple correlation procedures. In spite of the fact that we were dealing with ten national groups only and that these were not distributed as broadly along McClelland's scales as one might like, this exploration has been valuable because it shows rather convincingly that socialization experiences in the early lives of parents can have strong influences, not only on the development of their motives and values, but also on how they relate to their own children and thereby perpetuate the influence process. What is exciting for us is that we now begin to see some possible roots to the important nation-to-nation and social-class-to-social-class variations in child-rearing values that we encounter in our own investigation. For instance, we find that activity inhibition and affiliation orientations at the present level have a particularly strong effect on the degree of leniency or severity in parents' treatment of their children. Thus, the more a parental group is affiliative (for example, Italian, English, and Portuguese) or controlled (for example, English, American, and Japanese), the more that group is lenient and conciliatory toward discipline matters and to children's requests for aid. What is more, we find important social-class variations in the ways affiliation and activity inhibition are reflected in parents' child-rearing attitudes: affiliative middle-class parents discourage attention demanding but are selectively lenient on insolence outbursts only, whereas affiliative working-class parents are generally lenient on most discipline issues, prone to extend help, and encourage guest privileges, with no concern shown to attention demandings. Similarly, the effects of activity inhibition are more specific for the middle-class subgroups and more general for the working-class subgroups: controlled middle-class parents are lenient on discipline matters only, while controlled working-class parents are generally easygoing, being both lenient on discipline issues and conciliatory on aid issues.

Although fewer relationships were found with achievement, power, and other-directedness, still the patterns of these relationships are extremely suggestive and interesting. For instance, the more that children in a particular national setting are given freedom to demand attention, while being discouraged from being insolent, the more likely it is that their parents rank high in achievement. Or, the more that working-class subgroups of children are discouraged from demanding attention, the more likely it is that their parents rank high in power. Or, the more that middle-class subgroups of children are treated leniently when displaying social temper or disputing with same-age friends, the more likely their parents rank high in other-directedness.

These findings also make us look more attentively at the national profiles on McClelland's various indexes, for it is in these profiles that we may have the beginnings of each nation's uniqueness. Thus, England stands out among the ten nations we are working with because it ranks highest on other-directedness and on activity inhibition, very high on affiliation, but low on achievement. In contrast, France stands out by ranking highest on achievement, but lowest on affiliation and low generally on power, other-directedness and activity inhibition. Italy ranks highest on affiliation and power but low on other-directedness and achievement. In contrast, Greece ranks very high on achievement but lower on power and affiliation. English

Canada ranks high on achievement and power but low on other-directedness and activity inhibition. In contrast, French Canada ranks only average on achievement and low on power and affiliation. Finally, America ranks high on other-directedness and activity inhibition but low on affiliation. These profiles, therefore, make it clear that there are multiple sources of influence that shape the ways particular national groups of parents approach the matter of bringing up children.

Finally, it is encouraging for us to find that the simple dimensions on which we relied so heavily in our investigation seem to have their own individual characteristics. Some—like attention demanding, insolence, and social temper—entered into numerous pattern relationships with McClelland's indexes, while others—like requesting help, disputing with a guest or with a baby, or sex-role perceptions—entered less often, but where they did, they entered in intriguing combinations. It gives us a sense of satisfaction, then, that these simple scales may prove valuable to others who may want to build on what we have done here.

AN APPLICATION TO SCHOOLS: A COMPARISON
OF TEACHERS' AND PARENTS' VALUES

With our cross-national study of parental child-rearing values as a frame of reference, we turn in this final section to a possible practical extension of our findings to the school system. Here we focus attention on the match or mismatch of child-rearing values of Canadian teachers, on the one hand, and of parents from various national and social-class backgrounds, on the other. The idea that parent-school conflicts may have important consequences for the educational careers of students from minority-group or working-class backgrounds is far from new (McCandless 1967; Seely, Sim, and Loosley 1968). However, there is relatively little research evidence available on the specific areas of parent-teacher conflict that could affect students from various social backgrounds. Now that we have a large body of cross-national and cross-class data on a major area of parental values, the extension of our procedures to include groups of teachers seemed a logical and potentially valuable next step.

With this aim in mind, we focused on two relatively small groups of elementary teachers from Canada, one representing old-stock English Canadian and the other old-stock French Canadian backgrounds.

Since there are a large number of comparisons involved we will not present all of our results, but instead we will describe fully the French and English Canadian teacher-parent comparisons and then simply summarize the most interesting findings in the other comparisons. *

Overview of the Teacher-Parent Comparisons

We tried to keep the procedure used with the teachers as similar as possible to that used with parents. However, because most elementary teachers are females and most do not now have their own six-year-old children, a number of procedural modifications were necessary for the teacher samples.

French Canadian teachers responded in French to the French Canadian tape recording of the child's voice and English Canadian teachers in English to the English Canadian tapes. Instructions accompanying the tape recordings of the child's voice were the same for teachers as for parents, except that teachers were asked to imagine that they had a six-year-old child and to respond to the tape as if they were responding to their own child. Half were asked to imagine that they had a six-year-old boy and half a six-year-old girl. Because the teachers were interviewed in groups rather than individually, they were asked to write down their responses to the statements. Like the parents, all teachers also answered the two sex-role questionnaires. Coding of the teachers' responses followed the standard procedures already outlined.

The Teacher Samples

To qualify as English Canadian, teachers had to be English-speaking Protestants who were born and educated in Canada and who identified themselves as English Canadian rather than as members of any ethnic or cultural group. French Canadian teachers also had to have been born in Canada, to have had French as a mother tongue, to be at least nominally Catholic, and to identify themselves as French Canadian.

All French Canadian teachers were working in French-language elementary schools in the Montreal area, and all English

---

*Readers who are interested in pursuing the finer details of these studies may obtain the necessary tables and graphs by writing to us. A fuller description, as well as technical details of the comparisons, are available in the form of (A) tables and figures.

Canadian teachers were employed in English-language elementary schools in Montreal. It is noteworthy that the majority of French Canadian teachers came from working-class backgrounds, whereas half or more of the English Canadian teachers came from middle-class families. A complete description of the teacher samples is available in Tables A 13.2 and A 13.3.

We will begin by looking at the degree of value alignment between Canadian teachers and parents of working- and middle-class backgrounds. Because of the growing interest in Canada in "immersion" schooling (Lambert and Tucker 1972), in which children of one language background attend classes taught by teachers of a different language background, we will summarize the degree of match-mismatch in school-home values that might occur when an English Canadian child has a French Canadian teacher, or vice versa. In the final section we tackle the question of how well child-rearing values of neo-Canadian parents fit with those of English Canadian and French Canadian teachers.

French Canadian Teachers and Parents

Our first two comparisons involve French Canadian teachers and two separate groups of French Canadian parents—first, FC teachers versus FC middle-class parents, and then FC teachers versus FC working-class parents. (The results of these comparisons are given in Tables A 13.4 to A 13.7.)

French Canadian Teachers and Middle-Class Parents

Differences between the reactions of FC teachers and FC middle-class parents occurred for only two scales: help withholding ($\underline{F}$ = 7.85; $\underline{p}$ < .01) and guest restrictions ($\underline{F}$ = 3.29; $\underline{p}$ < .05). In each case multiple comparison tests comparing the mean responses of FC teachers, FC middle-class mothers, and FC middle-class fathers revealed that the teachers gave harsher responses than fathers or mothers.

The teachers' more restrictive attitudes toward help giving could result in part from their occupational experiences. If we consider again the taped statements included in the help withholding scale, it will be recalled that the scale is built around two incidents, one in which the six-year-old child makes repeated attempts to get help with a puzzle, and one in which the child asks the parent to get him (or her) a different puzzle. It could be that the teachers' experience with dividing their time and attention among the demands of a large number of children may have outweighed the instructions to respond as a parent dealing with only two children. Similarly, teachers may also have been influenced by a desire to foster independence, in a theoretically prescribed fashion, by not giving in too readily to the child's demands.

In addition to the overall parent-teacher differences, significant effects due to sex of child appeared for the scales of social temper control (F = 4.94; p < .05) and expected sex-role differences (F = 4.77; p < .05). What is intriguing about these differences is that they occurred in the responses of teachers and parents alike. Thus, the general working-class and middle-class French Canadian pattern, described at length in Chapter 2, in which temper outbursts in social situations are less tolerated from girls than from boys, seems to hold as well for FC teachers as for FC parents. The FC girl may be faced with uniformly harsh adult reactions to her temper outbursts, whether they occur at home or at school. FC boys, in contrast, apparently get by with considerably more before equivalent sanctions are applied by either parents or teachers.

A similar pattern held for sex-role expectations. In this case, FC middle-class parents of girls, particularly mothers of girls, and teachers who played the role of mothers of girls expected more boy-girl differences than did parents of boys or teachers playing the role of mothers of boys.

Generally speaking, then, the French Canadian elementary teachers, in spite of their predominately working-class backgrounds, responded very similarly to our sample of FC middle-class parents. The teachers differ from FC middle-class parents only on the help withholding and guest restrictions scales.

French Canadian Teachers and Working-Class Parents

The child-rearing values of our sample of FC teachers were more similar to those of FC middle-class than FC working-class parents. In fact the middle-class parents differed from the FC teachers on only two scales, while working-class parents and teachers differed on six of twelve scales.

The tendency for FC teachers to be less inclined than parents to give help (F = 4.89; p < .05) to a child playing with a puzzle held for the FC working-class parents as it did for their middle-class counterparts. Thus, it seems likely that FC children, regardless of their social-class background, face teachers who see giving direct aid to a child as less appropriate than FC parents do.

In addition, we observed teacher-parent differences on four of the five discipline scales: siding with baby versus child (F = 5.92; p < .05); social temper control (F = 6.03; p < .01); insolence control (F = 5.07; p < .05); and siding with guest versus child (F = 5.92; p < .01). In all four cases the mean responses of the FC teachers were lower than the mean responses of FC working-class parents, indicating that the teachers were more lenient than parents. These differences between the discipline responses of the FC working-class parents and teachers may reflect real differences in harshness or leniency, but it could also be that the FC teachers were playing the role of teacher in their reactions, in which case the contrast may not be so much a difference in harshness or lenience as a difference in the type of discipline the parents and teachers are inclined to use. Thus, the six-year-old FC working-class child who fights with a younger sibling or with a friend, or is insolent toward an adult, could find a different type of discipline used at school than at home. Some children might interpret this difference in discipline as a sign of lenience of teachers and thus, at least initially, be encouraged to try even more blatant forms of misbehavior at school than they would try at home. For other children the difference in discipline could be intimidating by its strangeness. In any case the contrasts suggest that FC working-class children are faced with new types of sanctions in the school environment, but whether these novel experiences turn out to be problems or challenges is not clear from these results.

For two of the discipline scales, namely, social temper control and siding with guest versus child, we observed that although FC teachers were generally more lenient than the working-class parents, teachers and parents alike showed a bias in favor of boys. Thus, both at home and at school it is likely that FC working-class boys who fight with peers are treated more tolerantly than girls who misbehave in the same fashion.

Parent and teacher responses to insolence provide an intriguing contrast to this rather uniform bias in favor of FC working-class boys. While FC teachers were generally more lenient toward insolence than FC working-class parents, there was also an interesting interaction in this case. FC working-class parents switched their bias to favor girls in the insolence situation while FC teachers again were biased in favor of boys. Overall, then, FC teachers gave harsher responses to girls than to boys in cases of both social temper and insolence, whereas FC working-class parents were harsher on social temper coming from girls and on insolence coming from boys.

Interestingly enough, although we found that FC teachers' responses to the taped episodes showed as many boy-girl differences as the FC working-class parents, still the teachers reported that they saw fewer boy-girl differences in comportment than the FC working-class parents did on the perceived sex-role differences scale ($F = 3.22$; $p < .05$).

In general, our sample of FC teachers was generally less prone to extend help to a six-year-old than FC parents of either social class were. FC teachers were also more restrictive than FC middle-class parents, but no different from FC working-class parents in response to the child's request to have a friend in to play. While the FC teachers' general approach to discipline did not differ markedly from that of FC middle-class parents, their discipline responses were significantly more lenient than those of FC working-class parents. FC teachers, like both FC middle- and working-class parents, treated quarrels involving girls more harshly than similar squabbles involving boys, but otherwise the teachers' responses to girls and boys were more like those of FC middle-class than working-class parents. Apparently our FC teachers, while themselves coming from working-class backgrounds, had child-rearing attitudes more like those of FC middle-class parents. Consequently, it is likely that the working-class FC child is faced with a greater number of home-school value differences, particularly in the area of discipline, than is the middle-class FC child who probably finds the values at school and home to be pretty similar except in the domains of help giving and guest privileges.

English Canadian Teachers and Parents

Our consideration of the English-speaking side of the Canadian picture also involved two comparisons: EC teachers versus EC middle-class parents and EC teachers versus EC working-class parents (statistical comparisons are in Tables A 13.8 to A 13.11).

English Canadian Teachers and Middle-Class Parents

For the child-baby dispute and the comfort issues, the EC middle-class mothers were relatively lenient and the EC middle-class fathers relatively harsh. The point of interest is that EC teachers took a middle ground, being at the same time harsher than the mothers and more lenient than the fathers. Compared to FC middle-class children who apparently face teachers who are in some ways harsher or more restrictive than either of their parents, the EC middle-class children have fewer school-home value conflicts to contend with, although, relatively, neither group has all that many value mismatches to cope with. In fact, value matches predominate. For example, EC teachers and EC middle-class parents shared a common bias toward girls when it came to giving comfort (F = 6.80; p < .01) and granting autonomy (F = 5.04; p < .05). This means that EC middle-class boys likely have clearer limits placed on their autonomy both at home and at school than do girls, and they are also more likely denied gestures of comfort whether at home or at school. It is as if the EC middle-class six-year-old boy is expected to be "man enough" not to seek comfort for a small injury although he is not perceived to be "man enough" to cross the street on his own. His sister, in contrast, seems better treated at school and at home when comfort is asked for and is given autonomy when she asks for it.

English Canadian Teachers and Working-Class Parents

Not surprisingly, many more teacher-parent value differences turned up for our EC working-class samples. On four discipline scales (siding with baby versus child [F = 15.51; p < .01], temper control [F = 14.87; p < .01], social temper control [F = 5.71; p < .01], and insolence control [F = 32.05; p < .01]), the EC teachers were less harsh than either mothers or fathers from EC working-class families. In other words, the EC working-class child who misbehaves at school is likely to find, like his FC counterpart, that teachers tend to use different and more lenient types of discipline than do his parents. They are also likely to find that teachers are more lenient than parents in terms of guest privileges (F = 4.82; p < .05), but when they clamor for attention, they are more likely to be indulged by mothers than by fathers or teachers (F = 5.47; p < .05). Thus, the EC working-class child who expects that teachers, being females, will respond like mothers may be in for a surprise on the attention issue.

EC teachers and working-class parents, particularly fathers, do not agree on the sex-role issue (F = 5.79; p < .01), and it is the parents who expect more sex-role differentiations. Whether this teacher-parent contrast in expectations generates problems for the working-class child is not clear, but the question is worth further exploration.

Interestingly, it is the parents of boys, in particular, who expect more sex-role differentiation, and on this point the parents are in agreement. Thus, EC teachers, as well as EC working-class parents, are more concerned about unisexism among boys than among girls. Teachers and parents also agree that insolent boys should be treated more harshly than insolent girls, as though they both worry more about confrontations with males than with females. However, parents and teachers diverge on the comfort issue, in that EC teachers are less prone to respond to comfort requests from boys than from girls, while EC working-class parents tend to deny comfort to children of either sex, if anything, denying comfort to girls more so than to boys (see Figure A 13.2). This means that

EC working-class girls are likely to find EC teachers more comforting than their parents, while EC working-class boys probably see little difference in the reaction of teachers and parents.

Summary of Canadian Parent-Teacher Comparisons

These Canadian parent-teacher comparisons, whether English Canadian or French Canadian, revealed that teachers from both language groups hold child-rearing values more like those of middle-class than working-class parents. This suggests that middle-class French Canadian and English Canadian six-year-olds can expect fairly similar responses from parents and teachers, while working-class children are likely to find more lenient discipline, or at least different types of discipline, at school than at home. Perhaps we have uncovered new sources of evidence for the current theory that middle-class children are better prepared for the school system than are working-class children. Hess and Shipman (1965) have demonstrated that the quality of mother-child interactions differs according to the social-class background of the family, and other studies have shown that the middle-class child is more likely to develop the cognitive (Whiteman and Deutsch 1968; Eson 1972) and linguistic (Bernstein 1961) skills needed for school. Our findings add another dimension to this evidence, for in addition to having an advantage in terms of cognitive and linguistic skills, it could well be that middle-class children also experience a greater continuity in the child-rearing attitudes of adults at home and at school than do working-class children. But whether these overlaps of cognitive, linguistic, and value domains from home to school should necessarily give the middle-class child the advantage is not clear to us. Contrasts in these domains could be capitalized on by teachers and converted into interesting novelties in the education process.

Implications for Cross-Language Schooling

With the teacher-parent comparisons of both French Canadian and English Canadian communities as a frame of reference, we wondered about teacher-pupil interaction in schools where the pupil and teacher are from a different ethno-linguistic background. In Quebec and Ontario, and other communities in North America, mixtures of this sort are common in "immersion" programs where, for example, English Canadian parents in substantial numbers now place their children in schools with monolingual French-speaking teachers. Does the fact that the teacher is a member of a different ethnolinguistic group necessarily increase the number of school-home value contrasts? To shed some light on this question we carried out a number of teacher-parent value comparisons where teachers and parents represented different ethno-linguistic backgrounds.

Overall, our results indicate that immersion schooling probably makes little difference in the number of school-home value contrasts faced by FC or EC children.* For example, the FC child, whether middle- or working-class, attending a French or an English school will probably face an adult who is more willing than his parents to give help with independent learning tasks, as these are reflected in our taped episodes for the helping scale. Furthermore, working-class Canadian children, whether FC or EC, are likely to face major parent-teacher differences in modes of coping with discipline whether they attend French- or English-language schools. Fortunately for the working-class Canadian child, these differences are in the direction of more lenience and patience at school than at home. As well, working-class children in both school systems are likely to encounter teachers who endorse sex-role equality, and this would be at odds to some degree to the values of both EC and FC working-class parents. Thus, regardless of mother tongue or language of instruction, working-class Canadian children face more value contrasts at school than do middle-class children, but the contrast on discipline matters could be a relief from the relatively harsh parental attitude they encounter at home. Incidentally, these findings constitute another example of the overriding influence of social class on child-rearing values, an influence that spreads from home to the community.

Value Matches and Mismatches of Canadian
Teachers and Immigrant Parents

With the Canadian surveys as backgrounds, we are now ready to explore the value matches and mismatches of Canadian teachers and parents, where the parents in this case are neo-Canadians representing a number of immigrant groups. Here we are concerned mainly with first-generation immigrant children attending Canadian schools, and we try to determine if they face essentially the same parent-teacher differences in attitudes toward socialization as do native-born Canadian children, or whether their cultural backgrounds generate unique patterns of parent-teacher value differences.

---

*The statistical analyses for these studies are available in Tables A 13.12 to A 13.19 and in Figures A 13.3 to A 13.6.

With this aim in mind, we compared teachers' responses with those of parents from four immigrant groups for whom adjustment to Canadian schools is of significance: Greek, Italian, Japanese, and Portuguese. Actually, our sample of Portuguese parents was living in New England, but because of the fast growing rate of Portuguese immigration to Canada, making this comparison especially valuable for Canadians, we will assume that these Portuguese parents are essentially like those who immigrate to Canada.*

Canadian Teachers and Greek Immigrant Parents

There are substantial numbers of Greek immigrants to Canada, and, except for religious schools, Greek children have teachers who are either English Canadian or French Canadian. Our results show that Greek immigrant (GI) children with English Canadian teachers face fewer home-school value contrasts than they do with French Canadian teachers. Contrasts, nevertheless, do show up even in the English Canadian school setting. For example, the EC teacher is less likely than the GI parent to respond to the child's request for help. At the same time the EC teacher is more lenient than the GI parent on child-baby disputes. Attitudes toward sex roles are also likely to constitute an area of school-home differences since the EC teachers make fewer differentiations between boys and girls than GI parents do.

Value contrasts are more numerous with a French Canadian teacher. First, FC teachers, much like EC teachers, are also less prone than GI parents to respond to the child's requests for help, and they make fewer sex-role differentiations. On the other hand, the FC teacher is more restrictive than GI parents on guest privileges. In addition, on discipline matters, FC teachers are more lenient with boys than with girls, a pattern which clashes with the view of GI parents, who tend either to be more lenient with girls

---

*As for the Canadian comparisons, all teacher-immigrant comparisons were based on the responses of nine mothers and fathers of girls and nine mothers and fathers of boys. All other statistical procedures for these comparisons followed the model described earlier in this chapter, that is, a series of 3X2 analyses of variance for each immigrant group, with mothers, fathers, and teachers taken as three separate groups of adult socializers. Tables A 13.20 to A 13.35 give the results for each of the teacher-immigrant comparisons, and Figures A 13.7 to A 13.16 depict the significant interactions; as mentioned earlier, these are available on request.

than boys or to treat both sexes alike. It is hard to say what effect the FC teacher's favoritism toward boys on discipline issues might have on Greek children, but the findings suggest that GI boys and girls alike face a novel discipline situation in the French Canadian classroom.

In summary, then, Greek immigrant children probably face fewer school-home value contrasts with an English Canadian than with a French Canadian teacher, at least insofar as the child-rearing attitudes tapped by our approach were concerned. When we compare the school-home value mismatches of Greek immigrant children with those we discovered for French Canadian and English Canadian children, it turns out that the working-class Greek immigrant child encounters fewer school-home value differences than the working-class Canadian child does.

Canadian Teachers and Italian Immigrant Parents

As with the Greek immigrant parents, the relatively large number of Italian immigrants to Canada meant that comparisons involving the two groups of Canadian teachers and Italian immigrant (II) parents would be relevant. What is most striking about these comparisons is the relatively large number of contrasts that appeared. Although Italian immigrant children encounter a fairly novel situation in school with either FC or EC teachers, the contrasts are fewer and less marked with FC than EC teachers, particularly in the area of discipline.

Canadian teachers, FC or EC, expect and perceive fewer sex-role differences than do Italian immigrant parents. Teachers are also less likely to respond to the child's requests for help, and less likely to grant guest privileges than II parents. Canadian teachers also differed from the II parents in their readiness to comfort a child, in the sense that the teachers tended to be more comforting than II fathers but less comforting than II mothers. In addition, the EC teachers shared the II parents' tendency to comfort girls more than boys.

Both teacher groups also tended to be milder disciplinarians than II parents, but here there were marked differences between FC and EC teachers. For example, French Canadian teachers were significantly more lenient than II parents in their reactions to insolence, and in contrast to II parents who react with equal severity to insolence from boys and from girls, the generally more lenient French Canadian teachers favored boys over girls on the insolence issue. Actually, II parents and FC teachers both tended to favor boys over girls in other discipline domains (social temper and child-guest dispute) and the FC teachers extended that favoritism to include insolence as well.

The picture is different for II children in English Canadian classrooms, for there they are likely to experience teachers' disciplinary lenience in a wider range of situations, and boys are likely to find themselves treated no differently than girls when they misbehave.

Basically, then, the II child is likely to face many of the same sorts of school-home attitude contrasts as Canadian working-class children do, and although these conflicts are likely to occur with both groups of Canadian teachers, the II child experiences fewer value conflicts in a French Canadian classroom.

Canadian Teachers and Portuguese Immigrant Parents

For the Portuguese immigrant (PI) parents, the group we described in detail in Chapter 11, we assume that Portuguese immigrants to Quebec will have essentially the same child-rearing values as those who immigrate to the United States. When we ask ourselves which teacher group, FC or EC, would be more like parents in their attitudes toward child rearing, the answer for the Portuguese child is not that clear-cut.

Again we found that the immigrant child is likely to find more lenient attitudes toward discipline at school than at home. If the teacher is English Canadian, she is likely to respond more leniently than PI parents to both temper displays and insolence, while a French Canadian teacher is likely to be more lenient than parents on the insolence issue only.

There is an interesting mismatch of values on the autonomy issue. Canadian teachers, FC or EC, react similarly to boys and to girls who make a bid for autonomy, and usually they comply. PI parents react quite differently, since PI mothers tend to comply with their sons' requests for autonomy and deny their daughters', while PI fathers favor the daughters' requests over the sons'. This parent-teacher value contrast is likely to be the source of more confusion for PI girls than PI boys, in that teachers and mothers alike tend to grant the PI boy's autonomy requests, whereas the PI girl is more likely to be given autonomy at school by one female socializer, but denied it at home by another female, the mother.

Another source of difference turns up on the sex-role issue, and again we find that Canadian teachers, FC or EC, expect fewer boy-girl differences in comportment than PI parents do. It would be valuable to explore the sex-role issue further and to see what impact the different views of sex roles at home and in the community has on the thinking of the Portuguese child.

Interestingly enough, French Canadian teachers shared many of the Portuguese immigrants' sex-linked preferences. Thus, both French Canadian teachers and Portuguese immigrant parents tend to extend more help to boys than to girls, and to be more lenient toward boys than to girls who are insolent toward an adult. Similarly, both FC teachers and PI parents were more likely to grant guest privileges to girls than to boys. Thus, in these respects, FC teachers are more similar to the PI parents in their child-rearing values than the EC teachers are. But in other respects (for example, on autonomy and social temper control), the French Canadian teachers show preferences to boys or girls that are quite different from those of PI parents. These intriguing patterns of results point to the potential value of follow-up studies with Portuguese families in North American settings.

Canadian Teachers and Japanese Immigrant Parents

As we compare the child-rearing attitudes of our sample of Japanese immigrant (JI) parents with those of our Canadian teachers, we get a glimpse of some of the special demands made on Japanese immigrant children who find themselves in Canadian classrooms. The JI group, it will be recalled, included middle-class families only.

A number of sharp contrasts emerged between the values of Canadian teachers and JI parents. In the first place, EC teachers show a greater willingness to comfort a six-year-old child than do JI parents, but they differ in the opposite direction on the child-guest dispute issue where they are more punitive than JI parents when the child in question is a boy. In other words, JI parents are particularly harsh with a disputative girl, whereas the EC teachers, who give essentially the same treatment to boys as to girls in the dispute episode, end up much more punitive than JI parents when it is a boy who starts the quarrel. The JI boy might well experience an important contrast between his expectations and those of an EC teacher when he becomes involved in a dispute with a peer. In general, EC teachers expect fewer sex-role differences than do JI parents, and this might be another instance of value mismatch that could affect the JI child at school. For example, on the temper control issue, a JI girl who displays temper is likely to encounter more severe reactions than is a boy who acts up in identical fashion. This is so because of a general tendency among Japanese parents, whether in Japan or in Canada as immigrants, to favor boys over girls on temper displays. This distinctive Japanese characteristic is discussed in detail in Chapter 12.

While JI parents tend to be harsher with daughters than sons in the case of a temper outburst, they are more prone to comfort daughters than sons. This relatively softer attitude toward girls is shared by our EC teachers who also extend more comfort to girls than boys. EC teachers also share with JI parents the tendency to extend more guest privileges to daughters than to sons.

In summary, the child-rearing attitudes of EC teachers contrast with those of JI parents in interesting ways: the EC teacher is more inclined than the JI parent to extend comfort when comfort is requested, and her attitudes toward attention bids are less conciliatory than those of JI mothers, being more like those of JI fathers. If a dispute develops between the child and a same-age friend, the JI girl can expect essentially the same reaction from EC teachers as from her parents, whereas her brother can expect to be treated with much more severity by EC teachers than by parents. Nevertheless, EC teachers and JI parents have common views about what is appropriate sex-role behavior, for example, that girls should be comforted and given more guest privileges than boys.

French Canadian Teachers and Japanese Immigrant Parents

What would happen in the realm of value mismatches if a child from a Japanese immigrant family in Canada were exposed to schooling with an FC teacher? We find that FC teachers, much like EC teachers, are more inclined than JI parents to extend comfort, and they expect fewer sex-role differences. At the same time, FC teachers are harsher than JI parents on insolence outbursts, and are less inclined to grant guest privileges.

The most striking outcome of these comparisons, however, is a case of value matching between FC teachers and JI parents—a tendency for both sets of socializers to be more severe disciplinarians with girls than with boys. This tendency shows itself on four separate value dimensions: temper control, social temper control, insolence control, and the child-guest dispute episode. In Chapter 12 we have already discussed this bias JI parents seem to have against girls who misbehave while being much more gentle with boys who provide the same degrees of provocation. What is noteworthy here is that FC teachers seem to share the same bias against socially aggressive girls. Thus, JI children might well find a family bias reinforced by the FC teacher.

Thus, we have found that in certain instances EC and FC teachers are more lenient than JI parents and in other instances more harsh and more demanding. Consequently, the JI child receiving his or her schooling in a Canadian context is likely to experience conflicting patterns of child-rearing values at home and at school. With an EC teacher, JI children will be denied attention, much as at home, but if they get into a quarrel with same-age acquaintances, they will meet with harsher disciplinary reactions from teachers than from parents. When insolent, JI children can expect harsher reactions from FC teachers than from parents and more restrictions placed on guest privileges. In general, both EC and FC teachers are in accord with the sex-role expectations of the JI parents, with certain important exceptions: in contrast to JI parents, EC teachers do not favor boys over girls when the children are socially aggressive. EC teachers do, however, share with JI parents the view that girls "deserve" more comforting and more guest privileges. It is different with FC teachers, because they seem to share the JI parents' bias that girls should be treated more harshly than boys when they become socially aggressive or insolent. Note that on these important value dimensions, the FC teacher could reinforce a potentially dysfunctional and unjust bias against girls that seems to characterize the JI family.

What sort of conclusions can we draw from these various comparisons of teachers' and parents' child-rearing values? Where might the expectations of the immigrant child that he presumably picked up from parents at home be at odds with those of Canadian elementary school teachers? The trends schematized in Tables 13.9 and 13.10 point to the following overall generalizations:

1. When a six-year-old's behavior calls for discipline, both FC and EC Canadian teachers were generally less harsh in their reactions than any of the groups of working-class immigrant parents that we have examined here. This overall difference in severity of reactions is likely due in part to the differences in social-class backgrounds of teachers and immigrant parents. But there is more to it than that for we found that Canadian teachers were also more lenient on discipline than were Canadian parents of the same social-class background.

2. This general trend for teachers to be more lenient than parents in matters of discipline does not hold for the Japanese immigrant group, the one middle-class immigrant sample examined in our study. In fact, the Japanese immigrant child will find that Canadian teachers, relative to parents, are more demanding on matters of discipline, this being the case with the FC teacher when the Japanese child displays insolence, and with the EC teacher when the JI child gets embroiled in a child-guest dispute.

3. Discipline aside, Canadian teachers, in general, are not more permissive or conciliatory than parents on matters calling for aid. In some instances, both Canadian groups of teachers are less conciliatory than parents, as, for example, when the Italian or the Greek immigrant child asks for help or for guest privileges. On the other aid dimensions, however, the child's request will consistently be met with greater leniency from the teacher. For

TABLE 13.9

Summary of Teacher-Parent Contrasts

(compared to a particular parental group, teachers are harsher (H), more lenient (L), and so on)

Parent Group: Teacher Group:	GI		II		PI		JI	
	FCT	ECT	FCT	ECT	FCT	ECT	FCT	ECT
Help Withholding	H	H	H,BF	H				
Siding with Baby vs. Child		L		L				
Temper Control				L		L		B=G
Social Temper Control	BF				BF			
Insolence Control	BF		L,BF	L		L	H	
Attention Denial				F>T>M			L	F>T>M
Comfort Withholding				L,B=G			L	L
Autonomy Control					B=G	L,B=G		
Guest Restrictions	H		H		H			
Siding with Guest vs. Child	BF			U				H,GF
Perceived Sex-Roles	U	U		U		U		
Expected Sex-Roles	U	U	U	U	U	U	U	U
Total Number of Contrasts	5	2	5	7	3	4	3	4

Note: In contrast to family pattern, teachers can: be harsher (H), more lenient (L), rank between parents (F>T>M), show more boy favoritism (BF), girl favoritism (GF), little or no favoritism (B=G), or have fewer sex-role expectations or perceptions (U).

Source: Compiled by the authors.

TABLE 13.10

Summary of Teacher–Parent Reactions to Boys versus Girls

(compared to a particular parental group, teachers share same boy favoritism (BF), or girl favoritism (GF), or show less boy–girl differences (U) on sex–role issues)

Parent Group:	GI		II		PI		JI	
Teacher Group:	FCT	ECT	FCT	ECT	FCT	ECT	FCT	ECT
Help Withholding					BF			
Siding with Baby vs. Child								
Temper Control							BF	
Social Temper Control		GF	BF		BF		BF	
Insolence Control							BF	
Attention Control								
Comfort Withholding				GF		GF		GF
Autonomy Control								
Guest Restrictions					GF			GF
Siding with Guest vs. Child			BF		BF		BF	
Perceived Sex–Roles	U	U		U		U	U	
Expected Sex–Roles	U	U	U	U	U	U	U	U

Note: BF=boy favoritism shared by teachers and parents; GF=girl favoritism shared by teachers and parents; U=teachers expect or perceive less boy–girl differences on sex–role issues than do parents.

Source: Compiled by the authors.

example, the Canadian teacher tends to be more prone to comfort the child than are the Greek or Japanese immigrant parents.

4. Canadian teachers differ from certain national parental groups in the way they deal with boys as compared to girls. This means that in some cases the Canadian teacher will reinforce a bias toward boys or toward girls that already exists in the child's family, while in other cases the teacher's attitudes will stand in sharp contrast to those of the parents. For instance, the FC teacher is generally more lenient with aggressive boys than with aggressive girls, and this bias reinforces a similar pattern already existent in the JI family; for the GI child, however, the FC teacher's reactions contrast with the relatively greater permissiveness that a GI girl may expect at home.

Thus, immigrant children in Canada will experience new types of adult-child relations with their Canadian school teachers. Whether there are or are not important mismatches in the values of parents and teachers depends on the sociocultural origin of the children's families. Interestingly enough, the parent-teacher contrasts in most cases seem to represent rather pleasant experiences for the immigrant children in the sense that they generally encounter in the teacher an adult more permissive than their parents. Still there are other instances where the teachers expect more of the immigrant child than parents do, and these teacher-parent differences could also act as a corrective for cases where there is too much parental attention or too much favoritism shown to boys or to girls.

Interesting and instructive as these comparisons are, they are only a start. They did not permit us to recommend greater or less leniency on the part of the teacher, or to recommend greater or less value overlap between teachers and parents. We don't know whether value matches between parents and teachers are necessarily better in any sense than value mismatches, if the mismatches are intelligently treated by the school system or the community at large. Perhaps this might be a good topic to explore in future research.

APPENDIX A
Coding Guidelines

SOME PRELIMINARY NOTES

    1. The codes for all statements have been set up so that higher scores represent harsher or more restrictive responses, and lower scores represent more lenient responses.

    2. "NP" stands for neutral point and signifies the point in each coding scheme above which a parent's response can be said to limit or to attempt to control the child's behavior. The NP for each coding scheme is indicated prior to the coding categories for each statement.

    3. Uncodable responses include all instances where a parent tries to preface his response by including conditionals about the setting, time of day, the child's prior behavior, and other things. For example, the statement "If I weren't busy, I'd help him" is such a conditional and is considered uncodable.

    4. Responses consisting of an unmodified "yes" or "no" are sometimes codable and sometimes uncodable depending on the specific statement involved. However, the codability of a "yes" or "no" remains the same within each coding scheme. The codability of these responses is indicated prior to the coding categories for each statement.

    5. If it is difficult to classify a remark, sometimes an examination of the overall mood of the parent in response to the other statements in that episode is helpful in determining the best coding.

    6. When a parent gives two separately codable responses, the harsher response should be coded unless the separately codable responses fall at opposite extremes of the coding scheme. If the responses are at opposite extremes the statement is considered uncodable.

    7. For final analysis a parent's answers to the individual statements are combined to yield scores for nine different scales: help withholding (statements 1, 2, 3, 11); comfort withholding (9, 10); temper control (7); insolence control (8, 13); siding with baby versus child (4, 5, 6); attention denial (9); autonomy control (12); guest restrictions (14); and siding with guest versus child (15, 16, 17). A tenth scale, social temper control (6, 17), which involves items already included in other scales, can also be analyzed to examine parental reactions to temper directed at other children. Because the scales vary in the number of statements they include and the code systems for each statement vary in number of categories, final analysis is done in terms of percentage scores rather than raw scores for each scale. The table below gives the formulas for obtaining percentage scores for each scale.

TABLE A.1

Formulas for Determining Percentage Scores for Each Scale

(cc#1 means coding category for response to statement 1,
cc#2 means coding category for response to
statement 2, and so on)

SCALE	FORMULA
Help withholding	$\dfrac{100}{4}\left(\dfrac{cc\#1}{3} + \dfrac{cc\#2}{5} + \dfrac{cc\#3}{5} + \dfrac{cc\#11}{8}\right)$
Comfort withholding	$\dfrac{100}{2}\left(\dfrac{cc\#9}{6} + \dfrac{cc\#10}{6}\right)$
Temper control	$100\left(\dfrac{cc\#7}{5}\right)$
Insolence control	$\dfrac{100}{2}\left(\dfrac{cc\#8}{6} + \dfrac{cc\#13}{6}\right)$
Siding with baby versus child	$\dfrac{100}{3}\left(\dfrac{cc\#4}{7} + \dfrac{cc\#5}{7} + \dfrac{cc\#6}{6}\right)$
Attention denial	$100\left(\dfrac{cc\#9}{6}\right)$
Autonomy control	$100\left(\dfrac{cc\#12}{6}\right)$
Guest restrictions	$100\left(\dfrac{cc\#14}{4}\right)$
Siding with guest versus child	$\dfrac{100}{3}\left(\dfrac{cc\#15}{7} + \dfrac{cc\#16}{7} + \dfrac{cc\#17}{6}\right)$
Social temper control	$\dfrac{100}{2}\left(\dfrac{cc\#6}{6} + \dfrac{cc\#17}{6}\right)$
"Hey, when are we going to eat?"	$100\left(\dfrac{cc\#18}{6}\right)$
"I'm hungry, may I go and get myself something to eat?"	$100\left(\dfrac{cc\#19}{5}\right)$

Statement 1: "Mommy/Daddy come look at my puzzle."

HELP WITHHOLDING SCALE

(Coders, ask yourself: Does the parent give or withhold help, that is, does he/she agree to look at the puzzle or not?)
NP (neutral point on scale) = 2.5

Coding:

0. Uncodable. If I weren't busy, I'd go. (Includes all statements where parent prefaces the response with a conditional; "no" and "yes" can be coded on this scale.)

1. Complete acquiescence. Yes; all right; I'm coming; I would go look; yes; to do what?; it looks nice; tout de suite; j'y vais; je viens; j'aide la plupart du temps; j'arrive; let me see.

2. "Yes" with reservations. (Note: 2.01. The decimals are used as a substitute for a, b, c, etc.; they are not numbers to be used in ANOVA. We use the decimals as a convenience in tallying frequencies of different types of restrictions or refusals.)

2.01 Short delay. One minute; just a second; yes, in a minute; un instant; minute j'y vais.

2.02 Greater reservation. Bring it here; show me; montre.

2.03 Question which does not imply "yes" or "no." Are you having problems?; what game?

2.04 Reluctantly or grudgingly; urges child to try himself. I'll look when it's finished; I can see it from here.

3. Refusal.

3.01 Refuse or ignore. Not now; ask your mother; don't bother me; no.

3.02 Long delay. When I have finished; later (no time period specified); wait; après; I'm busy; in a minute; I can't now.

Statement 2: "Mommy/Daddy help me."

HELP WITHHOLDING SCALE

(Coders, ask yourself: Does the parent give or withhold help?)
NP = 3.5

Coding:

0. Uncodable ("No" and "yes" can be coded on this scale.)

1. Help—direct and immediate, or statement implying immediate availability of parent, or question implying availability, or specific strategy, for example, "try this piece." I'm coming; what do you want; what do you want me to do; I'll see what's wrong; yes; let me see; what's the matter; what is your problem; just for a little while; just for awhile.

2. Help—partial, for example, parent uses term "let's" and assists or gives minimum help, for example, "Yes, look there's a piece missing. Look for it." Let's see; we'll do it together.

3. Short delay or reservation. Bring it here; OK, wait a second; maintenant? Neutral question, for example, "Are you having problems?" "How are you working it out?"; show it to me; in a minute; why?; pourquoi?

4. Urges child to try by himself with no parental help, or offers a very general solution, for example, "Regarde bien les morceaux," or a question implying try harder, for example, "Can't you do it alone?"; do it yourself; try it and I'll help you if it doesn't work.

5. Refusal

5.01 Refuse, ignore or long delay, for example, wait until I'm finished; don't bother me; do it by yourself.

5.02 Comment like "maybe" or "I don't know" or "ask your mother," such that end result is that child must continue alone or seek help elsewhere.

Statement 3: "Does this piece go here?"

HELP WITHHOLDING SCALE

(Coders, ask yourself: Does the parent give or withhold help, that is, Does he/she agree to look at the puzzle or not?)
NP = 2.5

Coding:

0: Uncodable ("No" and "yes" can be coded on this scale.)

1. Help—direct and immediate, or statement implying immediate availability of parent, or question implying availability, or specific strategy, for example, "Try this piece." I'm coming; what do you want; what do you want me to do; I'll see what's wrong; yes; I don't think so, let me see.

2. Help—partial, for example, use of "let's," and parent assists or gives minimum help, for exampe, "Yes, look there's a piece missing. Look for it." Let's see; we'll do it together; yes or let's see if it does; try corner different ways; let's try and find out.

3. Short delay or reservation. Bring it here; OK, wait a second; maintenant? Neutral question, for example, "Are you having problems?" "How are you working it out?"

4. Urges child to try by himself with no parental help or offers a very general solution, for example, "Regarde bien les morceaux," or a question implying try harder, for example, "Can't you do it alone?" Try it yourself first and if you can't do it yourself, I'll help; what do you think?; qu'en penses-tu?

5. Refusal.

5.01 Refuse, ignore, or long delay, for example, wait until I'm finished.

5.02 Comment like "maybe" or "I don't know" or "ask your mother," such that end result is that child must continue alone or seek help elsewhere. I don't know; I'd have to see it; it depends.

Statement 4: "Baby, you can't play with me. You're too little."

SIDING WITH BABY VERSUS CHILD SCALE

(Coders, ask yourself: Whom does the parent favor, the baby or the six-year-old?) NP = 3.0

Coding:

0. Uncodable (unmodified "yes" and "no" are uncodable on this scale).

1. Side with child; divert, remove, or restrict baby's intervention. I'll give him another toy. (Coders note that parent not child gives toy to baby); yes, that's right; baby is still too small; baby is not allowed to touch the game.

2. Compromise. Give him some pieces you don't need; he's too small; let him watch for awhile (note that parent doesn't say "play"); give him another toy; let's (parent and child) give a toy to baby; I'll take him in a minute; suggests a new game for both children.

3. Ignore or "work it out yourself" or comment which doesn't side with either baby or child. "He is as smart as you are"; tell your mother to take baby away; parent supervises; leave him alone (ignore him).

4. Side with baby; parent asks child only to adjust; parent diverts the child; child must interact positively with baby. You must share; it's for both of you; no, you must play with him; take care of him; show some interest toward him; be nice to him; big boys play with their little brothers; how about taking turns; you were young once.

5. Reprimand directed to child: parent abruptly terminates child's actions verbally. Disapproval, reproof, scolding. Stop that talk; I would scold him; that's enough; shut up!; that's not nice; don't be so selfish; apologize to him.

6. Threat of punishment to child. If . . . . . then . . . . . ; child's name!

7. Punishment.

7.01 Nonphysical punishment; or nonspecified punishment.

7.02 Physical punishment.

7.03 Sarcasm, which is really meant to humiliate or punish the child. (Note that there will be some sarcasm which is not this strong—a simple disagreement with the child (code 5), like "you're the one who's too little.")

Statement 5: "He can't play with my puzzle. It's mine."

SIDING WITH BABY VERSUS CHILD SCALE

(Coders, ask yourself: Whom does the parent favor, the baby or the six-year-old?) NP = 3.0

Coding:

0. Uncodable (unmodified "yes" and "no" are uncodable on this scale).

1. Side with child; divert, remove, or restrict baby's intervention. I'll give him another toy. (Coder note that parent not child gives toy to baby.) Take the puzzle where baby won't bother you; Chacun son jeu; ne jouez pas ensemble.

2. Compromise—asks both child and baby to adjust, or excuses baby in an attempt to pacify child. Give him some pieces you don't need; he's too small; let him watch for awhile

(note that parent doesn't say "play"); give him another toy; baby does not touch it; when you finish the game, lend it to him; I'll take him in a minute.

3. Ignores or says "work it out yourself," or comment which doesn't side with either baby or child. He is as smart as you are; when he gets bigger; not because it's yours, but because he might put it in his mouth; parent comes to play with baby with child's toy; don't let him spoil it, but don't hurt him, (England); parcequ'il est petit et toi tu es grand.

4. Side with baby—parent asks child <u>only</u> to adjust; parent diverts the child, child must interact positively with baby. You must share; it's for both of you; no, you must play with him; take care of him; show some interest toward him; be nice to him; big boys play with their little brothers; how about taking turns; suggests a new game for both children; show it to him; let him play for a few minutes; put it away; parent argues that baby is small, but still asks child to play with him.

5. Reprimand to child—parent abruptly terminates child's action verbally. Disapproval, reproof, scolding. Stop that talk; I would scold him; that's enough; shut up; that's not nice; don't be so selfish; apologize to him; reprimand to both baby and child; "let him" plus a reprimand.

6. Threat of punishment to child. If . . . . . then . . . . . ; child's name!

7. Punishment.

7.01 Nonphysical punishment; or nonspecified punishment.

7.02 Physical punishment.

7.03 Sarcasm, which is really meant to humiliate or punish the child. (Note that there will be some sarcasm which is not this strong—a simple disagreement with the child (code 4), like "you're the one who's too little.")

<u>Statement 6</u>: "Leave my puzzle alone or I'll hit you on the head!"

SIDING WITH BABY VERSUS CHILD SCALE
(also SOCIAL TEMPER SCALE)

(Coders, ask yourself: Does the parent side with the baby or the child? We are concerned with the parent's response to the child's threat of hitting the baby.) NP = 2.5

Coding:

> 0. Uncodable (unmodified "yes," "no," and "well" are un-
> codable on this scale).
>
> 1. Sides with child and overlooks threat of hitting baby; parent
> removes or diverts baby; ignores threat.
>
> 2. Compromise—parent asks both baby and child to adjust;
> parent excuses baby in an attempt to pacify the child; parent
> comes to supervise; parent suggests another activity for both
> baby and child. Don't break it, it costs money; what can we
> give baby to play with?
>
> 3. Sides with baby—diverting older child with no reprimand;
> asks child only to adjust; questions child's statement. You
> must share; be patient with him; bring her here quickly; why?
>
> 4. Reprimand. Disapproval, or stops child; moral reprimand;
> asks child to apologize. That would hurt the baby's head;
> don't do that; don't break it (alone).
>
> 5. Threat of punishment to child or to both baby and child.
> If . . . . . then . . . . . ; child's name!; you better not!
>
> 6. Punishment.
>
> 6.01 Nonphysical punishment like removing the game or
> sending the child to his room; or punishment which is not
> specified; separate children; put puzzle away.
>
> 6.02 Physical punishment.
>
> 6.03 Sarcasm.

Statement 7: "I don't like this game, I'm gonna break it."

TEMPER CONTROL SCALE

> (Coders, ask yourself: Does the parent control the child's
> temper?) $NP = 1.5$

Coding:

> 0. Uncodable (unmodified "yes" and "no" are uncodable on
> this scale).
>
> 1. Ignore, approve or neutral question, for example, Why
> don't you like it?; laughter from parent; break it, go ahead;
> neutral comment; what's the problem? Mary (wife) speak to
> your kid; break it, I'll throw it away.

2. Divert; suggestions for compromise; stopping child without reprimand; then why did you ask for it; put it away; t'es fatigué? Encourage to continue game, by cajoling, pleading; parent tries to make child see the consequences of his act, for example, If you break it, you won't have it any more; parent gives child a rational reason for not breaking it: If you don't want to play with it, put it away; (child is given a choice).

3. Reproof. Reproof; disapproval; scolding; moral reprimand; don't break it; parceque tu n'es pas gentille.

4. Threat of punishment. If . . . . . then . . . . . ; child's name! you better not!; if you break it, I won't buy you another.

5. Punishmnet.

5.01 Nonspecified or nonphysical, including removal of game by parent; I'm going to take it away; parent gives game away, child given a nap.

5.02 Physical.

5.03 Sarcasm which attempts to humiliate or frustrate child.

Statement 8: "I don't like this game. It's a stupid game and you're stupid mommy/daddy."

INSOLENCE CONTROL SCALE

(Coders, ask yourself: Does the parent control the insolence? We are concerned with parental reaction to insult to the parent.) NP = 1.5

Coding:

0. Uncodable (unmodified "yes" and "no" are uncodable on this scale).

1. Reaction restricted to puzzle; no reference made to insult; ignore; child told to continue puzzle; you don't understand the game; it's late and you're tired. Allows statement and attempts to understand it; expresses regret or surprise at statement about parent; laughter; je suis bête.

2. Delay, divert; child urged to play with something else; or parent comes to help child with game; child urged to put game away.

3. Question—In what way am I stupid? What's the matter?

4. Reprimand. Reprimand; disapproval; scolding. Je le gronde; stop it; that's enough; don't speak to me that way; you're the one who is stupid; I beg your pardon; tu es gentil; t'es fine ?; tu es bête; stopping child's train of thought.

5. Threat of punishment.

6. Punishment.

6.01 Nonphysical punishment or nonspecific punishment; parent gives game away; parent takes game away; I'm putting it away.

6.02 Physical punishment.

6.03 Sarcasm intended to frustrate or humiliate child.

Statement 9: "Ow, baby stepped on my hand!"

ATTENTION DENIAL SCALE

(Coders, ask yourself: Does the parent give or deny attention?) NP = 4.5

Coding:

0. Uncodable (unmodified "yes" and "no" are uncodable on this scale).

1. Side with child; comfort extended, including "I'm sorry"; parent asks baby to say he's sorry; parent removes baby. Poor dear; attention, bébé!; my poor darling, he didn't do it on purpose; show me your little finger, I'm going to blow on it; that's too bad, come here, I'll fix it; I would look at it; say you're sorry, baby.

2. Diminish pain by such statements as: It'll be all right in a minute; ça va passer.

3. Advise self-comfort, for example, blow on it; run some water on it; try not to think about it.

4. Interested statement such as "let me see" without comfort reference, for example, did he hurt you ?; did it hurt very much ?; question of neutral comment like: what's going on ?; what are you fussing about; distract or divert the child; show me, it's nothing; don't worry; come here; regarde cette belle image; tu as mal, est-ce OK ?

5. Excuse baby. It was an accident; he didn't do it on purpose; he's too young to understand; he did not mean to; he's very little.

6. Siding with baby; denial of pain, without comfort; ignore; "go see your mother"; reprimand; punishment of child. It's nothing; it's not serious; you're a big boy; that's life; I don't believe it hurts; let's see, you're not hurt; you are really impatient; listen, that's enough; you deserve it; I don't think he stepped on your hand; so, what?; watch where you put them; interest baby in something else. If parent excuses baby (5) and denies pain (6) we code it as 6; be patient; it's nothing, it will be all right in a minute; it will be all right; it is not very bad.

Statement 10: "Mommy/daddy, it hurts."

COMFORT WITHHOLDING SCALE

(Coders, ask yourself: Does the parent give or withhold comfort?) NP = 2.5

Coding:

0. Uncodable (unmodified "yes" and "no" are uncodable on this scale).

1. Side with child; comfort extended, including "I'm sorry"; parent asks baby to say he's sorry; parent removes baby. Poor dear; attention, bébé!; my poor darling, he didn't do it on purpose; show me your little finger, I'm going to blow on it; that's too bad.

2. Diminish pain by such statements as it'll be all right in a minute; ça va passer; don't cry; the pain will be over in a minute.

3. Advise self-comfort, for example, blow on it; run some water on it; try not to think about it.

4. Interested statement such as "let me see" without comfort reference, for example, did he hurt you?; did it hurt very much?; question or neutral comment like "what's going on?"; what are you fussing about; distract or divert the child; delay; show me; come over here a little; I would go see.

5. Excuse baby. It was an accident; he didn't do it on purpose; he's too young to understand; he did not mean to; he's very little.

6. Siding with baby; denial of pain without comfort; ignore; "go see your mother"; reprimand; punishment of child. It's nothing; it's not serious; you're a big boy; that's life; I don't believe it hurts; let's see, you're not hurt; you are really

impatient; listen, that's enough; you deserve it; I don't think he stepped on your hand; so, what?; watch where you put them; be patient.

Statement 11: "Mommy/daddy get me another puzzle."

HELP WITHHOLDING SCALE

(Coders, ask yourself: Does the parent give or withhold help?) NP = 2.5

Coding:

0. Uncodable ("yes" and "no" can be coded on this scale).

1. Complete acquiescence. Yes, which one would you like?; we'll look together; where are they?

2. Yes, with restrictions. Say "please"; if you pick up the other one first; (Note that this is a yes with restrictions not a delay).

3. Delay or encourage child to continue game, or divert child by suggesting another activity. Wait, it won't be long; we'll talk about it later; why don't you play with the one you have? question: get you another puzzle?; no, but play with something else (England); parent comes to supervise.

4. Parent tells child to get it himself. Go get it yourself; you know where they are, they're in your room; pick up the other and get it yourself.

5. No, with explanation. Not until you're finished with this one; one is enough; no, you should be patient.

6. No, without explanation. Long delay; I beg your pardon; ask your mother.

7. Threat of punishment.

8. Punishment.

8.01 Nonphysical or nonspecific punishment.

8.02 Physical.

8.03 Sarcasm, for example, who was your slave yesterday?

Statement 12: "It's not raining now, can I go across the street and play?"

AUTONOMY CONTROL SCALE

(Coders, ask yourself: Is the child allowed to cross the street?) NP = 3.5

Coding:

0. Uncodable ("yes" and "no" can be coded on this scale).

1. Permits. Yes; O.K.

2. Permits with reservations or warnings. Yes, put on your galoshes; yes, but be careful of the traffic; don't get muddy.

3. Parent gives an alternative to crossing the street alone, that is, yes, if accompanied by parent or older sibling (not necessary to have a yes or no); not on your own.

4. No, but parent suggests that child play in the yard or on this side of the street, for example, child can go outside, but may not cross the street.

5. No, with explanation. No, it is not safe; no, it's dangerous.

6. No, without explanation; ignore; divert; question: who are you going to play with?; "ask your mother."

Statement 13: "Why can't I? I'm gonna anyway."

INSOLENCE CONTROL SCALE

(Coders, ask yourself: Does the parent control the insolence? We are concerned with parental reaction to the insult to the parent.) NP = 1.5

Coding:

0. Uncodable ("yes" and "no" can be coded on this scale).

1. Acquiescence or short delay like "just a minute," "wait a minute."

2. Explanation of why parent said no before. I said "when I'm ready"; you're too young.

3. No, without explanation; diversion; ignore. Because I said so; no you're not; question.

4. Reproof, stopping. I would close the door; explanation plus reprimand.

5. Threat of punishment; threat and explanation.

6. Punishment.

6.01 Nonphysical or nonspecific.

6.02 Physical.

6.03 Sarcasm.

Statement 14: "Can Chris come in and play ?"

GUEST RESTRICTION SCALE

(Coders, ask yourself: Is the child given guest privileges ?)
NP = 2.5

Coding:

0. Uncodable ("yes" and "no" can be coded on this scale).

1. Agree. Yes, here or outside; yes; oui, s'il veut.

2. Agree, with qualification or short delay. For a little while; yes, but be nice to him; yes, if his mother says it's okay; yes, if you clean up after; yes, I'll phone his mother; yes, call his mother (with explanation); yes, if he can.

3. No with explanation; or long delay with explanation, for example, yes, but after dinner.

4. No without explanation; long delay without explanation, for example, tomorrow; diversion; question: who's Chris ?; ask your mother.

Statement 15: "Chris, let me put the pieces in myself, you watch me."

SIDING WITH GUEST VERSUS CHILD SCALE

(Coders, ask yourself: Whom does the parent favor, the guest or the child?) NP = 3.0

Coding:

0. Uncodable (unmodified "yes" and "no" are uncodable on this scale).

1. Side with child; divert, remove or restrict guest's intervention. I'll give him another toy (coders, note that parent, not child, gives toy to guest).

2. Compromise. Give him some pieces you don't need; he's too small; let him watch for a while (note parent does not say "play"); give him another toy; parent supervises without comment as to whose side he's on.

3. Ignore or "work it out yourself" or comment which doesn't side with either guest or child. He is as smart as you are; either share or get him another puzzle; why can't he; parent suggests a new game for both children; sharing and give another toy.

4. Side with guest; parent asks child only to adjust; parent diverts the child; child must interact positively with guest. You must share; it's for both of you; no, you must play with him; take care of him; show some interest toward him; be nice to him; big boys play nicely; how about taking turns.

5. Reprimand, to child; disapproval, reproof, scolding. Stop that talk; I would scold him; that's enough; shut up! That's not nice; don't be so selfish; apologize to him.

6. Threat of punishment, to child. If . . . . . then . . . . . ; child's name! if you don't let him, he'll want to go home.

7. Punishment.

7.01 Nonphysical punishment or nonspecific.

7.02 Physical punishment.

7.03 Sarcasm which is really meant to humiliate or punish the child; (note there will be some sarcasm which is not this strong, for example, a simple disagreement with the child, coded 4).

Statement 16: "Don't touch the pieces. You don't know how to do it."

SIDING WITH GUEST VERSUS CHILD SCALE

(Coders, ask yourself: Whom does the parent favor, the guest or the child?) NP = 3.0

Coding:

0. Uncodable (unmodified "yes" and "no" are uncodable on this scale).

1. Side with child; divert, remove, or restrict guest's intervention. I'll give him another toy; (coders, note that parent not child gives toy to guest).

2. Excuses guest in an attempt to pacify child. Give him some pieces you don't need; he's too small; let him watch for a while (note that parent doesn't say "play"); give him another toy; parent supervises without comment as to whose side he's on.

3. Ignore or "work it out yourself" or comment that favors neither guest nor child. He is as smart as you, why can't he? Parent suggests a new game for both children.

4. Side with guest; parent asks child only to adjust; parent diverts the child; child must interact positively with guest.

You must share; it's for both of you; no, you must play with him; take care of him; show some interest toward him; be nice to him; big boys don't fight; how about taking turns.

5. Reprimand, to child; disapproval, reproof, scolding. Stop that talk; I would scold him; that's enough; shut up; that's not nice; don't be so selfish; apologize to him.

6. Threat of punishment, to child; If . . . . . then . . . . . ; child's name! if you don't let him, he will want to go home.

7. Punishment.

7.01 Nonphysical punishment or nonspecified punishment.

7.02 Physical punishment.

7.03 Sarcasm which is really meant to humiliate or punish the child; (note there will be some sarcasm which is not this strong, for example, a simple disagreement with the child, coded 4).

Statement 17: "If you don't leave 'em alone I'll beat you up!"

SIDING WITH GUEST VERSUS CHILD SCALE
(also SOCIAL TEMPER SCALE)

(Coders, ask yourself: Does the parent side with the guest or the child? We are concerned with the parent's response to the child's threat of hitting the guest.) NP = 2.5

Coding:

0. Uncodable (unmodified "yes," "no," and "well" are uncodable on this scale).

1. Sides with child and overlooks threat of hitting guest; parent ignores statement; parent diverts guest.

2. Compromise: parent asks both guest and child to adjust; parent excuses guest in an attempt to pacify the child; parent comes to supervise; parent suggests another activity for both guest and child.

3. Sides with guest, diverting child with no reprimand; asks child only to adjust; questions child's statement. You must share; be patient with him; what will that help?

4. Reprimand: disapproval or stopping. That would hurt him; don't do that; moral reprimand; asks child to apologize.

5. Threat of punishment, to child or to both guest and child. If . . . . . then . . . . .; child's name! he'll hit you back; if you can't be nice, no one will want to play with you; if you're mean, he will want to go home; threat of sending guest home.

6. Punishment.

6.01 Nonphysical punishment, such as removing the game or sending the child to his room, or nonspecific punishment, separate children.

6.02 Physical punishment.

6.03 Sarcasm.

Statement 18: "Hey, when are we going to eat?"

(Optional item)

(Coders, ask yourself: Is the child given something to eat?)
NP = 2.5

Coding:

0. Uncodable ("yes" and "no" can be coded on this scale).

1. Comply, by giving a snack.

2. Ask child to adjust by waiting until dinner is ready; diverting child; delay child; asking child to wash his hands or set table. When it's ready; when it's time.

3. Ignore: ask your mother; no; why; you just ate.

4. Reproval; parent upset by child's tone of voice; scolding; moral reprimand; be calm.

5. Threat of punishment.

6. Punishment.

6.01 Nonphysical.

6.02 Physical.

6.03 Sarcasm.

Statement 19: "I'm hungry, may I go and get myself something to eat?"

(Optional item)

(Coders, ask yourself: Is the child allowed to serve himself?)
NP = 2.5

Coding:

    0. Uncodable ("yes" and "no" <u>can</u> be coded on this scale).

    1. Permits child to get something to eat by himself, with no restrictions.

    2. Permits child to take food himself, with restrictions.

    2.01 Restrictions on type of food; just a little bit.

    2.02 Restrictions on behavior; yes, but don't spill anything.

    3. Parent gets the child something.

    4. No, with explanation or delay, with explanation. Wait till the food is ready; wait until dinner.

    5. No, without explanation or delay, without explanation; diversion of child; ignore; ask your mother; wait a little longer.

APPENDIX B
Sex-Role Questionnaires

PERCEIVED SEX-ROLE DIFFERENCES QUESTIONNAIRE*

Instructions to be read aloud to parent:

In this questionnaire we would like to find out your feelings about differences between boys and girls. I will read you a number of statements which have been used by parents to describe differences they have observed between their sons and daughters. The statements apply to boys and girls between four and eight years of age who are either members of your family or of your friends' and neighbors' families.

For each statement please tell me the sex to which you feel the statement applies. If you feel a statement applies more to girls than to boys say the word "girls." If you feel it applies more to boys then say the word "boys." If you feel that there are no differences between girls and boys on a statement say the word "same."

For example, if I say, more likely to enjoy playing house—boys, girls, the same. How would you answer? If I say, more likely to be athletic—girls, boys, the same. How would you answer?

Instructions for interviewer:

(Now read the statements to the parent. After each statement, read the choices boys, girls, or the same in the order given on the answer sheet. Check the parent's answer yourself. Start with statement 1 and continue in order through statement 38.)

1. More likely to be self-assertive are:

    _____   _____   _____
    boys   girls   same

2. More likely to be persistent at tasks are:

    _____   _____   _____
    girls   same   boys

---

*Teachers received the same questionnaire but with instructions for written responses.

3. More likely to be defiant of punishment are:

        ————— ————— —————
        same   boys   girls

4. More likely to be demanding of your attention are:

        ————— ————— —————
        girls   same   boys

5. More likely to be rough and boisterous in play are:

        ————— ————— —————
        same   girls   boys

6. More likely to be patient with others are:

        ————— ————— —————
        same   boys   girls

7. More likely to have temper tantrums are:

        ————— ————— —————
        girls   same   boys

8. More likely to be well mannered are:

        ————— ————— —————
        girls   same   boys

9. More likely to be quiet and reserved are:

        ————— ————— —————
        girls   same   boys

10. More likely to defend themselves when attacked are:

        ————— ————— —————
        same   boys   girls

11. More likely to cry or become emotionally upset are:

        ————— ————— —————
        girls   same   boys

12. More likely to be dependent on others for help are:

        ————— ————— —————
        same   girls   boys

13. More likely to be thoughtful and considerate are:

        ————— ————— —————
        girls   same   boys

14. More likely to be competitive with others are:

$\overline{\text{same}}$ $\overline{\text{boys}}$ $\overline{\text{girls}}$

15. More likely to be easily frightened are:

$\overline{\text{boys}}$ $\overline{\text{girls}}$ $\overline{\text{same}}$

16. More likely to ask for love and affection are:

$\overline{\text{girls}}$ $\overline{\text{same}}$ $\overline{\text{boys}}$

17. More likely to do well in school are:

$\overline{\text{girls}}$ $\overline{\text{same}}$ $\overline{\text{boys}}$

18. More likely to be obedient are:

$\overline{\text{girls}}$ $\overline{\text{boys}}$ $\overline{\text{same}}$

19. More likely to be able to take care of themselves are:

$\overline{\text{boys}}$ $\overline{\text{girls}}$ $\overline{\text{same}}$

20. More likely to succeed at things they try are:

$\overline{\text{boys}}$ $\overline{\text{same}}$ $\overline{\text{girls}}$

21. More likely to be easily angered are:

$\overline{\text{girls}}$ $\overline{\text{same}}$ $\overline{\text{boys}}$

22. More likely to have good reasoning ability are:

$\overline{\text{same}}$ $\overline{\text{girls}}$ $\overline{\text{boys}}$

23. More likely to be popular are:

$\overline{\text{girls}}$ $\overline{\text{boys}}$ $\overline{\text{same}}$

24. More likely to seek comfort when hurt are:

$\overline{\text{boys}}$ $\overline{\text{girls}}$ $\overline{\text{same}}$

25. More likely to be a leader among the playmates are:

_____ _____ _____
same   boys   girls

26. More likely to be sensitive to the feelings of others are:

_____ _____ _____
boys   same   girls

27. More likely to do dangerous things are:

_____ _____ _____
girls   boys   same

28. More likely to be stubborn are:

_____ _____ _____
boys   same   girls

29. More likely to be helpful around the house are:

_____ _____ _____
same   boys   girls

30. More likely to be neat and clean are:

_____ _____ _____
boys   same   girls

31. More likely to enjoy mechanical things are:

_____ _____ _____
girls   boys   same

32. More likely to be physically active and athletic are:

_____ _____ _____
boys   same   girls

33. More likely to be noisy in play are:

_____ _____ _____
girls   boys   same

34. More likely to be creative and imaginative are:

_____ _____ _____
boys   same   girls

35. More likely to have well-rounded interests are:

_____ _____ _____
girls   same   boys

36. More likely to possess a good sense of humor are:

_____ _____ _____
same   girls   boys

37. More likely to be curious about things are:

_____ _____ _____
boys   girls   same

38. More likely to be well dressed are:

_____ _____ _____
same   boys   girls

EXPECTED SEX-ROLE DIFFERENCES QUESTIONNAIRE

Instructions to be read aloud to parent:

In the first part of this questionnaire you told me the differences that you felt exist between boys and girls. We realize that some parents think ideally there should be no differences between the sexes in these qualities. However, many parents do not always expect the same things from their sons as from their daughters. We have listed a number of qualities. We will ask you separately for boys and for girls how important it is for a child to be described by each quality. (At this point show the cardboard scale* to the parent and show him where he should point for each part of the example.) For example: If you feel it is very important for your boy not to enjoy playing house, you should point to the first space on the scale very important not to. If you feel it is somewhat important for your boy not to enjoy playing house, you should point to the second space on the scale important not to. On the other hand, if you feel that it is very important for your boy to enjoy playing house you should point to the last space of the scale very important to. If you feel that it is somewhat important for him to enjoy playing house, where would you point? (If parent doesn't understand give another example like "to be athletic".) Finally, if it doesn't matter to you whether your boy enjoyed playing house or did not enjoy it you would point to the middle space, unimportant.

_____

*A cardboard scale with different colors representing each answer was prepared for each language group.

The first list of qualities is to be rated for <u>boys only</u>;* the list will then be repeated for ratings of girls. If you do not have a son, pretend that you do and imagine how important the various qualities might be to you.

(Interviewer—put the cardboard with the picture of the boy on top of the scale and start reading the statements. For the first statement you should read it completely.)

For boys, is it <u>very important not to</u> (point at the space on the scale); <u>fairly important not to</u> (point at the corresponding space); <u>unimportant</u> (point at the corresponding space); <u>fairly important</u> (point at the corresponding space); or <u>very important to</u> (point at the corresponding space); be quiet and reserved?
(Check the parent's answer on your sheet.)

Go to statement No. 2; here again read the complete statement and check the parent's answer. You will have to read the complete statement as often as necessary until the parent understands the scale; only then can you drop the reading of the complete scale and read him only the statement itself. Proceed through item 38.

BOYS

	Very Important not to:	Fairly Important not to:	Un-important	Fairly Important to:	Very Important to:	
1.	'	'	'	'	'	be quiet and re-served.
2.	'	'	'	'	'	defend himself.
3.	'	'	'	'	'	be depen-dent on others.
4.	'	'	'	'	'	have temper tantrums.

*Half the subjects rated boys first and half rated girls first.

	Very Important not to:	Fairly Important not to:	Un-important	Fairly Important to:	Very Important to:	
5.	'	'	'	'	'	be thought-ful and consid-erate.
6.	'	'	'	'	'	do dan-gerous things.
7.	'	'	'	'	'	be easil frighten
8.	'	'	'	'	'	be com-petitive.
9.	'	'	'	'	'	do well in school
10.	'	'	'	'	'	seek comfort for minor hurts.
11.	'	'	'	'	'	be obedient.
12.	'	'	'	'	'	be suc-cessful.
13.	'	'	'	'	'	be sensi-tive to the feel-ings of others.
14.	'	'	'	'	'	be a lead-er among playmates.
15.	'	'	'	'	'	ask for love and affection.
16.	'	'	'	'	'	defy pun-ishment.

	Very Important not to:	Fairly Important not to:	Un-important	Fairly Important to:	Very Important to:	
17.	'	'	'	'	'	' be popular.
18.	'	'	'	'	'	' have high reason-ing ability.
19.	'	'	'	'	'	' be able to take care of himself.
20.	'	'	'	'	'	' be self-assertive.
21.	'	'	'	'	'	' be stub-born.
22.	'	'	'	'	'	' demand attention.
23.	'	'	'	'	'	' be rough and bois-terous at play.
24.	'	'	'	'	'	' be pa-tient with others.
25.	'	'	'	'	'	' be easily angered.
26.	'	'	'	'	'	' cry easily.
27.	'	'	'	'	'	' be well mannered.
28.	'	'	'	'	'	' be per-sistent.

Very Important not to:	Fairly Important not to:	Un-important	Fairly Important to:	Very Important to:	
29. ' _____ '	'	'	'	' '	be helpful around the house
30. ' _____ '	'	'	'	' '	be neat and clean
31. ' _____ '	'	'	'	' '	enjoy mechanical things.
32. ' _____ '	'	'	'	' '	be physically active and athletic.
33. ' _____ '	'	'	'	' '	be noisy in play.
34. ' _____ '	'	'	'	' '	be creative and imaginative.
35. ' _____ '	'	'	'	' '	have well-rounded interests.
36. ' _____ '	'	'	'	' '	possess a good sense of humor.
37. ' _____ '	'	'	'	' '	be curious about things.
38. ' _____ '	'	'	'	' '	be well dressed.

Now, we will ask you to give your ratings for girls. If you do not have a daughter pretend that you do and imagine how important the various qualities might be to you.

(Change the cardboard with the boy and put the cardboard with the picture of the girl on top of the scale. Read the first statement completely.)

For girls, it is <u>very important not to</u> (point at the corresponding space); <u>unimportant</u> (point at the corresponding space); <u>fairly important to</u> (point at the corresponding space) or <u>very important to</u> (point at the corresponding space). Be quiet and reserved?

(Check the parent's answer on your sheet.)

Go to statement No. 2; here again read the complete statement and check the parent's answer. You will have to read the complete statement as often as necessary until the parent understands the scale; only then can you drop the reading of the complete scale and read him only the statement itself. Proceed through item 38.

GIRLS

Very Important <u>not</u> to:	Fairly Important <u>not</u> to:	Un-important	Fairly Important to:	Very Important to:	
1.					be quiet and re-served.
2.					defend himself.
3.					be de-pendent on others.
4.					have temper tantrums.
5.					be thought-ful and consider-ate.

Very Important not to:	Fairly Important not to:	Un- important	Fairly Important to:	Very Important to:	

6. _____ do dan-
gerous
things.

7. _____ be easily
frightene

8. _____ be com-
petitive.

9. _____ do well
in school.

10. _____ seek
comfort
for mi-
nor hurts.

11. _____ be obedi-
ent.

12. _____ be suc-
cessful.

13. _____ be sensi-
tive to the
feelings
of others.

14. _____ be a lead-
er among
playmates.

15. _____ ask for
love and
affection.

16. _____ defy pun-
ishment.

17. _____ be
popular.

18. _____ have high
reasoning
ability.

	Very Important not to:	Fairly Important not to:	Un-important	Fairly Important to:	Very Important to:	
19.	'	'	'	'	'	' be able to take care of herself.
20.	'	'	'	'	'	' be self-assertive.
21.	'	'	'	'	'	' be stub-born.
22.	'	'	'	'	'	' demand attention.
23.	'	'	'	'	'	' be rough and bois-terous at play.
24.	'	'	'	'	'	' be pa-tient with others.
25.	'	'	'	'	'	' be easily angered.
26.	'	'	'	'	'	' cry easily.
27.	'	'	'	'	'	' be well mannered.
28.	'	'	'	'	'	' be per-sistent.
29.	'	'	'	'	'	' be helpful around the house.
30.	'	'	'	'	'	' be neat and clean.
31.	'	'	'	'	'	' enjoy me-chanical things.

	Very Important not to:	Fairly Important not to:	Un- important	Fairly Important to:	Very Important to:	

32. _____ be physcally active and athletic.

33. _____ be noisy in play.

34. _____ be creative and imaginative.

35. _____ have well rounded interests

36. _____ possess a good sense of humor.

37. _____ be curious about things.

38. _____ be well dressed.

Thank you. That's all as far as the questionnaire about boys and girls is concerned.

(After the questionnaire, if the parent has already heard the tape, proceed to the background information. If the parent has not yet answered the tape, say:)

Now my partner will play the tape for you while I ask your husband/wife some questions. Thank you for your answers.

BIBLIOGRAPHY

Aellen, Carole, and Lambert, Wallace E. "Ethnic Identification and Personality Adjustments of Canadian Adolescents of Mixed English-French Parentage." Canadian Journal of Behavioural Science 1 (1969): 69-86.

Ariès, Phillipe. Histoire des Populations Françaises et de leurs Attitudes Devant la Vie Depuis XVIIIe Siécle. Paris: Seuil, 1971.

_____. L'Enfant et la Vie Familiale Sous L'Ancien Régime. Paris: Seuil, 1973.

_____, in interview with P. Desgraupes. "L'Aventure Inconnue de la Famille." Le Point, nos. 148-153, July-August 1975.

Bell, Richard Q. "A Reinterpretation of the Direction of Effects in Studies of Socialization." Psychological Review 75 (1968): 81-95.

Bernstein, Basil. "Social Class and Linguistic Development: A Theory of Social Learning." In Education, Economy, and Society, edited by A. H. Halsey, J. Floud, and A. C. Anderson. New York: Free Press, 1961.

Blishen, Bernard R. "A Socio-economic Index for Occupations in Canada." Canadian Review of Sociology and Anthropology 4 (1967): 41-53.

Bronfenbrenner, Urie. "Socialization and Social Class through Time and Space." In Readings in Social Psychology, edited by E. E. Maccoby, T. M. Newcomb, and E. L. Hartley. New York: Holt, Rinehart and Winston, 1958.

_____. Two Worlds of Childhood: U.S. and U.S.S.R. New York: Russell Sage Foundation, 1970.

Campbell, Donald. "The Mutual Methodological Relevance of Anthropology and Psychology." In Psychological Anthropology, ed. F. L. K. Hsu. Homewood, Ill.: Dorsay Press, 1961.

Chalon, Jean. "Ma Mére, Mon Enfant." Le Figaro, Dec. 24. 1976.

Commission of Inquiry on the Position of the French Language and on Language Rights in Quebec. The Position of the French Language in Quebec: The Ethnic Groups, Vol. 3. Quebec: Government of Québec, 1972. (The Gendron Report.)

Devereux, Edward C., Bronfenbrenner, Urie, and Rodgers, Robert R. "Child Rearing in England and the United States: A Cross-National Comparison." Journal of Marriage and the Family 31 (1969): 257-70.

Devereux, Edward C., Bronfenbrenner, Urie, and Suci, George J. "Patterns of Parent Behavior in America and West Germany: A Cross-National Comparison." International Social Science Journal 14 (1962): 488-506.

Eson, Morris E. Psychological Foundations of Education. New York: Holt, Rinehart and Winston, 1972.

Garigue, Philippe. La Vie Familiale des Canadiens Français. Montreal: Presse de l'Université de Montréal, 1962. Translated abstract: "The French-Canadian Family." In Canadian Society, edited by B. R. Blishen et al. Toronto: Macmillan, 1968.

Guindon, Hubert. "Social Unrest, Social Class, and Quebec's Bureaucratic Revolution." In Canadian Society: Sociological Perspectives, edited by B. R. Blishen, F. E. Jones, K. D. Naegele, and J. Porter. Toronto: Macmillan, 1968.

Guterman, Stanley S. The Machiavellians. Lincoln: University of Nebraska Press, 1970.

Guthrie, George M., and Jacobs, P. J. Child Rearing and Personality Development in the Philippines. University Park: The Pennsylvania State University Press, 1966.

Harper, Lawrence V. "The Scope of Offspring Effects: From Caregiver to Culture." Psychological Bulletin 82 (1975): 784-801.

Henrot, T. Belgique. Petite Planète, Editions du Seuil, Paris, 1971.

Hess, Robert D., and Shipman, Virginia W. "Early Experiences and the Socialization of Cognitive Modes in Children." Child Development 36 (1965): 869-88.

Holmes, Roger. Legitimacy and the Politics of the Knowable. London: Routledge and Kegan Paul, 1976.

Lambert, Wallace E. "Culture and Language as Factors in Learning and Education." In the Fifth Western Symposium of Learning, Cultural Factors in Learning and Education, edited by Frances E. Aboud and Robert E. Meade, 1974: 91-122.

_____. "Social Psychological Approaches to the Cross National Study of Values." Paper presented at the International Conference on Subjective Culture, Lagonissi, Greece, 1968.

_____. "A Social Psychology of Bilingualism." Journal of Social Issues 23 (1967): 91-109.

_____. "What Are They Like, These Canadians? A Social Psychological Analysis." Canadian Psychologist 11 (1970): 303-33.

Lambert, Wallace E., Frankel, Hanah, and Tucker, G. Richard. "Judging Personality through Speech: A French-Canadian Example." Journal of Communication 16 (1966): 305-21.

Lambert, Wallace E., Hodgson, Richard C., Gardner, Robert C., and Fillenbaum, Samuel. "Evaluation Reactions to Spoken Languages." Journal of Abnormal and Social Psychology 60 (1960): 44-51.

Lambert, Wallace E., and Moore, Nancy. "Word Association Responses: Comparisons of American and French Monolinguals with Canadian Monolinguals and Bilinguals." Journal of Personality and Social Psychology 3 (1966): 313-20.

Lambert, Wallace E., and Tucker, G. Richard. Bilingual Education of Children. Rowley, Mass.: Newbury House, 1972.

Lambert, Wallace E., Yackley, Andrew, and Hein, Ruth. "Child Training Values of English Canadian and French Canadian Parents." Canadian Journal of Behavioural Science 3 (1971): 217-36.

Lambert, William W., Triandis, Leigh M., and Wolf, Marjorie. "Some Correlates of Beliefs in the Malevolence and Benevolence of Supernatural Beings: A Cross-cultural Study." Journal of Abnormal and Social Psychology 58 (1959): 162-69.

Lipset, Seymour M. "Value Differences, Absolute or Relative: The English-speaking Democracies." In Canadian Society: Sociological Perspectives, edited by B. R. Blishen, F. E. Jones, K. D. Naegele, and J. Porter. Toronto: Macmillan, 1968.

Maccoby, Eleanor, ed. The Development of Sex Differences. Stanford: Stanford University Press, 1966.

Mazzatenta, O. L. "New England's 'Little Portugal'." In National Geographic Magazine, 1975, Vol. 147, no. 1, 90-109.

McCandless, Boyd R. Children: Behavior and Development. New York: Holt, Rinehart and Winston, 1967.

McClelland, David C. The Achieving Society. New York: Van Nostrand, 1961.

_____. Power: The Inner Experience. New York: Irvington Publishers, 1975.

Metraux, Rhoda, and Mead, Margaret. Themes in French Culture: A Preface to a Study of French Community. Stanford: Stanford University Press, 1954.

Minturn, Leigh, and Lambert, William W. Mothers of Six Cultures. New York: Wiley, 1964.

Mowrer, O. Hobart. Learning Theory and Personality Dynamics. New York: Ronald, 1950.

Naegele, Kasper D. "Modern National Societies." In Canadian Society: Sociological Perspectives, edited by B. R. Blishen, F. E. Jones, K. D. Naegele, and J. Porter. Toronto: Macmillan, 1968.

Olson, Chet L. Personal communication, based on current work on this matter by Gordon A. Hale at the Educational Testing Service, Princeton, N.J., 1977.

Ossenberg, Richard J., ed. Canadian Society: Pluralism, Change and Conflict. Scarborough, Ontario: Prentice-Hall, 1971.

Parsons, Talcott, and Bales, Robert F. Family Socialization and the Interaction Process. Glencoe, Ill.: Free Press, 1955.

Phillipart, André. "Belgium: Language and Class Oppositions." Government and Opposition: A Quarterly of Comparative Politics 2, no. 1 (Oct. 1966-Jan. 1967).

Population: Mother Tongue. 1971 Census of Canada. Bulletin 1.3-4, April 1973.

Radke-Yarrow, Marion, Campbell, John D., and Burton, Roger W. "Reliability of Maternal Retrospection: A Preliminary Report." In Readings in Child Socialization, edited by K. Danziger. Oxford: Pergamon Press, 1970: 269-84.

Rens, Ivo. "Les Garanties Parlementaires Contre la Minorisation et la Revision Constitutionnelle en Belgique." Res Publica 7, no. 3 (1965): 189-221.

Riesman, David. The Lonely Crowd. New Haven, Conn.: Yale University Press, 1950.

Rokeach, Milton. The Nature of Human Values. New York: Free Press, 1973.

Rosen, Bernard C. "Race, Ethnicity and the Achievement Syndrome." American Sociological Review 24 (1959): 47-60.

_____. "Family Structure and Achievement Motivation." American Sociological Review 26 (1961): 574-85.

Rosen, Bernard C., and D'Andrade, Roy G. "The Psychosocial Origins of Achievement Motivation." Sociometry 22 (1959): 185-218.

Rothbart, Mary K., and Maccoby, Eleanor E. "Parents' Differential Reactions to Sons and Daughters." Journal of Personality and Social Psychology 4 (1966): 237-43.

Rudin, Stanley A. "The Psychology of Nations." Discovery (June 1965).

Sears, Robert R., Maccoby, Eleanor E., and Levin, Harry. Patterns of Child Rearing. Evanston, Ill.: Row, Peterson, 1957.

Seeley, John R., Sim, R. Alexander, and Loosley, Elizabeth. "Parent Education." Canada: A Sociological Profile, edited by W. E. Mann. Toronto: The Copp Clark Publishing Company, 1968.

Toynbee, Arnold J. A Study of History. New York: Oxford University Press, 1947.

Trevelyan, George M. English Social History. London: Longmans, Green and Company, 1942.

Triandis, Harry C. In association with Vasso Vassiliou, George Vassiliou, Yoshi Tanaka, and A. V. Shanmuggan. The Analysis of Subjective Culture. New York: Wiley, 1972.

Triandis, Harry C., Vassiliou, Vasso, and Nassiakou, Maria. "Three Cross-Cultural Studies of Subjective Culture." Journal of Personality and Social Psychology, Monograph Supplement 8, no. 4, part 2 (1968): 1-42.

Triandis, Harry C., and Triandis, Pola F. "The Building of Nations." Psychology Today 2 (1969): 31-35.

Underhill, Frank H. "The Image of Canada." Address presented at the University of New Brunswick Founder's Day. March 8, 1962. (Cited in Blishen et al., p. 484.)

Whiteman, Martin, and Deutsch, Martin. "Social Disadvantage as Related to Intellective and Language Development." Social Class, Race, and Psychological Development, edited by M. Deutsch, E. Katz, and A. R. Jensen. New York: Holt, Rinehart and Winston, 1968.

Whiting, John W. M., and Child, Irving L. Child Training and Personality: A Cross-Cultural Study. New Haven, Conn.: Yale University Press, 1953.

Whiting, John W. M., Child, Irving L., Lambert, William W., et al. Field Guide for a Study of Socialization in Five Cultures. Cambridge, Mass.: Laboratory of Human Development, 1955.

Whiting, Beatrice, ed. Six Cultures: Studies of Child Rearing. New York: Wiley, 1963.

Witkin, Herman A. "Studies in Space Orientation." Journal of Experimental Psychology 38 (1948): 762-82.

_____. "Social Influences in the Development of Cognitive Style." Handbook of Socialization Theory and Research, edited by D. A. Goslin. New York: Rand McNally, 1969.

_____. "Socialization and Ecology in the Development of Cross-Cultural and Sex Differences in Cognitive Style." Paper presented at 21st International Congress of Psychology, Paris, 1976.

Witkin, Herman A., and Berry, John W. "Psychological Differentiation in Cross-Cultural Perspective." Journal of Cross Cultural Psychology 6 (1975): 4-87.

Woolfson, P. "Traditional French Canadian Value Orientations and Their Persistence among the Franco Americans of Northeastern Vermont." Paper presented to the Northeastern Anthropological Association meetings, Burlington, Vermont, 1973.

Yackley, Andrew, and Lambert, Wallace E. "Interethnic Group Competition and Levels of Aspiration." Canadian Journal of Behavioral Science 3 (1971): 135-47.

AUTHOR INDEX

Aellen, Carole, 9
Ariès, Philippe, 7, 8

Bales, Robert F., 111
Bell, Richard Q., 2
Bernstein, Basil, 375
Berry, John, 65, 66, 97, 356
Blishen, Bernard R., 70, 87
Bronfenbrenner, Urie, 3, 8,
  58, 64, 356
Burton, Roger V., 9

Campbell, Donald, 3, 9
Chalon, Jean, 3
Child, Irving L., 3

D'Andrade, Roy G., 59
Deutsch, Martin, 375
Devereux, Edward C., 3

Eson, Morris E., 375

Frankel, Hannah, 9
Frasure Smith, Nancy, 8
Freud, Sigmund, 63, 78

Garigue, Philippe, 3, 85
Guindon, Hubert, 21
Guterman, Stanley S., 63, 64,
  79, 97
Guthrie, George M., 3, 9

Hamers, Josiane F., 8
Harper, Lawrence V., 2
Hein, Ruth, 9, 17, 60
Henriot, T., 97
Hess, Robert D., 375
Holmes, Roger, 4

Jacobs, Paul J., 3, 9

Klineberg, Otto, 10

Lambert, Wallace E., 4, 8, 9,
  10, 17, 60, 370
Lambert, William W., 2, 3, 9
Levin, Harry, 8, 79
Lipset, Seymour M., 141, 142,
  152, 154, 168
Loosely, Elizabeth, 368

Maccoby, Eleanor, 8, 9, 10,
  17, 18, 21, 24, 36, 68, 79
Mazzatenta, O. L., 264
McCandless, Boyd R., 368
McClelland, David C., 58, 59,
  60, 62, 83, 97, 167, 297,
  299, 305, 314, 356, 357,
  358, 359, 363, 366, 367
Mead, Margaret, 82
Metreaux, Rhoda, 82
Minturn, Leigh, 2, 9
Moore, Nancy, 9
Mowrer, O. Hobart, 78

SUBJECT INDEX

ABOUT THE AUTHORS

WALLACE E. LAMBERT is a professor of psychology at McGill University. He received his training at Brown University, Colgate University, and the University of North Carolina and for short periods at Cambridge University and l'Université de Paris. He served three years with the U.S. Army in the European theater of operations during World War II. He has been a visiting professor at numerous U.S. universities as well as at universities in France, the Philippines, and Thailand.

His research interests are in social and experimental psychology, cross-national studies, and psycho- and sociolinguistics, and these are reflected in numerous publications, including Social Psychology, a textbook written in collaboration with his brother, William W. Lambert; Children's Views of Foreign Peoples: A Cross-National Study, with Otto Klineberg; Bilingual Education of Children: The St. Lambert Experiment; Tu, Vous, Usted: A Social Psychology of Forms of Address; and French Speaker's Skill with Grammatical Gender: An Example of Rule-Governed Behavior; all three in collaboration with G. Richard Tucker; Attitudes and Motivation in Second Language Learning in collaboration with Robert C. Gardner; and Language, Psychology and Culture: Essays by W. E. Lambert, edited by A. S. Dil. He is a fellow in the Canadian Royal Society and a member of the National Academy of Education.

JOSIANE F. HAMERS is an associate professor at Université Laval and at the International Center for Research on Bilingualism where she teaches psycholinguistics and the development of language. After receiving a licence in experimental psychology at the Université Libre de Bruxelles in Belgium, she received a Ph.D. in psychology from McGill University in 1973, with a speciality in the psychology of language. For the next two years she was a research associate at McGill, conducting studies on cross-cultural psychology and on bilingualism. Her main research interests are in the psychology of bilingualism, bilingual education, second language teaching and acquisition, and cross-cultural psychology.

NANCY FRASURE-SMITH is a social psychologist from Albany, New York. After completing her Ph.D. thesis in the area of developmental sociolinguistics at the Department of Social Relations, Johns Hopkins University, she came to the Psychology

Department of McGill University as a National Institute of Mental Health postdoctoral fellow. At McGill she has been involved in a number of studies concerning social-class and language-group variation in parents' and children's attitudes toward child rearing. She is currently a research associate and project director at the Research Unit of the McGill University School of Nursing where she is working on the development of techniques to assess the impact of nurse-patient verbal interaction on patients' abilities to handle stressful life events.

RELATED TITLES
Published by
Praeger Special Studies